Citizen Refugee

This innovative study explores the interface between nation-building and refugee rehabilitation in post-partition India. Relying on archival records and oral histories, Uditi Sen analyses official policy towards Hindu refugees from eastern Pakistan to reveal a pan-Indian governmentality of rehabilitation. This governmentality emerged in the Andaman Islands, where Bengali refugees were recast as pioneering settlers. Not all refugees, however, were willing or able to live up to this top-down vision of productive citizenship. Their reminiscences reveal divergent negotiations of rehabilitation 'from below'. Educated refugees from dominant castes mobilised their social and cultural capital to build urban 'squatters' colonies', while poor Dalit refugees had to perform the role of agricultural pioneers to access aid. Policies of rehabilitation marginalised single and widowed women by treating them as 'permanent liabilities'. These rich case studies dramatically expand our understanding of popular politics and everyday citizenship in post-partition India.

Uditi Sen is a historian of colonial and post-colonial India. She studied history at Presidency University and Jawaharlal Nehru University in India before being awarded a DPhil in history from the University of Cambridge. She has taught history and South Asian studies in various institutions, including the European University Institute, the London School of Economics and Political Science and Hampshire College. In 2018, she joined the University of Nottingham as Assistant Professor of Liberal Arts.

Citizen Refugee

Forging the Indian Nation after Partition

Uditi Sen

University of Nottingham

CAMBRIDGE
UNIVERSITY PRESS

CAMBRIDGE
UNIVERSITY PRESS

University Printing House, Cambridge CB2 8BS, United Kingdom

One Liberty Plaza, 20th Floor, New York, NY 10006, USA

477 Williamstown Road, Port Melbourne, VIC 3207, Australia

314–321, 3rd Floor, Plot 3, Splendor Forum, Jasola District Centre,
New Delhi – 110025, India

79 Anson Road, #06–04/06, Singapore 079906

Cambridge University Press is part of the University of Cambridge.

It furthers the University's mission by disseminating knowledge in the pursuit of
education, learning, and research at the highest international levels of excellence.

www.cambridge.org
Information on this title: www.cambridge.org/9781108425612
DOI: 10.1017/9781108348553

First published 2018

Printed and bound in Great Britain by Clays Ltd, Elcograf S.p.A.

A catalogue record for this publication is available from the British Library.

Library of Congress Cataloging-in-Publication Data
Names: Sen, Uditi, author.
Title: Citizen refugee : forging the Indian nation after partition / Uditi Sen,
Nottingham University.
Description: Cambridge, United Kingdom ; New York, NY, USA : Cambridge
University Press is part of the University of Cambridge, [2018] | Includes
bibliographical references.
Identifiers: LCCN 2017061461 | ISBN 9781108425612
Subjects: LCSH: Refugees – India – West Bengal – History – 20th century. |
India – History – Partition, 1947 – Influence. | Hindus – India – West Bengal –
History – 20th century. | Citizenship – India – History – 20th century. | West
Bengal (India) – Politics and government – 20th century.
Classification: LCC HV640.4.I4 S47 2018 | DDC 305.9/06914095409045–dc23
LC record available at https://lccn.loc.gov/2017061461

ISBN 978-1-108-42561-2 Hardback

Contents

List of Figures and Maps	*page* vi
List of Tables	vii
Preface	ix
Acknowledgements	xii
Note on Spelling and Translations	xvi
Introduction	1
Part I Framing Policy	21
1 Unwanted Citizens in a Saturated State: Towards a Governmentality of Rehabilitation	23
2 Harnessed to National Development: Settlers, Producers and Agents of Hinduisation	71
Part II Rebuilding Lives	113
3 Exiles or Settlers? Caste, Governance and Identity in the Andaman Islands	115
4 Unruly Citizens: Memory, Identity and the Anatomy of Squatting in Calcutta	161
5 Gendered Belongings: State, Social Workers and the 'Unattached' Refugee Woman	201
Conclusion	241
Appendices	251
Select Bibliography	257
Index	276

Figures and Maps

Figures

1.1 Refugees from East Pakistan, 1950   *page* 22
1.2 Refugees from East Pakistan at Dandakaranya   22
2.1 Bengali Refugees at Calcutta Port, boarding a ship
    to Andaman Islands, 1949   70
3.1 East Bengali refugees build huts at the Andaman Islands   118
3.2 Refugees from East Pakistan at South Andaman Islands, 1951   118
5.1 Sketch plan of Bansberia Women's Home, c.1989 (not to
    scale)   231

Maps

0.1 India and Pakistan in January 1948   xviii
3.1 Andaman Islands showing settled areas in 1961   114

Tables

1.1 Chronological statement of exodus from erstwhile
    East Pakistan to India, 1946–70   *page* 42
1.2 Accepted schemes of residuary rehabilitation, 1962   60
2.1 Pattern of refugee resettlement in the Andaman Islands,
    1949–52   87
2.2 Displaced families settled in the Andaman
    and Nicobar Islands, 1953–71   106
3.1 Refugees settled in South Andaman Island, 1949–52   120

Preface

Officially, this book began as a proposal for doctoral research at the University of Cambridge. Yet, the seeds of this history had been sown long before I had the skills and resources to write it, in a sphere far removed from the archives, libraries and lecture halls that usually inspire historical research. My interest in understanding and interrogating partition's aftermath was born of growing up in Calcutta, in a middle-class and Anglicised family that was nominally Hindu, and traced its origins to eastern Bengal. Partition, or *deshbhag* in Bengali, was not something I encountered in history books. Surprisingly, it was also not part of family histories narrated by grandparents. Though both sides of my family traced their origins to East Bengal, the stories passed down across generations in our family were not of violence, displacement or migration. Instead, I grew up with humorous, irreverent and even scandalous anecdotes regarding, what seemed to me, an army of eccentric relatives I could barely keep track of. Yet, partition permeated my childhood. As far back as I can recall, most social interactions with Bengalis who were not family members soon led to an attempt to place each other within the partitioned landscape of Bengal. Someone would pop the question, *Ghati na Bangal?* (Are you a *Ghati* or a *Bangal?*) In this ordering of social difference that only made sense in a post-partition context, a *Ghati* was a Hindu whose family came from the western districts of Bengal, while a *Bangal* was a Hindu whose family came from the eastern districts of Bengal – those areas, that went to Pakistan and eventually became Bangladesh. At times, the question would be phrased as *edeshi na odeshi*, which literally translates as 'from this country or that'? Though I was born in a nursing home in Calcutta more than three decades after partition, the correct answer for me was that I was a *Bangal* from 'that country', an *odeshi*. If further probed to answer where I was from, I had been taught to recite the following stock answer: '*Gram* (village) Panchchar, Police Station Madaripur, *Jela* (district) Faridpur'. Reciting names of places in East Bengal that I had never seen, as proof of where I was from, seemed entirely natural in that social milieu. Growing up in Calcutta, partition was not a clutch of stories that

I had inherited. It became part of my identity, intertwined into my everyday social negotiations.

As I began to develop an academic interest in history and pursued the subject at Presidency University and Jawaharlal Nehru University (JNU), I began to realise that partition haunted the social and cultural landscape of Calcutta. These hauntings included the differences in *Ghati* and *Bangal* cuisine, the passionate rivalry in football between East Bengal and Mohun Bagan and a world of stereotypes, both positive and negative, regarding the 'other' community, which generated a lot of inappropriate but satisfying humour. When I sought to pursue a doctoral dissertation at the University of Cambridge, it was this everyday aspect of partition's aftermath, its myriad social and cultural manifestations, that I proposed to research. An early archival encounter with a 'forgotten' episode of refugee resettlement in the Andaman Islands disrupted my plans of writing this Calcutta-centric history. As I broadened the scope of my inquiry, I realised that the impact of millions of Hindu refugees from eastern Pakistan extended far beyond my hometown. In its final form, this book makes explicit these lesser known and under-explored consequences of the presence of millions of unwanted refugees from eastern Pakistan. In the process, it has strayed quite far from its origins in cultural history centred upon Calcutta. Yet, it is fundamentally shaped by a historical subjectivity born of the everyday presence of partition in the social milieu of Calcutta.

There are two fundamental ways in which the everydayness of partition, which I grew up with, has informed this book. Almost half of *Citizen Refugee* is built on analysis of refugee reminiscences and oral history. Looking back, I realise that it was my own intimate and everyday relationship with partition that inspired me to look for and understand other such intimate narratives, where history becomes intertwined with identity. The fact that I was able to identify respondents and conduct this research into partition's history 'from below' derives in no small measure from my own social location. The 'field' I started my research in was the familiar alleys and streets of my hometown, and my first informants were family and friends and their friends and family. I scrupulously avoided all suggestions to interview grand-aunts, distant uncles and in-laws, but gratefully accepted phone numbers and addresses of refugee leaders, introductions to scholars and social workers and most importantly, copies and photocopies of out-of-print autobiographies, pamphlets and souvenirs produced by refugee organisations. While my affiliation to Cambridge opened the doors of numerous archives and libraries in India and the UK, my social and familial affiliations gave me access to this intertwined world of memory, history and identity. In the ultimate analysis, this book is moulded by the creative encounter between the academic rigour of pursuing a PhD in history, and the personal impulse to make sense of the ways that partition continues to inform the personal histories and identities of millions of families.

Acknowledgements

In the course of conducting the research for this project and converting it into a book, I have been fortunate to accumulate many debts of gratitude, old and new, scattered across three continents. This book began as a proposal for MPhil research on Bengali refugee identity at JNU. It found its current focus of exploring the paradoxes and possibilities of the citizen-refugee in post-colonial India at the University of Cambridge, where an early version was submitted as a doctoral dissertation in 2009. The present book is born of substantive revisions and ongoing intellectual conversations with old mentors and colleagues in India and the UK, as well as new colleagues and mentors at the Five Colleges, in the USA. At each stage, I have enjoyed support that I am thankful for.

Tanika Sarkar mentored me into archival research and helped me to develop a feminist analytical framework at the beginning of my career at JNU. While I was fortunate to enjoy the support of Rosalind O'Hanlon and Chris Bayly in finding my intellectual feet at Cambridge, my doctoral dissertation took its final shape under Joya Chatterji. My research was inspired by Professor Chatterji's scholarship long before I met her and I was extremely fortunate to complete my doctoral dissertation under her. Joya Chatterji's insights, encouragement and unstinting support have been invaluable in completing the dissertation and in its long-winded path to becoming a book. The process of converting my thesis into a book manuscript gained new focus and impetus at the AIIS Dissertation to Book Workshop held at the 2013 Madison Conference in South Asian Studies. I am thankful to all the participants who read and discussed my work, as well as the workshop leaders, Susan S. Wadley, Geraldine Forbes and Pika Ghosh, for their invaluable guidance. I am grateful to Hampshire College for granting me leave from a busy teaching schedule that has enabled me to complete this book.

This project would simply not have been possible without the generous financial support I have received from a number of funding bodies. My doctoral research was supported by the Cambridge Commonwealth Trust, Richard Alford and Charles Wallace India Trust, Cambridge

Political Economy Society, Smuts Fund, Prince Consort and Thirlwall Fund, Holland Rose Fund and Clare College. I am grateful for the help and cooperation of the staff, archivists and librarians of the University Library and the Centre for South Asian Studies in Cambridge, the British Library and the School of Oriental and African Studies Library in London, the International Institute of Social History Library in Amsterdam, the National Archives and Nehru Memorial Museum and Library in Delhi and the Central Agricultural Research Institute and the State Library of Andaman and Nicobar Islands in Port Blair. The bulk of my research was carried out in various libraries and archives in Calcutta, including the National Library, the West Bengal State Archives, the Police (Intelligence Branch) Archives, the Centre for Women's Studies Library in Jadavpur University, the Jadunath Sarkar Resource Centre for Historical Research and the archive of the Centre for Studies in Social Sciences (CSSS). I thank the archivists and librarians of these institutions for guiding me safely through the maze of bureaucratic hurdles that greets researchers of the post-colonial state in West Bengal. I am particularly grateful to Kamalika Mukherjee of CSSS and Saktidas Roy of the Anandabazar Patrika Library and Archives for their guidance and help.

Conversations and interactions with a number of people have helped me to work out my ideas. I would like to acknowledge my debt to Tanika Sarkar, Samita Sen, Subhash Chakraborty, Gargi Chakravartty, Mrinalini Sinha and Asok Sen. Much of the material used in this thesis is derived from an alternative archive of oral history, popular memory and out-of-print vernacular publications, which are seldom stored in archives due to their relatively recent provenance. I acknowledge the incredible generosity of an army of friends, well-wishers and complete strangers who have helped me to locate these sources. I am especially grateful to Subhoranjan Dasgupta and Subhasri Ghosh for sharing with me transcripts of interviews with refugee women. I thank Mr Dan, the librarian of Havelock High School, for his help in locating respondents in the Andaman Islands. Above all, I thank the refugee-settlers of the Andamans for their time, their trust and their willingness to share their memories.

I have presented some of the research and key findings of this book at various conferences and colloquiums, and I have benefitted greatly from the thoughtful comments and questions from the participants and audiences. I am particularly grateful to the Centre for South Asian Studies at the University of Cambridge, where I first presented the main arguments of my thesis, and to the to the participants and organizers of the conference on "Meanings of Citizenship in South Asia", hosted by the Department of International Development at the University of Oxford, where I received extremely positive feedback on the connections I proposed between refugees, citizenship and Nehruvian development. My conceptualisation of women as residues of rehabilitation benefitted from critical feedback at the work-in-progress workshop on "From Subjects to Citizens: Society and the Everyday State in India and Pakistan 1947–1964", held at Royal Holloway, University of London, in 2009. I am thankful to the organisers and participants of "Caste Today: the Fifth Annual Contemporary India Seminar" at the University of Oslo, where I had the opportunity to further develop my explorations of how caste identity impacted partition refugees with feedback from an informed audience.

A version of Chapter 4 was published as "The Myths Refugees Live By: Memory and History in the Making of Bengali Refugee identity", *Modern Asian Studies*, 48:1, (2014), 37–76 and is reprinted with permission. Some of the quotes from oral history interviews with refugees re-settled in the Andaman Islands, which are used in Chapter 3, particularly those on pages 137, 138, 140, 142 and 152, appeared in a previous publication, "Dissident Memories: Exploring Bengali Refugee Narratives in the Andaman Islands" in Panikos Panayi and Pippa Virdee (eds.) *Refugees and the End of Empire: Imperial Collapse and Forced Migration during the Twentieth Century* (Basingstoke and New York: Palgrave Macmillan, 2011). I am grateful to the publishers and the editors for their permission to reuse this research.

No research thrives in isolation and this book has been nourished by several vibrant intellectual communities. I thank my teachers and friends in JNU, including Neeladri Bhattacharya, Radhika Singha, Majid Siddiqui, Tanika Sarkar, Rachna Singh, Shipra Nigam, Sanjukta Sundersaon, Mahesh Gopalan and Aditya Sarkar, for encouraging and enduring long debates on history and methodology that laid the foundations of this book. During my doctoral research at the University of Cambridge, I was fortunate to find a community of scholars who have remained supportive readers and informed critiques of my scholarship over the years. I am particularly thankful to William Gould, Rachel Berger, Eleanor Newbigin, Taylor Sherman, Zirwat Chowdhury and, above all, Erica Wald for their generosity in either reading through drafts or thinking through ideas. My friends and colleagues in the Five College Consortium have provided crucial support in the last leg of this marathon process. I am particularly grateful to Jennifer Hamilton for her unwavering support, Yael Rice for her invaluable company in weekends spent writing and Hiba bou Akar for always making time for my last-minute request to read drafts. I would also like to thank Amrita Basu, Pinky Hota, Amina Steinfels, Kavita Datla, Krupa Shandilya, Sujani Reddy, Nusrat

Chowdhury and Sahar Sajdadi for a heady combination of good food, mentorship and nights out dancing – all crucial ingredients for completing a book. Finally, I would like to thank Lucy Rhymer of Cambridge University Press, for her support and enthusiasm for this project.

I thank my mother, Indrani Sen, for encouraging my every endeavour. She has been my unofficial research assistant in Calcutta and this project has benefitted massively from her ability to dig up a 'contact' almost anywhere, including the Andaman Islands. I thank my sister, Ishani Sen, and my brother-in-law, Santanu Datta, for their unconditional support. I regret that my grand-uncle, Asok Sen, did not live to see the completion of this project. It is only in his absence that I have come to fully appreciate how far his incisive comments, suggested readings and gentle critiques have informed the analytical trajectory of this book. I would like to dedicate this book to the memory of my father, Udayan Sen, who glorified my teenage precociousness with the motto of 'plain living and high thinking'.

Last, but not least, I thank Onni Gust, my strongest critic, most reliable reader and partner in intellectual growth for over a decade. Their patience, support and love has kept me sane and seen this project through.

Note on Spelling and Translations

In recent decades, several states and cities of South Asia have been renamed to reflect non-Anglicised pronunciations. Most of these changes in names amount to changes in spellings, such as Kolkata instead of Calcutta and Odisha instead of Orissa. However, during the period under research, i.e. 1947 to 1971, the older names and spellings were in use. In order to avoid confusion and to maintain consistency, I have used the older spellings throughout the text. For example, I use Calcutta instead of Kolkata.

All the interviews with refugees in the Andaman Islands were conducted in Bengali. The oral histories of refugee women living in permanent liability camps were accessed primarily as transcripts written in Bengali. In addition, this book also draws upon numerous Bengali sources on refugee life in and around Calcutta, ranging from pamphlets and autobiographical accounts to collections of oral history. Instead of reproducing the Bengali original, I have translated the interviews that are cited in the text. Occasionally, specific words and phrases have been reproduced in the original Bengali, accompanied with a translation. This is mostly designed to retain some of the texture and cadence of the interviews. In order to ensure readability, and in keeping with common practice, I have avoided the use of diacritical marks while transliterating Bengali words and phrases into the Roman script. I have attempted to replicate Bengali pronunciation, as far as possible, using the Roman script.

Map 1.1 India and Pakistan in January 1948

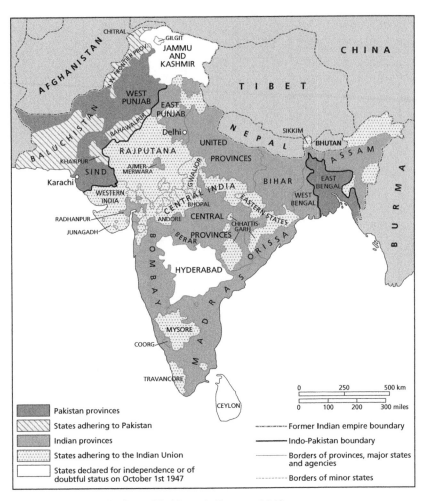

Map 0.1: India and Pakistan in January 1948

Introduction

*And what happened in Palestine . . . . was then repeated in India on a large
scale involving many millions of people. Since the Peace Treaties of 1919 and
1920 the refugees and the stateless have attached themselves like a curse to all
newly established states on earth which were created in the image of the nation-
state. For these new states this curse bears the germs of a deadly sickness.*

Hannah Arendt[1]

Indian independence took the form of the partitioning of British India
into Muslim-majority Pakistan and Hindu-majority India. The twinning
of partition with independence has long disrupted any celebratory narrative of the arrival of the nation-state in South Asia.[2] In northern India, and
especially in Punjab, it was accompanied by communal violence that was
unprecedented in its scale and brutality.[3] In the divided provinces of
Bengal and Assam, minorities usually faced covert forms of social and
political marginalisation that occasionally escalated to violent riots.[4] All
over this partitioned landscape, millions of minorities felt 'stranded' on

[1] Hannah Arendt, *The Origins of Totalitarianism* (London: André Deutsch, 1986), p. 290.
[2] Historians of India have struggled to contain the contradictory motifs of national birth and
partition within a singular narrative. Mushirul Hasan, in 'Memories of a Fragmented
Nation: Rewriting the Histories of India's Partition' in *Inventing Boundaries: Gender,
Politics and the Partition of India* (New Delhi, 2000), pp. 26–44, clearly privileges fiction
as the ideal means for capturing the popular history of partition. In 'Partition, Pakistan and
South Asian history: In search of a narrative', *The Journal of Asian Studies*, 57, 4 (1998),
1068–95, David Gilmartin suggests approaching partition as a moment of re-negotiation
of the relationship between high politics and everyday life in South Asia. Gyanendra
Pandey, in *Remembering Partition: Violence, Nationalism and History in India* (Cambridge,
2001), deconstructs the unitary notion of a single political partition into its multiple
meanings and negotiations while Ranabir Sammadar, in *Reflections on Partition in the
East* (New Delhi and Calcutta, 1997), argues that South Asia's discontent with the
settlement of 1947 might well warrant the renaming of the post-colonial period as 'post-
partition' times.
[3] For details see Swarna Aiyar, '"August Anarchy": The Partition Massacres in Punjab,
1947', *South Asia: Journal of South Asian Studies* 18:1 (1995), 13–36; Paul R. Brass, 'The
Partition of India and Retributive Genocide in the Punjab, 1946–47: Means, Methods,
and Purposes 1', *Journal of Genocide Research*, 5: 1 (2003), 71–101.
[4] See Nilanjana Chatterjee, 'Interrogating Victimhood: East Bengali Refugee Narratives of
Communal Violence', (http://www.swadhinata.org.uk/document/chatterjeeEastBengal%
20Refugee.pdf, accessed 18 August 2015).

the wrong side and fled to their putative homelands. This gave rise to a refugee crisis of staggering proportions and complexity. While no accurate numbers are available of Hindu and Sikh minorities who left Pakistan for India, or of Muslims who left India for Pakistan, the total number of refugees is estimated to be anything between 11 to 18 million.[5] In recent decades, histories of partition have privileged quotidian negotiations of this political rift, highlighting themes of displacement, loss and violence.[6] These new histories explore partition as a process instead of an event, where the long-term struggle to rebuild lives and communities continues well beyond 1947.[7] A particularly rich analytical prism is provided by regional studies that investigate the long afterlife of partition in directly impacted geographies, which are variously conceptualised as divided polities, fractured trade networks, new borderlands or 'capitol landscapes'.[8] The figure of the displaced minority, variously classified as migrants, refugees, displaced persons, *muhajirs* and evacuees, emerges

[5] For a discussion of the inconsistent practices of enumeration of partition refugees, especially in Bengal, and the contradictory figures thrown up as a result see Abhijit Dasgupta, 'The Puzzling Numbers: The Politics of Counting "Refugees" in West Bengal', *SARWATCH*, 2:2 (2002), 64–73. In recent years, demographic data has led 'official' figures to be progressively revised upwards. The figure of eleven to eighteen million is taken from Prashant Bharadwaj, Asim Ijaz Khwaja and Atif R. Mian, 'The Partition of India: Demographic Consequences', June 2009, available at SSRN: http://ssrn.com/a bstract=1294846. A higher figure of 20 million is mentioned in Joya Chatterji, 'From Imperial Subjects to National Citizens: South Asians and the International Migration Regime since 1947' in Joya Chatterji and David Washbrook (eds.) *Routledge Handbook of the South Asian Diaspora* (London and New York: Routledge, 2013), p. 187.

[6] Gyanesh Kudaisya and Tai Yong Tan, *The Aftermath of Partition in South Asia* (London: Routledge, 2004); Anjali Gera Roy and Nandi Bhatia, *Partitioned Lives: Narratives of Home, Displacement, and Resettlement* (Delhi: Pearson Education India, 2008); Amritjit Singh, Nalini Iyer, and Rahul K. Gairola, *Revisiting India's Partition: New Essays on Memory, Culture, and Politics* (Lanham, MD: Lexington Books, 2016); Urvashi Butalia (ed.), *Partition: The Long Shadow* (New Delhi: Zubaan/Penguin, 2015); Yasmin Khan, *The Great Partition: The Making of India and Pakistan* (New Haven and London: Yale University Press, 2008); Deepti Misri, *Beyond Partition: Gender, Violence, and Representation in Postcolonial India* (Champaign, IL: University of Illinois Press, 2014).

[7] Of particular importance is the term 'long partition' used by Vazira Zamindar, which shifts the emphasis from partition's impact to looking at partition as a long-term process. See Vazira Fazila Zamindar, *The Long Partition and the Making of Modern South Asia: Refugees, Boundaries, Histories* (New York: Columbia University Press, 2007).

[8] Willem van Schendel, *The Bengal Borderland: Beyond State and Nation in South Asia* (Anthem Press, 2005); Sarah F. D. Ansari, *Life After Partition: Migration, Community and Strife in Sindh, 1947–1962* (Oxford: Oxford University Press, 2005); Ravinder Kaur, *Since 1947: Partition Narratives Among Punjabi Migrants of Delhi* (New Delhi: Oxford University Press, 2007); Joya Chatterji, *The Spoils of Partition: Bengal and India, 1947–1967* (Cambridge and New York: Cambridge University Press, 2007); Ilyas Chattha, *Partition and Locality: Violence, Migration, and Development in Gujranwala and Sialkot, 1947–1961* (Karachi : Oxford University Press, 2011); Haimanti Roy, *Partitioned Lives: Migrants, Refugees, Citizens in India and Pakistan, 1947–65* (New Delhi: Oxford University Press, 2012); Debjani Sengupta, *The Partition of Bengal: Fragile Borders and New Identities* (Delhi: Cambridge University Press, 2016).

as a central figure in these histories. The centrality of displaced persons in histories of partition is not merely born of the scale and complexity of the refugee crisis unleashed by the hurried division of British India; it is also indicative of a peculiar feature of partition refugees. The refugees who sought shelter in India and Pakistan in the aftermath of partition claimed to be *both* refugees and citizens of their putative homelands. This allowed partition refugees to occupy a visible and central place in the post-partition polities of South Asia. The significance of this simultaneous iteration of refugee-ness and national belonging is the point of departure of this study. This unlikely conjuncture transformed the project of rehabilitation of partition refugees into a richly contested sphere of governance where refugee visions of rights and belonging clashed with official ideals of governance and citizenship.

The political leadership of India and Pakistan did not anticipate any large-scale movement of minorities. As a result, in both India and Pakistan, policy lagged behind ground realities. When refugees started pouring in from Punjab, along with reports of 'stranded' minorities facing mass slaughter, the authorities were forced to improvise. In the face of escalating violence and complete polarisation along ethnic and religious lines, initial hopes of restoring peace in Punjab and repatriating refugees rapidly gave way to a bilateral military operation to evacuate stranded minorities. The Hindu and Sikh minorities who were rescued in this manner and brought 'home' to India could not be excluded from the emerging community of citizens. The evacuation of minorities from Punjab was completed by January 1948.[9] In the eyes of the state, this was an exceptional measure, adopted in order to deal with an emergency situation. It nevertheless drew force from prevalent discourses of ethno-nationalist belongings, in which India and Pakistan were seen as the respective homelands of Hindus and Muslims.[10] The evacuated minorities, who were initially housed in government-administered refugee camps, were seen to belong to the new nation-states. In post-partition India, this led to equivalence between becoming a Hindu or Sikh refugee and becoming a de facto citizen. The violent arrival of the nation-state in

[9] For details see U. Bhaskar Rao, *The Story of Rehabilitation* (Department of Rehabilitation, Ministry of Labour, Employment and Rehabilitation, Government of India, 1967), pp. 4–29.
[10] These discourses had deep roots in colonial historiography and nineteenth century literature that consistently portrayed Muslims as outsiders and invaders in India. For example, see Shahid Amin, 'Representing the Musalman: Then and Now, Now and Then', in Shail Mayaram, M. S. S. Pandian, Ajay Skaria (eds.) *Subaltern Studies XII: Muslims, Dalits, and the Fabrications of History* (New Delhi: Permanent Black and Ravi Dayal Publisher, 2005).

South Asia thus gave birth to the paradoxical figure of the citizen-refugee. Families displaced by partition became refugees and staked a claim to citizenship long before the new rulers of India had managed to define either a partition refugee or an Indian citizen.

The refugee crisis that engulfed post-partition South Asia posed a fundamental challenge to the emerging nation-states. The question posed by the millions of refugees who crossed the newly minted international borders of India and Pakistan was one which lies at the heart of the modern political system. The post-war international order of nation-states seeks to organise populations into national groups, each with their own sovereign state, or homeland. The modern refugee is the product of a world where the ground realities of multi-ethnic societies contradicts the political ideal of a seamless congruence between the territory and population encompassed by a state and the political community of a nation. Given that the nation, as an 'imagined community',[11] has seldom been free from ethnic or religious markers of belonging, where do ethnic and religious minorities belong? This question has been answered differently by various philosophers and political scientists, depending on the particular minority group they study, and the specificity of the historical context. Many scholars, beginning with Hannah Arendt, have cited India's post-partition refugee crisis as an example that illustrates how nation-states inevitably fail to shelter ethnic and religious minorities. A brief survey of this literature presents a curious anomaly. The partition of India is repeatedly evoked as an example of how nation-states generate refugees. However, this evocation is selective. Post-partition South Asia did not merely generate a large number of refugees; it also absorbed an overwhelming majority of these refugees within the rank of citizens. Thus, to cite partition refugees as an example of the inevitable incommensurability between nation-states and ethnic minorities is to tell only half the story. The history of rehabilitation of millions of refugees in South Asia calls for a more nuanced understanding of the relationship between emerging nation-states and refugees in the twentieth century.

Arendt argued, based on her experience of the first half of the twentieth century, that nation-states were prone to creating, through expulsion from their ranks of citizens, the 'curse' of refugees and stateless people. For Arendt, this expulsion was a symptom of the rise of totalitarianism, or the emergence of a kind of state that dealt with diversity through the expulsion of people who did not fit a prefigured ideal of citizenship. Arendt analysed the predicament of Jewish refugees in post-war Europe

---

[11] Benedict Anderson, *Imagined Communities: Reflections on the Origin and Spread of Nationalism* (London: Verso, 1991).

to illustrate what she believed to be the inevitable fate of all minorities in modern nation-states. Writing in 1948, she cited the millions displaced in India and Pakistan as proof of her indictment of all states 'built in the image of the nation-state'.[12] Arendt's theorisation of the impossibility of minority belonging has been understandably influential within refugee studies, as it is usually displaced minorities who populate the category of the refugee. Aristide Zolberg expands Arendt's insight to argue that nation-building is a refugee-generating process that is neither limited to totalitarian regimes, nor unique to the twentieth century. He argues that the homogenising impulse of states can be traced back to early modern Spain and France, when nationalism first emerged as an organising principle of political power in Western Europe. The same process, with important variations, has been repeated in the demise of multi-ethnic empires in Eastern Europe and colonial empires in Asia and Africa.[13] Zolberg explicitly cites the partition of India as the 'classic case' that illustrates how the birth of new nation-states transformed minorities into refugees fleeing from violence.[14] Giorgio Agamben builds upon Arendt's insights to argue that the figure of the refugee is not just representative of minorities who cannot belong, but an embodiment of the unresolved crisis of the contemporary political order of nation-states that reduces anyone who is not a national to 'bare life' – a human being devoid of political rights.[15] Within this particular trajectory of thought, the refugee emerges as the radical outsider. They are the essential opposite of citizens and nationals. Becoming a refugee, in this context, is usually read as an experience of loss – of homes, of political rights *and* of citizenship. However, becoming a refugee in post-partition India did not only connote loss. While displacement was a formative experience for all partition refugees, it was not coterminous with the process of *becoming* refugees. Millions of minorities who were forcibly displaced from their homes in the wake of a violent partition became refugees, both by their own accounting and in official records, only *after* they crossed the new national borders. To become a refugee in post-partition India was not only to be displaced. To become a refugee was to claim the right to relief and rehabilitation from the state. In other words, in post-partition India, the displaced became refugees in order to stake a claim to their putative

---

[12] Arendt, *The Decline of the Nation-State and the End of the Rights of Man* (1986).

[13] Aristide R. Zolberg, 'The Formation of New States as a Refugee-Generating Process', *Annals of the American Academy of Political and Social Science*, 467(1983), 24–38.

[14] Aristide R. Zolberg, Astri Suhrke and Sergio Aguayo, *Escape from Violence: Conflict and the Refugee Crisis in the Developing World* (Oxford, New York: Oxford University Press, 1989).

[15] Giorgio Agamben, *Homo Sacer: Sovereign Power and Bare Life*, trans. Daniel Heller-Roazen, 1st edition (Stanford, CA: Stanford University Press, 1998).

homeland. The constraints and possibilities of refugee life in South Asia have always exceeded Eurocentric formulations of refugees as stateless outsiders and abject victims.

The partition refugees' claim to be citizens of their host states gained traction due to contingent circumstances. The need to grant citizenship to the minorities evacuated from divided Punjab was one of many ingredients that went into the making of the citizen-refugee. Partition refugees evoked shared communitarian ties with the host society and a historical loyalty to Indian or Pakistani nationalism as a basis of belonging. Though the partitioning of British India into Muslim-majority Pakistan and Hindu-majority India was sold as a 'solution' to the problem of providing adequate rights to the Muslim minority, in effect, it offered no real solution for minority belonging. Once the dust settled over the borders, millions of Muslims were 'left behind' in India while several million Hindus found themselves in Pakistan. Partition deepened the vulnerability of minorities by recasting them as people out of place. Yet, the founding fathers of India and Pakistan neither anticipated nor encouraged the movement of minorities. While Sardar Patel was content to lament their pain and loss,[16] Muhammad Ali Jinnah waxed eloquent on the 'sacrifices' made by those 'left behind'.[17] By migrating, minorities refused to be sacrificed. Instead, they claimed affective belonging to their putative homelands, demanded compensation for their displacement and loss of homes, and expected to become citizens in the host societies. The new nation-states disapproved of such migration and exhorted minorities to stay put, but they were powerless to stop migration across still largely notional borders. The categorical denial of citizenship to migrants was technically impossible, given that the laws and statutes conferring Indian and Pakistani citizenship were yet to be formulated. More importantly, this was a political impossibility. In both India and Pakistan, the partition refugees' claim to moral citizenship enjoyed considerable support, not just among their co-religionists, but also amongst bureaucrats and politicians. The exchange of minority populations in Punjab was enabled by this atmosphere. Once accomplished, it provided validation for the moral citizenship of displaced minorities that spilled beyond the frontiers of Punjab. It became a popular demand that resonated across the partitioned landscape of India and Pakistan. This is not to suggest that all minorities chose to, or even wanted to migrate. For many, migration

---

[16] Sardar Patel's speech delivered on 15 August 1947, as cited in *Andandabazar Patrika*, 28 January 1964.

[17] Jinnah's speech 'Those Who Gave Great Sacrifices' delivered on 9 June 1947, cited in Tahir Hasnain Naqvi, 'The Politics of Commensuration: The Violence of Partition and the Making of the Pakistani State', *Journal of Historical Sociology*, 20:1 &2 (2007), p. 56.

offered no remedy for a profound loss ushered in by the new borders that divided families, disrupted livelihoods, and dismantled shared cultural worlds. Yet, becoming a refugee, in post-partition India and Pakistan, was also a step towards national belonging. This study begins in the immediate aftermath of displacement, mapping the complexity of the intertwined processes of becoming a refugee and becoming a citizen in independent India.

Becoming Refugee, Becoming Citizen: The Status of Displaced Hindus in India

This book focuses on the Hindu minorities who left East Bengal, or the eastern wing of Pakistan, between 1947 and 1970, and sought refuge in West Bengal. Though migration continued and even reached crisis levels after 1970, the refugees who fled civil war in Pakistan cannot be regarded as partition refugees. They were the result of yet another process of national determination in South Asia, and marked the violent birth of Bangladesh in 1971. Between 1947 and 1970, migration across the Bengal frontier continued in fits and starts. There was no comprehensive process of enumeration, and official estimates of East Bengali migrants who sought refuge in India between 1946 and 1970 vary between 5.8 million[18] and 4.1 million.[19] West Bengal alone took in over 3.9 million refugees.[20] Though the patterns of displacement and official response varied significantly across these twenty-three years, this period nevertheless enjoys a certain coherence due to the ability of Bengali refugees to make claims upon the local and national government as de facto citizens. For all Hindu migrants the path to citizenship passed through official acknowledgement of refugeehood. However, the government of India was particularly reluctant to accept the refugee status of Hindu migrants from East Bengal. As a result, the Bengali refugee's long-term struggle to wrest relief and rehabilitation from a recalcitrant state emerges as a key site for the articulation of the limits and possibilities of Hindu belonging in post-colonial India.

If we go by official declarations and constitutional guarantees alone, then the inclusion of Hindu and Sikh refugees within the body of Indian

---

[18] Pran Nath Luthra, *Rehabilitation* (New Delhi: Publications Division, 1972).

[19] Committee for Review of Rehabilitation Work in West Bengal, *Report of the Working Group on the Residual Problem of Rehabilitation in West Bengal* (Calcutta, 1976).

[20] This is the official figure, as mentioned in Pran Nath Luthra, *Rehabilitation*, 1972; and cited in Chatterji, *Spoils of Partition* (2007), p. 112. This number possibly reflected the number of registered refugees, and the actual number of minorities who claimed refuge in West Bengal is likely to be much higher.

citizenry appears to be a deceptively straightforward process. Discussions within the Constituent Assembly rapidly led to a broad-based consensus that Hindu and Sikh minorities fleeing violence in Pakistan belonged in India.[21] In 1950, their right to belong to India was enshrined in the constitution. Article 5 allowed citizenship by registration to all those who had migrated to India from Pakistan, provided they had arrived in India before the commencement of the constitution.[22] But the influx of refugees continued well beyond 1950 and informed subsequent discussions on citizenship. The question of refugee belonging re-emerged as a dominant concern in 1955, moulding the tenor and texture of the debate around the Citizenship Bill. Pandit Pant, the Home Minister, was eager for a swift passage of the bill in order to ensure that the 'tens of thousands of displaced persons' who 'have come over and are still coming to India from Pakistan' could be given their full rights as citizens, including the right to vote in the forthcoming elections.[23] However, representatives from West Bengal, such as B. K. Das, criticised the bill for demanding the cumbrous and bureaucratic process of registration from destitute refugees, who might not have possessed the necessary papers. Instead of registration, Das wanted the bill to provide a definition for displaced persons that would declare all displaced persons to be citizens of India. Pant refused, insisting that registration was necessary to avoid confusion. However, he was also quick to clarify that the bill did not propose to endow partition refugees with a new right, or monitor their eligibility for citizenship. The right of citizenship, according to him, was 'already there'.[24] In other words, India's Citizenship Bill formally acknowledged the contradictory category of the citizen-refugee. For displaced Hindus from Pakistan, being seen as refugees or displaced persons by the Indian state opened up a pathway to citizenship through registration.

Pandit Pant's reassurance that all refugees already had the right to citizenship left a vital question unanswered. Who counted as a bona fide refugee in post-partition India? There was no simple answer to this question. This was partly because the government of India was forced

---

[21] For an analysis of how the presence of partition refugees impacted the formulation of legal citizenship in India, see Joya Chatterji, 'South Asian Histories of Citizenship, 1946–1970,' *The Historical Journal* 55:4 (2012), 1049–71.

[22] Refugees of Indian descent who arrived before 19 July 1948 were exempted from the process of registration. The full draft of the Constitution of India is available at http://india.gov.in/my-government/constitution-india.

[23] Statement by Pandit Pant in the Lok Sabha, as reported in the *Amrita Bazar Patrika*, 12 August 1955. For details of how partition refugees were included in India's electoral roll, see Ornit Shani, *How India became Democratic: Citizenship and the Making of the Universal Franchise*, Cambridge, (New York, Melbourne, New Delhi, Singapore: Cambridge University Press, 2018).

[24] Ibid.

to deal with the refugee crisis on an emergency basis and policies for relief and rehabilitation preceded any clear definition of a partition refugee. The official term used to describe partition refugees was 'displaced persons', which was in keeping with the terminology used by the United Nations Relief and Rehabilitation Administration to refer to refugees born of the Second World War. By 1951, the Geneva Convention had put in place a Eurocentric definition of refugees that included European displaced persons but excluded those displaced by partition in India.[25] Within India, 'displaced persons' and 'refugees' continued to be used interchangeably in various official documents and declarations. While displaced persons or DPs was the preferred and more accurate term for official purposes, in everyday parlance and in the contemporary press, the displaced minorities were more frequently called refugees. Various vernacular iterations of refugee identity, such as *ashrayprarthi*, *sharanarthi* and *udvastu*, proliferated in the public sphere.[26] Displaced Hindus overwhelmingly described themselves using one of these terms, or as a refugee – a word that passed untranslated into vernacular speech. Self-identified refugees often constituted a far broader category than officially recognised DPs. Given that this study pays equal attention to the top-down iteration of policy and the process through which displaced minorities sought to belong, I use the broader category of refugees instead of the bureaucratically sanctioned 'displaced persons' to refer to displaced Hindus from eastern Pakistan.

In the aftermath of partition, there was no attempt to create a pan-Indian definition of a displaced person, or a refugee. This was not just the result of bureaucratic oversight. There was also a marked reluctance, on the part of the government, to come up with a clear definition of partition refugees. The lack of clarity allowed the government of India to maintain an inclusive official stance, where in theory citizenship was within the reach of all displaced persons or DPs. Yet, in order to officially count as a DP, those displaced by partition had to meet a host of discriminatory criteria, which the local authorities could change at will by periodically issuing new circulars that imposed new requirements and preconditions. As a result, questions around migration, minority belonging and citizenship continued to animate politics and policies in post-colonial India. Did minorities displaced from all parts of Pakistan count as de facto citizens of India? What would happen to those who migrated after 1950, or after

---

[25] For details of this process of exclusions see Pia Oberoi, *Exile and Belonging: Refugees and State Policy in South Asia* (New Delhi: Oxford University Press, 2006), pp. 11–43.

[26] *Ashrayprarthi* and *saranarthi* both translate as those who seek refuge/shelter. The former was used largely in Bengali, while *saranarthi* was used in Bengali and Hindi. *Udvastu* is a Bengali term, meaning those removed from homelands, or the uprooted.

1956, when the new Citizenship Act came into force? Was proof of facing persecution or violence in Pakistan an adequate or necessary criterion for becoming a refugee? Could Muslim migrants from Pakistan count as refugees in India? The official refusal to articulate clearly who could and could not be a partition refugee had the benefit of displacing these unresolved questions into the sphere of everyday governance. Contestation was rife over issues of *who* could count as a partition refugee, *how* official recognition was conferred, and *what* such recognition entailed in terms of relief and rehabilitation.

Neither India not Pakistan had any intention of accommodating all minorities 'left behind' on the other side. Pakistan, while upholding its foundational ideal of a homeland for South Asian Muslims in theory, refuted it in practice by arguing that it was only prepared to provide for Muslim refugees from Punjab and North West Frontier Provinces.[27] This selective acceptance of some but not all Muslim refugees was explicitly justified by Pakistan on grounds of national economic interests.[28] The situation in avowedly secular India was more complicated. In post-partition India, the national leadership found itself walking a tightrope between various contradictory notions of national belonging. In the immediate aftermath of Partition, India's first prime minister, Jawaharlal Nehru, took an uncompromising stand against those who called for a 'Hindu Raj' and the evacuation of all Muslims from India by describing such beliefs as 'sectarian' and 'fascist' in numerous public speeches and declarations.[29] However, his principled commitment to a secular polity was undone by his response to partition refugees. In May 1948, Sardar Patel, the Home Minister of India, sounded the alarm bell regarding the arrival of Muslims from Pakistan. He warned Nehru of 'considerable discontent both among the public, in general, and refugees in particular, in regard to our failure to prevent the inflow'.[30] Nehru's

---

[27] At the inter-dominion conference held at Lahore on 5 October 1948, Liaqat Ali Khan, the prime minister of Pakistan, sought to restrict the accountability of the Pakistan government to the Muslim refugees from Punjab and North West Frontier Province only. Cited in Zamindar, The *Long Partition* (2007), pp. 41–4. For further details on the strategies adopted by Pakistan to restrict migration of Muslims from India see pp. 79–119 and 161–226. Also see Omar Khalidi, 'From Torrent to Trickle: Indian Muslim Migration to Pakistan, 1947–97', *Bulletin of the Henry Martin Institute of Islamic Studies*, 16:1 & 2 (1997), 32–45; and Ansari, *Life after Partition* (2005).

[28] Zamindar, The Long Partition (2007).

[29] For examples see Nehru's address to Congress workers in Delhi on 3 October 1947, as reported in *The Hindu* and his speech at a public meeting in Delhi on 6 October 1947, as reported in *The Hindustan Times*. Both have been reproduced in S. Gopal (ed.), *Selected Works of Jawaharlal Nehru, Second Series, Vol. 4* (New Delhi: Jawaharlal Nehru Memorial Fund, 1984), pp. 118–19 and 124–6.

[30] Vallabhbhai Patel to Jawaharlal Nehru, 4 May 1948, Durga Das (ed.), *Sardar Patel's Correspondence, Vol. 6* (Ahmedabad: Navajivan Publishing House, 1972), pp. 319–20.

response made it clear that Muslim migrants from Pakistan could not join the ranks of refugees in India. He declared that '[r]egarding the influx of Muslims from Pakistan, our policy is clear enough. The difficulty comes in implementing it, especially on the Sind-Rajputana border. We are asking the Military to take some steps in that border to prevent large numbers coming through.'[31] When public policy is read in conjunction with private correspondence, it becomes clear that the refusal to clearly define the contours of the partition refugee allowed the government of India to resort to various bureaucratic means to prevent Muslim migrants from entering the ranks of refugees. Apparently non-sectarian categories of governance, such as displaced persons and refugees, were in practice tied to ethnic markers.[32] This allowed a pragmatic validation of the primacy of Hindu belonging in India to flourish beneath public assertions of a secular polity that did not discriminate between Hindu and Muslim citizens. Given that all bona fide refugees were also citizens in post-partition India, the refusal to grant refugee status to Muslim migrants indirectly achieved their exclusion from Indian citizenship. Thus, despite broad public statements promising citizenship to all displaced persons from Pakistan, Hindu migrants alone counted as citizen-refugees in post-partition India.

The early exclusion of Muslim migrants from Pakistan from the ranks of genuine refugees prepared the ground for a more systematic disenfranchisement of India's Muslim residents. Recent scholarship has demonstrated how in post-partition India, it became a virtual impossibility for Muslim minorities to fully belong.[33] They were unilaterally categorised as 'evacuees' or 'intending evacuees' for Pakistan and the draconian Evacuee Property legislation allowed the authorities to appropriate Muslim property for 'public purposes', that included rehabilitation of Hindu refugees, without recourse to legal appeal.[34] In sum, when compared to displaced Muslims, Hindu minorities from Pakistan appear to be privileged insiders. As Gyan Pandey has argued, by virtue of being Hindu, they constituted the imagined core of the Indian nation.[35] Vazira Zamindar draws a sharp

---

[31] See letter from Jawaharlal Nehru to Vallabhbhai Patel, 12 May 1948, Ibid., pp. 367–8.

[32] The ethnically marked category of the refugee in post-partition India is also a key point of departure in Zamindar, *The Long Partition* (2007).

[33] See, for example, Claire Alexander, Joya Chatterji, and Annu Jalais, *The Bengal Diaspora: Rethinking Muslim Migration* (Routledge, 2015); Taylor C. Sherman, *Muslim Belonging in Secular India: Negotiating Citizenship in Postcolonial Hyderabad* (Cambridge University Press, 2015); and Gyanendra Pandey, 'Can a Muslim Be an Indian?', *Comparative Studies in Society and History*, 41:4 (1999), 608–29.

[34] For details see Zamindar, *The Long Partition* (2007) and Chatterji, 'South Asian Histories of Citizenship, 1946–1970,' (2012), 1049–71.

[35] Pandey, 'Can a Muslim Be an Indian?' (1999).

contrast between the deeply ambiguous position of Muslim refugees and the relatively straightforward path to Indian citizenship enjoyed by displaced Hindus and Sikhs: 'They could migrate to the territory of India and become Indian citizens'.[36] There is no doubt that in the aftermath of partition, there was an increasing tendency to equate being Indian with being Hindu. However, the actual process of becoming citizens was far from straightforward for Hindu refugees. Not all displaced Hindus who migrated to India were welcomed into the body of citizens.

The political obligation to acknowledge the Hindu refugees' right to citizenship had to be balanced against pragmatic considerations of the financial burden placed upon the nascent nation-state by millions of refugees. Official declarations that validated the Hindu refugees' right to belong were often undermined by a range of bureaucratic interventions designed to limit the actual number of refugees. This was particularly true of displaced Hindus from eastern Pakistan who found themselves negotiating a veritable obstacle course of preconditions, such as date of entry, necessary documentation and arbitrary last dates of registration, in order to be acknowledged as refugees. Though Hindu migrants could and did lay claim to being citizens of India, their ability to wrest substantive belonging depended upon their ability to gain recognition as genuine refugees. This recognition came relatively easily to refugees from western Punjab. In the immediate aftermath of partition, the entire infrastructure of providing relief to refugees, including the creation of a central Ministry of Rehabilitation and a range of policies, such as the exchange of minority populations and compensation for lost property, evolved in response to the crisis in Punjab.[37] The policies of inclusion designed for refugees from Punjab were later extended to Hindu refugees from Sind and Baluchistan. Thus, for Hindu refugees from western Pakistan, the path to citizenship was indeed relatively straightforward. This was by no means true for Hindu refugees from eastern Pakistan. The Punjab model of rehabilitation was dependent on the expulsion of Muslim minorities as 'evacuees', and was not replicated in divided Bengal or Assam. The result was that refugees from eastern Pakistan were greeted by an apathetic state and a hostile society. Viewed from the east, a wide gap emerges between the Hindu refugees' status as de facto citizens and their lived reality of displacement.

The East Bengali Hindus' quest to become citizens of India had divergent outcomes in different parts of India. A long history of anti-Bengali

---

[36] Zamindar, *The Long Partition* (2010), p. 53.
[37] For an official account that clearly displays this Punjab-centrism, see Bhaskar Rao, *The Story of Rehabilitation* (1967).

sentiments in Assam saw Bengali-speaking migrants branded as foreigners, notwithstanding their Hindu background.[38] In sharp contrast, there was little or no hostility towards the influx of Bengali refugees in Tripura throughout the 1950s.[39] The vast majority of East Bengali Hindus sought refuge in the state of West Bengal, where they also shared a linguistic identity with the host population. Despite such affinities, they faced a hostile and apathetic government that questioned whether they were refugees at all. What ensued was a prolonged struggle waged by displaced Hindus from East Bengal to obtain official recognition as refugees and/or substantive rehabilitation – both crucial to the process of becoming citizens. Policy declarations that allowed citizenship to all displaced Hindus from Pakistan does not capture the full complexity of this process. The Hindu refugees' quest to belong to India was a complex process riddled by contradictions that are yet to be fully explored. In order to understand this process, it is necessary to look eastwards, beyond the spectacular violence of divided Punjab and its emergency resolution through an exchange of population.

'Thick' Citizenship: The Rival Meanings of Rehabilitation

The equivalence between being a partition refugee and being a citizen changed the meaning of refugee rehabilitation in post-partition India. According to Ajit Prasad Jain, the central minister in charge of rehabilitation between 1950 and 1954, rehabilitation was a process designed to achieve 'the disappearance of all distinction' between refugees and other nationals.[40] Given that partition refugees were already acknowledged as de facto citizens and guaranteed voting rights, the erasure of 'all distinction' between them and other citizens did not denote a juridical change in their status. Instead, it denoted a project of state intervention into the social and economic lives of partition refugees, designed to restore them to normality. Schemes and policies of refugee rehabilitation are therefore best understood as part of a massive project of normalisation. However, this raises an obvious question – what did a 'normal' Indian citizen look like? There was no pre-figured standard of 'normal' socio-economic life for citizens of

---

[38] For details see Sanjib Baruah, *India Against Itself: Assam and The Politics of Nationality* (Philadelphia, PA: University of Pennsylvania Press, 1999) and Sujit Chaudhuri, 'A God-sent Opportunity? in Seminar No. 510, *Porous Borders, Divided Selves: a Symposium on Partitions in the East*, February, 2002, (http://www.india-seminar.com/2002/510/510%20sujit%20chaudhuri.htm, last accessed 5 August 2015).

[39] Gayatri Bhattacharyya, *Refugee Rehabilitation and Its Impact on Tripura's Economy* (New Delhi: Omsons Publications, 1988).

[40] Cited in Prafulla Kumar Chakrabarti, *The Marginal Men: The Refugees and the Left Political Syndrome in West Bengal* (Calcutta: Naya Udyog, 1999), p. 255.

India. Through planning for rehabilitation, the Indian state generated multiple articulations of what the everyday 'normal life' of citizens could look like. The bureaucratic and political elite involved in authoring policies used this process to indulge their paternalistic ambitions of forging ideal members of the Indian nation-state out of refugees. Seen from the perspective of the state, the regime of rehabilitation was not only a normalising project, but also a creative one that articulated top-down visions of an ideal Indian citizen. However, partition refugees were not passive recipients of state policy. They brought with them their own aspirations of belonging and expectations from the state. The regime of rehabilitation became a sphere of governance characterised by clashes between rival ideals, aspirations and expectations around belonging and citizenship in post-colonial India. I read policies and practices of rehabilitation to tease out these subjective, experiential and idealised aspects of citizenship, that can collectively be called 'thick' citizenship, as opposed to 'thin' or formal aspects of citizenship, such as the right to vote and legal status.[41]

Bureaucrats who set out to rehabilitate refugees expected them to embody a range of desirable qualities and behaviours. Bengali refugees who relied on the state for rehabilitation were the most vulnerable to these scripts of thick citizenship, which the post-colonial state sought to inscribe on refugee bodies. This is not to suggest that rehabilitation was a neat or unidirectional process free from contestations. It was a polyphonic and dynamic sphere of governance that involved considerable negotiation between different levels and departments of government, which often had contradictory agendas. Joya Chatterji has traced at length how refugee rehabilitation in West Bengal was severely compromised by the differences between Dr B. C. Roy's government on one hand, and Nehru and the central Ministry of Rehabilitation on the other.[42] Even within the same level of government, different ministries often found themselves at odds with each other. For example, the Ministry of Relief and Rehabilitation could often find its schemes scuttled by the economising drive of the Ministry of Finance. Moreover, the actual shape that policies took was invariably informed by the specific interpretations of the men-on-the-spot, a process that Michael Lipsky has conceptualised as 'street-level bureaucracy'.[43] In order to capture this dynamic and

---

[41] For a summary of the multiple ways in which the distinction between 'thick' and 'thin' citizenship is evoked within theorisations on citizenship, see Will Kymlicka and Wayne Norman, 'Return of the Citizen: A Survey of Recent Work on Citizenship Theory', *Ethics*, 104:2 (1994), 352–81.

[42] Chatterji, *Spoils of Partition* (2007).

[43] Michael Lipsky, *Street-Level Bureaucracy: The Dilemmas of the Individual in Public Service* (New York: Russell Sage Foundation, 1983).

contingent texture of the regime of rehabilitation I draw upon a wide range of sources including the records of various ministries, published reports and surveys, debates in legislative assemblies and the memoirs or testimonies of street-level bureaucrats. I argue that despite multiple contestations, a singular ideal of citizenship gradually came to be dominant within the regime of rehabilitation. Refugees were increasingly recast as hyper-masculine and productive agents of post-colonial development. By living up to this ideal, they could transform themselves into desirable members of the nation-state from the deviant figure of the citizen-refugee.

Idealised visions of citizenship were not new in South Asia. Multiple and rival ideals of belonging had co-existed in late colonial India. These notions of 'thick' citizenship included ideals of Islamic or Muslim belonging,[44] of Hindu homelands,[45] the liberal feminist vision of the universal Indian citizen unmarked by caste, class or ethnicity,[46] and an increasingly irrelevant colonial vision of a loyal subject-citizen.[47] The transfer of power from the crown to independent governments in 1947 was the watershed that marked the symbolic transition from colonial subjects to self-governing citizens. However, the specific iteration of citizenship in India, whether as legal status, identity, or as social and political rights, has been a contested and long-term process. Recent scholarship on Indian citizenship has largely focused on this dynamic aspect of citizenship by exploring how the actualisation of citizenship in India has been, and continues to be, informed by contingent histories. There is a broad consensus among historians and political scientists that

---

[44] For a range of conceptualisations of Muslim belonging see Farzana Shaikh, *Community and Consensus in Islam: Muslim Representation in Colonial India, 1860–1947* (Cambridge: Cambridge University Press, 1989); Akbar S. Ahmed, *Jinnah, Pakistan and Islamic Identity: The Search for Saladin* (London: Routledge, 1997); Faisal Devji, *Muslim Zion: Pakistan as a Political Idea* (London: Hurst Publishers, 2013); Venkat Dhulipala, *Creating a New Medina: State Power, Islam, and the Quest for Pakistan in Late Colonial North India* (Cambridge: Cambridge University Press, 2014).

[45] For various iterations of Hindu nationalism in colonial India, see Tanika Sarkar, *Hindu Wife, Hindu Nation, Community, Religion, and Cultural Nationalism* (New Delhi: Permanent Black, 2001); William Gould, *Hindu Nationalism and the Language of Politics in Late Colonial India* (Cambridge: Cambridge University Press, 2004); and Christophe Jaffrelot, *Hindu Nationalist Movement and Indian Politics, 1925 to the 1990s* (London: Hurst Publishers, 1996). There is surprisingly little work on the impact of Hindu nationalism on the partition of India. Exceptions are Joya Chatterji's *Bengal Divided: Hindu Communalism and Partition, 1932–1947* (Cambridge: Cambridge University Press, 2002); and Neeti Nair's *Changing Homelands: Hindu Politics and the Partition of India* (Cambridge, MA: Harvard University Press, 2011).

[46] See Mrinalini Sinha, *Spectres of Mother India: The Global Restructuring of an Empire* (Durham, NC and London: Duke University Press, 2006).

[47] For an exploration of the idea of the subject-citizen, see Niraja Gopal Jayal, *Citizenship and Its Discontents: An Indian History* (Cambridge, London: Harvard University Press, 2013), pp. 27–50.

the decade between 1946 and 1956 was a generative period for the cluster of ideas, rights and legal definitions that constitute Indian citizenship. Bookended by the convening of the Constituent Assembly and the passage of the Citizenship Act, this decade was also marked by the violence and dislocation of partition. However, different scholars have evaluated the significance of this period, and particularly, the impact of partition and its accompanying refugee crisis on histories of citizenship in divergent ways.

Joya Chatterji has traced how the political crisis of managing partition refugees gradually and definitively shifted the contours of legal citizenship in India from *jus soli*, i.e., citizenship by birth, towards *jus sanguinis*, or citizenship by heredity. The result was a peculiar form of citizenship that combined these two principles and was designed to elevate Hindu migrants to full citizens while simultaneously reducing Muslim residents to second-class or abject citizens.[48] Anupama Roy argues that the historical context of partition produced several liminal categories of people, who were neither fully citizens, nor entirely foreign. Within this category she includes not just displaced persons, but also minors, Pakistani wives and abducted women. Roy understands the Indian Citizenship Act as a moment of encompassment. It negotiated the conflict between the ground reality of differential access to citizenship and its universal promise by offering different 'possibilities' of becoming citizens to different groups – through birth, descent or registration.[49] Ornit Shani explores a similar idea of differential citizenship, drawing upon James Tully's notion of diverse citizenship.[50] This body of work largely focuses on the impact of partition migration on the legal aspects of citizenship. Niraja Jayal's survey of the changing citizenship regime in India does not fit this mould. Jayal not only explores the question of legal citizenship for partition refugees, but also explores what substantive citizenship looked like for different groups of migrants. She maps how the concept of citizenship, both as a cluster of rights and as an identity, changed over time.[51] This study builds upon Jayal's approach of mapping diverse expressions of the idea of citizenship. However, it does so by exploring the clash between statist and popular idioms of citizenship within the regime of rehabilitation. Official reports of rehabilitation were replete with dense descriptions of the qualities that could enable a partition refugee to become a citizen of India. In this top-down vision, refugees

[48] Chatterji, 'South Asian Histories of Citizenship, 1946–1970' (2012), 1049–71.
[49] Anupama Roy, *Mapping Citizenship in India* (New Delhi, Oxford and New York: Oxford University Press, 2010).
[50] Ornit Shani, 'Conceptions of Citizenship in India and the 'Muslim Question'', *Modern Asian Studies*, 44:1, (2010), 145–73.
[51] Jayal, *Citizenship and Its Discontents* (2013).

were celebrated for demonstrating the civic virtues of self-reliance. However, most refugees who looked to official aid fell short of this ideal. The dominant ask within the regime of rehabilitation was not for self-rehabilitation, as Ravinder Kaur suggests.[52] Instead, refugees were required to demonstrate their willingness to engage in productive labour and to actively contribute to projects of national development. In fact, their access to rehabilitation depended upon their ability to perform this role of productive citizens furthering national development. Imposed selectively upon vulnerable refugee bodies, this was a far cry from any universal vision of active, participatory citizenship.

In stark contrast to this top-down ideal, refugees usually expressed their belonging to India in the language of rights or as an identity marked by both ethnicity and history. To understand refugee narratives of belonging I draw upon oral history interviews, autobiographical texts and a scattered archive of popular histories, pamphlets and memorandums which have been preserved in the personal collections of refugees. What emerges is a deeply fractured experience of rehabilitation where the ability of refugees to resist, utilise or adapt to policies varied widely depending on their class, caste and gender backgrounds. These divergent negotiations of the regime of rehabilitation challenges received wisdom on the agency of East Bengali refugees. Existing literature tends to equate the agency or resistance of refugees in West Bengal with the emergence of various refugee associations and their social role in building refugee colonies as well as their political role in fostering a refugee movement.[53] This narrative not only suffers from an overt focus on the capital city of Calcutta, but is also guilty of selectively feting urban, middle-class men as the authors of radical patterns of popular protest. All others tend to be portrayed as victims. Expanding the analytical lens to include the voices of rural refugees, peasants from depressed caste backgrounds and women destabilises this binary division of Bengali refugees into agents and victims. It also expands our understanding of refugee resistance and agency beyond the narrow format of oppositional politics and organised protest. Refugee reminiscences reveal a richly textured encounter between the state and its citizen-refugees where *all* refugees mobilised a range of everyday strategies to derive the best from a hostile regime of rehabilitation.[54] They bent

---

[52] Ravinder Kaur, 'Distinctive Citizenship: Refugees, Subjects and Post-colonial State in India's Partition,' *Cultural and Social History*, 6:4 (2009), 429–46.

[53] For example, see Pradip Kumar Bose (ed.), *Refugees in West Bengal: Institutional Practices and Contested Identities* (Calcutta: Calcutta Research Group, 2000) and Chakrabarti, *The Marginal Men* (1999).

[54] This draws upon James C. Scott, *Weapons of the Weak: Everyday Forms of Peasant Resistance* (New Haven, CT: Yale University Press, 1985).

as well as broke rules, greased palms as often as they threw bombs, and appealed to sympathetic bureaucrats no less than they protested against apathetic ones.

This book is divided into two sections. The first part consists of two chapters and traces the official response to the crisis of rehabilitation in West Bengal. Chapter 1 explores the evolution of policies between 1947 and 1971. It counters the dominant perception of rehabilitation in the East as a collection of knee-jerk reactions and ill-planned, piecemeal schemes. Instead, it traces the emergence of a coherent governmentality that informed policy. It seeks to explain *why* East Bengali refugees were treated as an unwanted population and how this initial reluctance gave way to schemes specifically designed for their rehabilitation. These schemes were scattered across India and extended the impact of partition migration far beyond the frontiers of West Bengal. Chapter 2 focuses on one such scheme – the resettlement of Bengali refugees in the Andaman Islands. It began in 1949 as the opportunistic use of refugees to meet labour shortages in the Andaman Islands. By 1952, it was transformed into a five-year scheme of 'Development and Colonisation', which continued till 1961. The Andaman Islands functioned as an unlikely laboratory for crafting policy, where through trial and error, the limits and possibilities of transforming East Bengali refugees into productive citizens were mapped out. The connected histories of rehabilitation in West Bengal and development in these Islands points to the inadequacy of regionally bound analytical frameworks for understanding the Bengali refugee experience. The national government played an increasingly dominant role in authoring policies of rehabilitation. The implementation of schemes of dispersal saw the involvement of actors from multiple states, including Orissa, Bihar, Andhra Pradesh, Chhattisgarh, Uttaranchal and even Gujarat. In sum, the wide dispersal of Bengali refugees gave partition's aftermath a pan-Indian scope.

The second part of this book consists of three chapters and traces how East Bengali refugees negotiated the regime of rehabilitation. Displaced Hindus from eastern Pakistan were a heterogeneous group and policies impacted them differently depending on their gender, class and caste backgrounds. The compulsion to perform ideal citizenship fell disproportionately upon refugees who had the least resources and had to rely on aid from the state. By contrast, refugees from urban and middle-class backgrounds could draw upon their social and cultural capital to successfully resist state diktat. Chapters 3 and 4 explore the divergent negotiation of the regime of rehabilitation by refugees from different class and caste backgrounds. Chapter 3 is based on interviews with *Namasudra* peasants who were dispersed to the Andaman Islands and provides an insight into how the poorest among the refugees negotiated the regime of rehabilitation. Chapter 4 analyses the reminiscences and autobiographies of the *bhadralok* refugees who built the Bijoygarh squatters' colony in the outskirts of Calcutta. These two sections of West Bengal's refugee population were socially and culturally distinct, and generated very different textures of memory and identity. Taken together, these two chapters mitigate against any singular understanding of the Bengali refugee experience.

When compared to the growing body of scholarship on regional histories of partition and its aftermath, there are very few studies that explore class and caste difference *within* particular refugee groups. Ravinder Kaur's work is a noted exception. She demonstrates how class background determined the speed and pattern of travel for Punjabi refugees and how caste hierarchies marked the organization of space and relationships within the refugee camps of Delhi.[55] When it comes to refugees from East Bengal, the impact of class and caste difference upon patterns of migration is well-documented.[56] However, the impact of caste upon patterns of rehabilitation is yet to be explored in a systematic manner. Received wisdom largely understands caste as a divisive factor that fractured the social life within urban refugee colonies and splintered refugee politics.[57] Annu Jalais demonstrates how the massacre of the refugees who had settled illegally in the Marichjhapi region of Sunderbans was enabled in no small measure by the upper-caste disdain for Dalit lives.[58] Within this literature, caste difference is mobilised episodically, in order to either explain the limits of refugee organisation or the excesses of state repression. This study breaks new ground by demonstrating how caste difference did not merely inform how refugees experienced rehabilitation, but was also a constitutive element in the formulation and implementation of policy.

Though politicians and bureaucrats skirted around issues of class and caste difference that fractured refugee communities, the role of gender difference found a prominent place within policy. The Indian state actively acknowledged the special needs of single and widowed refugee women. Chapter 5 explores the place of refugee women with the regime of rehabilitation. By exploring the experiences of East Bengali women who

[55] Ravinder Kaur, 'The Last Journey,' *Economic and Political Weekly*, 41: 22 (2006), 2221–8; and *Since 1947: Partition Narratives Among Punjabi Migrants of Delhi* (Oxford: Oxford University Press, 2007).

[56] See Chatterji, *Spoils of Partition* (2007).

[57] Manas Ray, 'Growing Up Refugee', *History Workshop Journal*, 53:1, (2002), 149–79; and Chakrabarti, *Marginal Men* (1999).

[58] Annu Jalais, 'Dwelling on Morichjhanpi: When Tigers Became "Citizens", Refugees 'Tiger-Food', *Economic and Political Weekly* 40, no. 17 (2005): 1757–62.

were admitted to permanent liability or PL camps, it complements the ground-breaking scholarship by Urvashi Butalia, Ritu Menon and Kamla Bhasin that exposed the gendered violence suffered by refugee women, but focused almost exclusively on Punjab.[59] It reads state paternalism towards 'unattached' refugee women as bureaucratic violence that was designed to preserve the performance of full citizenship as a male prerogative in India.

Though all displaced Hindus from eastern Pakistan strove to become citizen-refugees, not all of them succeeded. This book chronicles both the successes and failures of East Bengali refugees in their struggle to rebuild lives. It maps the bureaucratic violence of state policy that reduced thousands of displaced families to marginal lives, by denying them official recognition as refugees and substantive rehabilitation. For many this entailed joining the ranks of the undocumented. For others, the denial of official aid, in the form of adequate loans or well-planned rehabilitation schemes, was the greater loss that plunged generations into poverty. For some refugees, success entailed resisting official polices, while for others, it entailed being able to sign on to a resettlement scheme of their choice. Yet others felt trapped in ill-planned schemes that either imposed point-less hardship, or doled out mere relief in lieu of substantive rehabilitation. In all these contexts, refugees presented themselves as citizens of India and claimed adequate relief and rehabilitation from the government as a political right. The Hindu refugees' quest to belong thus generated multiple scripts of everyday citizenship that evolved in dialogue and contestation with the official, top-down vision of an ideal Indian citizen.

[59] Ritu Menon and Kamla Bhasin, 'Abducted Women, The State and Questions of Honour', and Urvashi Butalia, 'Community State and Gender: On Women's Agency During Partition' in *Economic and Political Weekly*, 'Review of Women's Studies', 24 April 1993, 2–11 and 12–21; Ritu Menon and Kamla Bhasin, *Borders and Boundaries: Women in India's Partition* (New Delhi, 1998) and Urvashi Butalia, *The Other Side of Silence: Voices From the Partition of India* (New Delhi, 1998).

Part I

Framing Policy

Refugees from East Pakistan.

Figure 1.1: Refugees from East Pakistan, 1950
(Source: ABP Archives)

Refugees from East Pakistan at Dandakaranya.

Figure 1.2: Refugees from East Pakistan at Dandakaranya
(Source: ABP Archives)

1 Unwanted Citizens in a Saturated State
Towards a Governmentality of Rehabilitation

Introduction

Though nearly seven decades have elapsed since the partition of India, the crisis of rehabilitating the refugees born of this political fissure is yet to be relegated to the pages of history. The figure of the partition refugee haunts every decadal memorialisation of India's independence as the embodiment of the human cost of partition.[1] Contrary to the official claim that India's refugee problem was largely resolved by 1965 (which paved the way for the dissolution of the central Ministry of Rehabilitation), thousands of Hindu refugees from Pakistan still await rehabilitation and full inclusion as citizens in locations as diverse as Rajasthan and West Bengal.[2] This is particularly true of the eastern region. In Assam and Tripura, the arrival of thousands of Bengali refugees led to fears of being swamped by outsiders and informed the growth of movements championing indigenous or local rights.[3] Many of the Bengali refugees dispersed to rehabilitation sites in Orissa and Bihar were not registered as Indian citizens. For decades, they have been convenient

---

[1] For example see Dan McDougall, 'The Forgotten Refugees who wait for Justice after 60 Years' *The Observer*, 5 August 2007, and Andrew Whitehead's award-winning radio series, *India: A People Partitioned*, that was aired by BBC World Service to mark the fiftieth anniversary of India and Pakistan's independence (http://www.andrewwhitehead.net/ind ia-a-people-partitioned.html, accessed on 10 August 2015).

[2] For Rajasthan see Vishwajeet Singh Bhati, '"Derelict": Pakistani Hindu Refugees in Rajasthan and Gujarat', Refugee Watch Online (A Co-Publication of Refugee Watch), 29 July 2013, (http://refugeewatchonline.blogspot.co.uk/2013/07/derelict-pakistani-hindu-refugees-in.html, accessed on 20 April 2015) and for West Bengal see Central Working Committee, *Sammilita Kendriya Bastuhara Parishad, Panchadash Rajya Sammelan, (United Central Refugee Council, Fiftieth State Assembly)*, Bardhaman, 6–7 September, 1997 (Calcutta: UCRC,1997) and Anil Sinha, *Pashchim Bange Udvastu Upanibesh, (Refugee Colonies of West Bengal)*, (Calcutta: Book Club, 1995).

[3] For the impact of Bengali refugees upon the economy and politics of Tripura, see Gayatri Bhattacharya, *Refugee Rehabilitation and its Impact on Tripura's Economy*, (New Delhi/Guwahati: Omsons Publications, 1988) and Harihar Bhattacharya, 'The Emergence of Tripuri Nationalism, 1948–50', *South Asia Research*, 9:1 (1989), 54–71. For Assam's opposition to the resettlement of Bengali refugees see Sanjib Baruah, *India Against Itself: Assam and the Politics of Nationality* (Philadelphia, PA: University of Pennsylvania Press, 1999).

scapegoats of xenophobic politics and periodically threatened with expulsion on account of being foreigners.[4] The unresolved 'problem' of rehabilitating refugees from East Pakistan thus continues to inform, to a lesser or greater degree, the regional politics in the receiving states.

The beginning of this 'problem' can be traced to particular patterns of displacement and migration from eastern Pakistan into Tripura, Assam and West Bengal, which continued, with breaks and in spurts, for twenty-five long years between 1946 and 1971. Though the stream of migrants has far from dried up, the emergence of Bangladesh radically altered the status of migrants from eastern Bengal. A bilateral understanding between India and Bangladesh redefined all future migrants as illegal infiltrators, thus bringing to an end the era of cross-border migration when a Hindu refugee from eastern Pakistan could claim to belong to India.[5] The period before 1971 was characterised by a broad political consensus regarding the displaced Hindu's right to full Indian citizenship. The Citizenship Act of 1956 formally acknowledged this right through special provisions which allowed displaced persons from Pakistan to register as Indian citizens.[6] This allowed East Bengali refugees who entered India before 1971 to articulate their need for relief and rehabilitation as a political right, which they felt entitled to as new citizens of a nation. This was particularly true of West Bengal, where the Bengali refugee's struggle to belong was bolstered by emotive evocations of a shared language and (Hindu) cultural heritage. Yet, the new rulers of West Bengal were far from eager to either admit a large number of displaced Hindus from East Bengal, or to make provisions for their relief and rehabilitation. As a result, the regime of rehabilitation in West Bengal evolved as a deeply contested field of negotiation between the post-colonial state and its citizen-refugees. This chapter analyses the regime of rehabilitation in West Bengal between 1947 and 1971 as an evolving and multi-authored set of practices and policies. It argues that underlying the many shifts and apparent inconsistencies that marked West Bengal's regime of rehabilitation was the gradual crystallisation of a rationale for the proper governance of partition refugees, or a governmentality of rehabilitation.[7]

---

[4] Syed Ali Mujtaba, 'Partition Refugees Targeted as Bangladeshi Infiltrators', *Global Politician Magazine*, 11 January 2006, (http://www.globalpolitician.com/22273-bangladesh accessed on 8 June 2009).

[5] For details of this shift see Antara Datta, *Refugees and Borders in South Asia: The Great Exodus of 1971* (London: Routledge, 2012).

[6] Joya Chatterji, 'South Asian Histories of Citizenship, 1946–1970,' *The Historical Journal*, 55:4 (2012), 1049–71.

[7] Here, the Foucaultian concept of governmentality is used in its broadest sense, indicating a way or system of thinking about the nature of the practice of government, i.e. who can

Eight Million 'Extra Mouths' to Feed: Development and The Denial of Relief, 1947–1948

Though it seems incredible in hindsight, the government of West Bengal had failed to anticipate any migration of minorities from Pakistan. In the immediate aftermath of partition, Dr Pratulla Chandra Ghosh, the first Premier (equivalent of Chief Minister) of the truncated province of West Bengal, was busy trying to resettle those displaced by the 1946 Calcutta riots.[8] When reports started appearing in the vernacular dailies regarding the exodus of Hindus from East Bengal, the government was caught unawares.[9] Amongst these early migrants many had property, relatives or the means to rent houses in Calcutta, but they struggled to find a living. The new government was already struggling to find employment for several hundred government servants who had 'opted' for West Bengal and was in no position to find additional employment for refugees.[10] Those lower down the economic scale – artisans, peasants, agriculturists and the indigent amongst the educated – were reduced to squatting on the railway platforms and pavements of Calcutta. Vivid reports in the press made it impossible for officials to wish away this human misery. P. C. Ghosh was pushed to pledge government help for the '*asrayprathi*', literally, 'those who sought shelter'.[11] The content of this 'help' was limited to requisitioning a few houses and abandoned military barracks in and around Calcutta, which the government then rented out to refugees. As many failed to pay rent, the practice was discontinued. However, taking their cue from the government, the refugees started occupying the various military barracks and huts in and around Calcutta, which had been lying empty since the Second World War. This largely middle-class squatting in various empty houses in Calcutta was the precursor to the *jabardakhal* (forced acquisition) movement that later became the distinctive feature of the refugee experience of West Bengal.[12]

In the absence of any clear directives from the government, ad hoc measures employed by local administrators and bureaucrats were the saving grace for thousands who could not fend for themselves. Fortunately, refugees were not a new phenomenon in Bengal. In April 1947, the Relief Department of undivided Bengal had hosted roughly 94,342 Muslim

---

govern, what is governing, what or who is governed, and towards what end. Michel Foucault, *Security, Territory, Population: Lectures at the Collège de France*, trans. Mr Graham Burchell (Basingstoke: Palgrave Macmillan, 2009).

[8] *Jugantar*, 3 September 1947.   [9] *Jugantar*, 7 October 1947.

[10] *Jugantar*, 23 September 1947.   [11] *Jugantar*, 12 October 1947.

[12] For details see Anil Sinha, *Udvastu upanibesh (Refugee Colonies)* (1995) and Prafulla K. Chakrabarti, *The Marginal Men: The Refugees and the Left Political Syndrome in West Bengal* (Calcutta: Naya Udyog, 1999).

refugees, displaced by the 1946 riots in Bihar, in thirty-nine refugee camps.[13] Their temporary stopover in Muslim League-ruled Bengal provided important administrative precedent for dealing with refugees at the local level. Faced with a new crisis, district officials reopened camps to provide shelter and relief to refugees. In some cases, local officials even took the initiative to rehabilitate refugees. Hiranmoy Bandyopadhyay's description of the refugee problem in the district of Jalpaiguri, where he served as a district administrator between August 1947 and 1948, offers one such example. As the rising tide of refugees spilled over from various abandoned buildings of Jalpaiguri town and into the railway station, Bandyopadhyay requested help from local social workers in devising a more durable solution. A committee was formed to formulate rehabilitation schemes. Refugees were divided into agriculturists and non-agriculturists. The latter were settled on *khasmahal* lands[14] while the former were allocated privately owned agricultural land. This entire process was completed by 1948, long before the authorities in Writers' Building had come up with any plan for rehabilitation. However, by Bandyopadhyay's own admission, this initiative was very much an exception to the rule.[15] In most places, state officials drew the line at opening camps and instituting relief at government approved rates. The majority of refugee from East Bengal either had to fend for themselves, or were left to languish in camps improvised out of empty storehouses, jute mills and factories.

Dr Ghosh's premiership came to a premature end in January 1948, amidst allegations of bias towards East Bengali migrants. His expulsion from office had more to do with factionalism within the West Bengal government than with any manifest sympathy for refugees.[16] Nevertheless, his unceremonious exit illustrated the antipathy of the majority within the Bengal Congress towards migrants from East Bengal. After Dr B. C. Roy took over as the Premier, indifference towards refugees gave way to active marginalisation. In the first annual budget of West Bengal, no funds were allocated for the relief of migrants from East Bengal. Instead, the Finance Minister, Nalini Ranjan Sarkar, offered them 'the deepest and most sincere sympathies' on behalf of Dr Roy's government:

---

[13] Mr Masihuddin Ahmed, (on behalf of Mr AFM Abdur Rahman, Minister in Charge of Relief Department), *Question on Bihar Refugees in West Bengal*, Bengal Legislative Assembly, First Session 1947, pp. 255–7.

[14] A category of land where the ownership remains with the government and is leased out to individuals for various purposes.

[15] Hiranmoy Bandypadhyay, *Udvastu (Refugee)* (Calcutta: Sahitya Samsad, 1970), pp. 11–21.

[16] For details on this coup and the politics of the Hooghly group, see Joya Chatterji, *The Spoils of Partition: Bengal and India, 1947–1967* (Cambridge and New York: Cambridge University Press, 2007), p. 49.

With the limitations imposed on us by the new political changes, it may not be possible for us to render all the relief they may need or all that we may wish to render them in the new predicament, but I give vent to our sincere feelings when I say that they have our deepest and most sincere sympathies in the situation they find themselves in and that their interest and welfare shall ever remain a matter of vital concern to us. Whenever necessary and wherever possible and to the full limit of constitutional proprieties, we shall use all our good offices with our neighbouring Dominion to secure for them political and economic justice.[17]

The message was clear: East Bengali Hindus should not expect anything more than sympathy if they chose to come to West Bengal. As long as they remained in East Bengal, the government was prepared to exert diplomatic pressure on Pakistan. Sarkar went on to lament that partition, by limiting the area of West Bengal, had increased the problems of over-population, particularly in the cities. He blamed the 'steady influx of people from East Pakistan' for further compounding an already difficult situation. 'Since the influx from East Bengal is mostly swelling the population in the towns, West Bengal's problems of food supply, housing, education and public health as also of finding employment for large blocks of floating population are rapidly growing in magnitude and complexity.'[18] Though the Finance Minister did not say it in so many words, the failure to allocate funds for refugee relief in a budget which harped upon 'productive expenditure' and 'expenditure on beneficent activities' clearly suggested that the refugees were an undesirable presence.

This characterisation of refugees as obstacles to economic development was an innovation by the independent government of West Bengal. Relief measures had been inadequate for those displaced by the communal riots of 1946 and for the victims of the famine of 1943.[19] Nevertheless, expenditure on relief had never before been characterised as detrimental to the development of a region. However, as the post-colonial state set out to deliver the promise of 'development' to its people, a new arithmetic of development infused governance. Sarkar's hope for West Bengal was that it would enjoy its full opportunities of 'development and progress' as 'part and parcel of the great Indian Union'.[20] The first annual budget of West Bengal was a forward looking one, focused on outlining a future 'Development Programme', whose main objective was to 'raise the

---

[17] Nalini Ranjan Sarkar, Finance Minister, *Finance Minister's Statement on Budget for 1948–49*, West Bengal Legislative Assembly, 17 February 1948, p. 17 (henceforth WBLA).

[18] Ibid., p. 18.

[19] See Paul R. Greenough, *Prosperity and Misery in Modern Bengal: The Famine of 1943–1944* (New York: Oxford University Press, 1982), pp. 127–36.

[20] Sarkar, *Statement on Budget for 1948–49*, 17 February 1948, p. 20.

standard of living of the masses'.[21] 'Two obvious factors' conditioned the degree of success of these plans, namely, 'production of more wealth and its equitable distribution amongst the people'.[22] It followed that any increase in the population of West Bengal through immigration would further impoverish the region by increasing the number of claimants upon its meagre resources. Once refugees came to be seen as additional population, their presence in West Bengal could only be viewed as detrimental to the development of the state. The hostile response of the West Bengal government to an influx of refugees from eastern Pakistan had its foundations in this logic of good governance that privileged economic development.

The Congress leaders were not yet prepared to publicly proclaim that the needs and aspirations of refugees from eastern Bengal went against the principles of good economic governance. This argument was explicitly made, as early as 1948, by members of the Muslim League. Janab Mudassir Hossain berated the government of West Bengal for not fully appreciating the threat posed by refugees from eastern Pakistan to the fragile economy of West Bengal.[23]

Sir, the gentlemen who have come from East Bengal are all middle class gentlemen; they are not producers; they will not and cannot help you in production . . . Find land for those persons and influence them to till the land and produce more food for themselves . . . But if you want them to remain in this province of ours as parasites or only as settlers and feed them from the sources of this province that will be no good. It will further enhance the difficulties and will further impoverish West Bengal which is already a poor province.[24]

The larger goal of Mudassir Hossain's much longer speech was not to vilify the refugees, but to question the complacency of the ruling government. In his opinion, the Congress was being too quick to celebrate independence in a truncated province, without fully facing up to the consequences of partition. His words were echoed by Janab Musharruf Hossain, a member of the Muslim League elected from the district of Jalpaiguri, but with very different motives. Musharruf Hossain, like many other leaders of the Muslim League who chose to stay on in West Bengal, struggled to find a new political language, divorced from the two-nation

---

[21] Ibid., p. 31.   [22] Ibid.

[23] In post-partition Bengal many Muslim politicians astutely repudiated their allegiance to the Muslim League, which was allowed to die a quiet death. As a result, many of the elected Muslim politicians in the legislative assembly of West Bengal appear as 'independents' during this period, solely representing the grievances of their community. Eventually, many such 'independent' candidates were accepted within the folds of the Bengal Congress. See Chatterji, *Spoils of Partition* (2007), pp. 171–81.

[24] Janab Mudassir Hossain, *General Discussions of the Budget*, WBLA, 20 February 1948, p. 79.

theory, to champion the interests of the Muslim minority who stayed on in West Bengal. His main goal was to prevent harassment of his Muslim constituents by the police and Congress workers on grounds of being disloyal. Instead of pleading for justice, he argued that the harassment of Muslims in West Bengal could backfire badly for West Bengal if it actually forced them to migrate to East Pakistan. He pointed out that East Bengali Hindus outnumbered Muslims of West Bengal by 8 million. So if West Bengal's 5.3 million Muslims were transferred to East Bengal, leading to a corresponding influx of Hindus from East Bengal, the truncated province would be left with a situation that was 'economically unsound'.

If 80 lakhs more of people are transferred from East Bengal to West Bengal without an inch of land with them, what will be the food position of West Bengal? At present West Bengal cannot feed its own population. Suppose you transfer 80 lakhs more of people from East Bengal, can you feed them?[25]

This portrayal of refugees as harbingers of doom for West Bengal has to be seen in the light of their tendency to grab lands and property owned by the Muslim minority.[26] Rumours were rife of a possible transfer of populations in divided Bengal, and there were prominent voices, such as Syama Prasad Mookerji, who argued for it. This obviously heightened the insecurity of the local Muslim community. This discussion is significant because it points to the early iteration of a discourse of governance that primarily saw refugees as additional or extra population. Within this discourse, the most relevant information about refugees was their economic attributes – their occupational backgrounds, urban or rural origins and the cost of hosting them, in terms of land and resources.

The West Bengal government's apathy towards refugees and the reluctance to allocate resources for their relief and rehabilitation begins to make sense when seen in this light. For those in power, the question of rehabilitation of the few thousand who had arrived in 1948 became inextricably linked with the fearful possibility of the millions who could follow in their wake. In the immediate aftermath of partition, the authorities in West Bengal feared rather than desired the possibility of a Punjab-like exodus of Hindu minorities from East Bengal. The belief had grown that such an influx would cripple the economy of West Bengal, which simply did not have enough land to accommodate all the Hindus 'left behind' in East Bengal. In the immediate aftermath of partition, an

---

[25] Janab Musharruf Hossain, *General Discussions of the Budget*, WBLA, 23 February 1948, p. 98.

[26] Joya Chatterji, 'Of Graveyards and Ghettos: Muslims in Partitioned West Bengal,' in Mushirul Hasan and Asim Roy (eds), *Living Together Separately: Cultural India in History and Politics* (New Delhi and New York: Oxford University Press, 2005), pp. 222–49.

insecure present drove the Muslim League leaders to express this belief in public, while Nehru and B. C. Roy contemplated this fearful possibility in private. In a letter to Dr Roy, written merely two months after the latter's ascendance to premiership, Nehru expresses his resolve to adhere to a 'clear policy' regarding refugees from eastern Pakistan.[27]

East Bengal will continue to feel neglected and bypassed so long as the centre of gravity is in western Pakistan. The centre of gravity is bound to continue to remain in the West, and this will lead to eastern Pakistan drifting further and further away.

Western Pakistan, I think, is likely to continue, though I hope that in future our relations with it will grow closer and there may be some common subjects like defence.

It is for this reason, among others, that it is wrong to encourage any large-scale migration from East Bengal to the West. Indeed, if such a migration takes place, West Bengal and to some extent the Indian Union would be overwhelmed.[28]

In suggesting the likely continuance of western Pakistan alone, Nehru betrays his belief that eastern Pakistan was unlikely to last as a political entity. It is unclear if Nehru saw eastern Pakistan's inexorable drift away from the 'centre of gravity' in the west leading to the formation of a separate nation in the future, or if he believed that it would lead to the reunification of Bengal. What was clear was that he believed state-aided evacuation of Hindu minorities from East Bengal to be either unnecessary, given this political eventuality, or unadvisable as it might jeopardise friendly relations with Western Pakistan. However, his final and clinching argument for following a policy designed to prevent the large-scale migration of Hindus from East Bengal was exactly the same as the 'limitations' cited by West Bengal's Finance Minsiter and the fears expressed by Muslim League members. The large numbers involved in such a migration would 'overwhelm' not just West Bengal, but the entire Indian Union. In post-partition West Bengal, the prevention of migration from across the frontier took precedence over providing for those who did cross over.

The government of West Bengal lacked the means to prevent large-scale immigration of minorities from East Bengal. Despite a series of bilateral talks, it was impossible for India to guarantee security and full inclusion in civic life of Pakistan for the 12 million Hindus 'left behind' in East Bengal, which would, in theory, make migration unnecessary. The second possibility was to try and prevent their entry at the border. But the border between India and eastern Pakistan was over 4,000 km

---

[27] S. Gopal (ed.), *Selected Works of Jawaharlal Nehru, Second Series, Vol. 5* (New Delhi: Jawaharlal Nehru Memorial Fund, 1984), pp. 161–2.
[28] Ibid.

long and far from being policed, had not even been demarcated in 1947.[29] West Bengal lacked both the means to police its new frontier and the regulations necessary to prevent or control cross-border migration. Both these strategies were attempted in later years, with varying degrees of success, in order to check the rising numbers of refugees from eastern Pakistan. However, in the immediate aftermath of partition, the only means of discouraging migration that the government of West Bengal had at its disposal was to make an example out of the few who did cross over. The outright denial of rehabilitation and provision of as little relief as possible to partition refugees became state policy in this context.

The new minister in charge of refugee relief in Dr Roy's cabinet was Nikunja Behari Maity, a champion of the Mahishya community of West Bengal and one of the most strident proponents of the rights of the 'sons of the soil' and landowners.[30] Unsurprisingly, his brief tenure (1948–9) was characterised by a single-minded determination to spend as little as possible on refugees.[31] In November 1948, the government declared that only those who had entered West Bengal between 1 June 1947 and 25 June 1948 would be eligible for relief. By December 1948, the government declared that no new refugees would be registered after 15 January 1949, thus further limiting an already narrow official definition of 'refugee'.[32] Joya Chatterji, while tracing these cynical attempts of the West Bengal government to limit its liability, argues that the characterisation of refugees as victims and relief as charity enabled the government to arbitrarily deny relief, since charitable aid could not be demanded as a right.[33] However, the reduction of relief to charity was not the only justification for its denial. The authorities of West Bengal explicitly justified their refusal to provide aid to Hindu migrants from East Bengal by characterising immigration as detrimental to the economic development of the state.

The post-colonial state distinguished itself from its colonial predecessor not just on the grounds of self-rule, but more so by what self-rule was

---

[29] Willem van Schendel, *The Bengal Borderland: Beyond State and Nation in South Asia* (London: Anthem Press, 2005), p. 53.

[30] See Chatterji, *Spoils of Partition* (2007), pp. 221–2.

[31] During this period there was no separate Ministry of Relief and Rehabilitation in West Bengal and refugees were administered through the old Relief Department. Maity's role in administering refugee relief ended in June 1949, with the creation of a separate Ministry of Relief and Rehabilitation. For details see Chakrabarti, *Marginal Men* (1999), p. 16 and Hiranmay Bandyopadhyay, *Udvastu (Refugee)*, p. 53.

[32] For details of this phase, see 'Right or Charity? The Debate over Relief and Rehabilitation in West Bengal', Suvir Kaul (eds), *The Partitions of Memory: The Afterlife of the Division of India*, (Delhi: 2001), pp. 74–110.

[33] Ibid.

supposed to achieve: the promise of national economic development.[34] By the 1940s, thinking about economic development in India had become entangled with thinking about population and poverty. The connection between population and poverty has a long history dating back to the Malthusian view of famines as necessary and 'natural' checks on populations exceeding the capacity of the land to provide for their needs. In the Indian context, Malthusian pessimism was complicated by a complex interface between economic nationalists and imperial apologists. The denial of development and prosperity to Indians due to colonial exploitation was an old theme, dating back to nineteenth-century economic nationalism. What was relatively new and peculiar to the twentieth century was the imperial apology that blamed Indians for their own poverty, arguing that it was 'overpopulation' and not underdevelopment that kept India poor.[35] This particular framing of the population of India as an obstacle in her path to achieving economic growth gained popularity during the 1930s and 40s, not just amongst colonial administrators, but also amongst influential Indian economists, such as Gyan Chand and Radhakamal Mukerjee.[36] By the time the post-colonial state embarked on its career of engineering national development, the problem of 'overpopulation' and the necessity of controlling the natural rate of growth through family-planning had become embedded in the logic of good governance.[37] Within this discourse of development and population, refugees could only be seen as unwanted additions to the existing problem of overpopulation.

Far from being two radically different policy regimes, the different responses of the post-colonial state to the refugee crisis in the west and in the east were actually the positive and negative manifestations of a singular governmentality of rehabilitation that pitted refugee needs

---

[34] There is an extensive literature on this subject. For examples see T. J. Byres (ed.), *The State and Development Planning in India, SOAS Studies on South Asia* (Delhi; New York: Oxford University Press, 1994), Sukhamoy Chakravarty, *Development Planning: The Indian Experience* (Oxford: Clarendon Press, 1987) and L. Rudolph and S. Rudolph, *In Pursuit of Lakshmi: The Political Economy of the Indian State* (Chicago, IL: University of Chicago Press, 1987).

[35] Sarah Hodges, 'Governmentality, Population and Reproductive Family in Modern India', *Economic and Political Weekly*, 39: 11 (2004), 1157–63.

[36] For example, see Gyan Chand, *India's Teeming Millions: A Contribution to the Study of the Indian Population Problem* (London: G. Allen & Unwin Limited, 1939) and Radhakamal Mukerjee, *The Political Economy of Population* (New York: Longmans Green, 1943). For their role in developing the study of population and demographics in India see Rajendra K. Sharma, *Demography and Population Problems* (Delhi: Atlantic, 1997), pp. 71–92 and Hodges, 'Governmentality, Population and Reproductive Family', 1160.

[37] Mohan Rao, *From Population Control to Reproductive Health: Malthusian Arithmetic* (New Delhi, Thousand Oaks and London: Sage Publications, 2004).

against nationalist aspirations of rapid economic development. An exchange of populations in the western sector allowed the state to absorb the majority of the refugees, who were agriculturists, in a manner consistent with this governmentality. They became the new hands who could till the fields left behind by evacuee Muslims.[38] In the eastern sector, the fact that the population of Hindus in East Bengal exceeded that of Muslims in West Bengal by 8 million decided their fate. Refugees from eastern Pakistan could only be 'extra mouths' to feed and the entire regime of rehabilitation in West Bengal was crafted to somehow prevent the fearful possibility of being overwhelmed by these unwanted extra millions. By the end of 1948, by government estimates, a little over 1 million refugees had entered West Bengal, and a majority of them did not enter government camps.[39] Yet, policy responses remained focused on the need to avert a future influx of eight million instead of responding to the present crisis.

A Flawed Beginning: The Three Patterns of Dispersal in 1949

Rehabilitation had taken its own informal course in West Bengal while the state followed a policy of drift and denial of relief to refugees. Every single abandoned army barrack and camp in Calcutta, originally built to house the Allied troops during the Second World War, was occupied by refugees by 1949. The squatters at Lake, Jodhpur, Jadavpur, B.R.O, Alipore and Durgapur camps organised committees to resist eviction and negotiate with authorities. This was followed by the emergence of central coordinating committees such as DKBS or *Dakhsin Kalikata Bastuhara Samgram Parishad* (South Calcutta Refugee Council of Action) and NBVK or *Nikhil Banga Vastuhara Karma Parishad* (All Bengal Refugee Council of Action).[40] Through these organisations refugees started petitioning the government for rehabilitation. Simultaneously, some smaller associations such as the Tollygunge Refugee Association and Jadavpur Refugee Camp Association started organising illegal squats on fallow land, eventually leading to the establishment of Gandhi colony and

---

[38] For a study of how displaced families were effectively used to further agricultural development in Punjab, see Gyanesh Kudaisya, 'The Demographic Upheaval Partition: Refugees and Agricultural Resettlement in India, 1946–67', *South Asia*, 18: SpecialIssue, (1995), 73–94.

[39] Committee of Review of Rehabilitation work in West Bengal, West Bengal, Report on Rehabilitation Loans to the Displaced Persons from Erstwhile East Pakistan in West Bengal (New Delhi: Ministry of Supply and Rehabilitation, 1974).

[40] Chakrabarti, *Marginal Men* (1999), pp 48–53.

Bijoygarh colony respectively.[41] The government was far from unaware of this growing world of refugee associations and their increasingly radical measures of self-help. Bidhan Chandra Roy was rumoured to have given tacit approval to the establishment of Bijoygarh colony. But government aid for this growing population of refugees was limited to meagre loans, designed to encourage them to be self-supporting. According to Saroj Chakrabarty, the personal assistant of Dr Roy, hundreds of unemployed young men sought interviews with the Chief Minister, then known as the Premier, hoping for some help.

Most of them were refugees and they had no money even for their day to day existence. They were asked to go to the wholesale markets, prepare a list of articles they could sell together with their prices and the Premier would provide them with small funds either from his own resource or from the Industries Department or the Refugee Relief Department . . . In so doing he not only solved their daily needs but instilled in them a spirit of self-reliance and hope.[42]

The dogma of self-reliance was eventually imposed upon destitute refugees who had taken shelter in government camps. On 6 November 1949, Dr Roy appealed to the refugees to formulate concrete schemes for their own rehabilitation within a month, after which all relief from the state would be discontinued.[43] Thus, by the end of 1949, the focus of policy had shifted from denial of relief to the question of rehabilitation. Several developments in 1949 aided this shift.

The government of India had so far prioritised discouraging migration from eastern Pakistan. Central to this policy was the deliberate refusal of rehabilitation and the provision of bare minimum relief, based on the conviction that anything more could be construed as encouraging migration. By the end of 1949, a mere 70,000[44] out of an estimated total of 1,338,842[45] refugees in West Bengal were in government camps. Even the minimal relief of maintenance grants disbursed at the rate of a maximum of 60 rupees per family represented a significant recurring cost for the government of India. In lieu of freeing itself from this

[41] Indu Baran Ganguly, *Colonysmriti: udvasu colony pratishthar gorar katha (Memories of Colonies: The Early Days of the Establishment of Refugee Colonies)* (Calcutta: Sanjib Printers, 1997), pp. 31–4. The genesis of Bijoygarh colony is taken up in detail in chapter 3.

[42] Saroj Chakrabarty, *With Dr. B. C. Roy and Other Chief Ministers: A Record Up to 1962* (Calcutta: Bensons, 1974), p. 81.

[43] Ibid., p.110.

[44] Hiranmoy Bandypadhyay, *Udvastu, (Refugee)*, (Calcutta: Sahitya Samsad, 1970), p.46.

[45] See table 1.1. This total is compiled from figures provided in 'Appendix 1: Chronological statement of exodus from erstwhile East Pakistan to India' in Committee of review of rehabilitation work in West Bengal, *Report of Rehabilitation Loans to the Displaced Persons from Erstwhile East Pakistan in West Bengal* (1974).

recurring cost, the government was prepared to sanction a loan of six million rupees towards rehabilitation.[46] Rehabilitation in West Bengal began as a time-bound project, constrained by a fixed deadline for the closure of government camps. Initially October 1949 was fixed as the date of closure, which was later extended to December 1949. This ultimatum finally prompted B. C. Roy to set up a Ministry of Refugee Relief and Rehabilitation in June 1949. In order to speed up work and meet the deadline, he personally took charge of the ministry and decided to appoint the same person as the Commissioner of Rehabilitation and as the Secretary of Relief. This role fell to Hiranmoy Bandyopadhyay, whose autobiographical account, *Udvastu* (Refugee), provides rich details of the ministry's activities between 1949 and 1955. Bandyopadhyay cites these administrative innovations as proof of Dr Roy's commitment to the welfare of refugees.[47] However, contemporary events in West Bengal suggest that Dr Roy's new-found urgency in rehabilitating refugees might have been influenced by other, less benevolent, considerations.

In 1948, India's military takeover of the princely state of Hyderabad fuelled anti-Hindu sentiments in eastern Pakistan and led to a rise in the number of refugees. The spike in migration had little or no impact on policy. During this period, Dr Roy's ministry merely encouraged self-help amongst the refugees by disbursing paltry loans for trade and business. The following year witnessed a perceptible drop in the rate of migration from eastern Pakistan. The ministry, ostensibly set up to cope with the rapidly increasing and complex problems of the displaced persons from East Pakistan, was actually constituted during this period of comparative quiet. Far more significant were political developments in Calcutta. On 14 January 1949, Calcutta witnessed its first rally of refugees when 15,000 marched to Sealdah station under the banner of NVBKP. The situation deteriorated rapidly once the students decided to strike in support. A day of violent student demonstrations was followed by brutal police repression in which five students were killed. The scandal led to outrage in the media and crisis within the state assembly, with Sarat Bose demanding the resignation of Dr Roy's ministry. While Sarat Bose was easily placated by promises, the simmering discontent amongst the refugees could not be so easily appeased.[48] The threat posed by the politicisation of refugees was brought home to the government in no uncertain terms. It is likely that Dr Roy's new-found zeal in solving the refugee problem was born of this realisation. It is in this context that the dispersal

---

[46] Bandyopadhyay, *Udvastu (Refugee)*, (1970), p. 31.   [47] Ibid., p. 32.
[48] For details of this incident see Chakrabarty, *With Dr. B. C. Roy*, p. 113 and Chakrabarti, *Marginal Men* (1999), pp. 53–6.

of refugees out of Calcutta emerged as a strategy designed to prevent the politicisation of East Bengali refugees. Dr Roy came up with a scheme of dispersal of refugee students from Calcutta that envisioned setting up institutions of higher education outside the city. He defended the scheme as a means of diluting the centralisation of higher education in Calcutta, where 40 of West Bengal's 89 colleges were located.[49]

This sequence of events in 1949 corroborates, to some extent, Joya Chatterji's assertion that Dr Roy 'looked at refugees through the prism of politics'.[50] In its earliest iteration, dispersal focused on refugee students and had little to do with the thousands awaiting rehabilitation in camps. But with time, a strategy born of the need to prevent solidarity between refugees and students became a general means of dealing with refugees. In the process, dispersal acquired new meanings. At its most banal, it meant discharging refugees from camps. This process of dispersal was inevitably accomplished via a mad rush to shut down camps, and was seldom designed to minimise political fallouts. A third variation of dispersal involved pushing refugees outside the state of West Bengal. The two later patterns more often than not swelled the ranks of malcontents in West Bengal and cannot be adequately explained through the prism of politics.

The decision to close all camps in 1949 left the government of West Bengal with the difficult task of dispersing 12,500 refugee families within a few months. West Bengal's new Ministry of Refugee Relief and Rehabilitation proceeded to categorise the refugees into occupational groups, such as agriculturists, weavers, fishermen and non-agriculturist middle class. This was followed by the rushed dispersal of refugees from camps to rehabilitation sites deemed to be conducive to the pursuance of their original occupation. Here, with some initial aid from the government, they were expected to become self-sufficient citizens.[51] All refugee families settled in rural areas were promised a plot of land measuring 4 to 10 *cottahs*[52], a house-building loan of Rs 500 and one month's maintenance. Those classified as agriculturists were entitled to 10 *bighas*[53] of land while 'businessmen' had to make do with an additional month's maintenance. However, the West Bengal government made the provision of land conditional upon its availability. In practice, the refugees were

[49] Dr Bidhan Chandra Roy, Premier, *Demands for Grants: Expenditure on Refugees*, WBLA, 4 October 1950, p. 200.

[50] Chatterji, *Spoils of Partition* (2007), p. 131.

[51] Bandyopadhyay, *Udvastu (Refugee)*, 1970, pp. 46–55.

[52] Also spelt as katta or kattha, this is a traditional unit of land area in South Asia that is equal to 1/20 of a bigha or roughly 720 square feet.

[53] A traditional unit of measure for a land area in South Asia with wide regional variations. In Bengal, one bigha is equal to 20 cottahs, with each cottah being 720 square feet.

dispersed from camps with loans and were expected to procure land at their own initiative. Dr Roy admitted that while 9,600 families were 'rehabilitated' in rural areas; a mere 2,000 had received cultivable land.[54] A colony of 500 families of fishermen was established at Majherchar, on the shores of the river Bhagirathi. The Chouhatta village near Rajpur was selected for the resettlement of 200 weavers and their families based on its proximity to markets in Howrah and Calcutta.[55] Both the settlements suffered from the absence of supportive infrastructure, such as facilities of storage, public transport and supply of raw materials, without which such large concentrations of a single occupational group could not attain self-sufficiency. A review conducted in 1972 revealed that most of the fishermen settled at Majherchar had given up fishing and worked as factory workers, vendors, small traders and casual day labourers.[56] Given that cutting costs was the motive force behind these hastily planned dispersals, most of these schemes failed to achieve substantive rehabilitation of refugees.

When it came to the rehabilitation of middle-class refugees, the government simply ran out of ideas. The families awaiting rehabilitation in the camps of Habra and Baigachi were quite simply relocated to plots of land near Habra, in a bizarre settlement named Kalyangarh that was neither rural nor urban. In an area which had no conceivable means of employment for urban professionals, the government sought to justify its scheme by expecting refugees to make a living out of a combination of 'planting trees, growing some crops, and maybe even keeping some cows'. Similarly, the camp at Gayeshpur was converted to an urban settlement.[57] In sum, these schemes added a floating population of over 7,000 families of 'agriculturists' to West Bengal, who had some money but no land and were likely to flock to the cities in search of employment. As for the middle classes, their ad hoc resettlement on empty tracts of land effectively recruited them to the growing refugee movement. Within a couple of years, the vernacular press carried reports of protests by refugees settled at Gayehspur and Habra, who complained against the absence of livelihood.[58] The dispersal of refugees to remote 'empty' tracts not only ignored their economic rehabilitation, it also failed to minimise political activity amongst the refugees.[59]

[54] Dr Bidhan Chandra Roy, Premier, *Amendments to Motion*, WBLA, 8 February 1950, pp. 71–5.

[55] Bandyopadhyay, *Udvastu (Refugee)*, pp. 48–55.

[56] Committee of Review of Rehabilitation Work in West Bengal, *Report on Development of Fisheries for Rehabilitation of Old Migrant Families in West Bengal*, 10th Report (New Delhi: Ministry of Supply and Rehabilitation, 1972).

[57] Bandyopadhyay, *Udvastu (Refugee)*, pp. 48–55.   [58] *Hindustan Times*, 12 June 1953.

[59] For an argument which privileges the political imperatives of dispersal see Joya Chatterji, 'Dispersal' and the Failure of Rehabilitation: Refugee Camp-dwellers and Squatters in West Bengal', *Modern Asian Studies*, 41:5 (2007), 995–1032.

The idea of dispersing refugees outside West Bengal was the last to be articulated. On 1 March 1949 the government of West Bengal hit upon a unique plan to solve its refugee problem. It declared that of the 1.6 million refugees in West Bengal, no more than 100,000 would be rehabilitated within the state. The rest were to be sent to Assam, Bihar, Orissa, Coochbehar and Tripura.[60] Given that no more than 70,000 had entered the camps of West Bengal, it was unclear as to how and on what basis the government would organise the expulsion of hundreds and thousands of refugees scattered in different parts of West Bengal. Nevertheless, this idea of dispersal beyond the state steadily gained popularity with Dr Roy's government. It is possible that B. C. Roy's enthusiasm for this form of dispersal derived from the government of India's one-off recruitment of Bengali refugees to an unrelated scheme of settling agriculturists in the Andaman Islands. In 1948, the national Rehabilitation and Development Board decided to throw open a scheme of resettling agriculturists in Andaman Islands to refugees from East Bengal.[61] Dr Roy saw in this one-off scheme the possibility of a long-term solution. The government of West Bengal sent an exploratory party to the Andaman Islands in October 1948. Led by Nikunja Behari Maity, this group toured the Islands and reported that it was extremely favourable for refugee resettlement.[62] This offered an unexpected outlet for West Bengal's unwanted refugee population. It is perhaps not a coincidence that the new plan of systematic dispersal of Bengali refugees to neighbouring states was announced two days before 11 March, when 200 refugee families set sail for the Andaman Islands. Dr B. C. Roy was personally present at the Kidderpore dock to bid farewell to, what he hoped, would be the first of many batches. Moreover, J. K. Roy, the Deputy Refugee Rehabilitation Commissioner, accompanied them to ensure smooth resettlement.[63] The importance Dr Roy accorded to refugee resettlement in the Andamans and his excitement over it did not derive from the actual numbers settled on the Islands, which remained insignificant. The real importance of the scheme was in the precedent it set.[64] From the middle of 1948, the Congress government of West Bengal changed its tone. Refugees were still unwanted in West Bengal, but the earlier exhortations encouraging the Hindu minority to stay put in

---

[60] *Jugantar*, 2 March 1949.

[61] Development-Colonisation, Settlement: Proposal to Settle West Punjab Refugees in Andaman Island, File No. 259/47-AN, Government of India, Ministry of Home Affairs, Andamans Branch, 1947, National Archives of India, New Delhi.

[62] Surajit Chadra Sinha, *Report on the Possibilities of Further Resettlement of East Pakistan Refugees in Andaman Islands* (Calcutta, Refugee Rehabilitation Department, Government of West Bengal, 1952), p.3.

[63] *Jugantar*, 12 March 1949.   [64] For a detailed discussion of the scheme see chapter 2.

Pakistan gave way to the increasingly insistent demand that Bengali refugees must be resettled outside West Bengal.

Thus, Bidhan Roy's enthusiasm for dispersing refugees outside West Bengal was not merely born of his perception of refugees as a politically combustible group. It also derived from a governmentality of rehabilitation that saw refugees as additional and unwanted population and can be traced back to his discussions with Nehru in early 1948. In Dr Roy's mind, the main factor that limited the resettlement of refugees in West Bengal was availability of land. As early as March 1948, he had realised that it would be impossible to completely prevent migration from East Bengal. The prospects of being saddled with this additional population had led him to argue that the disputed regions of Manbhum and Dalbhum in Bihar should be allotted to West Bengal in order to facilitate the rehabilitation of those refugees who came over despite the best efforts of the state. He was dissuaded from this scheme by Nehru's promise to find 'areas for the rehabilitation of people from East Bengal ... outside West Bengal wherever this is suitable.'[65] In August 1948, Dr Roy was already in conversation with the governments of neighbouring provinces regarding the dispersal of Bengali refugees. By then, Nehru had become sceptical of the success of such schemes. He confessed that 'it is difficult to induce most provinces to absorb more refugees. We have been pressing them to do so for a long time.'[66] But Dr Roy succeeded where the central government had failed, informing Nehru that 'Orissa and other native states which have been absorbed into the province, would be glad to have our refugees.'[67] Convinced that the East Bengali refugees would hamper the development of the state and unable to dissuade migration, he resorted to dispersing the refugees to 'empty' lands outside West Bengal. The core of the policy was to make 'our' refugees 'their' problem. However, dispersal born of parochial self-interest was bound to find little favour with the central government or with other provincial governments. This led the government of West Bengal to argue that since it had been a national decision to partition the province of Bengal, the refugees born of the consequences of this partition also had to be a national responsibility. The nationalisation of Bengal's refugee crisis had two components. Firstly, all costs for the relief and rehabilitation of refugees had to be borne by the central government, with the government of West Bengal merely acting as the agent distributing relief. Secondly, the central

---

[65] S. Gopal (ed.), *Selected Works of Jawaharlal Nehru, Second Series, Vol. 5* (New Delhi: Jawaharlal Nehru Memorial Fund, 1984), pp. 162–3.

[66] Jawaharlal Nehru to Dr. B. C. Roy, 16 August 1948, Saroj Chakrabarty, *With Dr. B. C. Roy*, p. 107.

[67] Dr. B. C. Roy to Jawaharlal Nehru, 22 August 1948, Ibid., p. 108.

government had to arbitrate to ensure that other provinces took in their fair share of refugees for rehabilitation.

The theory justifying the dispersal of refugees outside West Bengal gained ground in the years following 1950, and especially during the tenure of Renuka Ray as West Bengal's Minister in charge of Relief and Rehabilitation (1952–7). Between 1950 and 1958, the government of West Bengal succeeded in forcing the central Ministry of Rehabilitation to take primary responsibility for the rehabilitation of East Bengali refugees. Several factors enabled this shift, including fundamental changes in the pattern and scale of migration, which is discussed in the later sections. Contrary to received wisdom, the patterns of relief and rehabilitation that evolved in West Bengal speak of a resounding success for Dr B. C. Roy's government. Far from being the hapless administrator of centrally dictated policy, his government forced the central government to change its policy of studied apathy towards refugees from eastern Pakistan. The direct result of this shift in policy was the Dandakaranya scheme. It was run by the autonomous Dandakarnaya Development Authority and funded entirely by the government of India. It envisioned dispersal outside West Bengal as the sole path to rebuilding lives for the majority of East Bengali refugees languishing in camps in West Bengal. The United Central Refugee Council (UCRC) launched an agitation against the relocation of refugees to Dandakaranya, and accused the government of forced dispersal. They prepared an alternative proposal for the rehabilitation of camp refugees based on the meticulous study of the plot-by-plot survey of landholdings in Bengal conducted in 1944–5 under the supervision of A. H. M. Ishaque, the Development Commissioner of undivided Bengal.[68] Besides quoting figures of available cultivable waste from the Ishaque Report, the UCRC's alternative proposal also listed large landholdings for compulsory acquisition and redistribution amongst the refugees. Dr B. C. Roy issued a spirited response to this proposal, countering UCRC's claims with his own set of statistics designed to prove that the state had indeed run out of 'free' land. He explained how the statistics in the Ishaque Report were misleading, playing off the needs of landless labourers and *bargadars* of West Bengal against the needs of refugees, and clarified that the high cost of reclaiming the mostly poor quality or saline land available in the western districts and

---

[68] A. H. M. Ishaque, *Agricultural Statistics by Plot to Plot Enumeration in Bengal, 1944–45*, 3 Parts (Calcutta: Superintendent Government Printing, 1946). Figures from this survey were used extensively by both the UCRC in *An Alternative Proposal for Rehabilitation of Camp Refugees: Memorandum Submitted by UCRC to Dr, B.C. Roy, Chief Minister, West Bengal, on 11.8.58, United Central Refugee Council Pamphlet*, (Calcutta: UCRC, 1958) and by Dr B. C. Roy in his statement in response to UCRC.

Sunderban made it impossible to rehabilitate refugees within the rates stipulated by the central government. His conclusions were non-negotiable:

economic necessity does and should outweigh most considerations ... It is abundantly clear that from all that has been said above that paucity of land is the biggest obstacle in the way of rehabilitation of displaced persons within West Bengal .... The conclusion is inevitable that West Bengal cannot possibly absorb a large section of the agriculturists from camps.[69]

In other words, West Bengal was already saturated with refugees and could not make room for any more. These claims of saturation dated back to 1948 and are remarkable for their tenacious grip on the bureaucratic imagination. The fact that the state could and did absorb hundreds and thousands of refugees between 1947 and 1957 did little to alter the claims of the government. Dispersal of refugees outside West Bengal was primarily designed as a pre-emptive solution to West Bengal's perceived saturation; it was not the last resort of an overwhelmed state.

The Genesis of the Unending Trail: 1950–1951

By the late 1950s, it had become common practice in West Bengal to lament the continuous nature of migration from East Bengal. The authorities blamed this 'unending trail' of refugees, which ebbed and flowed without warning, for repeatedly throwing their plans of rehabilitation out of gear.[70] However, this pattern of migration became evident only after the riots of February 1950. Unprecedented in East Bengal in its scale and ferocity, the February riots of 1950 proved to be a watershed in the history of refugee rehabilitation in West Bengal. It ended the federal government's wilful blindness to East Bengali refugees and cut short the government of West Bengal's satisfaction over the successful closure of camps. By the end of 1951, there were over 1 million new refugees in West Bengal (see table 1.1). The problem of rehabilitation in West Bengal had reached a scale and complexity which could no longer be resolved by arbitrary deadlines for hasty closure of camps and withdrawal of relief.

[69] *Rehabilitation of Camp Refugees, Statement issued by Dr. B. C. Roy, Chief Minister, West Bengal* (Calcutta: Government of West Bengal, 1958), p. 8.

[70] Khushwant Singh, *The Unending Trail* (Delhi: Rajkamal Publications, 1957). This sentiment is expressed quite succinctly by Renuka Ray, when she entitles the section of her autobiography on refugee rehabilitation in West Bengal 'And Still they Come'. *My Reminiscences: Social Development During the Gandhian Era and After* (Calcutta: Stree, 2005), pp. 130–47.

Table 1.1: *Chronological Statement of Exodus from Erstwhile East Pakistan to India, 1946–70*

Year	Persons
1946	58,602
1947	4,63,474
1948	4,90,555
1949	326,211
1950	1,172,928
1951	47437
1952	531440
1953	76123
1954	121364
1955	240424
1956	581000
1957	6000
1958	4898
1959	6348
1960	97128
1961	10847
1962	13894
1963	16295
1964	693,142
1965	107,906
1966	7665
1967	24,527
1968	11,614
1969	9,763
1970	2,51,160
TOTAL	5283334

The figures are replicated without amendment from the original.
Source: Committee of Review of Rehabilitation Work in West Bengal, *Report of Rehabilitation Loans to the Displaced Persons from Erstwhile East Pakistan in West Bengal,* New Delhi, 1974, p. 63.

Police harassment of prominent Hindus of Barisal and alarming deterioration of communal relations in the Bagerhat district of Khulna triggered a renewed exodus from the middle of January in 1950.[71] Over 1,000 refugees at Bongaon station brought news of pogroms against Hindus.[72] By 1 February there were 10,000 'new' refugees in West Bengal. More poured in with every passing day. As soon as the vernacular press carried

[71] *Jugantar,* 17 January 1950.   [72] *Jugantar,* 20 January 1950.

news of violence in East Bengal, the predictable pattern of retaliatory violence flared in Calcutta and parts of West Bengal. The repercussions in East Bengal were far more serious. Riots spiralled outwards from Dhaka into its suburbs, to Jamalpur and Kishoreganj sub-division of Mymensingh district, the town of Chittagong and its suburbs, Feni in Noakhali, Sylhet, Barishal and Tippera.[73] Survivors of pillage, rape and mass murders flooded West Bengal along with their fear-crazed neighbours, making it impossible for the central government to argue that there was no crisis in the East. As for the government of West Bengal, there was a perceptible softening of attitude. Affective ties between Hindus of East and West Bengal, sympathetic press coverage and heightened solidarity along communal lines produced a wave of sympathy towards the refugees. Far from discouraging migration, Dr B. C. Roy sent in specially hired trains and steamers to rescue Hindus stranded at railheads and steamer stations in East Bengal.[74] Exploiting his personal influence with Airways India Limited, he also airlifted to safety 16 plane-loads of refugees from Dhaka airport.[75] In this the provincial government acted without consulting the central authority. In the aftermath of the February riots, speculation was rife in West Bengal regarding a possible exchange of populations in the East. This might have inspired Dr Roy's ad hoc evacuation of stranded minorities.

Nehru dampened this wave of sympathy by categorically denying any possibility of an exchange of minority populations between the two Bengals. Writing to Dr Roy on 17 February, Nehru declared that the 'business of shifting millions of people is entirely beyond our capacity. The mere attempt will create enormous difficulty and conflict.'[76] This was a crucial reprieve for West Bengal's Muslim community, but paved the way for the policy to push back thousands of East Bengali migrants. While ruling out the exchange of populations, Nehru declared that Bengal would henceforth receive top priority.[77] However, in terms of actual content of policy, Nehru and the Congress had run out of ideas. Nehru's initial response to the crisis of 1950 was to wait and watch.

I might give you my own appraisal of the general situation. I think that the months before monsoon are rather critical. If we pass that period, the tension and the possibility of a major conflict will gradually get less. If we pass the next seven or eight months, that possibility will be even less [sic].[78]

---

[73] For details see *Indian Commission of Jurists, Committee of Enquiry, Recurrent Exodus of Minorities from East Pakistan and Disturbances in India: A Report to the Indian Commission of Jurists by its Committee of Enquiry* (New Delhi: 1965).
[74] Hiranmoy Bandyopadhyay, *Udvastu (Refugee)*, pp. 82–3.
[75] Saroj Chakrabarty, *With Dr. B. C. Roy*, p. 154.   [76] Ibid., p. 157.
[77] *The Amrita Bazar Patrika*, 24 February 1950.
[78] Saroj Chakrabarty, *With Dr. B. C. Roy*, p. 158.

While the tide of East Bengali refugees rose inexorably, this disastrous decision to wait out the crisis was elevated to the level of national policy. Mohanlal Saksena, the central minister in charge of rehabilitation, convened a conference at the Raj Bhavan in Calcutta on 2 March. At this conference, Saksena declared that the government of India had decided to provide temporary relief for refugees on the grounds that they would return to East Bengal as soon as normalcy was restored. Refugee camps, renamed as 'transit camps', were set up close to the border in anticipation of the eventual return journey.[79] A flurry of diplomacy at the highest levels produced the Nehru-Liaquat Ali Pact of 8 April 1950. Its basic thrust was to reverse the tide of refugees by ensuring firstly, the security of minorities and secondly, the free movement of people and goods across the Bengal borderland. The pact provided for a new post of Minority Affairs Minister and the establishment of minority commissions in East and West Bengal. Though these were genuine institutional innovations geared towards protecting and reassuring the minorities, in the absence of a system of accountability and given the clear lack of political will in implementation, it brought little relief for the minorities. What it did do, with considerable success, was to buy the Indian government some reprieve from arranging for the rehabilitation of thousands of displaced families.

Armed with the Nehru-Liaquat Pact, the authorities sat back to wait and watch in the hope that the refugees would return across the open borders. Where many of the sympathisers of East Bengali refugees had been hoping for some sort of an exchange of population, this policy understandably led to dismayed protests. The vocal protests of a minority of politicians and bureaucrats sympathetic to the plight of refugees tend to obscure the fact that East Bengalis were unwelcome intruders in the eyes of the vast majority. The sympathy whipped up by the press for the suffering Hindus of East Bengal proved to be ephemeral and had little purchase outside Calcutta. In Nadia, the staunch opposition of local farmers and landowners led to riots,[80] while the Sonarpur-Bagjola scheme, which had envisioned resettling 10,000 agricultural families had to be abandoned after resettling a mere 400 families in the face of stiff local resistance.[81] It did not matter how much violence the refugees had suffered. They were still unwanted in West Bengal and treated as a problem by the government of India. Nevertheless, the

---

[79] For a vivid account of government initiatives to deal with the influx in 1950, see Bandyopadhyay, *Udvastu (Refugee)*, pp. 59–64.

[80] For the details of conflict between refugees and locals in the border district of Nadia see Subhasri Ghosh, 'The Impact of Immigration on West Bengal, 1947–71', unpublished PhD thesis, Jawaharlal Nehru University, (2006).

[81] *Rehabilitation of Camp Refugees* (1958).

refugees came. With the government of West Bengal announcing a net influx of 460,610 Hindu migrants into West Bengal between the second week of April and the end of August in 1950, it was evident that the Nehru-Liaquat Pact had failed to secure its objective.[82]

Underlying the apparent difference of opinion between the champions of East Bengali refugees and authorities reluctant to offer rehabilitation was a shared understanding of the nature of rehabilitation. For those sympathetic to the plight of refugees, the demand for proper rehabilitation went together with the demand for an exchange of population. For those against it, the refusal to exchange populations entailed the denial of rehabilitation. Neither could imagine making room for refugees in West Bengal unless a comparable number were evacuated. In contemporary West Bengal the support for exchange of population was not limited to S. P. Mookerjee and the right wing. Many, including Hiranmoy Bandyopadhyay, regarded it as a 'natural' or 'inevitable' solution, while disappointment cut across political affiliations amongst those sympathetic to the plight of East Bengali Hindus.[83] Even Asok Mitra, the eminent demographer, admitted in retrospect that he would have preferred the 'fresh start' provided by the unspeakable carnage and brutality in the west to the 'periodic carnage and a running sore' that crippled West Bengal.[84] In other words, thinking about refugee rehabilitation had become inextricably linked to thinking about the management of population and resources in independent India. During the 1950s, there was widespread consensus for an interventionist state that could act as an engine of development. Governance was designed to deliver the promise of national growth. Any policy that advocated a massive increase in population without a commensurate increase in finite national resources was, simply put, bad planning. It was this tendency to think about refugees as additional population within the broad scheme of national development that led both the supporters and detractors of rehabilitation for East Bengali refugees to link it to the question of transfer of population.

The communists provided the sole exception to this broad political consensus, since they opposed both an exchange of population and the dispersal of refugees outside West Bengal. Their alternative vision of rehabilitation is best encapsulated in UCRC's memorandum submitted to Dr B. C. Roy in August 1958, at the height of the agitation launched to protest the dispersal of refugees outside West Bengal. They argued that

[82] Chakrabarty, *With Dr. B. C. Roy*, p. 169.

[83] Bandyopadhyay, *Udvastu (Refugee)*, pp. 61–72. Also see Renuka Ray, *My Reminiscences*, pp. 130–4.

[84] Asok Mitra, *The New India: 1948–55, Memoirs of an Indian Civil Servant* (Bombay: Popular Prakashan, 1991), pp. 140–2.

there was enough cultivable wasteland available in West Bengal, especially in the Sunderbans region, where the resettlement of refugees would also achieve local development.[85] This argument had few takers beyond the camp refugees. The government dismissed it as impracticable while even the most politicised refugees who lived in the squatters' colonies failed to mobilise to defend the rights of the camp dwellers.[86] Interestingly, the Communist leaders abandoned this alternative vision as soon as a Left Front coalition, led by the Communist Party of India (Marxist), won the elections in 1977. Once in power, they succumbed to the same rationale of governance that privileged the 'economy' and resisted any new influx of refugees into West Bengal in the absence of a corresponding rise in available resources. Ross Mallick traces this dramatic reversal of policy, which he attributes to the new government's unwillingness to allow a new influx of refugees to hamper the economic recovery of West Bengal by 'diverting scarce resources from other development projects'.[87] This tendency to disenfranchise refugees in the name of development was nothing new. The Communists were merely the last group to arrive at this Consensus on what constituted good governance when it came to refugees.

The February riots gave the government of West Bengal the leverage it needed to elicit the cooperation of the central government in the project of rehabilitating the refugees who were already in West Bengal. At the conference held on 2 March, the government of India finally agreed to bear the full costs for the relief of all refugees from East Bengal. The neighbouring states of Assam, Bihar and Orissa were instructed to rehabilitate their share of Bengali refugees. Dr B. C. Roy's attempts at dispersing West Bengal's load of refugees now received a seal of approval from the central government. A Branch Secretariat of the central Ministry of Rehabilitation was opened in Calcutta. It took full responsibility for the administration and eventual rehabilitation of the refugees in Coopers Camp at Ranaghat, the largest refugee camp in West Bengal.[88] Though the official policy was to encourage refugees to return to East Bengal, the mounting cost of providing relief to these families led Ajit Prasad Jain (who had replaced Mohanlal Saksena as the central Minister of Rehabilitation) to press for the speedy rehabilitation of refugees. What followed repeated the pattern of rehabilitation that had emerged in 1949.

[85] *An Alternative Proposal by UCRC*, 1958.
[86] For an indictment of the squatters for this failure see Chakrabarti, *Marginal Men*, pp. 178–9.
[87] Ross Mallick, *Development Policy of a Communist Government: West Bengal Since 1977* (Cambridge and New York: Cambridge University Press, 2007), p. 100.
[88] Bandyopadhyay, *Udvastu (Refugee)*, pp. 64–7.

The drive to rehabilitate refugees was preceded by an official redefinition of a bona fide refugee designed to limit state liability. On 7 November 1950, the central government declared 30 November to be the last date for receipt of claims for maintenance grants from refugees.[89] In December 1950 the government of India announced that it would rehabilitate all of West Bengal's 252,000 refugees and close the camps by 30 April 1951. The inevitable shortcomings of hasty dispersal followed. A desperate search for 'empty land' for distribution to those enumerated as cultivators was paralleled by lack of any clear policy towards traders, professionals and other non-agriculturist groups. A variety of loans, earmarked for building houses, purchasing homestead land and setting up small businesses stood in for the rehabilitation of these groups.[90] Dispersal outside West Bengal remained a popular theme and small batches of refugees continued to leave for the Andaman Islands. These departures were turned into occasions for favourable propaganda by the government of West Bengal. Senior officials and ministers addressed these refugees on the eve of their departure and they were showered with various gifts ranging from shoes and seeds to traditional musical instruments such as *khols* and *kartals*. The press was invited to ensure positive coverage.[91] Thus, the increasing involvement of the once apathetic central authorities did little to alter the content or pattern of refugee rehabilitation in West Bengal.

However, the sheer scale of the crisis in 1951 prevented a hasty closure of camps. The rehabilitation officials of West Bengal failed to find land to accommodate over 200,000 refugees. A new innovation, the Bynanama scheme, was implemented which encouraged refugees to locate and buy plots directly from landowners. Despite such innovations the state failed to achieve its goal. In December 1951, there were still 80,000 refugees living in various camps in West Bengal.[92] Every month more refugees applied for admission to camps. Adding fuel to this fire was the renewed influx of East Bengalis from June 1951, which was triggered by economic distress.[93] To further complicate matters, those who had been dispersed for rehabilitation to Bihar and Orissa in 1950 started returning to West Bengal in their thousands.[94] By the end of 1951, it had become abundantly clear that despite diplomatic intervention, reassurances and denial of rehabilitation, the government had little power to deter the steady influx of refugees from East Bengal. The only way to stop this unending

---

[89] *Jugantar*, 10 November 1950.   [90] Bandyopadhyay, *Udvastu (Refugee)*, pp. 139–48.
[91] Ibid., pp. 148–55. Several favourable reports and editorials were published by the pro-government *Anandabazar Patrika* during this period.
[92] Bandyopadhyay, *Udvastu (Refugee)*, p. 145.   [93] Chakrabarti, *Marginal Men*, p. 3.
[94] Bandyopadhyay, *Udvastu (Refugee)*, pp. 171–3.

trail would be to seal the eastern frontier of India. From 1952, the regulation of movement of minorities from East Bengal into India became an integral part of government strategies to resolve the crisis of rehabilitation in West Bengal.

Closing the Door on Refugees: 1952–1957

Few in West Bengal had expected the Nehru-Liaquat Pact to deliver. So for the authorities in Writer's Building, the failure of the pact had little or no impact on the direction of policy. The new Rehabilitation Minister, Renuka Ray, fell back upon tried and tested methods of limiting West Bengal's liability towards refugees. In August 1952, she demanded speedy allocation of increased funds from the central government for the rehabilitation of refugees who were already in West Bengal. When it came to fresh arrivals, she reiterated the old demand that refugees must go outside the state.[95] She advised those who remained in West Bengal to have faith in the motto of self-help instead of depending on the government.[96] However, within this cluster of familiar schemes and policies, a new theme began to come into prominence. In 1952, the government of West Bengal drew up plans to send 5,000 refugees to Orissa of which 2,400 were to be employed as labourers in constructing the Hirakud dam.[97] This dam, originally planned as a scheme of post-war reconstruction, was re-launched by Nehru in 1948 as a project promoting the all-round development of Orissa.[98] Its labour needs were huge, with 25,000 labourers working on it for eight years. This army of workers was mobilised from all over India.[99] For the government of West Bengal, the Hirakud dam provided a convenient outlet for disposing of several thousand refugee families. By dispersing refugees as labourers to Hirakud, it repeated a pattern first seen in the Andaman Islands. In these schemes of dispersal, refugees were portrayed as agents furthering projects of national development. Thus, Bengali refugees could earn their share of national resources by contributing to the nation's development. By 1953, policies of relief and rehabilitation were informed by the ethos of productive labour. The relief camps of West Bengal were replaced by work-site camps, where all able-bodied men were expected to work in lieu of

---

[95] *Amrita Bazar Patrika*, 2 August 1952.   [96] Ibid., 18 August 1952.
[97] Ibid., 3 August 1952.
[98] For details, see N. V. Sovani and Nilkanth Rath, *Economics of a Multi-purpose River Dam: Report of an Inquiry Into the Economic Benefits of the Hirakud Dam* (Pune: Gokhale Institute of Politics and Economics, 1960). Also see Balgovind Baboo, *Technology and Social Transformation: The Case of the Hirakund Multi-Purpose Dam Project in Orissa* (New Delhi: Concept Publishing, 1992).
[99] Baboo, *Technology and Social Transformation* (1992), p. 28.

wages.[100] The 'work' provided in these camps seldom amounted to anything more than the aimless drudgery of digging earth and breaking
stones, and was soon reduced to a formality. While Bengali refugees
were put to work in the Andaman Islands and Orissa, within West
Bengal, the dominant theme continued to be denial of rehabilitation.
In the middle of 1954, West Bengal's Ministry of Rehabilitation decided
that rehabilitation of newcomers was no longer possible within the province. The government agreed to merely house the refugees who entered
the state after June 1954 while they awaited rehabilitation in other areas of
India.[101] After 1954, the government of West Bengal limited its activities
to providing rehabilitation for those who had entered West Bengal in the
previous years.

Thus, by 1954, the West Bengal government's persistent claim of
'saturation' had reached its logical conclusion in the blanket denial of
rehabilitation to all future refugees. West Bengal had been proclaiming its
inability to cater to refugees since 1948. However, for the government of
India to accede to this refusal, a more rational basis than the saturation of
West Bengal was required. Between 1949 and 1955, a series of piecemeal
innovations led to a new formula for organising the rehabilitation of
Bengali refugees. Dispersal became not only the means of relieving pressure from West Bengal, but also a strategy by which the cheap labour
provided by refugees could be used in various planned projects of development. In other words, a governmentality of rehabilitation that privileged national development and enumerated refugees as additional
population could have positive as well as negative manifestations.
Within West Bengal, the East Bengali refugees remained unassimilable
to a rationale of rehabilitation that privileged economic productivity and
national development. For policies that strove to actually harmonise the
rehabilitation of refugees with national development it is necessary to look
beyond West Bengal, in sites as diverse as the Hirakud Dam, the
Andaman Islands and Dandakaranya. Projects and schemes that sought
to recast East Bengali refugees as productive labour and harness them to
national development largely evolved at the national level, outside the
social and political contexts of displacement in West Bengal. This is
explored separately in the next chapter. Here, the focus remains on
West Bengal's persistent refusal to accommodate refugees that created
the conditions for these scattered resettlement schemes.

---

[100] A Note on Rehabilitation in the East, Renuka Ray Papers, Subject File No. 2, Nehru
Memorial Museum and Library, New Delhi. Henceforth NMML.
[101] Renuka Ray to Morarji Desai, October 29 1960, Renuka Ray Papers, Subject File No. 6,
NMML.

The vast majority of the refugees in West Bengal were self-settled and a significant proportion of them lived in illegal squatters' colonies. Till 1951, Dr B. C. Roy's government had held on to the impossible ambition of evicting thousands of displaced families living in these colonies, partly to placate landed interests, and partly to disperse from the outskirts of Calcutta this politically flammable population. This attempt of the state was a spectacular failure.[102] The Eviction Bill, drafted by the government with the explicit purpose of providing a juridical process for the demolition of the squatters' colonies, instead became the catalyst for a massive refugee agitation led by the communist-dominated UCRC and the largely socialist RCRC.[103] By 1952, the government had reached a stalemate with the squatters and was forced to re-word the Eviction Bill to recognise the refugees' right to alternative accommodation. Though unable to evict the refugees, the government remained unwilling to regularise their illegal occupation. Thus, the regularisation of squatters' colonies made very little progress in West Bengal. If rehabilitation within West Bengal was slow, dispersal of refugees from its camps was non-existent. By December 1955, the population of the camps in West Bengal had risen to 237,000 from its previous count of 139,000 in December 1954.[104]

Alarmed at the prospect of being left to manage this rising number of refugees, the government of West Bengal now refused to provide even temporary accommodation. A new policy was formulated by which new arrivals would be dispersed to camps set up at rehabilitation sites in Madhya Pradesh, Bihar, Orissa, Vindhya Pradesh and Rajasthan.[105] In January 1956, Dr B. C. Roy suggested that East Bengali refugees should be settled outside West Bengal in corporate groups of 4,000–5,000 people in integrated rural-cum-industrial schemes.[106] This was precisely what the Dandakaranya Scheme, envisioned by S.V. Ramamurthy a year later, set out to achieve.[107] Formulated by the central Ministry of Rehabilitation and implemented by a specially constituted autonomous body named the Dandakaranya Development Authority, it was the central government's response to Dr B. C. Roy's persistent demand that West Bengal's refugee problem should be resolved on a 'national' basis. Thus, by 1956, the government of West Bengal had

---

[102] See Chakrabarti, *The Marginal Men* (1999), pp. 79–117.

[103] RCRC or Refugee Central Rehabilitation Council was a rival refugee organisation which enjoyed the support of refugee colonies dominated by the RSP, KMPP, Forward Block (Leela Roy Group), Revolutionary Communist Party of India (Soumen Tagore group) and the Socialist Party. Ibid., p. 88.

[104] *The Statesman*, 29 January 1954.   [105] *Hindustan Standard*, 31 January 1956.

[106] *Amrita BazarPatrika*, 29 January 1956.

[107] *Dandakaranya Project, Ministry of Rehabilitation, 97th Report of the Parliament Estimates Committee*, 2nd Lok Sabha, 1957–1962, (New Delhi: Government of India, 1960).

pushed the argument of national responsibility for East Bengali refugees to its logical conclusion. Henceforth, not just the cost of relief of East Bengali refugees, but also the planning and execution of their rehabilitation would be the responsibility of the government of India.

B. C. Roy's success in nationalising West Bengal's refugee problem shifted the liability of rehabilitating refugees from East Pakistan on to the central government. In order to check the rising costs on refugees, the government of India now looked to nip the problem in its bud, by restricting the movement of minorities across the Bengal border. These attempts dated back to 1952, when the government of India announced plans for passports for East Pakistanis. The result was counterproductive. Fear of being cut off in Pakistan led thousands of Hindu refugees to rush to West Bengal. Despite Pakistan's decision to postpone the introduction of passports, India unilaterally introduced the scheme on 15 October, largely in order to stop this renewed influx.[108] A system of migration certificates was introduced for those who wanted to migrate to India. Though theoretically introduced to 'alleviate the hardship of minorities', in practice the system was used by the government to regulate the entry of Hindu minorities into eastern India. This system failed to stem the tide. Every month, thousands of families applied for and obtained certificates of migration. In West Bengal, they were joined by another 40,000 families in possession of fake migration certificates, who nevertheless had to be accommodated on 'compassionate' grounds.[109]

In 1956 the government of India attempted to restrict the issue of migration certificates to only those who could prove a direct threat to their life, or to the honour of 'their women', in East Bengal. This scheme fell through due to opposition from bureaucrats.[110] In 1957, new prohibitive instructions were relayed to the Deputy Commissioner of Dacca. He was instructed to not issue any migration certificates unless the applicants had relations in West Bengal willing to look after them. Moreover, migrants now had to declare that they would not claim any rehabilitation benefits in West Bengal.[111] These new instructions, which removed even the pretention of relief for minorities, finally had the desired effect. It drastically reduced the number of refugees entering West Bengal. In 1957, the number of 'fresh arrivals' in West Bengal

---

[108] P. C. Sen to Jawaharlal Nehru, 9 October 1952, Saroj Chakrabarty, *With Dr. B. C. Roy*, p. 210.

[109] *Relief and Rehabilitation of Displaced Persons in West Bengal* (Calcutta: Government of West Bengal, 1957).

[110] For details see Roy, *Partitioned Lives*.

[111] Renuka Ray to Morarji Desai, 29 October 1960, Renuka Ray Papers, Subject File 6, NMML.

dropped to 6,000 from 581,000 in the previous year.[112] Having engineered this drop in migration from East Pakistan, the authorities in Delhi
proceeded to cite the declining numbers as proof of the end of the refugee
crisis. In December 1957 it announced that after March 1958, migrants
would no longer be registered as refugees.[113]

The Final Dispersal: 1957–1962

After 1957, the government of India was left with the formidable task of
finding land and livelihood for over 200,000 refugees languishing in the
camps of West Bengal. Its solution was the Dandakaranya project, which
was launched with much fanfare in December 1957. In theory, the project
was meant to develop 'backward' tracts in central India. But its involvement with the local population was restricted to granting land to 495
tribal families.[114] In fact, the project was designed to solve West Bengal's
refugee problem once and for all.[115] The agriculturists and non-
agriculturist refugees who had languished for years in the camps of
West Bengal were now recast as agricultural pioneers of this largely barren
tract in central India. Even at its most optimistic, Dandakaranya project
envisioned the rehabilitation of 20,000 displaced families from the camps
of West Bengal. However, the Dandakaranya Development Authority
faced considerable opposition from the governments of Orissa and
Madhya Pradesh in obtaining land. This significantly reduced the final
area of the project and therefore, the number of families it could accommodate. The revised target envisioned settling a maximum of 12,000
families by March 1961.[116] This did not deter the Ministry of
Rehabilitation from serving notice to the considerably larger population
of refugees in the camps of West Bengal.

The Ministry of Rehabilitation came up with a cynical method to
resolve the massive disparity between the total number of families who
awaited rehabilitation in the eastern zone, and the number of families who
could be accommodated at Dandakaranya. In 1957, after a detailed
survey of the refugee population living in camps declared that for

---

[112] See Table 1.1.
[113] *Relief and Rehabilitation of Displaced Persons in West Bengal* (1957).
[114] Nandini Sundar, *Subalterns and Sovereigns: An Anthropological History of Bastar,
1854–1996* (Delhi: Oxford University Press, 1997), pp. 196–7.
[115] The project envisioned the development of the districts of Bastar in Madhya Pradesh
and Koraput and Kalahandi in Orissa, which were all regarded as backward areas in
need of development. It was a project of agricultural colonisation with elaborate plans of
setting up new villages, building roads and railways, providing irrigation and establishing small-scale industrial production centres.
[116] *Dandakaranya Project Report* (1960).

rehabilitation to be effective, the size of the problem had to be cut down.[117] A ruthless 'screening' of the camp population followed, which had the explicit goal of denying rehabilitation to as many refugees as possible. Families with any alternative source of income, no matter how inadequate for subsistence, were deemed to no longer require rehabilitation. Refugees who had already received any kind of government assistance, such as house building or trade loans, were disqualified from applying. There was particular anxiety around those who had left, deserted, or been expelled from refugee camps. As far as the state was concerned, these people had forfeited their right to rehabilitation and relief officials were instructed to block all attempts by these men and women to re-enter camps.[118] Since the ceiling of the monthly dole was fixed irrespective of family size, it had been a common practice amongst refugees to split larger families into two or three units in order to receive sufficient relief. The screening process resolved to weed out such irregularities as illegal. The nuclear family as the unit of rehabilitation was rigidly imposed upon refugees whose affective families and networks of relatedness did not necessarily confirm to bureaucratic definitions. A variety of familial dependants, such as nephews, nieces, aunts, uncles and grandparents, were regularly included in their joint families by East Bengali Hindus. The screening paved the way for their rejection. In theory, the state had pledged to stand in as the patriarch and provider of the old, the infirm and the unattached women, who were collectively branded as 'permanent liabilities'. However, in the final screening process of 1957–8, many such dependants, especially older women, were simply abandoned.[119] The government of West Bengal made a feeble attempt to prevent the forced disintegration of refugee families by 'tagging' familial dependants on to the statutory refugee families. However, the Dandakaranya Development Authority refused to cater to an additional 1,611 refugees 'tagged on' to 1,137 families on the grounds that they were not 'ex-inmates' of relief camps in West Bengal. The result was that 'aged parents, wives, minor sisters and daughters and adult sons of widows were separated from their families'.[120]

---

[117] *Jugantar*, 20 April 1960.

[118] This became particularly relevant after the fresh influx of refugees in 1964–5, who were called 'new migrants'. For details of this policy see Parliament Estimates Committee, *Reception, Dispersal and Rehabilitation of New Migrants Arriving in India from East Pakistan since 1st January 1964, Ministry of Rehabilitation, 71st Report of the Parliament Estimates Committee, 3rd Lok Sabha, 1964–65* (New Delhi: Government of India, 1965).

[119] Interview with Ashoka Gupta and Nalini Mitra, conducted by Dr. Subhoranjan Dasgupta, 2000, Personal Collection of Subhoranjan Dasgupta. Henceforth PCSD.

[120] Parliament Estimates Committee, *Dandakaranya Project, Ministry of Rehabilitation, 72nd Report of the Parliament Estimates Committee, 3rd Lok Sabha, 1962–67* (New Delhi: Government of India, 1965), pp. 45–6.

By August 1958, the population in the camps of West Bengal had been whittled down to 35,000 families. Of these, West Bengal was expected to rehabilitate 10,000 while the remaining 25,000 families would be dispersed, mainly to Dandakaranya. In July 1958, the ministry declared that all camps would be closed by July 1959 and relief would be discontinued.[121] This declaration was greeted by massive protests by camp refugees who were opposed to summary dispersal. This movement, led by various left-wing parties and involving several *Namasudra* leaders, such as Jogendranath Mondal, Apurbalal Mazumdar and Hemanta Biswas, was riddled with internal contradictions and factions.[122] Ultimately, it failed to either significantly alter government policy, or inspire support from the general population of West Bengal, which by now included the refugees living in various squatters' colonies. This failure signalled the end of an era of autonomous refugee movements in West Bengal, which were relatively free from calculations of electoral profit. The Left champions of refugee rights had to be satisfied with the meagre assurance that no refugees would be forced to depart for Dandakaranya. This was cold comfort for the thousands of refugee families stuck in 74 camps in West Bengal. They had weathered years of neglect born of a moribund policy that did little more than re-name camps, from rural or urban to 'work-site' and finally, 'transit' camps as proof of a new 'approach' to rehabilitation.[123] The Sonarpur transit camp, in the outskirts of Calcutta, was the first to be shut down, in March 1959, initiating a process of gradual closure of camps over the next few years. This process ended with the closure of the transit camp at Bongaon, a much traversed border-crossing between India and East Pakistan, in March 1962.[124] Throughout this period, the residents of camps were issued with notices that asked them to either follow the instructions of the government and enlist for dispersal to Dandakaranya, or leave the camp after receiving six month's dole.[125] By June 1962, in the eyes of the state, there were no more camps in West Bengal. However, only 5,268 families had actually moved to Dandakaranya.[126] The West Bengal government launched a number of schemes, such as the Herobhanga scheme at Sunderbans, to rehabilitate its quota of 10,000 refugee families. Between July 1958 and March 1960

[121] *Jugantar*, 24 April 1960.   [122] Chakrabarti, *Marginal Men*, pp. 162–207.

[123] Committee of Review of Rehabilitation Work in West Bengal, *Report on Rehabilitation of Displaced Persons from East Pakistan at Ex-Camp-Sites in West Bengal* (New Delhi: Ministry of Supply and Rehabilitation, Department of Rehabilitation, 1969).

[124] Ibid.

[125] For details of these notices and the resistance of refugees see Chakrabarti, *The Marginal Men* (1999), pp. 177–207.

[126] *Dandakaranya Project Report* (1965).

it boasted the successful rehabilitation of 10,086 families, thus exceeding its quota.[127] In other words, for most refugees who had sought official aid in West Bengal by entering refugee camps, rehabilitation took the form of summary expulsion through 'screening' or a disappearance from official records once they had received six month's maintenance allowance. This did not deter the central Ministry of Rehabilitation from taking pride in its success. The ministry was now converted to a department within the Ministry of Works Housing and Supply. This was considered to be sufficient for dealing with 'residual' problems.

The state's so-called 'success' in the sphere of rehabilitation was authored at the expense of tremendous suffering of thousands of refugees. Most clung on to the hollow shells of the erstwhile camps of West Bengal, eking out a living as best as they could.[128] The minority who reached Dandakaranya were forced to carve out a precarious existence in the dry jungles of the region. Between 1959 and 1961, over 5,000 refugee families were relocated from camps in West Bengal to a variety of worker's camps established within the Dandakaranya Development Area. These work centres were constructed by the Dandakaranya Development Authority, mostly along the few existing roads in the area, in the hope that the refugees would find work in repairing roads. Nearly one-third of the 62 work centres constructed to receive refugees were dismantled due to the low number of arrivals.[129] The actual resettlement of refugees in new villages and the disbursement of agricultural land took years to accomplish and suffered from significant setbacks due to inadequate irrigation in an area prone to draughts.[130] The Dandakaranya project was marred by bad planning and power-struggles within a top-heavy administration from its very inception. The project, however flawed, served the interests of the Congress government of West Bengal in more ways than one. It not only allowed the authorities to get rid of its unwanted refugee population by 1962, but also provided a ready site for the dispersal of all undesirable refugees in the future. The Dandakaranya project was the final element in a three-pronged resolution of West Bengal's refugee crisis that consisted of tighter border controls, denial of official relief and rehabilitation within West Bengal and a ready site of dispersal of all new migrants outside the state. It proved to be a resilient set of technologies of governance for the management of East Bengali refugees that served the authorities in West

---

[127] *Jugantar*, 20 April 1960.
[128] For a detailed report on the condition of refugees in ex-campsites see Committee of review of rehabilitation work in West Bengal, *Report on Rehabilitation of Displaced Persons from East Pakistan at ex-camp sites in West Bengal* (1969)
[129] *Dandakaranya Project Report* (1965).
[130] *Reception, Dispersal and Rehabilitation of New Migrants* (1965).

Bengal right up to 1971, when the emergence of Bangladesh provided a definitive break in India's post-partition policy regime.

The Failure of Residuary Rehabilitation: 1958–1971

Until 1958, the entire energy of the authorities in West Bengal had been focused upon somehow disrupting the unending trail of refugees from East Bengal, and ideally, also pushing out of their 'saturated' state as many of them as possible. Between 1958 and 1962, it achieved a degree of success in both spheres. After 1958, in order to obtain a migration certificate and enter West Bengal legally, East Bengalis had to formally give up any claim to relief and rehabilitation. As a result, new refugees quite simply disappeared from official records. During this period, the word 'migrants' gained ground in official records. They comprised a new category of displaced minorities from East Bengal who could still migrate across the porous borders, with or without migration certificates. However, in the eyes of the state, they had lost any claim upon its resources for relief or rehabilitation. Those who confessed to still needing government aid for rehabilitation were dispatched to Dandakaranya after a brief sojourn at reception centres in West Bengal. This official solution to West Bengal's refugee problem proved to be remarkably resilient. With minor modifications, it withstood the Hazratbal crisis of 1964, when widespread riots in East Bengal generated a mass exodus of fear-crazed Hindus that was reminiscent of the crisis in 1950. 'Residual' rehabilitation emerged as the defining feature of the regime of rehabilitation in West Bengal during the 1960s. This was nothing short of an official acknowledgement of the inadequacy of the relief and rehabilitation offered to refugees who had entered West Bengal before 1958 and had stayed on. In theory, it sought to right this historic wrong by completing the unfinished project of their economic and social rehabilitation. In practice, it achieved spectacularly little. This was partly because the Congress government lacked the political will to undo the patterns of neglect and apathy towards refugees that had, by now, become entrenched within the bureaucratic apparatus of the state. But more importantly, its past success in repeatedly denying rehabilitation to all but the narrowest possible definition of refugees now came back to haunt all negotiations with the central government for additional funds towards 'residual rehabilitation'. The latter evoked the same strategy of imposing arbitrary conditions and restrictive definitions to whittle away the numbers eligible for rehabilitation, and therefore, the funds due to the government of West Bengal.

The first clear sign that the post-1958 period was qualitatively different from the preceding decade was a newfound concern, on the part of the

Congress government, regarding the well-being and rehabilitation of the 'non-camp' refugee population. This constituted the vast majority of refugees in West Bengal. So far, the authorities had done little for these refugees, beyond offering them a series of loans and lecturing them on the virtues of self-sufficiency. Nevertheless, a decision taken in 1957 to refuse any kind of assistance to future migrants from East Bengal was paralleled by the claim that more than 50 per cent of West Bengal's refugee population was partially rehabilitated and required further aid.[131] The government of West Bengal published a brochure in 1958, which claimed that out of 420,000 families who had previously received some form of rehabilitation, 210,000 needed further assistance. The central government responded to these claims by asking the government of West Bengal to prepare an estimate of the total cost of residuary rehabilitation of displaced persons living within the state. Initially, the government of West Bengal calculated residuary rehabilitation in the narrowest possible terms, by simply adding up the amount required to clear all pending and estimated future application for loans made by refugees. The figure cited was 71 million rupees, of which 36.68 million was to be disbursed as loans to 36,328 refugee families who had already applied for loans by 1959. The remaining 34.32 million would be required to process future loan applications, possibly for house-building, from squatters who had been relocated. The government of India was unwilling to sanction the full amount, arguing that given the lapse of time, it was unlikely that all applicants still needed the loans. It sanctioned a much-reduced sum of 22.8 million rupees towards pending loans and asked the government of West Bengal to review the entire question of residuary rehabilitation in West Bengal.[132] However, by the end of 1959, the lay of the land had changed significantly. It was clear that the authorities in Delhi intended to wrap up the central Ministry of Rehabilitation. It is possible that the impending disappearance of the central ministry finally jolted the government of West Bengal out of its passivity. Faced with the prospect of losing a ministry to which they could periodically return with appeals for more funds, the government of West Bengal suddenly changed its tune. Instead of its usual pattern of paltry loans, minimum relief and hasty dispersal, it now attempted to undertake a comprehensive view of rehabilitation that included not just loans, but also new schemes of creating employment

---

[131] The summary of these developments is drawn from two reports prepared by the Committee of Review of Rehabilitation Work in West Bengal. These are the *Report of Rehabilitation Loans to the Displaced Persons* (1974) and *Report on Rehabilitation of East Pakistan Displaced Persons Through Poultry Schemes in West Bengal* (New Delhi: Ministry of Supply and Rehabilitation).

[132] *Report on Rehabilitation Through Poultry Schemes*, p. 7.

and development of refugee colonies. The new Minister of Relief and
Rehabilitation, Prafulla Chandra Sen, put forward a claim of 426 million
rupees for the final 'liquidation' of the refugee problem in West Bengal.
On 4 March 1961, he presented details of the West Bengal government's
plans of rehabilitation in the Legislative Assembly, addressing people who
had so far been portrayed as an unwanted burden as his refugee 'brothers
and sisters'.[133]

This unprecedented attentiveness towards the needs of non-camp
refugees represented a radical shift in Congress policy towards refugees
in West Bengal. It seems that the blanket denial of relief and rehabilitation
to all future migrants from East Bengal had finally freed the authorities
from the fear that provision of adequate relief and rehabilitation for those
already in the state would trigger a deluge of all of East Bengal's remaining
population of Hindu minorities – the dreaded 8 million 'extra mouths' to
feed. This opened up some space, within the regime of rehabilitation, for
the admission that the real problem of rehabilitation lay outside the
refugee camps. In West Bengal's overcrowded towns and in a range of
refugee colonies of various categories – urban and rural, legal and illegal,
self-settled, private and government sponsored – thousands of refugees
struggled to make ends meet. However, given the past record of mismanagement and apathy, not many were convinced of this sudden change of
heart. Opposition members elected from constituencies where there was
a high concentration of refugees, such as PSP's Haridas Mitra, elected
from the Tollygunje constituency, marshalled evidence of their continuing neglect.[134] The communist opposition, which included staunch supporters of refugee rights, such as Samar Mukhopadhyay, the secretary of
UCRC, joined them in suggesting that the Congress ministry's new
concern for refugee welfare was nothing more than a ploy to woo refugee
votes on the eve of the election of 1962.[135] Hare Krishna Konar, who had
been actively involved in the recent unsuccessful agitation against the
closure of camps and the dispersal of refugees to Dandakaranya, summed
up the mood in the assembly with his wry remark that if an election could
be conducted annually in West Bengal, then maybe some solutions could
emerge for the refugees.[136] Thus, by 1961, the refugee vote had become
an important factor in the electoral politics of West Bengal and both the
Congress and the communists were prone to accusing each other of

---

[133] Prafulla Chandra Sen, Minister of Relief and Rehabilitation, *Demand for Grant No: 42,
Major Head: 57-Miscellaneous-Expenditure on Displaced Persons, etc.*, WBLA, 4 March
1961, pp. 3–5.
[134] Haridas Mitra, *Demand for Grants*, WBLA, 4 March 1961, pp. 17–20.
[135] Samar Mukhopadhyay, *Demand for Grants*, WBLA, 4 March 1961, pp. 13–17.
[136] Hare Krishna Konar, *Demand for Grants*, WBLA, 4 March 1961, p. 39.

privileging politics over the genuine welfare of refugees when it came to policies of rehabilitation.

Whatever the motives behind the Congress government's attempt to formulate new and comprehensive schemes for the rehabilitation of all pre-1958 refugees, very little actually came of it. The only part of residuary rehabilitation that was swiftly completed was the disbursement of pending loans, though here too the amount distributed fell far short of the amount requested. It covered 24,531 of the estimated 36,328 applicants. The denial of assistance to over 11,000 applicants was born of a combination of red tape and bureaucratic nit-picking on the part of the central authorities, and administrative apathy within West Bengal's Ministry of Relief and Rehabilitation. A brief description of how the two levels of government dealt with one category of loan – the contributory house-building loan – is useful as it illustrates the patterns of intergovernmental conflict, mismanagement and apathy that set the tone for the entire project of residuary rehabilitation. The government of India initially declared 3,338 of the 5,923 applicants ineligible for the house-building loan. It argued that these refugees had violated the criteria of the loan by beginning to construct houses in anticipation of money. Persuaded out of this resolve by the government of West Bengal, the central authorities now decided to sanction money towards the loan applications of the truant builders alone, in the process arbitrarily excluding the other 2,585 applicants. Equally arbitrary was the decision to sanction only half of the estimated cost in 1959. The balance was to be sanctioned upon evidence of smooth disbursement of the allotted amount. However, the state government failed to follow up with any further demand for funds, or proof of distribution. It took another 15 years and another review of rehabilitation work in West Bengal for this lapse to be acknowledged.[137] This pattern was repeated, on a much larger scale, in every single sphere of residuary rehabilitation in West Bengal.

Arbitrary refusal to sanction or disburse adequate amounts, in the name of 'economy', permeated every sphere of residuary rehabilitation. The government of India finally sanctioned 213 million rupees, which was roughly half of the total amount required for residuary rehabilitation. The state government was expected to submit detailed schemes for utilising these funds. A flurry of paperwork followed and nine separate kinds of schemes were prepared for the rehabilitation of partially rehabilitated families, at a combined cost of 117.2 million rupees (see Table 1.2). There was a clear focus on substantive rehabilitation through the generation of additional income and employment. Towards this end,

---

[137] *Report of Rehabilitation Loans to the Displaced Persons* (1974).

Table 1.2: *Accepted Schemes of Residuary Rehabilitation, 1962*

No	Schemes	No of Families Covered	Amount Accepted (in lakhs or 00000s)
1	Irrigation facilities and supply of better seeds and manure	29000	100
2	Additional agricultural land	2500	34
3	Supply of tools and implements	4721	17.37
4	Supply of milk cows	5500	40
5	Supply of poultry birds and ducks	3600	
6	Small scale and cottage industries	1000	
7	Supply of bullock carts	1300	2.60
8	25 industrial estates in rural areas	12500	178.12
9	Medium industries to be financed by RIC (Rehabilitation Industries Corporation)	67000	800.00

The figures are replicated without amendment from the original.
Source: Ibid.

the schemes included the establishment of small-scale and cottage industries, training refugees to raise poultry and an ambitious plan of establishing no less than 25 industrial estates in rural areas. However, the vast majority of these remained paper schemes.

A review of official attempts to promote industries for refugees, conducted in 1971, revealed that not a single one of the 25 proposed industrial estates was actually established in rural West Bengal. Most of the funds allotted were distributed to industrialists in exchange of a promise to employ a certain number of displaced persons. These promises were not kept.[138] The situation was no better when it came to the regularisation and development of refugee colonies, for which the state government had requested funds to the tune of 81.66 million rupees. Of this, 56.2 were to be spent on the development of 528 government-sponsored colonies and the remaining would go towards the regularisation of various squatters' colonies. The government of India decided to allot only 47.9 million on the grounds that past experience suggested that sixty percent of the estimated cost would be enough to meet the actual costs. While the government of West Bengal vehemently protested this reduced assessment, it failed to make much headway with the funds it received. By 1974,

[138] Committee of Review of Rehabilitation Work in West Bengal, *Report on Establishment of Industrial Estates in West Bengal for the Rehabilitation of Displaced Persons from East Pakistan in West Bengal* (New Delhi: Ministry of Supply and Rehabilitation, 1971).

development works had been completed in only 102 government-sponsored colonies and nine squatters' colonies.[139]

To cut a long story short, new policies for West Bengal's old migrants achieved very little in terms of their rehabilitation. This failure was far more significant than earlier shortcomings as the schemes proposed in the 1960s did not merely repeat old patterns. Besides focusing exclusively on the refugees outside camps and taking a holistic view of rehabilitation, these schemes were also marked by a new way of imagining the displaced population from East Bengal. Within these schemes, for the first time, the possibility of refugees aiding rather than inhibiting the economic development of West Bengal was articulated. They were not imagined as additional population claiming a share of scarce resources. Instead, they were seen as clusters of workers who could be used to set up new industrial estates, as artisans who could aid in the expansion of cottage industries and as petty entrepreneurs, such as poultry farmers, who could generate their own employment. Yet, in the ultimate analysis, neither the government of West Bengal nor the government of India could break out of entrenched practices. Constant and arbitrary reduction of necessary funds by the central government in the name of economy fuelled acrimony between different levels of governance and delayed implementation of schemes. Closer to home, the bureaucrats and administrators within West Bengal's Ministry of Relief and Rehabilitation continued with old patterns of apathy. Sanctioned funds were not fully utilised and perfectly good schemes, such as poultry farming, were scuttled by the obdurate refusal to provide manpower to run the scheme.[140] In other words, within West Bengal's regime of rehabilitation, partition-refugees were given little or no opportunity to become productive citizens. They remained an unwanted extra population. As late as March 1961, Prafulla Chandra Sen harboured hopes of a different, more desirable solution to West Bengal's refugee problem that did not involve the implementation of residuary schemes. While defending the potential of the Dandakaranya scheme in the legislative assembly of West Bengal he confessed to a conviction, largely unsupported by existing reports, that the scheme could absorb 'not just 20/25 thousand families, but one or two lakh families.'[141] He believed that 'now, if we can send those 18 thousand camp families, then the doors and windows will open. Those who have

---

[139] Committee of Review of Rehabilitation Work in West Bengal, *Report on Development of Colonies of Displaced Persons from Erstwhile East Pakistan in West Bengal* (New Delhi: Ministry of Supply and Rehabilitation, 1974).

[140] *Report on Rehabilitation Through Poultry Schemes* (1970).

[141] Prafulla Chandra Sen, Minister of Relief and Rehabilitation, *Demand for Grants*, WBLA, 4 March 1961, pp. 47–8.

received partial rehabilitation here, especially agriculturists, it will be possible to take them too to Dandakarnaya.'[142] With dreams of dispersal alive and well in the highest echelons of governance, it is small surprise that schemes of residual rehabilitation failed miserably.

New Migrants, Old Policies: 1962–1971

Paper schemes of residuary rehabilitation were not the only distinctive feature of the 1960s in West Bengal. During this period, the government also enjoyed unprecedented success in denying rehabilitation to new migrants. Officially, there were no longer any refugee camps in West Bengal, nor were migrants from East Bengal recognised as refugees after 1958. This allowed the ministers in charge of rehabilitation who engineered and oversaw this radical disenfranchisement, Prafulla Chandra Sen (1957–61) and his successor, Abha Maity (1962–7), to hide behind rules and regulations. Throughout the 1960s, they continued to press the central authorities to accept more refugees from West Bengal. When it came to expanding the ranks of potential settlers of Dandakaranya, they were more than willing to request a reconsideration of existing regulations. Thus, by the end of 1962, the government of India had agreed to accept refugees who had previously refused to go to Dandakaranya, provided they were agriculturists. The government of West Bengal also requested the central authorities to arrange for the rehabilitation for new '*udvastu*' or refugees who were displaced by the riots in Rajshahi district and started entering India in April 1962. An agreement was reached to send 1,008 Santal families to Dandakaranya.[143] However, when it came to the needs of newcomers who remained in West Bengal, Abha Maity was quick to clarify that 'these *udvastu* (refugees) who have come ... have not been recognised as *udvastu* (refugees) according to our rules.'[144] She further clarified that West Bengal had provisions to prevent starvation deaths through the process of 'ordinary relief', provided at the district level. These families of not-refugees were free to avail of such relief in case of dire need. By the time a new refugee crisis hit West Bengal in 1964, the government was well-versed in this bureaucratic game that could turn East Bengali refugees into non-refugees in West Bengal, but resurrect them as refugees entitled

---

[142] Ibid.

[143] Abha Maity, Minister of Relief and Rehabilitation, *Rehabilitation of Refugees in Dandakaranya*, WBLA, 8 March 1963, p. 167.

[144] Abha Maity, Minister of Relief and Rehabilitation, *Questions and Answers: Rehabilitation of Refugees in Murshidabad District*, 5 April 1963, p. 630.

to rehabilitation as soon as they left the confines of the saturated state. This sleight of hand was raised to the level of official policy in 1964.

By January 1964, it was clear that a cycle of riots in the two halves of Bengal, triggered by the Hazratbal incident, had placed West Bengal in the throes of a refugee crisis that resembled the crisis of 1950 in scale and intensity. Once more, there was a wave of sympathy for co-religionists and brethren on the other side. The Calcutta-based Bengali press, including the pro-Congress *Anandabazar Patrika*, reminded their readers of assurances that were once given by Congress stalwarts, such as Sardar Patel, to East Bengali refugees.[145] Letters to the editor poured in advocating exchange of populations as the only real solution.[146] There were also important differences from the crisis of 1950. Over a decade of partition migration had increased the numbers of divided families, and the newspapers were overwhelmed by queries about missing relatives on the other side. Also, unlike 1950, fleeing minorities had to negotiate a functioning international border, with all the trappings of checkpoints and guards on both sides who demanded the stipulated documents. With newspapers carrying graphic reports of harassment of fleeing Hindus by East Pakistan's border security, a popular clamour built up for opening up the borders[147] and freeing Hindus 'trapped behind Pakistan's iron curtain'.[148] The government of West Bengal was unwilling to dismantle the policies and regulations that had delivered a measure of success in stemming the tide of refugees from East Pakistan. Instead, Prafulla Chandra Sen, who had succeeded Dr B. C. Roy as the Chief Minister, sought early and complete involvement of the government of India. An emergency meeting of ministers was convened in Calcutta that was attended not just by Mehr Chand Khanna, who was now the Minister of Works, Housing and Rehabilitation, but also by the central ministers of Finance and Home Affairs. Prafulla Sen, Abha Maity, numerous other ministers of West Bengal and Atulya Ghosh, who was a member of the Congress Working Committee and widely acknowledged as West Bengal's 'kingmaker' behind the scenes, presented a united front in their insistence that the impending influx, estimated to be at least a million, had to be the central government's responsibility.[149] At this stage, West Bengal was joined by Assam and Tripura, with all three states claiming to have reached a point of saturation with refugees. By February 1964, the government of India had caved in to these

---

[145] See for example *Anandabazar Patrika*, 28 January 1964.
[146] Several such letters appeared in Anandabazar Patrika and Amrita Bazar Patrika in January and February 1964.
[147] *Anandabazar Patrika*, 31 January 1964.   [148] *Anandabazar Patrika*, 26 January, 1964.
[149] *Anandabazar Patrika*, 28 January, 1964.

demands. The conditions for obtaining migration certificates were relaxed, leading to 35,000 people obtaining migration certificates in a single day. The decision was taken to expand the Dandakaranya project so that the 'new refugees' could be resettled there.[150] Abha Maity hastened to set up 'reception centres' at Banpur and Petrapole border-crossings where refugees were given 'gratuitous relief' that included clothing, blankets, milk powder, etc. Those who required state assistance were dispatched, preferably within two days of their arrival, to Dandakaranya by train.[151] Only those who gave up all claims to official aid were free to remain in West Bengal. In the early days of the crisis, the vast majority – 14,502 out of 18,172 – chose to give up all claims to relief and stay.[152] As the number of refugees seeking official aid grew, two more reception centres were started at Hasnabad and Banpur and in April 1964, the central Ministry of Rehabilitation was resurrected to deal with this crisis. By September 1964, these temporary shelters housed 169,226 refugees, awaiting dispersal.[153]

The deluge of refugees in Dandakaranya created a crisis of resources at Mana, where camps were hastily erected to receive them. However, the government of West Bengal could congratulate itself in successfully washing its hands of this crisis. There was no public outcry against this policy of compulsory and hasty dispersal of new migrants. Nor was there any significant opposition to this policy within the legislative assembly. Prafulla Sen's government weathered a crisis of over 600,000 refugees without reopening a single refugee camp or offering rehabilitation to a single refugee family. West Bengal was no longer a space of home-coming for East Bengali Hindus. It had been reframed, within administrative discourse, as a space of transit and at best, of temporary refuge. In the ultimate analysis, this remarkable success of the West Bengal government proved to be counterproductive. Most of the 'new migrants' chose to stay on in West Bengal, thus continuing older patterns of resettlement. Not all who gave up claims to official relief had adequate means to rebuild their lives. For many, the relatives and friends they sought to join lived in insecure and illegal settlements. When new migrants made their 'own arrangements', they actually swelled the ranks of squatters in refugee colonies, ex-campsites and occupied houses in Calcutta. Their ineligibility for rehabilitation benefits would eventually become an

[150] *Anandabazar Patrika*, 8 February 1964.
[151] Abha Maity, Minister of Relief and Rehabilitation, *Starred Questions: Refugees from East Pakistan*, WBLA, 20 February 1964, pp. 391–3.
[152] Ibid.
[153] Abha Maity, Minister of Relief and Rehabilitation, *Questions and Answers: New Arrival of Refugees*, WBLA, 9 September 1964, p. 817.

intractable problem that delayed the regularisation of colonies and squats.[154]

During the 1960s in West Bengal, citizen-refugees from East Bengal were fractured into multiple categories based on their relationship to the regime of rehabilitation. The first category was the 'old migrants' or refugees from East Pakistan who came in before 1958. Their putative claim to belong to India was affirmed by the government of West Bengal through provision of a measure of relief and rehabilitation, however inadequately implemented. It is important to remember that this homogenous category of old migrants was a retrospective rationalisation of a more complex ground reality. The lived experience of the old migrants was marked by successive arbitrary redefinitions of the statutory refugee, i.e., a refugee entitled to government aid. This could lead the same refugee families to fall in and out of the sphere of state-sanctioned rehabilitation over time. Take for example displaced families who entered West Bengal after 15 January 1949, one of many state-imposed cut-off dates for counting refugees, and before February 1950, when riots and mass migration led to the reopening of camps. These families would have initially been excluded from the ranks of refugees. However, once schemes of 'residual rehabilitation' of 'old-migrants' were launched in 1959, these families became eligible for official aid. The second category is a curious one of non-refugees. They were the thousands who entered West Bengal between 1959 and 1963. They inhabited a precarious space as putative citizens who were deliberately ignored by the state. The government of West Bengal continued to affirm their right to belong by arguing that they could, like any other citizen, avail of the ordinary relief provided for the destitute at district level. Yet, the refusal to acknowledge them as refugees created obstacles in their path to legal and substantive citizenship that was dependent upon being officially acknowledged as displaced persons from East Pakistan. However, even this category of non-refugees was not a stable one. Once a non-refugee agreed to leave West Bengal, he could become a refugee and traverse the established route to full citizenship through resettlement schemes, albeit outside West Bengal. The third category of 'new migrants' referred to those who entered West Bengal after January 1964, and technically,

---

[154] By the 1970s, the Committee of Review of Rehabilitation Work in West Bengal was constrained to argue for the rehabilitation of ineligible refugees on grounds of 'compassion' and realism in various reports. For details see *Report on Development of Colonies of Displaced Persons* (1974); *Report on Rehabilitation of Displaced Persons From East Pakistan Living at Bagjola Group of Ex-camp Sites in West Bengal* (New Delhi: Ministry of Supply and Rehabilitation, 1970); and *Report on Rehabilitation of Displaced Persons From East Pakistan at Ex-camp Sites in West Bengal* (New Delhi: Ministry of Supply and Rehabilitation, 1969).

covered all those who entered West Bengal right up to 25 March 1971. This cut-off date was also imposed retrospectively, by the Indira-Mujib Agreement of 1972. The main goal of this bilateral agreement was to organise the repatriation of the estimated 7–10 million refugees who entered India in 1971, fleeing the Liberation War in East Pakistan. Acknowledging that all those who entered before that date had a right to belong was largely an unintended consequence of negotiations directed towards repatriation. Before 1972, only those who had entered India during the Hazratbal crisis of 1964 had been eligible for temporary relief within West Bengal and rehabilitation outside it. Those who chose to stay on in West Bengal, or those who came in the late 1960s, were studiously ignored by the government of West Bengal. Their claims upon the state for acknowledgement of quasi-legal lives and for the regularisation of illegal settlements picked up pace only after 1971 and continues to this date.

Conclusion

The watershed of 1971 signalled the end of the era of the citizen-refugee in India. Unlike their predecessors, Hindu and Buddhist minorities who migrated to India from Pakistan after March 1971 were no longer treated as putative citizens. They were marked as foreigners and temporary sojourners. Future migrants from Bangladesh came to be characterised as *anuprobeshkaris* or infiltrators in West Bengal. However, as this historical survey of government response to migration from East Pakistan illustrates, the transformation of the citizen-refugee, variously and interchangeably categorised as migrants, refugees and displaced persons since 1947, to the Bangladeshi 'infiltrator' was not a sudden affair. The non-refugee of the 1960s anticipated the illegal infiltrator of later years.

This chapter traces the evolution of the regime of relief and rehabilitation of partition refugees in West Bengal over a period of 24 years. This dynamic approach reveals the many contradictions and multiple re-writings that made West Bengal's regime of rehabilitation a formidable bureaucratic maze for refugees to negotiate. These shifting sets of practices and policies resist any notion of authorship by individual politicians or bureaucrats. Instead, what can be traced is the gradual crystallisation of a governmentality of rehabilitation. At first glance, state response towards refugees in West Bengal appears to repeat the same patterns between 1947 and 1962. Inadequate relief and long periods of administrative apathy are followed by sudden decisions to shut down camps. In 1949, 1951–2 and 1959–62, rehabilitation was a rushed affair, far more concerned with the hasty closure of camps than with the welfare of displaced families. Yet, underlying this apparent stagnation, was a steady accumulation of policies and practices informed by a rationality of governance that imagined East Bengali refugees as extra population in a saturated state. Governmental innovation consistently strove to safeguard the future prosperity of West Bengal by excluding these unwanted millions who threatened the state's development. The mechanism for excluding refugees evolved gradually, over a decade of trial and error, beginning in 1947. The first iteration of refugees as undesirable citizens was in 1948. This was followed by persistent attempts, between 1949 and 1952, to push the refugees out. The strategies used included denial of relief and rehabilitation, insistence on voluntary return, and haphazard attempts of dispersal outside West Bengal. Between 1952 and 1958, there was a gradual reform of regulations governing cross-border migration in the Eastern frontier, designed to stem the tide of refugees. The same period saw the parallel iteration of the need for a 'national' resolution for West Bengal's refugee problem, which was window-dressing for West Bengal government's determination to disperse refugees outside the state. Between 1958 and 1962, these disparate strategies coalesced together. With the government of India agreeing to take full responsibility for rehabilitating refugees outside West Bengal, the inauguration of the Dandakaranya scheme, new regulations restricting migration from East Pakistan and the rapid closure of camps, West Bengal's regime of rehabilitation fully reflected the theory of saturation of the state, which had been in vogue since 1948. The 1960s were largely a period of ruthless implementation of this top-down solution to West Bengal's refugee problem, characterised by a refusal to reopen camps, the compulsory dispersal of all those who entered government 'reception centres' to Dandakaranya, and a denial of relief and rehabilitation to the majority who remained in West Bengal.

In other words, by 1962, a way of thinking about refugees and their rehabilitation had gained ground in West Bengal that made future resettlement of refugees within the state an undesirable prospect that simply did not pass the test of good governance. This orientation of policy outlasted multiple changes of guard at the Writers Building in Calcutta, including several Congress ministries, unstable coalition governments interspersed by President's rule and last, but not least, a Left Front government led by the Communist Party of India (Marxist). It found its most brutal expression in the violent expulsion of refugees who attempted to 'return' to West Bengal from Dandakaranya after a pro-refugee left-wing government came to power in 1977. The face-off between the police and refugees who had deserted rehabilitation sites in central India to build an illegal settlement in the riverine island of Morichjhanpi took the form of a massacre, with an estimated 4,128 refugee families or 17,000 refugees killed and the survivors frogmarched back to their designated sites of resettlement.[155] This further reinforces the core argument of this chapter, that policy responses towards partition refugees are inadequately understood as politically motivated actions of specific individuals or political parties. They have deeper roots in ways of thinking about population, resources and territory that can, and in the case of West Bengal, did, transcend political differences.

The regime of rehabilitation in West Bengal was not merely the product of a contestation between the government of West Bengal and East Bengali refugees. The government of India played a crucial role in the evolution of this regime. West Bengal's success in adopting a policy that required refugees to leave West Bengal in order to access rehabilitation would have been impossible without the active support of the central government. In 1948, Nehru had argued that large-scale dispersal of refugees outside West Bengal, though desirable, was an unfeasible project. Yet, by 1954, the government of India had accepted resettlement outside West Bengal as the core principle of solving West Bengal's refugee problem. This reversal of policy was enabled by a radical re-imagining of East Bengali refugees as agents of national development in marginal areas. This reframing of East Bengali refugees as potentially productive citizens can be traced to the unlikely location of the Andaman Islands. Between 1949 and 1952, these Islands witnessed repeated opportunistic deployment of Bengali refugees to serve multiple agendas of nation-building. This apparently marginal history of refugee resettlement in the Andamans is taken up in the next chapter.

In the ultimate analysis, the successful denial of rehabilitation to the majority of refugees who entered West Bengal was a hollow achievement. The mere denial of adequate official aid did nothing to discourage future migrants. All it did was to make official policies of resettlement and dispersal irrelevant to the vast majority of refugees, who did not or could not find refuge in government camps. The government of West Bengals' hard-won victory of dispersing refugees outside West Bengal actually applied to the minority in government camps. Here too, the state's power was restricted to shutting down camps. The actual dispersal of refugees, against their will, was rendered a political impossibility by the active support of refugee rights by a growing communist opposition within the legislative assembly. A minority of East Bengali migrants who

---

[155] For details see Annu Jalais, 'Dwelling on Morichjhanpi: When Tigers Became "Citizens", Refugees "Tiger-food"', *Economic and Political Weekly*, 40: 17 (2005), 1757–62; and Ross Mallick, 'Refugee Resettlement in Forest Reserves: West Bengal Policy Reversal and the Marichjhapi Massacre,' *The Journal of Asian Studies*, 58: 1 (1999), 104–25.

had the means to rebuild lives joined the general population of West Bengal and maintained a careful social distance from the refugees who were pushed to the margins of society by hostile policies. In squats, colonies and ex-campsites entire families lived on the margins of legality. They were Prafulla Chakrabarti's 'marginal men', who provided fertile grounds for the spread of anti-establishment sentiments and Left ideology. In these quasi-legal settlements, the distinctions between old and new migrants, refugees and non-refugees broke down, creating mixed settlements of people who did not fit the contours of civil society. Their sheer numbers eventually forced the government to engage with and regularise patently illegal strategies of survival – a process that provides the case study for Partha Chatterji's articulation of the concept of political society.[156] The regime of rehabilitation outlined above is not only crucial to understanding governmental rationality; it also provides the necessary context for exploring the range of strategies employed by East Bengali refugees to negotiate this hostile regime of rehabilitation 'from below'.

---

[156] In *The Politics of the Governed: Reflections on Popular Politics in Most of the World* (New York: Columbia University Press, 2004), Partha Chatterjee draws heavily upon Asok Sen's study of a mixed informal settlement of refugees and non-refugees in South Calcutta, *Life and Labour in a Squatters' Colony, Occassional Paper No. 18*, (Calcutta: Centre for Studies in Social Sciences, 1992), to flesh out the everyday patterns of interaction between state and political society.

Refugees from East Bengal at Calcutta Port, being sent to Andaman.

Figure 2.1: Bengali Refugees at Calcutta Port, boarding a ship to Andaman Islands, 1949
Source: ABP Archive

2 Harnessed to National Development
Settlers, Producers and Agents of Hinduisation

Introduction

On 14 March 1949, a group of 495 East Bengali refugees arrived at the Kidderpore dock of Calcutta from a transit camp at Andul, a small town in the Howrah district of West Bengal. Consisting of 132 families, they were the first batch of refugees sent to the Andaman Islands for resettlement.[1] Their departure was part of a scheme, envisioned and funded by the Ministry of Home Affairs, that proposed resettling 200 refugee families in the Andaman Islands.[2] Though they were a tiny fraction of the estimated 70,000 who awaited rehabilitation in various camps of West Bengal, Dr Bidhan Chandra Roy, the Chief Minister of West Bengal, hailed their departure as a milestone.[3] He chose to be personally present on the eve of their departure, and hailed them as *'agradut'* or the first heralds of a new age, and as *'banibahak'* or ambassadors of Bengal.[4] In uncharacteristic hyperbole, he predicted that these refugees would become the architects of a new Bengal in the Andaman Islands.[5] To Dr Roy, these sparsely populated islands represented a space which had unparalleled potential of absorbing West Bengal's 'extra' population of refugees.[6] His hopes were only partially borne out. By

---

[1] *'Purbobonger asrayprarthider pratham daler Andaman yatra'*, (The First Batch of Refugees from East Pakistan set out for the Andamans), *Anandabazar Patrika*, 15 March 1949.

[2] Though 202 families were initially selected for resettlement, interviews and later surveys show that only 197 families actually made the journey. The details of this scheme can be found in *Financial Sanction for Scheme of Resettling 200 Refugees*, File No. 8/1/50-AN, Andaman Files, Ministry of Home Affairs, Government of India (henceforth Andaman Files), 1948, National Archives of India (henceforth NAI).

[3] Hiranmoy Bandypadhyay, *Udvastu, (Refugee)*, (Calcutta: Sahitya Samsad, 1970), p. 46.

[4] For a detailed analysis of the representations of refugees headed towards Andaman Islands in the Bengali press, see Uditi Sen, 'Memories of Partition's 'Forgotten Episode', *Südasien-Chronik/South Asia Chronicle, Fokus/Focus: Revisiting Partition Seventy Years Later: Of Layered Echoes, Voices and Memories*, 7 (2017), 147–78.

[5] *Anandabazar Patrika*, 15 March 1949.

[6] For details of Dr B. C. Roy's schemes to disperse refugees see chapter 1.

1971, the government of West Bengal, in collaboration with the central government, had managed to dispatch no more than 3,540 refugee families to the Andaman Islands.[7] Despite its limited scale, this experiment of resettling Bengali refugees in the Andamans is key to understanding the governmental rationality that informed an emerging regime of rehabilitation of partition refugees. It constituted the first clear departure from the central government's policy of studied neglect towards refugees in West Bengal. In the late 1940s and early 1950s, even as official policy stressed temporary relief followed by voluntary repatriation as the desired solution to West Bengal's refugee problem, the government of India willingly invested large sums on resettling a select few of the very same refugees in the Andamans. These remote islands, directly ruled by the government in Delhi and largely free of the ethnic and linguistic politics that disrupted projects of refugee of rehabilitation elsewhere in India, provided a laboratory of sorts for a critical transformation of Bengali refugees within official discourse. From an unwanted drain on limited resources and extra mouths to feed, they became colonisers, skilled agriculturists and desirable settlers. In this chapter, I trace the historical conjunctures, administrative opportunism, and governmental rationality that enabled this shift.

It is difficult to imagine a more remote or unlikely location for resettling refugees than the Andaman Islands. The Andaman Islands are the northern cluster of two groups of islands that constitute the Andaman and Nicobar archipelago. They are located in the Bay of Bengal at a distance of 560 miles from the mouth of the river Hooghly in West Bengal. The 300-odd islands of the Andaman group can be divided into two zones: the Great Andamans, which consists of the four largest islands, namely the North, Middle and South Andaman and Baratang Islands; and numerous outlying smaller islands. Port Blair, in South Andaman Island, is its principal port and administrative headquarters. It was the site of the infamous cellular jail and the nucleus of a penal settlement, established by the British in 1858.[8] A long history of transportation of rebels and freedom fighters to these islands earned them notoriety within popular and nationalist histories as the Bastille of the East and the dreaded

---

[7] Figures compiled from various files of the Andamans Section of the Ministry of Home Affairs, Government of India, NAI, New Delhi.

[8] The jail was built between 1896 and 1910 in order to shore up the punitive element of transportation to the Andamans, which, the authorities felt, was suffering due to the successful rehabilitation of convicts as 'self-supporters'. For details see Satadru Sen, *Disciplining Punishment: Colonialism and Convict Society in the Andaman Islands* (New Delhi: Oxford University Press, 2000), pp. 8–10; and L. P. Mathur, *Kalapani: History of Andaman and Nicobar Islands with a Study of India's Freedom Struggle* (Delhi: Eastern Book Corporation, 1985), pp. 20–54.

'*kalapani*' or 'black waters'. In 1947, it was incorporated into the Union of India as its only type D province. It was ruled directly by the central Ministry of Home Affairs through a Chief Commissioner, who was the highest executive authority in the Andaman and Nicobar Islands. In 1956, the Islands were re-organised as a Union Territory, but the pattern of direct, non-representative rule continued. Though the penal settlement had been abolished by 1947, Andaman's association with exile persisted. This negative image was reinforced by its remote location and forested interiors inhabited by 'hostile' tribes.

A long history of colonial occupation, marked by missions to 'pacify' and 'civilise' the indigenous tribes on one hand, and the expansion of settlements using convicts or criminalised communities on the other, had produced a schizophrenic population profile in the Andaman Islands.[9] The settled population of the Islands was confined to the area around Port Blair and the isolated settlement of Mayabunder in Middle Andaman Island. The ex-convicts and their descendants, known as the 'Local Born,' and a circulating population of administrators, forest-workers and traders lived in and around Port Blair, in the South Andaman Island. Two distinct criminalised groups – Mappila (or Moplah) rebels[10] and Bhantus, a 'criminal tribe'[11] – were settled in South Andaman Island during the 1920s. Though following the general theme of rehabilitation of criminals through exile and labour, these later settlements were also designed to provide much-needed manpower for expansion of forestry and agriculture. The Karens, settled in the Webi region of Middle Andaman Island in 1925, were the only group of settlers who had

[9] For histories of the penal colony in the Andaman Islands, see Sen, *Disciplining Punishment* (2000), and colonial rule in the Andaman Islands see Clare Anderson, *The Indian Uprising Of 1857–8: Prisons, Prisoners and Rebellion* (London; Anthem Press, 2007). For a broader history of imperial rule in the Andamans, see Aparna Vaidik, *Imperial Andamans: Colonial Encounter and Island History* (Basingstoke and New York: Palgrave Macmillan, 2010).

[10] About 1,400 Mappilas were brought to the Andamans as prisoners following the Mappila Rebellion of 1921 in Malabar. In 1926, some more prisoners along with some free settlers came to the Andamans voluntarily. Though the Mappila population was essentially a part of the convict settlement of the Islands, they did not intermingle socially with other convicts and retained their specific cultural traits. For details see Probhat Kumar Sen, *Land and People of the Andaman: A Geographical and Socio-economical Study With a Short Account of the Nicobar Islands* (Calcutta: The Post-Graduate Book Mart, 1962), pp. 73–96 and Taylor C. Sherman, 'From Hell to Paradise? Voluntary Transfer of Convicts to the Andaman Islands, 1921–1940,' *Modern Asian Studies* 43, no. 2 (2009): 367–88.

[11] The Bhantus, or Bhatus were a Central Indian community, notified as a so-called 'criminal tribe' by the Criminal Tribes Act of 1871, who were transported to the Andaman Islands for rehabilitation. At the time of independence, about 224 Bhantus lived in complete isolation from the Andamanese Indians and sustained themselves through agriculture, foraging and sea-fishing. For details see ibid.

travelled to the Andamans as free migrants.[12] Other than these pockets of settlements, the rest of the Andaman Islands were covered in dense tropical forests. The forests were home to the indigenous communities of the Andamans, namely, the Great Andamanese, the Jarawa, the Onge and the Sentinelese. Each of these tribes had been shaped by histories of 'pacification' and by colonial ethnography, albeit in different ways. The 'friendly' Great Andamanese, who lived around the settlement of Port Blair, were forged by colonial violence – a conglomeration of the survivors of the ten tribes that had once inhabited the Great Andaman archipelago. The Onges of Little Andaman Island and the Jarawas, who inhabited the western regions of South and Middle Andaman Islands, had both been treated as a threat and subjected to years of expeditions designed to 'tame' them. While the Onges had been 'tamed' by 1885 and appeared in official records as a 'friendly' tribe in 1947, the Jarawas remained 'hostile' and unapproachable.[13] The Sentinelese, who live on the North Sentinel Island, had largely been spared the incursion of outsiders due to their distant location.[14] To sum up, Dr B. C. Roy's evocation of the Andaman Islands as a new Bengal was an audacious re-imagination of a space that must have appeared to be a remote and hostile destination to refugees looking to rebuild lives. It had neither the infrastructure nor the manpower essential for a large-scale project of refugee resettlement. Yet, successive batches of Bengali refugees were resettled in the Andaman Islands, at significant cost, between 1949 and 1971.

---

[12] Very little is known about the history of Karen migration to the Andaman Islands. They were Christians who came over from the Burmese mainland and were guided by a certain Rev. Thru Luggie in their choice of a site of settlement in the Middle Andamans. See Sen, *Land and People of the Andaman* (1962), p. 80.

[13] Several scholars have explored the complicity between colonial knowledge production and the domination of the aboriginal tribes of the Andaman Islands. For the Jarawas, see Vishvajit Pandya, 'Jarwas of Andaman Islands: Their Social and Historical Reconstruction', *Economic and Political Weekly*, 37, No: 37, (2002), 3830–4. For the Onges, see Sita Venkateswar, *Development and Ethnocide: Colonial Practices in the Andaman Islands* (Copenhagen: International Work Group for Indigenous Affairs, 2004) and for the Great Andamanese and Jarawas see Satadru Sen, *Savagery and Colonialism in the Indian Ocean* (London and New York: Routledge, 2010) and Vishvajit Pandya, 'In Terra Nullius: The Legacies of Science and Colonialism in the Andaman Islands', paper presented at *Science Society and Nature, Nehru Memorial Museum and Library Public Lecture Series*, 22 May 2013.

[14] It is important to note that all of the above names are given by outsiders. Jarawa means 'stranger' in Aka–bea-da, and the British adopted the name from the Great Andamanese who fought against the Jarawas. The Jarawas call themselves Aang, while the Onge call themselves 'En-iregale', which means perfect person. It is not known what the Sentinelese call themselves. An appreciation of these distinctions has moved into mainstream discussions on tribal welfare and survival in recent years. See http://www.survivalinternational.org/tribes/jarawa.

There were three clear phases in the evolution of policies designed to resettle refugees on the Andaman Islands. The period between 1949 and 1952 saw several small, ad hoc schemes for settling refugees that largely focused on replenishing the population of existing villages in South Andaman Island.[15] In 1952, these gave way to an integrated 'Colonisation and Development Plan' that combined refugee rehabilitation with development of the Islands.[16] Colonisation, in this context, meant agricultural expansion carried out under the aegis of the state through the establishment of new villages.[17] This policy was continued till 1961 and constituted the core of the first and second five-year plans for the Andaman Islands. After 1961, refugee resettlement in the Andaman Islands petered out. Despite a renewed refugee crisis in the eastern region leading to the reconstitution of the Ministry of Rehabilitation in April 1964, the policy of colonising the Andamans using East Bengali refugees was discontinued from 1965. A team of experts, commissioned by the new ministry, declared that resettling East Bengali refugees could no longer further the development of the Andamans.[18] Two more refugee settlements were established in North Andaman and Little Andaman, in 1967 and 1969–71 respectively. But these were one-off schemes that failed to influence general policy. A thick description of refugee resettlement in the Andaman Islands and the quotidian negotiation of settlement schemes from below is taken up in the next chapter. Here, I focus on tracing the genesis and evolution of policy. However, even at this level, the success or failure of any policy of settlement depended on the response it evoked from targeted populations of potential settlers.

The transition from ad hoc schemes that brought in batches of Bengali refugees to replenish labour in the Andaman Islands to a sustained policy of using refugees as colonisers occurred in 1951/2. During this period, West Bengal was reeling from the impact of anti-Hindu riots that had affected large parts of eastern Bengal in 1950. This had unleashed a pattern of mass migration that was to continue, with ebbs and flows, for several years, and came to be lamented as the 'unending trail' of refugees. The heydays of refugee resettlement in the Andamans (1952–61) coincided with a period of escalating tension between the government of West

---

[15] Progress reports on the rehabilitation of displaced persons in Andamans, File No: 8/3/53-AN, Andaman Files, 1953, NAI.

[16] Ibid.

[17] See B. H. Farmer, *Agricultural Colonization in India Since Independence* (London: Oxford University Press, 1974).

[18] Inter-departmental Team on Accelerated Development Programme for Andaman and Nicobar Islands, *Report by the Inter-departmental Team on Accelerated Development Programme for Andaman and Nicobar Islands* (Delhi: Ministry of Rehabilitation, Government of India, 1966).

Bengal and the central government in Delhi over whether the rehabilitation of Bengali refugees was to be primarily a regional or national responsibility. As discussed earlier, it was not until 1956 that Dr Roy's argument
that West Bengal's refugee crisis was a national issue and should be,
therefore, the primary responsibility of the government of India, gained
traction in official circles. By then, the resettlement of selected Bengali
refugees was well underway in the Andaman Islands. In other words,
refugee resettlement in the Andamans anticipated and informed a
national policy designed to solve the refugee crisis born of the partition
of Bengal. The manner in which these remote islands came to be a
generative space for a national pattern of governance of Bengal's refugee
crisis was largely accidental and involved the opportunistic use of Bengali
refugees as labourers, settlers, agriculturists, and even agents of surrepti-
tious Hinduisation. Its enduring significance was to recast the unwanted
citizen-refugee from East Bengal into a productive citizen, who could be
harnessed to myriad projects of post-colonial nation-building.

A Marriage of Convenience: Partition Refugees and The Quest for Willing Settlers

The Andaman Islands was probably the only territory in colonial India
where post-war reconstruction was more than mere propaganda.[19] The
islands were re-occupied by the British in October 1945, after three years
of Japanese occupation, which were marked by severe deprivation and
torture of the civilian population.[20] Post-war reconstruction in the
Andaman Islands centred entirely upon the settled populations and
ignored the indigenous tribes. It involved repairing basic infrastructure,
providing medical relief and provisions to a severely malnourished population, and rejuvenating economic activities, especially forestry and
agriculture.[21] All this required labour, traditionally a scarce resource in
the Andaman Islands, that was further depleted by the dislocation of war.
Reports of local shortage of labour in the Andamans reached the colonial
authorities in Delhi at a time when governmental discourse was still
saturated with the propaganda around post-war reconstruction. This
included various schemes of providing alternative employment to

---

[19] Sanjoy Bhattacharya and Benjamin Zachariah, '"A Great Destiny": The British Colonial
State and the Advertisement of Post-war Reconstruction in India, 1942–45', *South Asia
Research*, 19: 1 (1999), 71–100.

[20] For details see Jayant Dasgupta, *Japanese in Andaman & Nicobar Islands: Red Sun Over
Black Water* (Delhi: Manas Publications, 2002).

[21] 'Operation Crocker: A little bit of Peace' in *Noel Kennedy Patterson Papers*, Mss Eur F180/
1, Asia and Africa Records, British Library, London.

demobilised soldiers. The result was a scheme, formulated in November 1945, that proposed settling 100 ex-servicemen and their families in the Andaman Islands.[22] Though the basic feature of this scheme – expanding agriculture through voluntary settlement – survived the political uncertainties and demographic upheavals between 1946 and 1949, the first batch of voluntary settlers sent to the Andamans consisted not of soldiers, but of refugees from East Bengal. This section maps out the various factors, some purely accidental, and others deriving from the dominant concerns of contemporary governance, which brought Bengali refugees to the attention of the bureaucrats who administered the Andaman Islands.

The colonial administration of the Andaman Islands has historically been dependent on importing labour from the mainland of India and Burma. Between 1789 and 1796, when the East India Company first occupied the Andamans, they envisioned it as a safe harbour for British vessels at Port Cornwallis, with a colony of settlers around it. The labour was provided by settlers from mainland India and a handful of deported convicts. This initial attempt had to be abandoned due to high mortality and general bad health among the settlers. In the 1850s, a spate of reports regarding the murder of shipwrecked seamen by the aboriginal tribes of the Andamans reopened the question of British occupation of the Islands. Though this initiative to occupy the Andamans owed its origins to British imperial needs of securing naval supremacy and trade routes in the Bay of Bengal, the simultaneous suppression of the revolt of 1857, and the resultant need to imprison large numbers of captured rebels sealed Andaman Islands' fate as a penal settlement. In 1858, the Andaman Islands were formally reoccupied as a British colony.[23] While the earlier, abortive attempt had used some convicts as cheap labour, this time the establishment of a penal settlement was seen as an end in itself. Among Indians, its colloquial name, *kalapani* or 'black waters', soon evoked the terrors of transportation and exile. However, as land was cleared of forests and cultivation progressed, the labour needs of the growing settlement began to supersede penal considerations. The earlier impetus of developing the Andamans and building a colony of settlers started gaining an upper hand. The convicts became the captive labour force that could drive forward this development.

---

[22] *Development-Colonisation, Settlement: Proposal to Settle West Punjab Refugees in Andaman Island*, File No. 259/47-AN, Andaman Files, 1947, NAI.

[23] See Clare Anderson, *The Indian Uprising of 1857–8*, 2007 and *Legible Bodies: Race, Criminality and Colonialism in South Asia* (Oxford: Berg, 2004); and Satadru Sen, *Disciplining Punishment* (2000).

Thus, from its very inception, the British project of developing the Andaman Islands depended upon unfree labour. In the twentieth century, another form of labour that approximated local systems of indenture joined the convicts. The Catholic Labour Bureau in Ranchi recruited coolies on six-month contracts from the Oraon, Munda and Kharia tribes of the Chotanagpur region to provide an unskilled labour force for the Forest Department.[24] But willing settlers who could expand agriculture in the Islands were harder to come by. The administration once more turned to unfree populations, leading to mass resettlements of criminal groups, such as the Bhantus and Mappila, from the mainland of India. Though successful, these schemes proved to be politically untenable and had to be abandoned.[25] As a result, the convicts became the only dependable source of agricultural settlers. The minuscule free population, consisting of administrators, supervisors, clerical staff, traders, and their respective families, was vastly outnumbered by ex-convicts. By far the largest section of the settled population consisted of the 'first class' convicts, who had earned the status of 'self-supporters' through good behaviour.[26] They were often encouraged to marry or bring their wives over from the mainland, and settle in the islands as a family unit. Basically, the colonial government followed a policy of developing the Andaman Islands through an enlarged population of convicts, ex-convicts and their descendants, the 'Local Born'.

The Second World War radically disrupted this pattern of administration. Between March 1942 and October 1945, Japanese forces occupied the Andaman Islands. As a result, the infrastructure of the islands sustained heavy damage. While the retreating British forces blew up the telegraph office and the wireless station of Port Blair, the three-year Japanese occupation left the civic amenities of the Islands in utter disarray

---

[24] See Aparna Vaidik, 'Working the Islands: Labour Regime in Colonial Andamans (1858–1921)' in Marcel van der Linden and Prabhu Mohapatra (eds) *Towards Global History: New Comparisons* (New Delhi: Tulika, 2008), pp. 189–253 and Philipp Zehmisch, 'A Xerox of India? Policies and Politics of Migration in an Overseas Colony', *Working Papers in Social and Cultural Anthropology*, LMU Munich, 2:1, 2012.

[25] Taylor C. Sherman, 'From Hell to Paradise? Voluntary Transfer of Convicts to the Andaman Islands, 1921–1940', *Modern Asian Studies* 43: 2, (2009), 367–88.

[26] Since 1925 the convicts sent to the Penal Settlement of Andamans were administered through a three-class system based on the rules framed by Raffles, known as the Penang rules, followed in the Penal Settlement of Sumatra. The majority of the convicts were to be placed in the third class on their arrival in the island. They were subjected to hard physical labour and had no freedom at all. The best among the third-class convicts after a period of time, during which they had to maintain a good conduct, were promoted to a second class. The second-class convicts were employed as *sardars* or *tindals* over the other convicts. After a satisfactory conduct in the second class for a specific period they were to be promoted to the first class and given tickets of leave for becoming self-supporters. See L. P. Mathur, *Kalapani* (1985).

and considerably damaged the cellular jail. Moreover, it wrought havoc on the well-being of the local population. A reign of summary mass executions and systematic starving of civilians reduced the population of the islands from 34,000 to 18,000. A mercy ship sent in by the British authorities in September 1945 found beri-beri, malnutrition and scabies rampant in the islands. The hospitals were full of people suffering from malaria and dysentery, without any supply of drugs.[27] In these circumstances, it was no longer possible to maintain a penal settlement in the Andamans. Moreover, the cellular jail of Port Blair had outlived its utility as a site of incarceration of political prisoners of British India. One of the first decisions taken by the British, after their re-occupation of the islands on 8 October 1945, was to abolish the penal settlement.[28] Free pardon was granted to all the convicts and they were offered repatriation at government expense.[29] Between 1945 and 1946, approximately 4,200 people took advantage of this offer, further depleting the population of the Andamans to approximately 14,500.[30]

The abolition of the penal settlement in the Andamans did not amount to a withdrawal of British interests from the islands. Britain was still keen to retain the Andaman and Nicobar Islands as a crown colony in the interests of Commonwealth defence.[31] Relief and rehabilitation of the local population assumed prime importance. In light of the rapid decline in population, the islands badly needed labourers and cultivators. As the villages emptied of ex-convict and convict settlers, large tracts of agricultural land lay fallow in South Andamans. The need to find new settlers for the Andaman Islands coincided with the large-scale demobilisation of Indian soldiers who had served in the Second World War, giving rise to a scheme to settle ex-servicemen in the Andamans. The scheme envisaged the colonisation of 900 acres of land with 100 ex-servicemen and their families. Several inducements, such as allotments of 8–9 acres and grants of Rs 1,300, were built into the scheme to attract settlers. In return, each

---

[27] *Report on Medical Work in the Andaman and Nicobar Islands by Major GES Stewart, IMS, lately Senior Medical Officer of Port Blair*, File No: 304/48-AN, Andaman Files, 1948, NAI.

[28] Ibid.

[29] Government of India, *Administration Report on the Andaman and Nicobar Islands, 1945–46* (Delhi, 1946).

[30] Arthur Henderson, Under-Secretary of State for India, *Hansard, House of Commons Debates, 440*, 14 July 1947, cc46–62.

[31] Field Marshall Viscount Wavell to Pethick-Lawrence, 13 July 1946, in N. Mansergh, E. W. R. Lumby and Penderel Moon (eds) *Constitutional Relations Between Britain and India: The Transfer of Power 1942–47, Vol VIII* (London: Her Majesty's Stationery Office, 1970) (henceforth TP, Vol. VII, etc.)

ex-serviceman had to be prepared to invest Rs 500 of his own money.[32] Despite wide publicity in the press, the scheme had few takers. Meanwhile, the military lobby in London lost the battle to hold on to the Andaman and Nicobar Islands.[33] With independence, the new rulers of the Andamans inherited from the British the problem of chronic shortage of labour as well as the moribund scheme designed to solve it.

By November 1947, only 20 people had volunteered to go to the Andamans, leading to speculation in the Ministry of Home Affairs about the inadequacy of incentives offered.[34] The Chief Commissioner suggested that ex-soldiers were not prepared to invest Rs 500. According to him, assistance to the extent of Rs 2,500 per family would be required to attract settlers from the mainland. This view was echoed by the Ministry of Home Affairs, which felt that further publicity of the scheme would bear no fruit unless greater financial incentives were included.[35] Such explanations, however, failed to recognise that the proposed scheme, by attempting to recruit voluntary settlers, envisioned a radical departure from established patterns of settlement of the Andaman Islands. Administrative fantasies of discontinuing transportation to the Andaman Islands and developing it as a free colony were not new. Back in the 1920s, the government of India had attempted to discontinue transportation and instead develop the Islands as a free colony. These plans never materialised due to opposition from provincial governments, unwilling to lose the convenience of sending off a section of their convict population to the Andaman Islands. The result was a curious system of inducing convicts and other criminalised groups, such as Mappilas and Bhantus, to 'volunteer' for resettlement in the Andamans by promising them various inducements and a second chance at building a free life.[36] The scheme to settle ex-servicemen drew upon this tradition, but with one critical difference. The targeted population was already free. Without the threat of confinement in the Indian mainland, a journey to the Andamans clearly lost much of its appeal. The national government of a newly independent country could hardly return to colonial practices of recruiting convicts as settlers. Given the reputation of the Andaman Islands as a place of torture and exile for revolutionaries, it would be

---

[32] *Development-Colonisation, Settlement*, File No. 259/47-AN, Andaman Files, MHA, 1947, NAI.

[33] See Document Nos. 221, 239, 244 and 345, *TP*, Vol. XI, 31 May – July 1947.

[34] *Development-Colonisation, Settlement*, File No. 259/47-AN, Andaman Files, 1947, NAI.

[35] Ibid.

[36] Taylor C. Sherman, 'From Hell to Paradise? Voluntary Transfer of Convicts to the Andaman Islands, 1921–1940', *Modern Asian Studies* 43: 2, (2009), 367–88.

political suicide for the national government to be seen to continue the carceral habits of their colonial predecessors.

By late 1947, optimism was giving way to despair within administrative circles. The bureaucrats of the Ministry of Home Affairs were desperate to find willing settlers. It was feared that as time passed by, the forest would reclaim the fallow fields. 'No time should be lost if colonisation of Andamans by the Indian farmers is to be encouraged,' declared R.N. Philips, the Under-Secretary to the Government of India.[37] This increasingly desperate search for willing settlers coincided with the rising tide of refugees from western Pakistan. By September 1947, resolving multiple and unforeseen crises born of the partition of India had become the top priority of the authorities in Delhi. Two new administrative authorities, namely, the Ministry of Relief and Rehabilitation and the Emergency Cabinet Committee, were constituted in early September to deal with the refugee influx and the crisis in Punjab.[38] Just as the work of recovery and reconstruction in the Andaman Islands had been combined with schemes of settling demobilised soldiers in a post-war context, in post-partition India, the ground was ripe for combining the refugees' need for land with the official quest for tillers. The idea of settling refugees in the Andaman Islands was put forward in two different contexts simultaneously. At an intra-departmental meeting of the Ministry of Home Affairs held on 23 September 1947 officials considered sending refugees to the Andamans, mainly keeping in mind the acute need for labourers and agriculturists for the development of the island. A note detailing the developmental potential and climatic conditions of the Andamans was sent to the Ministry of Relief and Rehabilitation, requesting the latter to investigate the possibility of rehabilitating refugees in the islands. Meanwhile, in a parallel development, the Ministry of Agriculture came up with a proposal to raise a civil pioneer corps from the poorest refugees, who could then be used to reclaim forested areas in Andamans.[39] The idea was to keep the refugees suitably employed pending their rehabilitation. The chief concern in both these proposals was the development of the Andaman Islands, though the rehabilitation of some refugees would no doubt be achieved in the process. Though these schemes amounted to little more than administrative opportunism, they linked the project of developing the Andaman Islands to the hitherto unrelated problem of finding land for a rising number of refugees in the Indian mainland. At the

---

[37] *Development-Colonisation, Settlement*, File No. 259/47-AN, Andaman Files, 1947, NAI.
[38] U. Bhaskar Rao, *The Story of Rehabilitation* (Labour, Employment and Rehabilitation, Government of India, 1967), pp. 11–12.
[39] *Development-Colonisation, Settlement*, File No. 259/47-AN, Andaman Files, 1947, NAI.

next meeting of the Emergency Cabinet Committee, the Andaman Islands came to be seen as one of the possible sites of rehabilitation.[40]

The idea of harnessing refugees to a project of developing the Andaman Islands was not just stray opportunism on the part of zealous bureaucrats. It reflected a broader tendency among India's political elite, especially Nehru, of attempting to link the project of refugee rehabilitation to national development. These suggestions, put forward in late 1947, in many ways anticipated the logic behind Nehru's brainchild, the Development and Rehabilitation Board, set up in February 1948, to address the concurrent challenges of rehabilitation and development together.[41] The problem of finding manpower for developing the Andaman Islands, quite by accident, provided the first concrete instance where the government of India explicitly sought to combine refugee rehabilitation with a project of development. In early 1948, as various concerned departments continued to debate the feasibility of sending refugees to the Andaman Islands, the Development and Rehabilitation Board also got involved. At this stage, the government of India was yet to acknowledge the existence of refugees from East Bengal. The refugees being courted by the Ministry of Home Affairs as potential settlers of the Andaman Islands were those who had migrated from western Pakistan. The Ministry of Home Affairs sent information supplied by the Chief Commissioner about the Andaman Islands to the East Punjab Government and the camp commandant of Kurukshetra,[42] hoping for their help in recruiting refugees. While the camp commandant of Kurukshetra did not respond, East Punjab's Rehabilitation Board declined the offer. The reasons cited included the high cost of transportation to the Andamans, the understandable preference of Punjabi refugees for land within East Punjab and last, but not the least, the availability of agricultural land both in and around the divided province as a result of a state-led exchange of populations and property. Once the attempt to find settlers among Punjabi refugees fell through, the Rehabilitation and Development Board asked the West Bengal government to investigate the possibility of settling refugees from East Bengal in the Andaman Islands. Accordingly, in March 1948 a modified version of the old scheme for finding settlers was thrown open to the general public, with preference given to refugees and to ex-servicemen.[43]

---

[40] Minutes of Emergency Committee Meeting held on 14 November 1947, ibid.

[41] Jawaharlal Nehru, 'The Rehabilitation and Development Board' in S. Gopal (ed.), *Selected Works of Jawaharlal Nehru, Second Series, Vol. 5* (New Delhi: Jawaharlal Nehru Memorial Fund, 1984), pp. 153–4.

[42] This was the largest refugee camp in Punjab, with a population of 300,000 by December 1947. For details see Bhaskar Rao, *The Story of Rehabilitation* (1967).

[43] *Development-Colonisation, Settlement*, File No. 259/47-AN, Andaman Files, 1947, NAI.

The government of West Bengal found volunteers 'willing' to travel to these remote islands with alarming alacrity in its refugee camps. By 5 August 1948, the ill-fated scheme of settling 100 ex-servicemen in the Andaman Islands was finally ready for implementation. In its modified form, it provided for the settlement of 25 each of ex-servicemen and ordinary citizens, and 50 refugees from East Bengal.[44] It is unlikely that this scheme was ever actually implemented. In subsequent surveys and in popular memory, the displaced families who left Calcutta in 1949 are repeatedly mentioned as the first batch of settlers to reach South Andaman Island. Nothing more was heard of ex-servicemen in the Andamans until 1965, when an official report proposed the inclusion of a large proportion of ex-servicemen in future colonisation schemes, keeping in mind the 'security angle dictated by the peculiar location of the islands away from the mainland'.[45] Even if the proposed mixed group of settlers existed only on paper, its convoluted history provides the missing link between late-colonial plans of settling ex-soldiers and the eventual pattern of re-settling Bengali refugees in the Andaman Islands.

To sum up, the government of India turned to Bengali refugees as possible settlers of the Andaman Islands as an emergency measure in order to save a failing scheme. The bureaucrats of the Ministry of Home Affairs were not concerned with finding land for the rehabilitation of Bengali refugees. Their goal was to take advantage of the adverse circumstances of refugees to repair the destruction and dislocation wrought by the Second World War and its aftermath in the Andaman Islands. A similar disinterest in the fate of refugees in West Bengal can be seen in the decisions and deliberations of the short-lived Rehabilitation and Development Board. Once it became clear that Punjabi refugees were not interested in travelling to the Andaman Islands, the Rehabilitation and Development Board decided against the rehabilitation of refugees in the Andaman Islands on a planned basis. Instead, the Board decided to allow refugees to participate in the scheme originally designed for ex-servicemen.[46] The refugees the Board considered planning for were those displaced from western Pakistan, while those allowed to participate in other, unrelated schemes of development were those from East Bengal. At this point, the Chief Minister of West Bengal, Dr B. C. Roy, was quite alone in his determination to disperse as many refugees as possible outside West Bengal. By 1950, he was offering to clear land in the Andaman Islands at the expense of the West Bengal government, provided he was

[44] Ibid.
[45] Inter-Departmental Team, Report on Accelerated Development Programme for Andaman and Nicobar Islands (1966).
[46] Development-Colonisation, Settlement, File No. 259/47-AN, Andaman Files, 1947, NAI.

allowed to use the land for resettlement of refugees.[47] Contrary to his hopes for the emergence of a 'new Bengal' in the Andaman Islands, the first batch of Bengali refugees sent to these Islands represented little more than a marriage of convenience between West Bengal's eagerness to get rid of its 'extra' population, and the Ministry of Home Affairs desperate search for 'willing' settlers. Yet, even in this opportunistic recourse to refugees as settlers, the post-colonial state betrayed ways of thinking about refugees that would come to have far-reaching impact on evolving policy.

In the eyes of the state, the partition refugees provided a pool of reserve labourers and agriculturists who had far greater mobility than the general population. The assumption was that having already been uprooted from their original social milieu, refugees had no real ties to the areas where they sought refuge, and could therefore be dispersed at will. U. Bhaskar Rao eulogises those displaced from western Pakistan as ideal refugees since they displayed 'a praiseworthy mobility – they were ready to spread themselves out over the whole country, as it were.'[48] This, he claimed, was in sharp contrast to the East Bengali refugees' reluctance to move beyond West Bengal, Assam and Tripura. Thus, by the 1960s, mobility or willingness to travel for resettlement was upheld as an attribute of the ideal refugee. In official discourse, Bengali refugees, on account of their 'character', failed to live up to this ideal. Yet, in the late 1940s, refugees awaiting rehabilitation in West Bengal were found to be uniquely 'willing' to travel for resettlement, unlike their Punjabi counterparts. These choices made by refugees have to be understood in terms of the specific conditions of displacement and not as manifestations of their character.

The refugees from West Punjab had hopes of being compensated with 'evacuee' lands and houses, left behind by the millions of Muslims who had fled to Pakistan. They therefore had good reason to refuse to go to the Andamans.[49] More importantly, both the provincial government of East Punjab and the central agencies concerned with rehabilitation believed that there was enough land in East Punjab to absorb most, if not all of those who were enumerated as rural refugees. Unlike them, the Bengali refugees were not entitled to compensation and had little hope of obtaining evacuee property. In sharp contrast to the situation in Punjab, the

---

[47] Minutes of Meeting, 12 September 1950, File No. 8/2/50-AN, Andaman Files, 1950, NAI.

[48] Bhaskar Rao, *The Story of Rehabilitation* (1967), p. 147.

[49] Letter from Mr Shrivastava, Deputy Secretary to the Ministry of Relief and Rehabilitation, Government of India, to Mr P. V. R. Rao, ICS, Joint Secretary of Ministry of Home Affairs, Government of India, 4 December 1947, File No. 259/47-AN, Andaman Files, 1947, NAI.

government of India took no initiative to develop a comprehensive plan of refugee rehabilitation for the eastern sector. As seen in chapter 1, the West Bengal government followed a minimalist programme of distributing relief and sanctioning loans. In early 1949, when refugee families from various camps in West Bengal agreed to travel to the Andaman Islands, they were yet to be offered any kind of rehabilitation. The conditions in the camps were also far from satisfactory. In 1951, a stray incident of smallpox infection among some refugees sent to the Andamans caused a furore within the administration. The resultant investigation left a rare trace in the archives of the voices of refugees who were usually portrayed as 'willing' settlers.

In January 1951, when 32 refugee families reached Port Blair, several of them were suffering from smallpox.[50] The discovery raised the spectre of an outbreak in the Islands. Further investigations revealed that the infected group had been forced to live in the same room with three refugees suffering from smallpox at the Ultadanga transit camp. When two of them died, the rest were forced to live for days with decomposing bodies. In response to their repeated requests for removal of the bodies, the camp superintendent had rebuked the refugees, saying they had entered the camps 'to die'.[51] It is significant that when given the opportunity to write a petition voicing their complaints, the refugees highlighted the abuse and neglect they had suffered in a refugee camp. None suggested that they had been forced to travel to the Andamans, or expressed any desire to return to West Bengal. At the same time, it is clear that their decision to travel to the Andamans was informed in no small measure by their desperation to escape the refugee camps. Denied rehabilitation in West Bengal and shoved into crowded and unhygienic refugee camps, the East Bengali refugees in many ways provided the closest approximation to a captive labour force. Much like convicts who 'volunteered' to travel to the Andamans, the 'willingness' of Bengali refugees to resettle in these remote islands has to be understood within its coercive context.

Refugees Recast: Growing Food and Producing Jute

As discussed above, the first scheme that made space for refugees in the Andaman Islands owed its origins to opportunism. However, instead of being a one-off measure to prevent deterioration of abandoned

[50] Official Note by E. C. Gaynor, Deputy Secretary to the Government of India, Ministry of Home Affairs, 10 March 1951, File No. 36/2/51-AN, Andaman Files, 1951, NAI.

[51] Petition by refugees to the Deputy Commissioner, Andaman and Nicobar Islands, Port Blair, 16 November 1951, Ibid.

agricultural land in the Andamans, it signalled the beginning of a pattern. The islands' administrators repeatedly turned to the refugee camps of West Bengal to recruit agriculturists and labourers. Between April 1949 and August 1951, the Ministry of Home Affairs sanctioned five separate schemes of resettling displaced families in the Andamans.[52] Later batches were resettled in lands newly cleared of forests. Some, such as the twenty-six displaced families who reached the Andamans on 20 May 1952, were employed as labourers to clear the land they had been promised.[53] While there was no uniform policy governing these piecemeal dispersals, a pattern began to nevertheless emerge. Between 1949 and 1952, the government of India increasingly saw East Bengali refugees as agents of agricultural expansion in the Andaman Islands (see table 2.1 for details). During these years, refugee resettlement in the Andamans saw the practical application of an emerging logic of governance that sought to harness refugees to projects of national development, by recasting them as agricultural pioneers.

In June 1952, this interweaving of refugee rehabilitation and agrarian expansion was written into policy with the adoption of a five-year Colonisation and Development Scheme. While refugees from East Pakistan continued to be negatively portrayed within administrative discourse as infantile creatures dependent upon government charity, in practice, they began to be mobilised as agents of agricultural colonisation of marginal lands. This was a crucial shift in the pattern of governing Bengali refugees as for the first time, albeit within the confines of the remote Andaman Islands, their presence could be harmonised with economic development instead of raising the Malthusian spectre of extra mouths to feed. In order to understand this transformation, it is necessary to look beyond the borders of West Bengal, where refugees remained the harbingers of economic doom for an overpopulated state, to the distant rulers of the Andaman Islands, based in Delhi, and the concerns and anxieties that dominated contemporary governance and politics.

The attempt to harmonise rehabilitation and national development was neither new, nor unique to the Andaman Islands. In 1948, Nehru created the Rehabilitation and Development Board to give concrete shape to his vision of looking at the 'two subjects' that faced independent India together, namely, the immediate crisis of refugee rehabilitation and the older issue of national development.[54] For Nehru, the blood-letting in Punjab and the refugee crisis unleashed by partition were sapping

---

[52] File No. 8/8/53-AN, Andaman Files, 1953, NAI.   [53] Ibid.

[54] Jawaharlal Nehru, 'The Rehabilitation and Development Board' in S. Gopal (ed.), *Selected Works, Vol. 5* (1984), pp. 153–4.

Table 2.1: *Pattern of Refugee Resettlement in the Andaman Islands, 1949–52*

Year	No of Families Sent	Specificities of Resettlement scheme
1949	198 families (in two batches)	Promised 10 acres each of agricultural land, livestock and maintenance dole of six to nine months
1950	(i) 65 agriculturist families	(i) Promised 10 acres each of agricultural land, livestock and maintenance dole of six to nine months etc.
	(ii) 28 families of labourers	(ii) Paid wages by the forest department to clear land. Promised land for settlement at a future date
1951	78 families (in two batches)	Allotted recently cleared land (with stumps sticking out) or jungle covered land for clearing
1952	51 families (in three batches)	Working as paid labourers to clear land

Source: Information taken from Surajit Chadra Sinha, *Report on the possibilities of further resettlement of East Pakistan refugees in Andaman Islands*, Calcutta, 1952,

distractions from the very essence of *swaraj* or self-rule – planned development to combat poverty, ignorance and unemployment. He was eager to settle the 'problems caused by the partition' and focus national energies on schemes that would benefit the people.[55] As he attempted to refocus on planned development, the presence of millions of uprooted families needing final resettlement appeared to be not just a daunting problem, but also one that offered an 'ideal opportunity for planning'.[56] The Board was created to give form to Nehru's vision of utilising partition refugees in broader processes of nation building. Nehru envisioned it as an autonomous executive and planning authority that would work in conjunction with various provincial governments to expedite schemes of national development. Its work would be to ensure that refugees awaiting rehabilitation were absorbed in schemes and projects where manpower was needed, instead of creating new settlements where 'resources have been more or less exhausted or have run to a saturation point'.[57] The Board proved to be an ineffectual and short-lived body. Far from functioning with greater speed than a normal department of government, which is

[55] Jawahralal Nehru, 'The Necessity of National Reconstruction', Speech at Kanpur, 16 December 1947, in S. Gopal (ed.), *Selected Works, Vol. 4* (1984), p. 218.

[56] Jawaharlal Nehru to Albert Mayer, 3 March 1948, in S. Gopal (ed.), *Selected Works, Vol. 5* (1984), p. 160.

[57] Jawaharlal Nehru, 'Organising Rehabilitation', extract from Note for the Rehabilitation Committee of the Cabinet, 13 January 1948, in ibid., p. 142.

what Nehru had intended, the Board failed to function at all.[58] However, the core idea behind it, that refugees should aid and not detract from national development, had much wider currency in post-colonial India. Its positive articulation was seen in East Punjab, where refugees were welcomed as tillers of 'agricultural land abandoned by Muslim migrants to Pakistan' that 'could not be allowed to lie fallow save at dire peril to the country's economy'.[59] Its negative expression was seen in West Bengal, a 'saturated' region which could not, and by the logic of good governance, should not, take in any more refugees.

The failure of the Rehabilitation and Development Board meant that Nehru's vision of centrally planned rehabilitation, which could identify and develop suitably under-populated areas through the resettlement of refugees, never took off. Planning did not move beyond the identification of Central Provinces, Orissa and Assam as possible sites for resettlement of refugees from 'Punjab or the Frontier Provinces or Sind'.[60] In many ways, such plans were deemed redundant since the resettlement of Punjabi refugees, the main pre-occupation of the national government, was largely accomplished through redistribution of evacuee land. Yet, the governmentality that sought to harness refugees to various projects of national development outlived Nehru's Rehabilitation and Development Board and permeated various levels and departments of governance. It came to be applied, in a decentralised and non-linear manner, to refugees from East Pakistan. The Andaman Islands was the first iteration of this direction of policy.

Resettling refugees in the Andaman Islands was an expensive affair. The 1949 scheme, which aimed at resettling 200 displaced families in the Andamans, consisted of an extraordinarily generous package of grants and loans. Besides free passage and funds to cover the cost of cattle, agricultural implements and building materials, the scheme also promised a maintenance allowance to each family for the first nine months. On top of these grants, the refugees received loans to purchase fodder (or tools in case of artisans) and to construct houses.[61] It cost the government of India Rs 5,045 to resettle each refugee family in the Andaman Islands.[62] The government's contemporary policy of withholding rehabilitation from East Bengali refugees and encouraging their repatriation

---

[58] L.C. Jain, *The City of Hope: The Faridabad Story* (New Delhi: Concept Publishing, 1998).

[59] Bhaskar Rao, *The Story of Rehabilitation* (1967), p. 48.

[60] Jawaharlal Nehru, 'Organising Rehabilitation', 13 January 1948, in S. Gopal (ed.), *Selected Works, Vol. 5* (1984), p. 142.

[61] Letter sent to Ministry of Home Affairs by Manmohan Kishan, Assistant Secretary to the Government of India, Ministry of Rehabilitation, File No. 33/1/50-AN, Andaman Files, 1950, NAI.

[62] Ibid.

throws into sharper relief this contradictory treatment meted out to the select few who opted to cross the *kalapani*.[63] Clearly, the desperation of some East Bengali refugees to escape the subhuman conditions of West Bengal's refugee camps was matched by the government of India's urgency to develop agriculture in the Islands. This urgency begins to make sense only when it is seen in the context of the simultaneous and apparently unrelated crisis in food supply, which became a national pre-occupation in independent India.

The crisis of rehabilitating millions of uprooted families was only one of the many unforeseen consequences of partition in India. Soon after independence, it became evident that the division of Bengal and Punjab had substantially reduced the availability of food. The fertile rice fields of eastern Bengal as well as the canal-irrigated regions of Punjab and Sind had fallen to Pakistan. This further widened the gap between domestic demand and production of rice and wheat. It increased India's dependence on imports to meet the shortfall.[64] Till 1946, the government of India had depended on a two-pronged strategy of rationing and imports to meet its chronic food shortage. But the reliance on other countries for food had begun to rankle nationalist leaders. Rajendra Prasad, the Minister for Food in India's interim government expressed his dismay in no uncertain terms.

It is a tragic sight to see India's representatives going from one end of the earth to another – literally from Persia to Peru – with the begging bowl in their hands for food which she ought to be able to produce.[65]

Clearly, decolonisation added new meaning to the impetus to increase food production, which dated back to 1942. In the summer of 1942, the Japanese occupation of Burma had severed the supply of rice from Burma. The British government of India initiated a 'Grow More Food' campaign in order to meet the shortfall. Besides recommending a switch-over from cash crops like cotton to food crops, and increasing productivity through irrigation, better seeds and manures, it also advocated the exten-sive cultivation of fallow and arable wastelands.[66] However, no definite

---

[63] See chapter 1 for contemporary government policy towards East Bengali refugees.
[64] For a historical summary of India's food policy see R.N. Chopra, *Food Policy in India: A Survey* (New Delhi: Intellectual Publishing House, 1988).
[65] Henry Foley Knight, *Food Administration in India, 1939–47* (Stanford, CA: Stanford University Press, 1954), p. 248. Also cited in Chopra, *Food Policy in India* (1988), p. 58.
[66] Chopra, *Food Policy in India* (1988), pp. 69–70. Also see Grow More Food Enquiry Committee, *Report of the Grow More Food Enquiry Committee* (Delhi: Government of India, Ministry of Food & Agriculture, 1952).

targets were set. In effect, the scheme achieved little before 1947.[67] With independence, this campaign gained new urgency.

In September 1947, the government of India appointed the Second Foodgrains Policy Committee under Sir Purshottamdas Thakurdas. In a significant departure from the First Committee, it was asked to not only advise the government on measures to increase domestic production and procurement, but to also investigate 'the extent to which reliance can and should be placed on imports'.[68] The final report of this committee, published in April 1948, recommended the liquidation of dependence on imports of food grains in orderly and planned stages. It recommended a massive drive to increase internal food production, at the rate of 10 million tons annually.[69] Unlike the colonial state, which had been content to combine imports with increased production, in independent India the Grow More Food campaign was redefined as the means to achieve self-sufficiency. In 1949, the campaign was relaunched on a national scale, with the declared goal of achieving self-sufficiency in food by 1952. While the methods recommended for achieving increased production did not vary substantially from those recommended during the Second World War, the national government was far more willing to sink money into the campaign. Expenditure on the Grow More Food campaign was stepped up from Rs 36.6 million in 1948–9 to Rs 97.6 million in 1949–50, and to Rs 154.4 million in 1950–1.[70] However, given the fact that food policy was primarily a state subject under the Indian Constitution, the Union Food Minister's position was one of "maximum responsibility with minimum control".[71] For achieving results, the central government had to rely on participating states. The Andaman Islands, being directly administered, was an exception to this rule. Here, the government of India was free to demonstrate its determination to achieve self-sufficiency in food through reclaiming fallow fields and by expanding cultivation.

The Ministry of Finance approved the scheme to resettle refugees in the abandoned paddy fields of Andamans in 1949, the same year that the national campaign to achieve self-sufficiency in food was launched. There is evidence to suggest that the urgency to promote paddy cultivation in the

[67] For a critique of this phase of the Grow More Food campaign, see K. G. Sivaswamy, 'Indian Agriculture – Problems and Programmes', *Pacific Affairs*, 23:4 (1950), 356–70.
[68] Chopra, *Food Policy in India* (1988), p. 62.   [69] Ibid., pp. 63–4.
[70] Foodgrains Enquiry Committee, *Report of the Foodgrains Enquiry Committee* (New Delhi: Ministry of Food and Agriculture, Department of Food, Government of India, 1957).
[71] Norman K. Nicholson, 'Political Aspects of Indian Food Policy', *Pacific Affairs*, 41:1 (1968), 34–50.

Andamans was derived from the contemporary resolve to grow food grains on an emergency basis. S. K. Gupta, who was the Deputy Commissioner of the Andaman Islands between 1948 and 1951, claimed credit for providing the clinching argument in support of refugee rehabilitation in the Andamans.

As a 'grow more food' measure and with a view to attainment of self-sufficiency in the matter of food, I suggested colonisation of these Islands early in 1948 – especially as at that time about 3,000 acres of abandoned holdings were available for settlement. The idea caught and the Government of India agreed to the West Bengal Government's proposal to rehabilitate displaced persons from East Pakistan in the Andamans.[72]

Between 1949 and 1951, increasing expenditure on schemes to grow more food was paralleled by a series of generous schemes designed to expand paddy cultivation in the Andamans. The latter were never described as being part of the Grow More Food campaign. The Central Tractor Organisation, set up to reclaim land for growing food, confined its activities to northern India.[73] In the Andaman Islands, the authorities relied on the felling activities of the Forest Department or the manual labour of the refugees to reclaim 1,671 acres for paddy cultivation by the end of 1952.[74] Besides a grant amounting to less than Rs 50,000, the project to colonise the Andamans received little from the funds earmarked for growing food.[75] Nevertheless, it is likely that the national policy of increased state investment in agricultural production provided the justification for the high expenditure of resettling refugees in the Andaman Islands at a time when the government of India was determined to spend as little as possible on rehabilitating East Bengali refugees.

In 1949, a team headed by H. R. Shivdasani was sent to the Andaman Islands by the Ministry of Home Affairs to prepare a report on the possibilities of 'developing' them. However, from the two questionnaires handed to the team before their departure, it is evident that the ministry had already decided upon the desired direction of development in the Islands (see Appendices I and II). While the first set of questions primarily posed detailed queries regarding the possibilities of agricultural

---

[72] See S. K. Gupta, 'Appendix A: Andaman and Nicobar Islands', in A. K. Ghosh, *Census of India, 1951. Vol. 17. The Andaman and Nicobar Islands* (Delhi: Manager of Publications, Government of India, 1955). Henceforth *1951 Andaman Islands Census*.

[73] The Central Tractor Organisation reclaimed 4.66 lakh acres of land for cultivation in Uttar Pradesh, Madhya Pradesh, Madhya Bharat, Bhopal and Punjab. For details see Grow More Food Enquiry Committee, *Report*, 1952, p. 39.

[74] File No: 8/3/53-AN, Andaman Files, 1953, NAI.

[75] See Appendix VI, Statement I, Grow More Food Enquiry Committee, *Report*, 1952, pp. 116–17.

colonisation of Andamans, the second set dealt entirely with the needs of potential cultivators and settlers. The resultant report, known as the Shivdasani Report after its author, told the administrators what they wanted to hear. Colonisation of Andamans was 'not only possible but desirable ... to promote self-sufficiency in food and labour requirements.'[76] He further declared, based on a lightning tour spanning a few weeks between 24 January and 19 February, that the 'soil is extremely fertile and there are no insurmountable difficulties in respect of tackling the questions of Supply, Public Health and Communications.'[77] According to Shivdasani, the Andamans required a population of 6,500 families or 39,000 persons (at an average of six to a family) to achieve self-sufficiency in food. He suggested providing land for 25,000 settlers or about 4,500 families at the rate of 7 acres per family, by the end of 1954. This was colonisation on a staggering scale, neither envisioned not attempted by the British in the Andaman Islands.

The recommendations of the Shivdasani Report set the course for the future development of the Andaman Islands. In 1952, the government of India sanctioned a five-year Colonisation and Development Scheme, which in essence accepted the recommendations of the report. It formed the core of the first five-year plan for the Andamans. In these islands, the government of India privileged agricultural colonisation above all other economic activities, such as fisheries, shipbuilding or trade, as the main vehicle of development. This left the authorities with the daunting task of finding 4,500 agriculturist families, well versed in the cultivation of food crops, especially paddy, and willing to pioneer cultivation on a distant island. It is this particular profile of the ideal settler which led to the selection of Bengali refugees. Though the initial exodus from East Bengal had been of middle class professionals, by the 1950s migration had taken on a mass character. The majority of the later migrants were agriculturists and a rising percentage came from schedule caste, specifically, *Namasudra* background.[78] This provided the Andaman administration with a seemingly inexhaustible supply of prospective agricultural settlers. The beleaguered government of West Bengal was only too happy to help in the dispersal of refugees to the Andamans. It facilitated the

---

[76] H. R. Shivdasani, *Report on the Possibilities of Colonization and Development of the Andaman and Nicobar Islands* (New Delhi: Government Press, 1949), p. 1 (henceforth *Shivdasani Report*).

[77] Ibid.

[78] For the changing socio-economic character of migrants see the Government of West Bengal Statistical Bureau, *Rehabilitation of Refugees: A Statistical Survey, 1955* (Alipore: Government of West Bengal, 1956) and see Joya Chatterji, *The Spoils of Partition: Bengal and India, 1947–67* (Cambridge and New York: Cambridge University Press, 2007), pp. 105–58.

transportation of refugee-settlers from various camps to the point of embarkation at Calcutta. The refugee camps in West Bengal emerged as a new catchment area for enlisting settlers for Andamans. Much like *sardars* (headmen or jobbers) recruiting coolies and factory labourers, the settlement officers or *tehsildars* of the Andamans travelled from camp to camp, cajoling refugees to sign up for resettlement in the Andaman Islands.

Between 1949 and 1952, the Andaman Islands provided the unlikely venue for the emergence of a new way of conceptualising East Bengali refugees. Within correspondence that circulated between bureaucrats and administrators of various central ministries, especially, the Ministry of Home Affairs and to a lesser extent, the Ministry of Rehabilitation, they were recast as potential settlers, agricultural colonisers and agents of development. This redefinition saw its first successful implementation in the Andaman Islands, but was not limited to it. Once the government of India realised the potential of Bengali refugees as agricultural pioneers, it repeatedly cast them in this role in different parts of India, with varying degrees of success.

In 1949, the price war between India and Pakistan led the latter to cut supplies of raw cotton and jute to India. In June 1950, the government of India added exhortations for cultivating jute and cotton to its recently launched campaign to grow more food.[79] The Bengali refugees, already portrayed as expert paddy cultivators who could be relocated to sites of intensive colonisation, were now singled out for their knowledge of jute cultivation. There is evidence to suggest that the government of India encouraged West Bengal's neighbouring states to take in refugees precisely on these grounds, i.e., their expertise in producing paddy and jute. In May 1949, the Home Minister, Sardar Vallabhbhai Patel, wrote to the Chief Minister of Assam, Gopinath Bardolai, regarding the possibility of bringing fallow land under jute cultivation. He encouraged Bardolai to look beyond local opposition to the influx of Bengali refugees because they were specialists in the cultivation of jute. He advised Bardolai to 'look at this question from the wider national interests. Jute is the only commodity in which we can accumulate substantial foreign exchange, which we need badly for the fruition of many of our developmental schemes.'[80] The resettlement of Bengali refugees in what is today Uttaranchal indulged in a similar utilitarian characterisation of the refugees. The government of United Provinces had come up

---

[79] For details of this scheme see Grow More Food Enquiry Committee, *Report* (1952).
[80] Vallabhbhai Patel to Gopinath Bardolai, 17 May 1949, in Durga Das (ed.), *Sardar Patel's Correspondence, Vol. 9* (Ahmedabad: Navjivan Publishing House, 1972), pp. 38–9.

with a plan of expanding jute cultivation in the Terai region. In this little-known scheme, 1,000 East Bengali refugee families 'proficient in jute cultivation' were resettled in the Kichchha village of Nainital district.[81]

By the mid-1950s, when the central government finally gave in to Dr B. C. Roy's demands and agreed to take direct responsibility for rehabilitating the majority of West Bengal's refugees, utilising refugees from East Bengal as agricultural pioneers was an entrenched practice. The infamous Dandakaranya project, launched in 1957 as a long-term solution to the problem of rehabilitating refugees from East Bengal, took its cue from the precedence set in the Andaman Islands. The scheme was envisaged as a massive project of agricultural expansion and colonisation to be implemented in the forested regions of Dandakaranya, spanning the contiguous districts of Bastar in Madhya Pradesh, and Koraput and Kalahandi in Orissa.[82] Once more Bengali refugees were cast in the role of pioneering agriculturists and treated as instruments for expanding sedentary agrarian settlements into land which had hitherto been covered in forests. There was, however, a crucial difference between the Dandakaranya project and earlier patterns of re-settlement of Bengali refugees outside West Bengal. In the Andaman Islands and Uttaranchal, refugees had been used to fill in an existing need for settlers and cultivators. The Dandakaranya project owed its origins to a national search for locating a tract of 'empty' land large enough to resettle 35,000 displaced families living in different camps in West Bengal. The project area was in effect carved out of the participating states of Orissa and Madhya Pradesh, who ceded the land to the autonomous Dandakaranya Development Authority with considerable reluctance. The project is usually seen as the brainchild of S. V. Ramamurthy, who was the adviser to the Planning Commission of India in 1956. However, both in the selection of sparsely populated and 'backward' tracts for the resettlement of refugees, and in the preference of creating an autonomous executive authority for its implementation, the Dandakaranya Project can be traced back to Nehru's original vision of a national plan for resettling partition refugees, which was first articulated by the long-defunct Rehabilitation and Development Board. Echoing Nehru's original vision and the limited, yet successful experiment of Andaman's colonisation, the declared goal of the Dandakaranya project

---

[81] For details of these schemes see Bandyopadhyay, *Udvastu (Refugee)* (1970), p. 250 and Tapan Bose and Rita Manchanda (eds), *States, Citizens and Outsiders: The Uprooted Peoples of South Asia* (Kathmandu: South Asia Forum for Human Rights, 1997).

[82] For refugee rehabilitation in Dandakaranya see K. Maudood Elahi, 'Refugees in Dandakaranya', *International Migration Review*, 15:1/2 (1981), 219–25 and Alok Kumar Ghosh, 'Bengali Refugees at Dandakaranya: A Tragedy of Rehabilitation', Pradip Kumar Bose (ed.), *Refugees in West Bengal: Institutional Practices and Contested Identities* (Calcutta: Calcutta Research Group, 2000), pp. 106–29.

was not refugee rehabilitation, but the dual goals of resettlement of refugees and the development of the entire region.

Thus, what began as moribund schemes and administrative opportunism eventually moulded national policy towards East Bengali refugees. In order to access rehabilitation, the displaced agriculturists of East Bengal had to prove their mettle as agricultural colonisers in independent India. Only then was the government of India prepared to invest in their rehabilitation. Conversely, the presence of thousands of displaced agriculturists fuelled visions of rapid development of 'backward' regions by bringing in outsiders, to the detriment of the various tribal communities who lived in these forested tracts. In Dandakaranya and in the Andaman Islands, the resettlement of East Bengali refugees was achieved at the expense of tribal dispossession and marginalisation, though there were considerable regional variations in the political, economic and ecological impact of this narrow and top-down vision of refugee-led development. In both regions, the voices of local tribal communities were entirely absent from the deliberations leading to the formulation of schemes of development powered by refugees. In the Andaman Islands the plan to resettle refugees faced stiff opposition from another quarter – the local population of settlers drawn from convicts and ex-convicts, pejoratively known as the 'Local Born'. The central government's insistence on pushing through with refugee resettlement despite local opposition reveals that refugees, on account of being Hindus, could also be harnessed to other less salutary and ethno-centric visions of post-colonial nation-building.

A Desirable Demographic: Religion and Security in The Andaman Islands

The government of India pushed through its scheme to colonise the Andaman Islands using Bengali refugees in the face of stiff opposition from the 'Local Born' population. Primarily the descendants of convicts who were settled the Andaman Islands, they rechristened themselves Andamanese Indians in 1948.[83] Though the protests never stood any chance of success, they provoked significant discussions within the Ministry of Home Affairs regarding what kind of settlers were the most 'suitable' for the Andaman Islands. Here, religious affiliations and ethnic identity came to play a central role. The bureaucrats in Delhi insisted on screening all potential settlers of the Andaman Islands, which brought them into conflict with not just the local population, but also the Chief

[83] The Andamanese Indians organised themselves during this period to demand special privileges on account of being the 'original' inhabitants of the islands.

Commissioner of the Andaman Islands, Inam-ul-Majid. This insistence on having the last word on who was a 'suitable' settler stemmed from an unstated policy of excluding all Muslims from schemes of colonisation and settlement in the Andaman Islands. In other words, the willingness, albeit constrained, of large numbers of Bengali Hindu refugees to settle in the Andamans made it possible for the Ministry of Home Affairs to pursue a covert agenda of securing a frontier region through demographic manipulation.

The representatives of the Local Born Association[84] reacted with tremendous anxiety to plans of resettling refugees in the Andaman Islands.[85] In October 1947, they met the secretary of the Ministry of Home Affairs, P. V. R. Rao, to express their misgiving regarding the influx of an alien community. In a memorandum of appeal they declared that 'colonisation by the Anglo-Indians or any one single community from outside or from riot-affected areas may prejudice the well-being of this small established community.'[86] This was followed by a letter to the Chief Commissioner of the Andaman and Nicobar Islands. The letter is remarkable in its bias against refugees.

By bringing men from riot-affected areas to these islands, the peace and tranquillity of this little island is liable to be disturbed. It is well known to you that these islands are free from communal feelings and it is our earnest desire to promote the same ... We therefore appeal that utmost care may kindly be exercised before arriving at a decision to settle in Andamans the people from riot-affected areas as it would be almost difficult if not impossible to discriminate between persons with and without communal feelings.[87]

Despite this characterisation of refugees as vectors of communal violence, it seems unlikely that the Andamanese Indians particularly disliked refugees. Given their small numbers, they were apprehensive of any plans for large-scale immigration. They feared being swamped by communities from the mainland and being reduced to a minority in their birthplace.

---

[84] The Local Born Association, organised in order to express the needs and grievances of this community, was renamed the Andamanese Indian Association in 1948. The organisation had considerable influence among the Andamanese Indians and petitioned the authorities on their behalf. *Report by Durga Prashad Tiwari, the Assistant Superintendent of Police, Port Blair*, in File No. 445/48-AN, Andamans Files, 1948, NAI.

[85] Secretary of the Local Born Association, Port Blair, to the Chief Commissioner, Andaman and Nicobar Islands, 5 December 1947, File No. 69/47-AN, Andamans Files, 1947, NAI.

[86] Minutes of Meeting held between Mr. P. V. R. Rao, Joint Secretary to the Government of India, Ministry of Home Affairs and the representatives of the Local Born Association, 22 October 1947, File No. 259/47-AN, Andamans Files, 1947, NAI.

[87] Secretary of the Local Born Association, Port Blair, to the Chief Commissioner, Andaman and Nicobar Islands, 5 December 1947, File No. 69/47-AN, Andamans Files, 1947, NAI.

The refugees were targeted simply because they constituted an immediate and real threat. The proposal to turn the Andaman Islands into a home-land for the Anglo-Indian community had failed to materialise due to the Anglo-Indian Association's opposition to any plans of mass emigration.[88] The repeated characterisation of refugees as 'communal' could have been a strategic ploy to get a favourable response from the Government of India.

The Andamanese Indians found an ally in Inam-ul-Majid, the first Indian Chief Commissioner of the Andaman and Nicobar Islands. Opinions on Majid varied widely. He was seen variously as a troublemaker who fomented communal divisions in the Andamans with his bias towards Muslims,[89] as 'a man of the people', and as an ardent supporter of the co-operative movement in the Islands.[90] It seems that much of the controversy surrounding Majid derived from his tendency to champion the interests of the local population, even at the cost of oppos-ing policies of the central government. Given that he was appointed by and answerable to the Ministry of Home Affairs, this naturally incurred the ire of his superiors. Echoing the anxiety of the Andamanese Indians, Majid insisted that persons who 'might create trouble' should not be allowed to enter. He wanted a central clearing house to ensure that all ex-servicemen selected for resettlement in Andamans had a good service record. When the government of India modified the 1945 scheme to allow refugees, Majid once more insisted upon a rigorous process of selection. Moreover, he wanted the local population of the Andaman Islands to have access to the proposed colonisation scheme.[91] Ultimately, the offi-cials of the Ministry of Home Affairs ignored the opposition of the Andamanese Indians and silenced dissent within its ranks by replacing Inam-ul-Majid with A. K. Ghosh in July 1949.[92] Though the ministry offered no explanation for its insistence on resettling refugees in the Andamans, its constant disagreements with Majid between August 1947 and July 1949 are quite illuminating. These wrangles over policy, especially on an apparently unrelated dispute over the desirability of Mappila settlement in Andamans, illuminate how Bengali refugees became unwitting agents of Hinduising the population of Andaman Islands.

[88] See House of Commons Hansard (debate), col. 311.HC Deb, 30 June 1947, Vol. 439. Column 925–6.

[89] *Report by Durga Prashad Tiwari*, File No. 445/48-AN, Andamans Files, 1948, NAI.

[90] N. Iqbal Singh, *The Andaman Story* (New Delhi: Vikas Publishing House, 1978), pp. 275–82.

[91] Unofficial Note by R. N. Philips, Under-Secretary to the Government of India, Ministry of Home Affairs, 21 July 1948, File No. 259/47-AN, Andamans Files, 1948, NAI.

[92] Singh, *The Andaman Story* (1978).

In 1948, reports that labourers belonging to the Mappila community had arrived in the Andamans sparked a heated discussion between the Ministry of Home Affairs and the local administration. Durga Prashad Tiwari, the Assistant Superintendent of Police in the Andaman Islands, accused Majid of facilitating the immigration of Mappila labourers to the Andaman Islands. His report went on to raise fears of a veritable conspiracy to increase the Muslim population of the Andamans, which could eventually lead to its cessation to Pakistan! Though riddled with wild speculation and rumours, the report was nevertheless taken seriously by the authorities in Delhi and is therefore worth quoting at some length.

Although gentlemanly and kindly in talk, it is alleged that he has always had a special consideration for Muslims. The appointment of Mr. Rizvi a *tehsildar*, as liaison officer at Calcutta is viewed with suspicion. Recently when the Chief Commissioner returned home from India, Rizvi accompanied him and returned home from Port Blair to Calcutta by Madras. On his way he met some leaders on the Hyderabad-Madras border. Another allegation is that he was personally sent by the Chief Commissioner to persuade the Moplahs to migrate to Andamans. Nothing can be said regarding the correctness of these allegations but it is a fact that a number of Moplahs have been brought to Andamans in the last two Madras boats. Questions are being raised as to why the Chief Commissioner brought in fanatical and dangerous Moplahs over and above the refugees from Punjab. The underlying motive is conjectured to be to increase the Muslim population of the Island so as to declare it a Muslim predominant place, free to choose accession to Pakistan. Muslim labourers from Noakhali and other West Bengal places are also present in Andamans in a good number.[93]

The same report also accused two prominent Muslim residents, Subhan Ali and Syed Ali, of pro-Pakistan leanings. This allegation was based on the flimsiest evidence – the suspects had not attended the flag salutation ceremony on Independence Day. The response of the Ministry of Home Affairs makes it difficult to dismiss this string of assumptions and allegations as the paranoid suspicion of an overzealous officer. The bureaucrats in Delhi dismissed the appointment of Rizvi as a liaison officer in Calcutta as any proof of bias on the Chief Commissioner's part. Rizvi had actually been transferred to Calcutta from Port Blair by the authorities in Delhi. However, the reason for his transfer was a suspicion that he was carrying out pro-Pakistan activities in Port Blair.[94] Moreover, the Ministry of Home Affairs reacted with undisguised alarm at the prospect of increasing immigration of 'fanatical and dangerous' Mapillas. Clearly, Tiwari was not alone in his anti-Muslim sentiments. Recent scholarship

---

[93] *Report by Durga Prashad Tiwari*, File No. 445/48-AN, Andamans Files, 1948, NAI.
[94] Unofficial Note by R. N. Philips, 21 July 1948, File No. 259/47-AN, Andamans Files, 1948, NAI. (Italics mine).

corroborates this routine suspicion of Muslims in post-partition India that permeated every level of governance and politics – from a solitary official of the Intelligence Bureau to the Home Minister of India, Sardar Patel.[95] The routine construction of Muslims as fifth columnists played a crucial role in how contingent histories of development and refugee rehabilitation intersected in the Andaman Islands.

The Home Ministry's response to the issue of Mappila immigration to the Andaman Islands is particularly revealing. In the immediate aftermath of independence, as various rumours of planned immigration from the Indian mainland gained currency in the Andamans, the Mappilas put in requests to increase their numbers by bringing in members of their community from the mainland. According to the Deputy Commissioner, they put great pressure on the local administration with the demand that they should be allowed to bring in relatives. It is likely that Majid's attempts to bring in Mappila settlers was in response to this demand from the community and not proof of any conspiracy to hand the Andaman Islands over to Pakistan. His attempts were blocked by the Ministry of Home Affairs, where a string of senior civil servants, such as the Secretary Mr Bannerjee and the Under-secretary, R. N. Philips, reacted with alarm. Regarding the reported arrival of Mappilas, Philips declared that 'If it is a fact, then Chief Commissioner may be advised to repatriate them at once *even if it may hamper our reconstruction work.*[96] Similar action may be taken in respect of Muslim labourers who came from Noakhali and other West Bengal places'.[97] Clearly, when faced with exaggerated fears of a Muslim influx, the drive to find labourers for post-war reconstruction in the Andaman Islands lost much of its urgency.

The official reason for the government's opposition to expanding the Mappila settlements was a patently absurd claim that there was not enough land. According to S. K. Gupta, 'the pressure on land became too great and the administration had to interfere'.[98] Permits already granted to intending settlers, presumably by Majid, were now screened and only 'those who really needed assistance on their land or in their trade were allowed to import relatives'.[99] The copious 'unofficial notes' of R. N Philips leave no doubt regarding the actual motives behind the administration's opposition to Mappila immigration. He stated that if the

[95] Gyanendra Pandey, 'Can a Muslim Be an Indian?', *Comparative Studies in Society and History*, 41: 4 (1999), 608–29.
[96] Italics added.
[97] Unofficial Note by R. N. Philips, 21 July 1948, File No. 259/47-AN, Andamans Files, 1948, NAI.
[98] S. K. Gupta, 'Appendix A' in A. K. Ghosh, *1951 Andaman Islands Census* (1955).
[99] Ibid.

allegations against Majid were true, then 'it is a very serious state of affairs as we have all along taken steps to see that *the population ratio in the islands is not disturbed by unauthorised and unlimited entry of Muslims into the islands.*'[100] This is no less than an admission to a consistent policy of demographic manipulation in favour of maintaining a Hindu majority. Though the records are not clear as to how the authorities in Delhi classified the population of the Andaman Islands, and what particular 'ratio' between these different groups it sought to maintain, it is clear that the entry of Muslims was 'unauthorised' and had to be limited at all costs. Though it is not openly stated, the opposition between desirable refugees and undesirable Muslim migrants, whether from Kerala or Bengal, suggests which particular feature of refugees made them preferred settlers. The refugees were, without exception, Hindu. Durga Prashad Tiwari was not the only one who saw Muslim migrants as a colonising force for Pakistan. All existing evidence and subsequent policies suggest that the Ministry of Home Affairs was invested in not just maintaining, but also significantly increasing a Hindu majority in the Andaman Islands. If excluding all Muslim migration as 'unauthorised' offered the means to maintain a Hindu majority, the presence of thousands of Bengali refugees 'willing' to settle in the Andaman Islands offered the perfect means of pursuing a covert agenda of increasing the Hindu population of the Andaman Islands. The value of refugees as desirable settlers became particularly evident in the face of opposition by Majid, who was certainly aware of this prejudice and did everything in his power to challenge the exclusion of Muslims. The correspondence between Majid and the authorities in Delhi is marked by repeated requests to include 'Local Borns', many of whom were Muslims. He consistently attempted to retain say in the selection of 'suitable' settlers and clearly did not share the central government's opposition to Muslim immigration.

The perception of Muslims as disloyal and as agents of Pakistan was hardly unique to the Andaman Islands. It was rampant in the years after partition and had very real consequences for Muslim refugees, for whom the right to return to temporarily abandoned homes in India was legislated away through the draconian evacuee property laws.[101] However, the prejudice against Muslim settlers in the Andaman Islands illustrates a more specific form of suspicion and mistrust, articulated in the borderlands and

---

[100] Unofficial Note by R.N. Philips, 16 October 1948, File No. 445/48-AN, Andamans Files, 1948, NAI, Italics mine.

[101] For details see Vazira Fazila Zamindar, *The Long Partition and the Making of Modern South Asia: Refugees, Boundaries, Histories* (New York: Columbia University Press, 2010) and Joya Chatterji, 'South Asian Histories of Citizenship, 1946–1970,' *The Historical Journal*, 55:4 (2012): 1049–71.

disputed territories between India and Pakistan. The general distrust of Muslims as fifth columnists was heightened by bitter disagreements between the new nations over the division of territory and the allocation of resources. While the dispute over Kashmir had escalated into a full-scale war, uncertainty regarding the political boundaries of India was widespread in 1948. Several princely states, such as Coochbehar, Tripura and Junagadh, were yet to declare their allegiance to either India or Pakistan. In September 1948, independent India resorted to military force to enforce Hyderabad's 'accession', fuelling rumours of retaliation by Pakistan.[102] Moreover, the Radcliffe Award that demarcated the boundary between India and eastern Pakistan had left both parties dissatisfied. There were intermittent border skirmishes and persistent rumours of a Pakistani invasion. According to a secret telegram sent by the central intelligence officer based in Calcutta, 'Secret information indicates possibility of Pakistan attack on Tripura State on same lines as in Kashmir. Infiltration of Muslim League supporters and dissemination of propaganda literature have begun within Tripura.'[103] According to another source, 'the Muslim League National Guards in East Bengal are carrying on open propaganda that Tripura State belongs to East Pakistan and that preparations are being made to invade Tripura.'[104] Given this atmosphere of suspicion and hostility, both India and Pakistan were eager to secure their borders. While both states had resorted to militarisation in the western frontier, in the east more insidious tactics of recruiting civilians to paramilitary bodies and clearing the border areas of infiltrators was pursued. The *Ansar Bahini* (Volunteer Army)[105] of Pakistan found its mirror twin in the *Bangiya Jatiya Rakshi Dal* (Bengal National Protection Brigade) of West Bengal.[106] In both the Bengals, local officials regularly hatched plans of cleansing the border areas of the 'other' community.[107] While these plans were seldom followed through in post-partition West Bengal, the suspicion of all Muslims as citizens or agents of Pakistan had an adverse effect upon their mobility and security.[108]

---

[102] For details see Taylor C. Sherman, *Muslim Belonging in Secular India: Negotiating Citizenship in Postcolonial Hyderabad* (Cambridge: Cambridge University Press, 2015).

[103] T.G. Sanjevi, Intelligence Buruau, New Delhi to V. Shankar, Private Secretary to Honorable Minister of Home Affairs, Durga Das (ed.), *Sardar Patel's Correspondence*, Vol. 5 (1972), p. 425.

[104] Ibid.

[105] Willem Van Schendel, 'Working Through Partition: Making a Living in the Bengal Borderlands', *International Review of Social History*, 46: 3, (2001), 393–421.

[106] Haimanti Roy, *Partitioned Lives: Migrants, Refugees, Citizens in India and Pakistan, 1947–65* (New Delhi: Oxford University Press, 2013).

[107] Willem van Schendel, *The Bengal Borderland: Beyond State and Nation in South Asia* (London: Anthem Press, 2005).

[108] See Chatterji, *Spoils of Partition* (2007), pp. 181–94.

In this insecure collage of provinces and princely states in various stages of national integration, the Andaman and Nicobar Islands was India's only type D province, directly administered by the central government. Though its allegiance to India was not disputed, at the time of independence its population was in steep decline. While the Japanese interregnum had nearly halved the population of the Islands, the period of post-war reconstruction saw further decline in numbers due to the abolition of the penal settlement. This was followed by a decision to pardon and offer free repatriation to all surviving convicts. By 1947, the Andaman Islands' civilian population was down to a mere 14,500.[109] Of these, 2,440 were Burmese and expected to be repatriated.[110] According to Iqbal Singh, among the 12,000 who remained, there were roughly equal numbers of Hindus and Muslims, with Hindus enjoying a slim majority of 500–600 people.[111] Since the religious break-up of Andaman's population is not available until 1951, there is no way to confirm this claim. What we know for certain is that the Muslim population of the Andaman and Nicobar Islands was entirely confined to the Andamans and numbered 4,783 in 1951.[112] Assuming that this population remained relatively stable between 1951 and 1947, and assuming that the figure of 12,000 Indians is accurate, the non-Muslim population of the Andaman Islands enjoyed a slim majority of 2,434 in 1947. Since the Karens and Anglo-Indians settled in these islands would be enumerated as Christians, it is likely that the actual difference between the numbers of Hindus and Muslims in the Andaman Islands was closer to Iqbal Singh's claims of a few hundred. Whatever the exact numbers, a majority of anything between 500 and 2,500 was a fragile one. It could easily be overturned through immigration. In the post-partition world of unsettled belongings and spiralling territorial disputes between India and Pakistan, this was hardly a situation that inspired confidence.

The government of India was acutely conscious of the importance of retaining control over the Islands for strategic and defence purposes. Given the contemporary political context, the government was particularly sensitive to the threat of Muslim spies and fifth columnists in the islands. In this ambience of paranoia, maintaining, and if possible, strengthening the slender Hindu majority in the Andaman Islands

---

[109] 'Ex-servicemen to be settled in the Andamans-Central government scheme of colonisation'; a rough draft of press release, November, File No. 259/47AN, Andaman Files, 1947.

[110] Under-Secretary of State for India, Arthur Henderson, *Hansard*, House of Commons Debates, 440, 14 July 1947, cc46-62.

[111] Singh, *The Andaman Story* (1978), p. 282.

[112] *1951 Andaman Islands Census* (1955), p. 49.

became a matter of national security. Though the paranoia about Muslim infiltration was not specific to the Andaman Islands, here it collided with the parallel impetus to bring in labourers and settlers from the Indian mainland. On the one hand, the authorities advocated large-scale immigration. On the other hand, it had to ensure that the thin majority of Hindus over Muslims was not only maintained, but also increased and consolidated. Before harnessing refugees to the schemes to develop the Andamans, the Ministry of Home Affairs was forced to follow a policy of constant scrutiny of potential migrants to screen out Muslims, as demonstrated by the Mapilla affair. The problems of following such a piecemeal procedure of population manipulation became evident in the very first attempt to regulate organised immigration.

While the first abortive scheme that allowed for settlement of ordinary citizens in the Andaman Islands was being drawn up, matters came to a head between the Chief Commissioner, Inam-ul-Majid, and the Ministry of Home Affairs over the issue of selecting 'suitable' settlers. Majid repeatedly tried to claim for himself a say in the selection procedure. He tried to extend the benefits of the scheme to those persons who had already migrated to Andamans with the intentions of settling down permanently, but who were unable to continue due to financial difficulty. He also reminded the ministry of the cosmopolitan character of the population of the Andamans and the need to maintain it.[113] His efforts earned him the allegation of being anti-refugee.[114] R. N. Philips, while agreeing that people already in the Andamans might be more efficient colonisers, refused to extend government aid to them on blatantly communal grounds.

What, of course, we will have to guard against will be to see that these settlers, who have already gone over to the islands do not belong to one particular community. We have already doubts about the loyalty of the Muslim residents of Andamans and it will be necessary to see that they do not form a great number of the category of persons whom the chief commissioner mentions.[115]

The Ministry, through its officials in Delhi, ultimately retained the power to ratify the Chief Commissioner's selection. Soon after, Majid was replaced by A. K. Ghosh, whose support for Bengali refugees ensured that there would be little resistance from him to large-scale immigration from the Indian mainland. There is no record of the final list of the first

[113] Chief Commissioner, Andaman and Nicobar Islands to the Minister of Home Affairs, 12 August 1948, File No. 259/47-AN, Andamans Files, 1947, NAI.
[114] Official Notes, 21 September 1948, File No. 259/47-AN, Andamans Files, 1947, NAI.
[115] Notes by R. N. Philips, Under-Secretary to the Government of India, File No. 259/47-AN, Andamans Files, 1947, NAI.

hundred mixed settlers of Andaman Islands, perhaps because the scheme was never implemented. However, it can be assumed with a degree of certainty that if such a list existed, an overwhelming number of 'suitable' settlers on it would have been Hindu.

This altercation brought to the fore the risks of trying to regulate the population ratio of Andaman Islands through a piecemeal process of weeding out Muslims. What the Ministry of Home Affairs needed was a policy that catered only to Hindus. The formal commitment to secularism in Nehruvian India stood in the way of formulating a discriminatory policy, which would openly exclude Muslims on account of their presumed disloyalty. The refugees offered a way out. A scheme designed exclusively for partition refugees could be easily justified on grounds of their need for rehabilitation. It also provided an effective and covert means of Hinduisation of the Andaman Islands. Unlike Assam, the Andaman and Nicobar Islands were directly ruled by the central government through the Andamans Section of the Ministry of Home Affairs. This facilitated the foregrounding of national security over and above considerations of regional aspirations and identity. Bengali refugees became the means to secure the Andaman Islands.

Sardar Patel, the Home Minister of India, had no qualms in expressing his suspicion of Muslims as potentially disloyal elements.[116] His intervention in a separate but similar context suggests that he was well aware of the unique potential of the refugees in 'right-peopling' the divided nation of India, especially its frontier regions, where the maintenance of a healthy Hindu majority was seen as essential to national security. In 1949, while encouraging the Chief Minister of Assam, Gopinath Bardolai, to utilise refugees in expanding jute cultivation in Assam, Patel argued that 'from your own point of view it would be better if you secured more Hindu immigrants who will affect in your favour the population ratio.'[117] Clearly, Patel was hinting that there could be more than one 'benefit' in allowing Hindu refugees from East Bengal to settle in Assam. Besides producing jute, the East Bengali refugees would also automatically increase the proportion of Hindus in the population of Assam, which Patel considered beneficial to local interests. The demographic situation in Assam was not as precariously balanced as that in the Andamans. More importantly, regional anti-Bengali sentiments drowned out any possibility of large-scale and state-sponsored resettlement of East Bengali refugees. Nevertheless, the formula of demographic

[116] Rafiq Zakaria, *Sardar Patel and Indian Muslims: An Analysis of his Relations with Muslims Before and After India's Partition* (Mumbai: Bhartiya Vidya Bhavan, 1996).
[117] Vallabhbai Patel to Gopinath Bardolai, 17 May 1949, in Durga Das (ed.), *Sardar Patel's Correspondence, Vol. 9* (1972), pp. 38–9.

manipulation that could be justified in the name of development and rehabilitation is clearly articulated. It was in the Andaman and Nicobar Islands that this formula found its full expression.

Between 1949 and 1953, the only people who were permitted to settle in the Andaman Islands were refugees from East Bengal. After 1953, the government of India attempted to include settlers from other regions, such as the Chotanagpur region of Bihar and the state of Travancore-Cochin, which became part of Kerala in 1956.[118] These attempts were partly the result of demands put forward by other states, especially Travancore-Cochin, for access to the colonisation scheme in the Andamans as a means of solving its problem of overpopulation. Partly, they were born of the need to maintain some degree of linguistic diversity in the population of the Andaman Islands, to guard against the very real possibility of the state of West Bengal laying a claim upon the Andaman Islands on the grounds of linguistic affinity.

Nevertheless, the argument for the special needs of refugees remained a strong one and a compromise was reached with 75 per cent of all cleared land being reserved for refugees from East Bengal. In practice, the enthusiasm of state officials for dispersing targeted populations to the Andaman Islands, such as the landless agriculturists of Kerala, was seldom matched by their people. Despite a generous package of land and loans offered to settlers who signed up for the Colonisation and Development Scheme, the Andaman Islands remained a far from appealing destination. Between 1953 and 1961, there was not a single year when settlers other than Bengali refugees made up the allotted quota of 25 per cent (see Table 2.2). Between 1953 and 1971, East Bengali refugees accounted for roughly 89 per cent of Andaman's colonisers.

Though the government of India did not directly tamper with the cosmopolitan social milieu of the Andamanese Indians, they were deliberately reduced to a minority through huge artificial growth in the population of the Andamans. The population of the Andaman and Nicobar Islands more than doubled over a single decade – from 30,971 in 1951 to 63,548 in 1961.[119] During the same period, i.e., between 1951 and 1960, approximately 2,293 refugee families or approximately 11,400 people (allowing for an average of five members in each family) were settled in the Andaman Islands alone. The ratio between Hindus and Muslims in the population of the Andaman Islands was altered irrevocably in favour of the former. The abundant supply of 'willing' Hindu settlers from the

---

[118] *Plans for taking settlers under five year colonisation scheme of Andamans during 1955*, File No. 8/22/54-AN, Andaman Files, 1954, NAI.

[119] Republic of India, *Census of India, 2001, Series 36, Andaman and Nicobar Islands, Final Population Totals* (New Delhi: Controller of Publications, 2003), p. 16.

Table 2.2: *Displaced Families Settled in the Andaman and Nicobar Islands, 1953–71*

Year	State of Origin	Number of Families	Area of Settlement	Region of Settlement
1953	East Bengal	97	Ferrargunj	South Andamans
1954	East Bengal	438	Rangat	Middle Andamans
	Kerala	35	Betapur in Rangat	Middle Andamans
1955	East Bengal	390	Ferrargunj & Rangat	South and Middle Andamans
	Kerala	37	Rangat	Middle Andamans
	Tamil Nadu	4	Rangat	Middle Andamans Middle Andamans
1956	East Bengal	357	Diglipur	North Andamans
	Kerala	52	Diglipur	North Andamans
1957	East Bengal	221	Diglipur	North Andamans
	Pondicherry	4	Rangat (Betapur)	Middle Andamans
1958	East Bengal	194	Mayabunder	North Andamans
	Kerala	6	Ferrargunj	South Andamans
1959	East Bengal	217	Mayabunder	North Andamans
	Tamil Nadu	14	Diglipur	North Andamans
	Bihar	120	Rangat (Baratang)	Middle Andamans
1960	East Bengal	250	Mayabunder	North Andamans
	Tamil Nadu	17	Diglipur (Milangram)	North Andamans
	Bihar	64	Diglipur (Ramnagar)	North Andamans
1961	East Bengal	228	Port Blair (Havelock)	South Andamans
	Kerala	14	Port Blair	South Andamans

Table 2.2: (*cont.*)

Year	State of Origin	Number of Families	Area of Settlement	Region of Settlement
	Bihar	13	Diglipur	North Andamans
1967	East Bengal	323	Mayabunder (Billiground)	North Andamans
1969–1971	East Bengal	375	Little Andamans	Little Andamans

Source: Figures compiled from various files of the Andamans Section of the Ministry of Home Affairs, Government of India, National Archives of India, New Delhi.

refugee camps of West Bengal enabled India's national government to disguise its blatant exclusion of Muslims from state-aided colonisation as a special consideration towards refugees. The political will to Hinduise the population of the Andaman Islands had little to do with West Bengal's refugee crisis. It was born of the prevalent anxiety regarding the loyalty of Muslims in independent India and a tendency among sections of India's political and bureaucratic elite, especially Sardar Patel, to 'right-people' frontier regions and key services, such as the police force, by replacing disloyal Muslims with Hindus. In the Andaman Islands, the ability to carry through this project of Hinduisation, justified in the name of national security, was provided by the thousands of Bengali refugees who languished in unhygienic and crowded camps strewn across West Bengal. It was through them, and through an opportunistic utilisation of their misery, that the government of India securely moored the Andaman Islands to independent India.

Conclusion

The history of refugee resettlement in the Andaman Islands provides a necessary corrective to received wisdom on partition refugees. The rehabilitation of refugees born of the partition of India is usually studied as an autonomous sphere, cut off from other contemporary agendas of governance. Scholars have acknowledged the impact of myriad political goals and calculations on the fate of refugees, such as a need to compensate for loss of governmental authority in post-partition Punjab and an ethnonationalist fear of being overwhelmed by Bengalis in Assam.[120] The entire

[120] Barua, S., *India Against Itself: Assam and the Politics of Nationality* (New Delhi: Oxford University, 1999).

pattern of relief and rehabilitation of East Bengali refugees in West Bengal is understood in terms of contemporary politics, ranging from the political motivations behind B. C. Roy's dispersal of refugees outside West Bengal,[121] to the communist infiltration of grassroots refugee organisations such as the UCRC.[122] There is little doubt that calculations of electoral gain or loss played a crucial role in the response of different political parties to West Bengal's refugee crisis. However, as this exploration of motives and agendas behind refugee resettlement in the Andamans reveals, patterns of rehabilitation of partition refugees were not just the by-product of self-serving political agendas. Rehabilitation, as a field of governance, was permeated by other contemporary agendas of nation-building and frequently overdetermined by the greater goal of national development.

Independent India viewed its burden of refugees through the lens of national development. Within West Bengal, the arithmetic of development was mainly used to disenfranchise refugees. However, as the pattern of colonisation of the Andaman Islands reveals, the tendency to privilege national development above rehabilitation did not necessarily entail a negative outcome for refugees. The determination of the national government to outdo its colonial predecessor in developing the Andamans opened up a space of opportunity for refugees. Those willing to don the mantle of pioneers in remote regions, such as the Andaman Islands and Dandakaranya, and face up to the associated risks and hardships, could gain access to significant state support. Schemes where Bengali refugees could contribute to national development by growing paddy and jute in different parts of the country evolved simultaneously with West Bengal's regime of rehabilitation. While the former recast refugees as productive citizens, the latter had the singular aim of protecting the state's political economy from the negative impact of too many refugees. The underlying rationality that imposed a certain coherence upon these contradictory responses was the conviction that rehabilitation had to be harmonised with the broader contemporary goal of nation-building. However, the meaning and context of nation-building and the requirements of projects of national development varied from place to place and shifted over time. Being Hindu privileged Bengali refugees as suitable settlers of the Andaman Islands within a discourse of nation-building that focused on security. In sharp contrast, being Bengali worked against them in Assam, where regional ethno-nationalism trumped any concern regarding

---

[121] Chatterji, *Spoils of Partition* (2007).
[122] Prafulla K. Chakrabarti, *The Marginal Men: The Refugees and the Left Political Syndrome in West Bengal* (Calcutta: Naya Udyog, 1999).

insecure borders. In sum, refugee rehabilitation in post-partition India was a complex and shifting sphere of state intervention that interacted in diverse and often unpredictable ways with contemporary processes of nation-building.

While independent India's pursuit of national development inevitably moulded its policies towards partition refugees, the reverse was also true. The presence of millions of partition refugees fed post-colonial dreams of rapid development of 'backward' areas. The Indian government's grand plans of large-scale colonisation and development of the Andaman Islands could not have been conceived, let alone implemented success-fully, without the pool of 'willing' settlers provided by thousands of refugees languishing in camps in West Bengal. The same was true of the Dandakaranya Development Project. Thus, the attempt to harmonise refugee rehabilitation and development generated a pattern of state inter-vention in 'backward' areas that privileged outsiders, in this case, Bengali refugees, as both the agents and the main beneficiaries of development. These 'backward' regions were invariably tribal areas, where Bengali refugees became the main agents for expanding settled agriculture and therefore, instrumental in the alienation of tribal communities from their lands. This had serious long-term consequences. In Tripura and Dandakaranya, this mode of development was directly responsible for the political alienation of local indigenous communities.[123] By far the most negative impact of refugee-led development has been borne by the 'primitive tribes' of the Andaman Islands. The Onges have been confined to a tiny settlement in Little Andaman Island to make room for Bengali refugees through a process that amounted to 'ethnocide.'[124] In the Middle Andamans, the Bengali settlers' growing needs of land and resources have put them in a collision course with the very survival of the Jarawas.[125]

In the immediate aftermath of partition, the architects of these schemes anticipated no negative outcomes. If anything, recasting East Bengali refugees as agricultural pioneers seemed to offer a productive way forward that could resettle thousands of displaced persons without hampering national development. The successful experiment in the Andaman

---

[123] For Tripura see Harihar Bhattacharyya, 'The Emergence of Tripuri Nationalism, 1948–50', *South Asia Research*, 9: 1 (1989), 54–71. For Dandakarnaya, see Saagar Tewari, *Guns Against Bows: Making Central India Through Development Narratives*, unpublished PhD thesis, Jawaharlal Nehru University (2009).

[124] Venkateswar, *Development and Ethnocide* (2004).

[125] Pankaj Sekhsaria and Vishvajit Pandya (eds), *The Jarawa Tribal Reserve Dossier: Cultural & Biological Diversities in the Andaman Islands* (Paris: UNESCO, 2010). and Uditi Sen, 'Developing *Terra Nullius*: Colonialism, Nationalism, and Indigeneity in the Andaman Islands', *Comparative Studies in Society and History*, 59:4 (2017), 944–73.

Islands paved the way for envisioning the Dandakaranya Development Project as a national solution to the crisis of rehabilitation in the eastern sector. In effect, the planners and policy makers of independent India were making space for refugees by re-imagining them as idealised citizens of the post-colonial nation: productive and hypermasculine agents of national development. However, the burden of conforming to this role fell disproportionately upon the poorer refugees. Given that West Bengal's refugee camps were resource-strapped and makeshift affairs, which were run with apathy at best and criminal neglect at worst, middle-class refugees avoided them at all cost. For the East Bengali refugees who had spent years waiting for rehabilitation in various camps, to be recast as agents of development was a tall order. It made state aid in rebuilding their lives conditional upon their ability to perform the role of pioneers. There were many who embraced this opportunity. But not everyone was willing to sign up for a pioneering adventure in remote and unfamiliar geographies. Neither did all refugees have the ability to perform this ideal of productive citizenship. The violence and dislocation of partition had broken apart many refugee families, and created a large number of widowed and abandoned women. A survey conducted in 1955 enumerated 491,000 single-member refugee families living outside government camps.[126] A hypermasculine ideal of rehabilitation, designed to re-establish the patrilineal heterosexual family, by definition excluded single men and women. Not all refugees in the camps were agriculturists, and given the deeply stratified agricultural economy of East Bengal, not all those who were classified as agriculturists had the ability to plough land. Moreover, those who entered government camps were usually the poorest among the refugees. Years of poverty, overcrowding and unsanitary conditions had led to a general decline of health among poorer refugees, both inside and outside camps. The government of West Bengal reacted with alarm to the high incidence of tuberculosis among East Bengali refugees, treating it as a public health hazard and making special provisions of free treatment and care. However, the poverty and malnutrition that lay at the root of the problem was never addressed, leading to a persistent pattern of disease among refugees.[127] Men with health issues were ill-suited to the role of pioneers, and this became one of the main challenges facing the administrators of Dandakaranya.[128]

---

[126] State Statistical Bureau, *Rehabilitation: A Statistical Survey* (1956), p. 2.

[127] For details see Committee of Review of Rehabilitation Work in West Bengal, *Report on Medical Facilities for New Migrants from East Pakistan in West Bengal* (New Delhi: Ministry of Supply and Rehabilitation, 1971), pp. 9–24.

[128] Saibal Kumar Gupta, who was the Chairman of the Dandakaranya project during the 1964 refugee crisis, blamed the government of West Bengal for the malnourished and

It is perhaps this regressive pattern of rehabilitation in West Bengal that demanded the most – in terms of initiative and stamina – from those refugees who had the least to spare that contributed to the negative image of Bengali refugees as a 'problem'. Received wisdom on the aftermath of the partition of Bengal understandably treats the official tendency to blame the 'camp refugees' for failures of rehabilitation with suspicion. Where government-sponsored studies accused refugees of dependency on dole, Joya Chatterji exposes a completely unviable scheme of resettlement in Jirat.[129] Similarly, where official publications lament the apparently inexplicable unwillingness of Bengali refugees to be resettled outside West Bengal, historians have sided with the refugees by arguing that such dispersals were often coercive and could, in some cases, amount to exile.[130] However, these sympathetic readings also have the unintended consequence of reducing camp dwellers to unidimensional victims of an apathetic regime of rehabilitation. This is partly because received wisdom largely relies upon reading against the grain of official records when it comes to analysing the experience of refugees who were dispersed from government camps. The voices of poor refugees who were settled outside West Bengal is entirely absent from this analysis. This is in sharp contrast to the wealth of material available on urban and middle-class Bengali refugees who avoided government camps so as to build illegal squats in and around Calcutta. Their struggles to rebuild lives and resist eviction have been richly represented in Bengali popular culture, through theatre, film and literature. In recent years, their voices and experiences have also been chronicled in a variety of popular vernacular publications, that range from memoirs and local histories to more systematic anthologies of interviews. This richness of material invariably informs historical scholarship, resulting in a Calcutta-centric bias. Histories of squatters' colonies tend to be rich explorations of refugee politics, memories and quotidian struggles. However, as soon as the focus shifts to government camps, this richness gives way to flattened descriptions of suffering and allegations of exile. The dispersed refugees are usually represented as hapless victims. The next chapter speaks to this imbalance within partition historiography. It focuses on refugees who had spent anything between a few months to several years in various refugee

sickly condition of the new migrants sent to the project site. See *Kichu smriti, kichu katha (A Few Memories, A Few Stories)* (Calcutta: Manasi, 1994), p. 122–6.

[129] Joya Chatterji, '"Dispersal" and the Failure of Rehabilitation: Refugee Camp-dwellers and Squatters in West Bengal', *Modern Asian Studies*, 41:5, 2007, 995–1032.

[130] For example, see Sabyasachi Basu-RoyChowdhury, 'Exiled to the Andamans: The Refugees from East Pakistan' in Pradip Kumar Bose (ed.), *Refugees in West Bengal: Institutional Processes and Contested Identities* (Calcutta: Calcutta Research Group, 2000), pp. 106–41.

camps in West Bengal before being sent off to the Andaman Islands. It combines archival resources with oral history interviews, conducted with a cross-section of refugees resettled in the Andaman Islands. Camp dwellers felt the full brunt of the regime of rehabilitation, ranging from apathy to dispersal. Since they had to become agents of national development in order to access rehabilitation, their voices are crucial in understanding how this particular pattern of rehabilitation was negotiated 'from below'. The next chapter attempts to bring to the study of refugee experiences of camp life and dispersal a richness and nuance that has hitherto been reserved for the histories of middle-class refugees of squatters' colonies. What emerges are innovative and contingent negotiations of a regressive regime of rehabilitation, and complex articulations of agency and identity, which far exceed any unidimensional understanding of exile or victimhood.

Part II

Rebuilding Lives

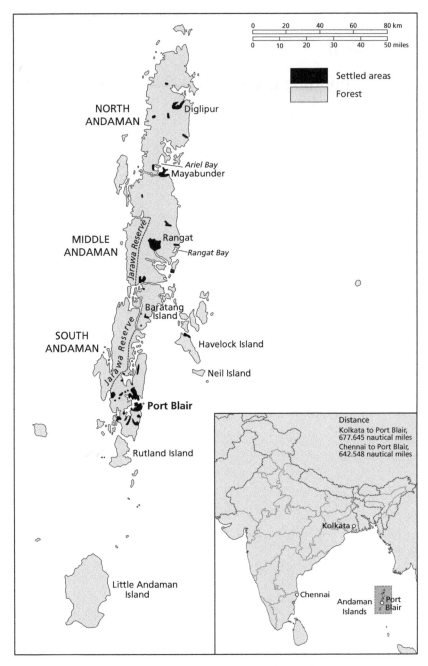

Map 3.1: Andaman Islands showing settled areas in 1961

3   Exiles or Settlers?

Caste, Governance and Identity in the Andaman Islands

Introduction

'Purbo-bonger mati to pray shesh- ekhon sob Andamaner mati ...'
'Those (born) of the soil of East Bengal are almost extinct – now all are of Andaman's soil ... '

Anonymous customer, Diglipur

This comment, which was casually thrown at me by a customer at a grocery shop in Diglipur, translates poorly into English. Diglipur is the headquarters of a *tehsil*[1] by the same name in the North Andamans. In my attempt to locate Bengali refugees who had been resettled in the valleys of Diglipur region between 1956 and 1961, shopkeepers of Diglipur market, servers in local 'rice-hotels'[2] and school teachers emerged as the most resourceful informants. Through a striking use of metaphor, the comment underlined the practical difficulty of locating such respondents. The customer represented people, much like Hindu deities of clay, as built of the soil of their birthplace. Refugees who had travelled to the Andamans from camps in West Bengal were thus composed out of East Bengali clay, unlike their descendants born in the islands. My fieldwork in Andamans was conducted in January 2007, when first-generation refugees were fast dwindling in numbers due to illness and old age. Nevertheless, 27 first-generation refugees spread over different villages of the Middle and North Andamans were willing to talk about their experience of being resettled in these islands. Conversational interviews, conducted in village huts, tea stalls and paddy fields, provided a variety of voices from below. Using

---

[1] The Union Territory of Andaman and Nicobar Islands is divided into two districts: the Andaman Islands and the Nicobar Islands. The Andaman Islands are further divided into five *tehsils* for the purpose of local administration.

[2] Basic, one-room eating joints which serve home-style Bengali food. The menu in such 'hotels' is limited to 'rice-plates' which include rice and accompaniments, sold usually in two pre-set combinations, one including fish and the other excluding it. Such hotels can usually be found near nodes of public transport or in markets, all over West Bengal. They cater to people of modest means, including traders and drivers and other workers in the informal economy.

refugee reminiscences in conjunction with official statistics, this chapter reconstructs this largely forgotten episode of refugee resettlement in the Andaman Islands.

Today, the Bengali population in the Andaman Islands consists of both resettled refugees and later migrants. The most recent disaggregated data comes from 1998, by which time there were 57,948 Bengali refugees in the Andaman Islands.[3] This is a predominantly rural population. Leaving aside a handful of refugee settlements in the tourist hub of Havelock Island, and some well-connected villages in the outskirts of Port Blair, the vast majority live in remote villages. This posed a few logistical challenges when it came to conducting oral history research. While roads were relatively well-maintained and many villages could be reached easily by foot from the nearest bus stop, the availability of overnight accommodation was limited to Port Blair, the tourist hub on Havelock Island and the three *tehsil* headquarters of Rangat, Mayabunder and Diglipur. This automatically limited the field of inquiry to villages which could be covered within a day's trip from these towns. This limited spatial focus was not a huge hindrance as my main goal was to locate and interview respondents from different batches of refugees sent to the Andamans between 1949 and 1971. A 'batch' consisted of all the refugees who began their journey from Calcutta together, aboard the same ship. Once in the Andamans, they got broken up into smaller groups and resettled in different areas of the Islands. Thus, neighbouring villages more often than not came from different batches and were settled in consecutive years. In the Andamans, the memory of this process structured the way the habitation of space was conceptualised in everyday conversations. Individual families and even entire neighbourhoods or villages were routinely described as the part of a particular batch, such as the 1949 batch or the 1953 batch. If there had been several trips in the same year, they are further distinguished as the first or second batch of a particular year. This peculiar pattern of settlement, and its continuing relevance in everyday negotiations of space and identity, lent itself well to the method of snowball sampling that I used to identify respondents.

My first informants in Havelock Island, Rangat and Port Blair were people closer to my own social milieu – middle-class professionals and

---

[3] Andaman and Nicobar Commission for Backward Classes, *Report of the Andaman and Nicobar Commission for Other Backward Classes* (2001), http://www.and.nic.in/Citizen%20Services/tw/obcPart%20V.pdf, last accessed on 15/5/2014. In this report, the refugees are called 'post-42 settlers'.

'mainlanders' who had migrated for work. The initial names and addresses of a handful of first-generation refugees came from the local librarian at Havelock Island, an administrative officer of the government of West Bengal who conducted annual audits in the Andaman Islands, and a school principal in Rangat. Due to the continuing relevance of a refugee's 'batch', the very first interview set off a chain reaction of identification of respondents.

Each interviewee was able not only to point me to possible respondents who were neighbours and friends, but also to provide information on surviving 'head-families'[4] of his own 'batch' settled in other villages. I started my enquiry in Havelock Island, followed by five days each in Rangat in Middle Andaman, and Diglipur in North Andaman. I ended my fieldwork in the villages around Port Blair, in South Andaman, where the earliest batches had been resettled. Here, both the numbers of surviving '*puraton lok*' or old-timers and their willingness to be interviewed dropped precipitously. As the vast majority of my interviewees were illiterate and wary of written forms, I proceeded with recorded verbal consent instead of thumb-prints on forms. These interviews were largely the 'hit and run' encounters,[5] typical of oral history research that uses popular memory to map the meanings and plebeian negotiations of a particular event or process, as opposed to the exploration of life stories of individuals.[6] While the refugee reminiscences collected in this manner by no means constitute an exhaustive survey of the memories and attitudes of Bengali settlers in the Andamans, they nevertheless provide valuable insight into how refugees who entered various camps in West Bengal negotiated the regime of rehabilitation. When read in conjunction with conventional archival sources, these reminiscences reveal how a project of dispersal from the camps of West Bengal was reinterpreted at the ground level, by officials and refugees, in unexpected and often ingenious ways.

---

[4] 'Head-family' was liberally used to refer to the male head of the household who was the main recipient of rehabilitation benefits on behalf of his family.

[5] Nita Kumar, *Friends, Brothers, and Informants: Fieldwork Memoirs of Banaras* (Berkeley, Los Angeles and London: University of California Press, 1992).

[6] Methodologically, I have drawn heavily upon Alessandro Portelli's approach to oral history, as seen in his 'The Peculiarities of Oral History', *History Workshop Journal* 12, No. 1 (21 September 1981): 96–107, and Alessandro Portelli, *The Death of Luigi Trastulli and Other Stories: Form and Meaning in Oral History*, First Edition (Albany, NY: State University of New York Press, 1990).

Refugees from East Bengal building huts at Andaman and Nicobar Islands.

Figure 3.1: East Bengali refugees build huts at the Andaman Islands.
Source: ABP Archives

Refugees from East Pakistan at South Andaman.

Figure 3.2: Refugees from East Pakistan at South Andaman Islands,
1951

Locating Refugee Voices: The Landscape and Social Milieu of the Andaman Islands

The 300-odd islands that constitute the Andaman archipelago are clustered into three groups: the Great Andaman, the Little Andaman and numerous outlying islets, many of which are unnamed and uninhabited. Though the Great Andaman region appears to be an undivided strip of land, stretching from north to south, narrow creeks divide it into four separate islands. These are called North, Middle and South Andaman. The much smaller Baratang Island is often treated as a part of Middle Andaman. In the Great Andamans, several forested hill ranges run parallel to each other from north to south. Numerous creeks and straits cut into these highlands. The ranges are interspaced by narrow valleys with freshwater streams flowing through them.[7] Colonisation of the Great Andamans spread from south to north and from coastal valleys and bays in the East to sites further inland and westwards.[8] In terms of patterns of resettlement, three clear phases corresponding to three main regions can be discerned. The refugees who arrived between 1949 and 1951 were settled entirely in South Andaman Island. The first batch of 198 refugee families were fortunate to be allotted cultivable lands which had either been abandoned by the 'Local Born' people fleeing Japanese repression, or left fallow due to repatriation of pardoned Indian and Burmese convicts in 1945.[9] Subsequent batches were allotted partly cleared or jungle land. They were expected to turn this land into paddy fields through their toil. By 1952 the Indian government had resettled 350 displaced families in South Andamans. They were mostly settled in already existing villages, in close proximity to the older settlers, such as the Andamanese Indians of Chauldhari, Burmese of Mamyo, Bhantus of Ferrargunj and Mappilas of Stewartganj[10] (see table 3.1).

---

[7] Parmanand Lal, *Andaman Islands: A Regional Geography* (Calcutta: Anthropological Survey of India, 1976).

[8] Unless stated otherwise, the summary of colonisation and resettlement that follows is pieced together from different files of the Andamans Branch of the Ministry of Home Affairs, Government of India, accessed at the National Archives of India, New Delhi.

[9] Government of India, *Administration Report on the Andaman and Nicobar Islands, 1945–46* (Delhi: 1946). The 'Local Born' was the term used to pejoratively refer to the descendants of convicts and ex-convicts in the Andaman Islands. They renamed themselves Andamanese Indians in 1948. However, by 2007 both nomenclatures of Local Born and Andamanese Indian had given way to 'pre-42 settler'.

[10] Detailed description of the first phase of refugee settlement is available in Surajit Chadra Sinha, *Report on the Possibilities of Further Resettlement of East Pakistan Refugees in Andaman Islands* (Calcutta: Anthropological Survey of India, 1952). I am grateful to Ananta Kumar Biswas for sharing his personal copy of this detailed report, as it could not be located in any other library or archive (henceforth *Report on East Pakistan Refugees*).

Table 3.1: *Refugees Settled in South Andaman Island, 1949–52*

No.	Villages/Areas	Total Population (Families)
1.	Manpur	147 (30 families)
2.	Tushnabad	25 (5 families)
3.	Colinpur	55 (13 families)
4.	Temple Myo	46 (9 families)
5.	Herbertabad	67 (12 families)
6.	Tirrur	68 (14 families)
7.	Chhauldari	182 (42 families)
8.	Craikabad Farm	34 (7 families)
9.	Port Mouat	21 (4 families)
10.	Brindaban	17 (3 families)
11.	Mathra	63 (14 families)
12.	Garacharama	18 (5 families)
13.	Monglutan	129 (24 families)
14.	Guptapara	134 (35 families)
15.	Humphreygunj	91 (16 families)
16.	Wandur	144 (32 families)
17.	Sipighat	35 (9 families)
18.	Shoal Bay	193 (51 families)
19.	Namunagarh	19 (6 families)
20.	Labour Barracks	13 (15 families)
21.	Nayashar	7 (44 families)
	Total	1,583 (350 families)

Source: Figures are taken from Surajit Chadra Sinha, *Report on the Possibilities of Further Resettlement of East Pakistan Refugees in Andaman Islands* (Calcutta: 1952), p.5

The second phase of settlement began in 1952, with piecemeal schemes giving way to a five-year policy of colonising the Great Andamans. The location and scale of refugee resettlement also changed. Between 1953 and 1955, colonisation focused upon creating new settlements in the Rangat and Betapore regions of Middle Andaman. In 1954 alone, 438 refugee families were settled in Rangat *tehsil*, thus more than doubling, in a single year, Andaman's population of refugee settlers. In 1956, a new phase of colonisation started in North Andamans with the opening up of the Kalpong river valley. Between 1956 and 1960, the areas around Diglipur remained the focus of refugee resettlement. Thus, the three phases of colonisation in the Andaman Islands corresponded to three distinct regions: the scattered ex-convict settlements and new villages of the South Andamans, new settlements near

Rangat Bay in the Middle Andamans, and new settlements in the Diglipur region of North Andaman, stretching inland from Ariel Bay (see map 3.1).

However, there were exceptions to this general pattern. In 1955, in response to a special request of the West Bengal government, the local administration of the Andamans found room for additional refugee families in the Ferrargunj region of South Andaman, and in the hitherto uninhabited Havelock Island.[11] With the settlement of another 181 families in 1961, Havelock developed into a distinctive and compact island society of Bengali refugees. Though the policy of resettling Bengali refugees was discontinued in 1964, there were several one-off settlement schemes offering various inducements to displaced families from East Pakistan. For example, between 1964 and 1966, a labour corps of 323 refugee families, named the *Rashtriya Viaks Dal* or National Development Corps, was put to work in North Andaman to clear a large valley of forests. In 1967, this led to a settlement consisting of several villages, known as Billiground.[12] Eighty-three refugee families, who were brought over as a permanent labour force for the rubber plantation at Katchal, ended up as waged labourers for the Forest Department on Neil Island.[13] As the area under colonisation expanded, so did the demand for Bengali-speaking clerks, administrators and medical compounders in the new settlement areas. Many educated single men among Bengali refugees were quick to apply for employment in such far-flung projects of rehabilitation, which simultaneously solved their twin problems of employment and accommodation. This provided another avenue for the migration of Bengali refugees to the Andamans. In 1950, 66 such educated young men reached Port Blair to take up employment under various departments of the administration of Andaman Islands.[14] Many among them, such as Benilal Samaddar, spent their entire working lives in the Islands and eventually settled there.[15] No systematic record of recruitment to the labour force of

---

[11] Administrative Report of the Andaman and Nicobar Islands, File No. 55/16/54-AN, Government of India, Ministry of Home Affairs, Andamans Branch, 1954, National Archives of India, New Delhi (henceforth Andaman Files, 1954 etc., NAI).

[12] Interviews with Nimchand Majumdar, Amulya Sutar and Kamalakanta Biswas, Harinagar village, Billiground, Middle Andaman, 31 January 2007.

[13] They were eventually given 2 hectares of agricultural land each and settled on Neil Island in 1967. This data was collected by Mr. A. K. Biswas for official use by the Bengal Association, Andaman and Nicobar Islands (BAANI).

[14] 'Memo No. 2/719, Office of the Labour Officer, Port Blair, 17/8/1950', personal collection of A. K. Biswas, Manglutan village, Andaman Islands.

[15] Interview with Benilal Samaddar, Rampur Village, Middle Andaman, 31 January 2007.

Andamans is available for the period of colonisation. The settlement records exclude not only the Bengali refugees who migrated for work, but also various one-off schemes of refugee resettlement between 1964 and 1971, which did not follow the pattern of colonisation. Moreover, once colonisation picked up pace, there were numerous instances of the friends and relations of the early settlers joining them in search of shelter and livelihood, without any government assistance. For example, Sushil Chandra Biswas of Kalsi village left Nehru Colony, one of the squatters' colonies of south Calcutta, to rebuild his life in Middle Andaman Island.[16]

At the final count, the Andaman Islands provided shelter to many more displaced families than the official number of 3,060 families. In everyday conversations, this diversity was evoked by referring to some families of East Bengali refugees as 'withouts'. In Andaman Islands' variant of spoken Bengali, the 'withouts' consisted of both self-funded East Bengali migrants and refugees brought over to the islands on a variety of work contracts who did not own land. Along with English words like 'settler' and 'batch', 'without' has also made its way into the local lingo, accruing its island-specific meaning in the process.

While recording the reminiscences of refugees in the Andamans, I attempted to select respondents who reflected the diverse patterns of resettlement. My respondents were drawn from four main regions of refugee resettlement: Diglipur and its surroundings in North Andaman, Rangat and its surroundings in Middle Andaman, the villages of Havelock Island in South Andaman, and Billiground in Middle Andaman.[17] They mostly consisted of men who had been the head of their respective households and the women who travelled with their husbands and children. The respondents from Diglipur and Rangat region correspond to the second and third phases of colonisation. Unfortunately, it was not possible to trace any first-generation refugees from the first phase of settlement around Port Blair. This gap is to some extent addressed by a detailed survey of the first phase of refugee resettlement conducted and published in 1952, under the aegis of the Anthropological Survey of India.[18] I obtained a copy of this study, which has been lost to archives in mainland India, from Ananta Kumar Biswas of Monglutan village, whose father was one of the earliest settlers of Andaman Islands. The interview with Mr Biswas yielded a wealth of information on the distinctive pattern of settlement in South Andaman

---

[16] Interview with Sushil Chandra Biswas, Kalsi Village, Middle Andaman, 3 February 2007.

[17] For a complete list of all interviews, see Bibliography.

[18] Surajit Chadra Sinha, *Report on East Pakistan Refugees in Andaman Islands* (1952).

Island.[19] Besides his childhood reminiscences, he also shared documents and facts and figures accumulated through a lifetime of amateur historical research into Bengali settlements. Several respondents from Havelock Island revealed the peculiar features of colonisation in the later years, when refugee settlements spread to the outlying smaller islands. The three interviewees of Billiground represent how top-down changes in policy affected the pattern of refugee resettlement in the Andamans after 1964.[20]

Despite this diversity of refugee experiences, born of changing patterns of settlement in the Andaman Islands, several common themes can be discerned in the reminiscences. The most immediate and striking commonality was in the pattern of self-identification. Without exception, the refugees resettled in the Andaman Islands referred to each other and self-identified as 'settlers'. As a result, my queries regarding the whereabouts of refugees or *udvastu* had to soon be modified to questions regarding *puraton* or old settlers in order to be legible in the social milieu of contemporary Andamans. Secondly, in every single narration of their journey to the Andamans, the erstwhile refugees chose to begin their reminiscences in a refugee camp in India. The names of ancestral villages left behind in eastern Pakistan were almost never mentioned, unless in response to a specific question. All the respondents spoke at length of the decision to enrol for the colonisation scheme. The refugees who finally reached the Andamans were mostly recruited from various camps in West Bengal, though a few were recruited from camps in Madhya Pradesh and Orissa. Their reminiscences contradict the notions of passivity and victimhood usually associated with East Bengali refugees who entered government camps. Every refugee-settler I interviewed described their journey to the islands as a choice. These narratives of choice go against the grain of administrative reports, which stress the careful selection of suitable refugees. They also challenge the characterisation of the journey to the Andamans as 'exile' or 'banishment', which was rampant in contemporary West Bengal, and continues to inform recent scholarship.[21] While reminiscing about their pasts, refugees in the Andamans dwelt on their minor victories over various figures of state authority, such as camp superintendents and settlement officials. Foregrounding these everyday

---

[19] Interview with Ananta Kumar Biswas, Manglutan Village, South Andaman, 10 February 2007.

[20] A complete list of the interviews is provided in the bibliography.

[21] For example, see Sabyasachi Basu-RoyChowdhury, 'Exiled to the Andamans: The Refugees from East Pakistan' in Pradip Kumar Bose (ed.), *Refugees in West Bengal: Institutional Processes and Contested Identities* (Calcutta: Calcutta Research Group, 2000), pp. 106–41.

acts of resistance brings to light how even a fundamentally repressive regime of rehabilitation cannot preclude the agency of those subjected to it.

Colonising the Andamans: Local Refiguring of National Policy

As described in chapter 2, refugee resettlement in the Andamans owed its origins to a marriage of convenience between the government of India's need to develop these islands and Dr B. C. Roy's determination to disperse East Bengali refugees. It paid little heed to the aspirations of the local population of Andamanese Indians, and lesser still to the welfare of the indigenous tribes of the Andamans. However, when it came to the execution of the colonisation scheme, local exigencies determined the pace and manner of implementation. Topography, climate, local infrastructure and the habits of governance born of the long history of exploiting forest resources in the Andamans, all played a role. Conflict of interest between the different agencies involved, innovations by ground-level officials, and above all, surprises thrown up by the largely unmapped terrain, shaped the project in unexpected ways. For the refugee families, the land on which they were resettled shaped their experience of rehabilitation and their memories. In order to make sense of their reminiscences, it is essential to locate them in the Andamans as they found it, not the increasingly popular tourist destination that they inhabit today.

The decision to establish a penal settlement in the Andamans had led to the planned clearing of forests in the area around Port Blair, which, like the rest of the islands, had been covered in dense forests in March 1858. Gradually, ad hoc clearance of forests to build the penal settlement gave way to an attempt to exploit the forests of South Andamans for timber. The Forest Department was established in 1877, and with the identification of Andaman Padouk or *Pterocarpus Dalbergioides* as commercially valuable timber, its activities expanded steadily.[22] By 1943, the department used nearly 100 elephants to extract timber and had expanded its activities to cover the Middle and North Andamans. It suffered from a perennial shortage of labour.[23] The expansion of settled agriculture in the Andamans lagged far behind the expansion of forestry. Cultivation was

---

[22] Forestry in the Andamans began with a rudimentary establishment of sixty convict labourers and seven elephants, confined to limited logging in the forests adjacent to the settlement in South Andamans. See *Report on Forest Administration in the Andamans, 1885–1948* (Delhi: Manager of Publication, Government of India, 1885–1948).

[23] Ibid.

confined to a few villages in South Andaman Island. This slow pace of settlement was largely due to the difficulty faced in attracting settlers from the Indian and Burmese mainland. Before 1949, isolated villages of Karens, stray relatives of ex-convicts, and a few families of labourers recruited from the Chotanagpur region who had settled near Port Bonington (later renamed Mayabunder) constituted the only agricultural settlements that existed outside South Andaman. The total population of the islands in 1948 was 15,532.[24] When the refugees arrived in the Andamans, more than nine-tenths of the island was covered in dense forest, interspersed with narrow clearings where the forest workers and bush policemen lived in temporary camps. The dense tropical forest and the island's peculiar topography of ridges and narrow valleys not only shaped the experience of rehabilitation in the Andamans, it also constituted the biggest challenge for planners and officials in charge of schemes of colonisation.

When the government of India sanctioned a scheme to resettle 200 refugee families in the Andamans, it did not explain how this was to be implemented.[25] The task of finding a way to implement the scheme was left to a team of experts, led by H. R. Shivdasani, who reached Port Blair on 24 January 1949. Besides Shivdasani, the team consisted of A. P. Hamilton, the Inspector General of Forests, R. L. Sethi, the Agricultural Commissioner, and De Mellow, the Superintendent Engineer of the Central Public Works Department. Within two months the team produced its report on the 'possibilities of colonization and development of the Andaman and Nicobar Islands'.[26] Contrary to its name, the report performed a limited function. The resettlement of Bengali refugees had already been sanctioned by the authorities in Delhi, as had the decision to expand agriculture in the Andamans to promote self-sufficiency in food. Shivdasani's team was merely expected to identify areas suitable for colonisation, outline a working plan for implementing it, and advise the government on ancillary requirements, such as transport, communications and

---

[24] Based on the total number of ration cards issued in February 1948. This number excluded the severely marginalised aboriginal people of the Islands, namely the Great Andamanese, Jarawas, Sentineles and Onges whose total population was estimated to be around 1,000 in 1953. For details see Appendix A of *Census of India 1951*, Vol. 17, *The Andaman and Nicobar Islands* (Republic of India, 1955), pp. xliii–xlvi.

[25] Manmohan Kishan, Assistant Secretary to the Government of India, Ministry of Rehabilitation to the Ministry of Home Affairs, File No. 33/1/50-AN, Andaman Files, 1950, NAI.

[26] H. R. Shivdasani, *Report on the Possibilities of Colonization and Development of the Andaman and Nicobar Islands* (New Delhi: Government Press, 1949), p. 1 (henceforth *Shivdasani Report*).

healthcare. However, practical constraints faced by Shivdasani and his team further limited the scope of their work.

No detailed surveys of the Andaman Islands existed in 1949. The surveys meticulously prepared between 1930 and 1935 had been lost during Japanese occupation. Using South Andaman's network of motorable roads,[27] the team could inspect most of the South Andaman sites listed as suitable for colonisation. However, in the Middle and North Andamans, it managed to reach only six of the forty possible sites of colonisation. Here, forest paths and tramlines used by the Forest Department to transport timber were the only means of reaching the inland river valleys flagged for settlement. To cut a long story short, this team of experts not only relied heavily on the Forest Department for transport and guidance, but also largely replicated the information provided by its officials with little or no verification. The sites recommended for settlement were often the forested valleys which had already been earmarked for clear-felling. The true genius of the Shivdasani Report was in setting out an action plan for implementing refugee resettlement where the 'present lack of knowledge' did not 'hold up the work of settlement.'[28] Shivdasani instructed the local administration to inform the authorities in Delhi about the extent of cleared land available in November every year. The report had to include details regarding the location and nature of land available by specifying if the land was 'flat land, terraced land, paddy cultivation land, garden land, coconut land'.[29] The number of settlers would be calculated accordingly and recruited in the period between November and February. The actual work of settlement was reserved for a relatively dry and cool period, between 15 February and 31 March each year. In other words, the hapless refugees were expected to fill in the blanks created by the felling and clearing activities of the Forest Department.

This pattern of settlement left ample room for conflict of interest between the needs of the settlers and the priorities of the Forest Department. The latter regarded the instruction to clear large tracts of forest for cultivation as an irksome imposition. Moreover, its officials inevitably selected to clear 'compartments' of forests rich in commercially valuable timber.[30] As the South Andaman forests had been

---

[27] In the South Andamans, the roads ended at Beadonabad in the west and Bumlitan in the south, beyond which the survey team had to continue on foot. For details see Shivdasani Report (1949), pp. 79–80.

[28] Ibid., p. 32.   [29] Ibid.

[30] Partly due to the absence of comprehensive surveys of forested lands and partly due to the constant changes in the nature of timber in demand, timber extraction in the Andamans has never followed a central working plan. Instead, surveys to evaluate the commercial timber contained in numbered sections of the forests have been undertaken on an annual

exhausted of valuable timber through selective felling during the 1930s, the Forest Department preferred working in the forests of Middle and North Andamans. But these areas were completely cut off from the older settlements of Port Blair and lacked even the basic amenities of sedentary life. Shivdasani did attempt to prioritise the needs of the refugees by insisting that the gradual outward extension of the zone of settlement was vital to the success of the colonisation scheme.

One of the essentials of success of the scheme is to start as close to existing habitation and headquarters as possible and then gradually extend outwards so that new comers do not feel lost. With this outward progress communication and other facilities should also continue to expand in the same direction. Thus it would be advisable if out of the area already described as available, as much as possible is first cleared in the South Andamans.[31]

This ideal of the gradual and continuous spread of colonisation was seldom adhered to in practice. It was followed only with regard to the first batch of settlers, and that too at Shivdasani's insistence. The Chief Commissioner, Inam-ul-Majid, advocated resettling the first batch of displaced families in the Rangat region of the Middle Andamans, since the forest there had already been worked heavily. Shivdasani strongly opposed this plan, insisting that the refugees be settled on 3,000 acres of previously cultivated land, lying fallow in South Andaman. According to him, the Rangat region would be unsuitable for the refugees as it was completely isolated. Shivdasani's concern for the well-being of refugees was largely born of practical calculations.

No one can deny that the success of the scheme will depend very much on the kind of reports the first settlers send about local conditions and treatment etc. received by them. The propaganda value of what happens to the first contingent is considerable ... They should be put on the most easily workable land and should be as near as possible to civilization.[32]

No such considerations were deemed to be necessary for later batches.

The land allotted to refugee families who arrived in the Andamans between 1950 and 1952 was far from 'easily workable'. There were often long delays in allotting land, and many refugees started working as forest labour in order to repay their loans. Seventy-eight families who reached the Andamans in 1951 were allotted plots that were either completely covered in jungle, or riddled with the tree stumps. Fifty-one refugees

basis. These enumerated sections, known as compartments, have then been worked out depending upon the availability of labour and transport.
[31] Shivdasani Report (1949), p. 34.   [32] Ibid.

who reached in 1952 were allotted forested land in the Shoal Bay region.[33] According to S. K. Gupta, some of the refugees who arrived in 1950 and 1951 'volunteered to go to jungle areas, which they will themselves clear and till.' He describes 'the little community of Mandals at Wandur, hacking away trees' as an encouraging and refreshing sight.-[34] However, according to Surajit Chadra Sinha, local officials put these refugees to work immediately after their arrival. 'Profiting by the experience of earlier settlements' the administrators 'gave them no respite to feed fat on cash doles.'[35] These conditions were largely born of the recalcitrance of the Forest Department, which was determined to not undertake commercially unprofitable clearance of forests. The condition of the land allotted forced the refugees to adopt 'jhum' or a variant of slash and burn pattern of cultivation in the initial years of settlement. They used spades instead of ploughs to turn the earth and scattered seeds over the virgin soil. Most spent the first few years burning leftover tree stumps to clear their plots. The refugee-settlers had to put in years of work clearing the land of tree stumps, roots and rocks before it could actually be ploughed.

In sum, the practical needs and rhythms of timber exploitation took precedence over the needs of the colonisers in the Andaman Islands. In the ultimate analysis, Shivdasani too privileged efficient forestry over the basic needs of the settlers. He conceded that despite its isolation, Rangat would have to be colonised in 1949–50, simply because 'a good deal of felling has been done there and if that area is not used in the next year much of the work already done will be lost by future growth of shrub and secondary jungle'.[36] He hoped that by 1951–2, with the spread of colonisation to the North and Middle Andamans, internal communications would improve and 'people settled further north will not feel cut off'.[37] His hope remained unfulfilled for years. Development of transport, roads and communication lagged far behind the work of refugee resettlement. The dispersal of Bengali refugees to remote settlement sites, lacking the most basic amenities of sedentary life, set the tone for the lived experience of rehabilitation in the Andaman Islands.

---

[33] Sinha, *Report on East Pakistan Refugees in Andaman Islands* (1952).

[34] 'Appendix A, The Andaman and Nicobar Islands, by Shri S. K. Gupta, IAS, Deputy Commissioner and Superintendent of Census Operations', *Census of India 1951, Vol. 17, The Andaman and Nicobar Islands* (Republic of India, 1955).

[35] Sinha, *Report on East Pakistan Refugees in Andaman Islands* (1952), p. 5.

[36] *Shivdasani Report* (1949), p. 34.   [37] Ibid.

The colonisation of Middle Andaman Island began in 1953 with 52 refugee families,[38] followed by an additional 408 families in 1954. After spending a few months in transit camps,[39] they were settled in Rangat, Nimbutalla, Amkunj, Tomachaung, Bomlungta and Panchwati.[40] In the South Andamans, the refugees were transported in lorries used by various government departments, to their transit camps.[41] In the Rangat region of the Middle Andamans, the settlement officers merely reversed the Forest Department's process of transporting timber in order to carry their human cargo of refugees to resettlement sites. The refugees were offloaded from the ship SS *Maharaja* onto an LCT or Landing Craft Tank. The Forest Department of the Andamans had acquired a few LCTs left behind by the Japanese occupation forces during the Second World War; and had used it since to transport timber from makeshift jetties of the Middle and North Andamans to the harbours of Port Blair or Mayabunder (Port Bonington). These rafts were now used to drop off refugees on beaches close to their colonisation sites. From there, the refugees walked to their transit camps, following the forest paths along which elephants had earlier dragged out timber. As colonisation proceeded inland, the settlers of more remote sites were ferried in on boats along creeks or rivers.

Once at their settlement sites, the refugees were stranded and clamoured for public transport. The government of India was slow to provide a public bus service in the South Andamans, where a few metalled roads already existed. However, in the North and Middle Andamans, the absence of roads made land transport impossible. By the end of 1956, only 1 mile of the planned 83 miles of new roads had been built. As a desperate measure, the Chief Commissioner, S. N. Maitra, converted a captured Chinese pirate boat into a passenger carrier. This provided rudimentary ferry service in the colonisation area.[42] By 1961, the situation had improved marginally, but was still far from adequate. A bi-weekly steamer service, connecting Port Cornwallis with Mayabunder and Port Blair, operated in tandem with a local ferry service in North Andaman Island. A proposed road connecting

---

[38] Interview with Jagabandhu Das, Dasarathpur Village, Middle Andaman, 1 February 2007.

[39] Transit camps similar to the barracks used to house labourers in forest camps were built in advance near the clear-felled land or jungles identified for resettlement. Each barrack was divided into ten rooms with attached verandahs, which could be used as kitchens. Each room was meant to house one refugee family.

[40] File No 55/16/54-AN, Subject: Administration Report of the Andaman and Nicobar Islands, Andaman Files, 1954, NAI.

[41] Interview with Mr. Ananta Kumar Biswas, Manglutan Village, South Andaman, 10 February 2007.

[42] File No 55/16/54-AN, Subject: Administration Report of the Andaman and Nicobar Islands, Andaman Files, 1954, NAI.

the Ariel Bay Jetty, from which the ferry operated, to the local town and administrative headquarters of Diglipur was yet to be built. In the Middle Andamans, a solitary unmetalled road connected the northern town of Mayabunder to southern regions, including Rangat. However, no buses plied this road and it was, therefore, of little use to local villagers. Walking long distances remained the only reliable means of transport in the new villages of Middle and North Andaman. In South Andaman, the fortunate few settled close to Port Blair enjoyed access to metalled roads and a rudimentary public bus service. The vast majority of Bengali refugees were hemmed in between dense jungles and the sea for the first ten or fifteen years. To succeed in this unfamiliar terrain, they were forced to adapt and innovate. Refugee memories of rehabilitation largely revolve around the hardship endured during the early days of colonisation, and the strategies they employed to rebuild their lives.

Selecting Suitable Settlers: Caste as an Administrative Tool

'Ei bhabe bachai korte korte ... shob paribarke niye jai ... Tabuo ora majhe majhei paliye ashar cheshta korto' ...
'In this manner I would select and take all the families .... Yet they would often try to run away'.

Sadhan Raha, tehsildar and settlement officer, Middle Andamans[43]

The resettlement of Bengali refugees in the Andamans did not start well. Of the 200 families selected in 1949, two never left Calcutta and ten more returned from the Islands. Sections of the press promptly reported this as a 'failure' of the scheme, leading to much consternation and soul-searching within the administration.[44] The Chief Commissioner of the Andamans, A. K. Ghosh, dismissed the reports as exaggerated. He explained that the majority had adapted well, and accused those who had returned of bad faith. 'They never had any intention of doing real work and returned as soon as the cash doles ceased'.[45] Besides criticising the 'malcontents' among the first batch of refugees, Ghosh placed the lion's share of the blame for this debacle upon the government of West Bengal. He argued that West Bengal's officials had selected the wrong type of people and had misled them regarding conditions in the Andaman Islands.

---

[43] *Anandabazar Patrika*, 15 January 2005.   [44] *Hindustan Times*, 11 September 1949
[45] 'Administrative Report on the Andaman and Nicobar Islands for the Period ending 15/10/49', in File No. 53/10/49-AN, Andaman Files, 1947, NAI.

The real trouble is that tall promises were made to them at the time of selection, and they were given to understand that they were coming to a land of plenty, a land as fertile and as easily worked as that they had recently abandoned. As a result, few of them expected to have to do pioneering work, or work so hard.[46]

Learning from this experience, the Chief Commissioner insisted that in the future, the final selection of all settlers was to be made by an officer of the islands' administration deputed to the mainland. This was meant to 'weed out' undesirables and ensure that the refugees selected were of 'the required type'. The careful selection of suitable settlers therefore became an integral part of the colonisation project.

By 1952, the selection of the 'right type' of men from the refugees scattered over various camps of West Bengal was seen as the key ingredient for successful resettlement. However, the records reveal little about what constituted the desired 'type'. Though A. K. Ghosh scathingly criticised the government of West Bengal for 'the type of persons sent', he did not elaborate his notions of a suitable settler. His successor as Chief Commissioner, S. N. Maitra, was more forthcoming. In a letter to the Home Ministry, he explained that unsuitable selections in the first batch consisted of agriculturists who were 'middle class men who had never used their hands for work' and 'artisans who did not know the use of the plough'.[47] In other words, the ideal settlers, in the eyes of the state, were people who were accustomed to manual labour and proficient in paddy cultivation. Middle-class men were considered to be wholly unsuitable. But by what means could officials ascertain the class and occupational background of refugees in government camps? Usually, middle-class refugees avoided entering government camps at all costs. Nevertheless, many well-to-do families, who had lost everything in the riots and lacked the social contacts essential for 'self-settlement', were forced to seek shelter in the camps. Inside the camps, every refugee family was subjected to the same regime of subsistence. In order to ascertain their occupational background, officials had little choice but to depend on the information provided by the refugees regarding their backgrounds. This led to frequent allegations of deception and suspicion of fraudulent claims. For selection to be effective, the officials required some independent means of ascertaining the social and occupational backgrounds of refugees. The

---

[46] A. K. Ghosh, Chief Commissioner, Andaman and Nicobar Islands to H. J. Stooks, Deputy Secretary to the Government of India, Ministry of Home Affairs, 24 September 1949, in File No. 53/10/49-AN, Andaman Files, 1949, NAI.

[47] S. N. Maitra, Chief Commissioner, Andaman and Nicobar Islands to the Secretary to the Government of India, Ministry of Home Affairs, New Delhi, 28 November 1953, in File No: 8/8/53-AN, Andaman Files, 1953, NAI.

responsibility for devising some means of effective selection fell upon Sadhan Raha.

In 1949, Raha was a *tehsildar* with the Andamans administration, though he was later promoted to the post of Assistant Commissioner of the Settlement Division of Middle Andaman. By his own admission, Raha decided to use caste as a convenient marker for identifying suitable settlers.[48] According to him, the refugees in the first batch were of the 'wrong' caste.

I saw that the upper caste people who had never farmed the land were not being able to work with the plough and bullocks, or the iron implements. Yet, in the Andamans, there was no way out of working with your own hands ... Hence, these people were failing to earn a livelihood and returning (to Calcutta).[49]

According to Raha, he was able to bring Dr B. C. Roy around to his view. After 1951, he had the full cooperation of the authorities in West Bengal and the active help of the state's Rehabilitation Commissioner, Hiranmoy Bandyopadhyay, in selecting 'suitable' refugees from the camps. There are no archival records of caste-based selection of settlers. His claims are largely corroborated by refugee reminiscences regarding the activities of the ubiquitous '*Rahasaheb*'. However, the strongest evidence of the systematic use of caste is provided by the results of Raha's intervention. The 178 families who were sent to South Andaman in 1949 were a mixed group in terms of caste. Nearly a third of these families were from dominant castes, consisting of 26 *brahmin* and 25 *kayastha* families. Many more belonged to traditionally non-agriculturist castes such as *napit* (barber) and *sutradhar* (or carpenter). The single largest group consisted of 85 *Namasudra* families, who were the erstwhile *chandals* or untouchables of the south-eastern marshy districts of eastern Bengal. After Sadhan Raha had taken charge of selecting suitable settlers, 51 refugee families reached Andamans in 1952. They were, without exception, *Namasudras*.[50]

Thus, in selecting 'suitable' refugees for the colonisation project of the Andamans, Sadhan Raha went one step further than weeding out the unsuitable castes. From the mixed population in the camps, he only selected *Namasudras* as colonisers. The *Namasudras* of Bengal often used high-caste surnames and had no obvious physical markers that distinguished them. Nevertheless, identifying caste background was easier than distinguishing genuine tillers of the soil from those who

[48] Sections of interview of Sadhan Raha, published in *Anandabazar Patrika*, 15 January 2005.
[49] Ibid.
[50] All figures are taken from *Report on East Pakistan Refugees* (Calcutta, 1952).

might have drawn their income from agriculture in East Bengal, but had never actually ploughed the land. Refugees often lied about their past occupations in order to increase their chances of rehabilitation.[51] However, the refugees were far less likely to lie about their caste background, especially if it entailed a demotion in caste status. The *Namasudras* also had a distinctive sociocultural profile which might have aided Raha in his selection procedure. The majority of poor *Namasudras* were illiterate and belonged to the *Matua* sect, founded by Harichand Thakur.[52] While devotion to Harichand Thakur could be easily ascertained from conversation, the evidence from oral history suggests that Raha certainly used illiteracy to identify 'suitable' settlers.

Lakshmikanta Ray of Sabari accused the authorities of selecting illiterate men on purpose. According to him, the authorities deliberately excluded any refugee who was educated as they believed that an uneducated population would be more compliant.

Later it came to such a pass that unless they could see (the man signing with) a thumbprint, they would not bring him. They would not bring the ones who could sign their names. There was an incident about this with a certain Biswas. It (the settlement) first happened at Port Blair. There was a B.A. pass amongst them – he was brought over, as refugee. An argument with the DC ensued. Then he said to Sadhan Raha, he was then the Tahsildar- 'Hey, why have you got these (people)? These who answer back to me? In English? Didn't I tell you to select and bring only those who get by with thumb prints?'[53]

Other informants confirm that there was indeed a graduate among the refugees settled near Port Blair. But his name was Benoy Chakraborty.[54] According to Benilal Samaddar, an educated refugee who had been appointed by the Labour Force Department of Andamans in 1950, the entire population of Bengali settlers in the Andamans had at most twenty men who had completed schooling and a single graduate.[55] While Lakshmikanta Ray's story might not describe a historical incident, it is a good indicator of how settlers felt disadvantaged by their high levels of

---

[51] See chapter 1.

[52] *Matua* was a plebeian sect of rural East Bengal, which drew upon the traditions of the *Bhakti* movement and repudiated Brahminical orthodoxy. It drew its following almost exclusively from the Namasudras. For details see Sekhar Bandyopadhyay, *Caste, Protest and Identity in Colonial India: The Namasudras of Bengal, 1872–1947* (London: Curzon, 1997), pp. 30–54.

[53] Interview with Lakshmikanta Ray, Sabari village, Middle Andaman, 1 February 200

[54] Interview with Benilal Samaddar, Rampur village, Middle Andaman, 31 January 2007; and list of settlers provided by A. K. Biswas from the records of the Bengali Association of the Andaman and Nicobar Islands.

[55] Interview with Benilal Samaddar, Rampur, Middle Andaman, 31 January 2007.

illiteracy. The contrast with the largely white-collar population of the squatters' colonies of Calcutta could not be starker.

All available evidence suggests that Sadhan Raha's literacy and caste-based selection of colonisers was a success, with rates of desertion plummeting among the colonisers.[56] The system worked largely because it exploited the conjuncture between social and economic inequalities that characterised East Bengal before partition. The *bhadralok* gentry consisting largely of the dominant castes (*brahman, kayastha and baidya*) had virtually monopolised ownership of the reclaimed low-lying districts of eastern Bengal.[57] Their rent-paying tenants were either Muslims or *Namasudras*. Though the capital for reclamation and colonisation had come from upper-caste Hindus, the labour, more often than not, had been provided by the *Namasudras*. With 95.71 per cent engaged as tenant-farmers, a more accurate description of this 'agricultural caste' would be 'peasant caste'.[58] Perhaps the *Namasudras* of East Bengal brought to the colonisation project of Andamans an ability to adapt born of older histories of colonisation, albeit of a very different land.

Though caste-based selection was the brainchild of Sadhan Raha, it was adopted enthusiastically by the government of West Bengal. Naren Haldar recalled strategies of recruiting colonisers targeted specifically at *Namasudra* refugees.

Here, amongst us Bengalis, you must have heard of Jogen Mandal? ... He came to our camp and addressed a meeting. He told us, if you want proper food, clothes etc., go to Andamans. There is no place like Andamans.[59]

Jogendranath Mandal was a prominent *Namasudra* leader who had established the Bengal branch of Ambedkar's Schedule Caste Federation. He was the sole schedule-caste member of the provisional cabinet of the new province of East Bengal, who resigned and sought refuge in India after the February riots of 1950.[60] By the 1950s, largely in response to the rising politicisation of refugees in West Bengal, the refugee camps had become heavily policed spaces. It would have been impossible for Jogendranath

---

[56] Sinha, *Report on East Pakistan Refugees in Andaman Islands* (1952).

[57] For a history of the dominance of the *bhadralok* in the Bengal delta see Iftekhar Iqbal, *The Bengal Delta: Ecology, State and Social Change, 1840–1943* (Basingstoke: Palgrave Macmillan, 2010).

[58] *Bandyopadhyay, Caste, Protest and Identity in Colonial India* (1997), p. 21.

[59] Interview with Naren Haldar, Nimbutala village, Middle Andaman, 1 February 2007.

[60] For the details of the political career of Jogendranath Mandal, see Bandyopadhyay's *Caste, Protest and Identity in Colonial India* (1997), Masayuki Usuda 'Pushed towards the Partition: Jogendranath Mandal and the Constrained Namasudra Movement' in H. Kotani (ed.), *Caste System, Untouchability and the Depressed* (New Delhi: Manohar, 1997), and Jagadischandra Mandal, *Mahapran Jogendranath Mandal*, Vols. 1 and 2 (Calcutta: 1975).

Mandal to address Naren Haldar inside a government-run work-site camp, in Bardhaman, without the active connivance of state authorities. Though he was reduced to a marginal figure in the political milieu of West Bengal, he retained a degree of influence among *Namasudras*. By allowing Mandal to address camp refugees, West Bengal's Ministry of Relief and Rehabilitation was clearly trying to use his influence over *Namasudra* peasants to convince the latter to enrol in the colonisation scheme of the Andaman Islands.

Over and above possessing first-hand knowledge of agriculture, the pioneering settlers of the Andamans were also required to be '*karmatha*' or able-bodied and '*parisrami*' or hard working. Here too, the *Namasudras* fitted the bill. They enjoyed a reputation for masculine prowess which Bengali men in general were believed to lack. The tribal population and Dalit of Bengal were the exceptions to the rule of the 'effeminate' Bengali man. Stereotypes born of colonial ethnography, such as the effeminate Bengali *bhadralok* and the masculine *Namasudra*, enjoyed wide currency in colonial Bengal, not just among administrators, but also in the self-representations of the *bhadraloks* and *Namasudras*.[61] The history of refugee resettlement in the Andaman Islands suggests that despite its public disavowal as a category of governance, caste lost none of its administrative potency in post-colonial India.[62] Stereotypes born of colonial ethnography often resonated with deeply ingrained local prejudices and found new currency among the bureaucrats and administrators of independent India. This might explain why Sadhan Raha's plan of caste-based selection found ready purchase with the government of West Bengal.

The reminiscences of the refugees resettled in the Andamans suggest that those 'selected' were acutely aware of the process and criteria of selection. Most respondents described how older and middle-aged men were usually excluded, and how *Rahababu* physically checked the arms and hands of refugees to ascertain their familiarity with manual labour. Many had found this process humiliating. In an essay that narrates the first '*Durgapuja*' or worship of the goddess Durga organised in Diglipur town, Dhirendranath Sadhak, a second-generation settler, links the humiliating selection procedure to a lack of social status. The essay begins with a conversation of Bimal Mandal, a refugee-settler of

---

[61] See John Roselli, 'The Self-image of Effeteness: Physical Education and Nationalism in Nineteenth Century Bengal', *Past and Present*, 86 (1980), 121–48; and A. K. Biswas, *The Namasudras of Bengal: Profile of a Persecuted People* (New Delhi: Blumoon Books, 2000).

[62] For both the public disavowal of caste tables from census reports of independent India and its persistence within administrative practices, see Asok Mitra, *The Tribes and Castes of West Bengal* (Alipore: West Bengal Government Press, 1953).

Diglipur with *Mastarda*,[63] a local teacher who was previously in the army. In response to *Mastarda's* instructions to prepare for the festival, Bimal replies:

What preparations can I make? Neither do I know how to write, nor do I have any knowledge. If it wasn't so, would Rahababu have brought me to the Andamans after pressing and probing my hands and arms?[64]

As a result of this peculiar pattern of selection, the majority of the new villages established in the Andamans were inhabited solely by *Namasudra* peasants. Far from seeing the absence of dominant castes as liberating, many colonisers found it inconvenient and unnatural. In the recent past, the *Namasudras* had launched a movement demanding social respect. Even in the remote Andamans, they lost none of their determination to secure social respectability. They demanded the customary services of *brahmins* (priests) and *napits* (barbers): the former to conduct the rites of birth, marriage and death, the latter to perform the lowly task of shearing hair and clipping nails, which no status-conscious *Namasudra* would stoop to. According to Narayan Dutta of Havelock, the government met the settlers' demands by including a few *brahmins* and *napits* in the later batches of colonisers.[65]

The Bengali society that emerged in the villages of the Andaman Islands is stamped with the distinctive sociocultural markers of the *Namasudra* community. The refugees built temples dedicated to Harichand Thakur and even named their settlements after their preferred deities. Harinagar, Radhanagar, Krishnanagar and Gobindanagar are some of the names chosen by the settlers. This offers a striking contrast to the urbane squatters of Calcutta who mostly chose secular names, such as Azadgarh and Bijoygarh. They also frequently chose to commemorate a national leader or nationalist hero in naming their colonies. Netajinagar, Gandhinagar, Khudiram Nagar, Bagha Jatin and Arabinda Nagar are all examples of this practice. Religion also played an important role in promoting social interaction across the scattered and remote settlement sites in the Andaman Islands. Each spring, devotees of Harithakur congregate in Havelock Island from all over the Andamans to participate in an annual extravaganza of *kirtan* or devotional songs. The social and cultural gulf that separates the *bhadraloks* from the *Namasudras* is no

---

[63] The English word master, pronounced *mastar*, is frequently used in colloquial Bengali to refer to a teacher. It is usually suffixed with *da*, meaning elder brother, or *mosai*, meaning mister to express respect.

[64] Dhirendranath Sadhak, '*Diglipurer pratham Durga Pujo* – 1958 (The first *Durga Pujo* of Diglipur)', *Dwip Bangla, sharadiya sankhya*, (Island-Bengal, Autumn edition), pp. 95–9.

[65] Interview with Narayan Dutta, Havelock Island, 28 January 2007.

less visible in these Islands. A small population of Bengali government servants posted at Port Blair mostly maintain a contemptuous distance from the peasants of rural Andamans.

Opting for the Andamans: Choice and Agency Among Camp Refugees

Raha saheb to anbe na, amra jor kore ashchi-
Raha saheb would not bring us (to the Andamans), we forced our way in
                                                        Naren Haldar, settler[66]

Despite the zeal of Sadhan Raha and the willing cooperation of the West Bengal government, the extent of actual control the authorities had over the selection process was limited by several factors. First, there were the constraints of working within a newly independent state. Despite its apathy towards refugees from East Bengal, neither the government of India nor the government of West Bengal could publicly afford to endorse the forced relocation of refugees to the Andamans.[67] The strong association of these islands with the colonial practice of transportation and imprisonment of freedom fighters made such an option impolitic. Instead, the state had to rely on propaganda and various tactics of persuasion to enlist settlers. This is borne out by the reminiscences of the refugees. Though several respondents spoke of government propaganda regarding the Andamans, none mentioned coercive dispersal. In actual practice, the 'selection' of refugees was largely a negative procedure. It was used to weed out unsuitable persons from among those refugees who had already signed up as potential colonisers. Secondly, though the state played an authoritative role in moulding the day-to-day life of the camp refugees, it had limited influence on the choices perceived and exercised by them. Every single respondent represented their journey across the *kalapani* as the result of a conscious choice. This choice, though severely constrained by a repressive regime of rehabilitation, was nevertheless informed by a variety of external factors, over which the state had no control. Thirdly, the interviews suggest that officials often failed to stick to the criteria of selection. A number of first-generation refugee-settlers bragged about forcing their way into the colonisation scheme, despite Sadhan Raha's opposition. This suggests that the resettlement of refugees in the Andaman

---

[66] Ibid.

[67] After 1964, the stance of the government of West Bengal had hardened considerably, with refugees being dispatched for Dandakaranya almost as soon as they arrived. However, the bulk of refugee resettlement in the Andamans happened during the 1950s, when the regime of rehabilitation had comparatively greater room for negotiation. For details on shifts in refugee policy, see chapter 1.

Islands is inadequately understood either as a 'forced diaspora'[68] or as 'exile'.[69]

Every single interviewee foregrounded their own agency in choosing to cross the *kalapani*. They narrated conversations or negotiations with state officials, which resulted in that decision. In these narratives, the officials appear to engage in a variety of interactions with the refugees. They ask camp refugees to enrol in the scheme, at times they provide encouragement and detailed information, and at other times they go to great lengths, including screening a documentary highlighting the richness of soil and abundance of crops in the Andamans. Gokul Biswas of Havelock Island recalled one such interaction. 'We had *Debmosai* from rehabilitation (ministry) ... he used to organise (rehabilitation), bring people. So he asked me, will you go to Andamans? (I said,) yes, I will go. Even if it's in London I will go!'[70] Jagabandhu Das narrated a similar conversation with Sadhan Raha.

At that time the tehsildar of this region was Raha *saheb*. He went (to our camp) and said some of you people will have to go to Andamans. We said, what will happen if we agree? What will you give us? Oh damn! (Raha exclaimed) The facilities that are available in Andamans, the government here will not be able to provide. Whatever may be required for a household, all of it will be given- a tin house,[71] plough cattle, plough, etc ...[72]

Both Naren Haldar[73] and Sukharanjan Mridha remembered making an informed choice to go to the Andamans over and above other possible sites of dispersal.

While we were at that camp, the call came- asking us where we would go for rehabilitation? (Among options) there was Andamans, Nainital, Coochbehar; then there was Madhya Pradesh, Andhra Pradesh. In this manner they called out. People could enrol their names for where they wished to go.[74]

---

[68] Joya Chatterji, *The Spoils of Partition: Bengal and India, 1947–67* (Cambridge and New York: Cambridge University Press, 2007).

[69] Sabyasachi Basu-RoyChowdhury, 'Exiled to the Andamans', in Pradip Bose (ed.), *Refugees in West Bengal* (2000), p. 130.

[70] Interview with Gokul Biswas, Havelock Island, 29 January 2007.

[71] The 'tin houses' the settlers speak of were actually wooden houses with asbestos roofs, which were promised to them as a part of the colonisation scheme. In some areas, such as Rangat, the authorities built the houses out of the total monetary grant allotted to every family. In other areas, such as Havelock Island, the authorities provided the settlers with the necessary materials and the cost of labour and they were left to construct their own houses.

[72] Interview with Jagabandhu Das, Dasarathpur Village, Middle Andaman, 1 February 2007.

[73] Interview with Naren Haldar, 1 February 2007.

[74] Interview with Sukharanjan Mridha, Kalsi Village, Middle Andaman, 4 February 2007.

In sum, refugee voices from the Andamans contradict received wisdom, as well as Calcutta-centric popular memory, where dispersal to the Andaman Islands is primarily seen as an act of exile or banishment.

These reminiscences provide valuable examples of how refugees in government camps negotiated the prospect of dispersal outside West Bengal. Communist accusation of political motivations behind the Congress government's insistence on resettlement outside West Bengal, coupled with the failure of rehabilitation in multiple sites in Bihar, Orissa and Madhya Pradesh, has led historians to highlight the coercive aspects of this policy.[75] However, for refugees stuck in crowded and unhygienic camps, the prospect of dispersal was not necessarily unwelcome. Moreover, while B. C. Roy's insistence on the saturation of West Bengal enforced a second process of displacement upon the most vulnerable among the refugees, who were completely reliant on government help for rehabilitation, it nevertheless left them some element of choice regarding their eventual destination. The process of dispersal of camp refugees to the neighbouring states of Bihar, Uttar Pradesh and Orissa, which had started in 1949, continued till 1960. The reminiscences of the refugees resettled in the Andamans suggest that refugees living in various camps of West Bengal were not only aware of the multiple sites of dispersal, but also kept track of the relative merits and demerits of different schemes. They resisted dispersal to patently irreclaimable lands, such as Dandakaranya, while opting for a handful of better schemes. Uttaranchal, for example, was an extremely popular destination among the refugees. After 1960–1, the situation changed dramatically for the worse. A re-evaluation of policy led to the closure of the rehabilitation ministries in all states except West Bengal. After 1961, the 'problem' of rehabilitating West Bengal's camp refugees became a 'residual' issue and was linked to the Dandakaranya project. The latter had always been unpopular among the refugees, who now became desperate to cling on to West Bengal at all costs. Thus, it was only after 1960 that options started drying up for the refugees awaiting rehabilitation in the camps of West Bengal.[76] Until then, they had exercised limited freedom in choosing rehabilitation sites. When it came to the Andaman Islands, the pressure upon local officials to resettle land before it was reclaimed by the forest made the refugees indispensable. Far from being exiled to the Andamans, the refugees were cajoled and persuaded by the officials responsible.

[75] See for example Joya Chatterji, 'Dispersal' and the Failure of Rehabilitation: Refugee Camp-dwellers and Squatters in West Bengal', *Modern Asian Studies*, 41:5, (2007), 995–1032.

[76] For details of this shift in policy, see chapter 1.

The bureaucrats and administrators in charge of implementing the Colonisation and Development Scheme were extremely conscious of the need to elicit the active participation and enthusiasm of the refugees. The ill-repute of *kalapani* and the fear of crossing the sea posed a significant hurdle. B. K. Samaddar remembered how the people in his camp, though initially attracted by Raha's description of the scheme, baulked at the prospect of crossing the sea. 'But then they reconsidered. He (Sadhan Raha) persuaded us once more- that it was a good place, that we would not face any problems in procuring fish or food, that we would get a lot of land; that we would benefit from it ... '[77] Sujata Mandal echoed these fears. 'I had no desire to come to the Andamans. Because it was *kalapani*, so far off, we would not be able to return- across the seven seas! I was scared'.[78] Gokul Biswas was the only one among 1,800 refugee families in Ashoknagar camp who agreed to travel to the Andamans. He vividly recollected the horrified reaction of his neighbours and friends.

It was almost like having a brand on my head! Hey, has your father killed a man? The people around me (said) – you will go to Andaman Nicobar? To *kalapani*? But people don't go there unless they commit murder! The government does not allow them to (go). Andaman- *kalapani*! Just the name was enough to scare people.[79]

Besides the considerable persuasive skills of Sadhan Raha, the refugees recounted other strategies, such as Jogendranath Mandal's exhortation at Shakho camp, which has already been discussed. By far the most ingenious government ploy of recruiting settlers for the Andamans emerges from the accounts of the refugees settled near Rangat, between 1953 and 1955.

After 1952, as the piece-meal schemes of earlier years gave way to a five-year plan of colonising the Andamans, there was a massive surge in demand for refugees. In 1954 alone 438 refugee families were settled around Rangat bay, followed by another 350 in 1955.[80] Given the infamy of the Andamans as place of exile, which was further bolstered by contemporary communist propaganda against the dispersal of refugees to the Andaman Islands, it was a difficult task for officials to recruit hundreds of refugee families. During this period, a documentary film of sorts on the richness of agricultural land in the Andamans, described by the refugee-settlers of Rangat as 'cinema' or 'bioscope', was screened at various refugee camps. This played a major role in inducing Sujata to overcome her fears.

[77] Interview with B. K. Samaddar, Nimbutala Village, Middle Andaman, 1 February 2007.
[78] Interview with Sujata Mandal, Janakpur Village, Middle Andaman, 4 February 2007
[79] Interview with Gokul Biswas, 29 January 2007.
[80] Figures compiled from various Andaman Files, NAI. Also see Table 2.2.

Then one day they showed us a cinema- showed us through bioscope the conditions in Andamans ... People were not willing to come ... So they showed this at Kashipur camp. After watching this I said- no, that's a land of golden crops; such beautiful crops of paddy, coconut trees, betelnut trees, gigantic pumpkins! Basically they showed us all the fields and gardens, all that was being grown around Port Blair. Then I said- if we go there, we will be able to live. So then we came to Andamans.[81]

A similar story was narrated by Sukharanjan Mridha and his wife, who came to the Middle Andamans in 1955, a year after Kalipada and Sujata Mandal. 'You know what they would show us? They would show us movies. On the movie screen they would show such things that people would forget all apprehensions.'[82] However, the hopes raised by rice paddies and giant pumpkins rapidly dissolved when the refugees encountered the ground realities of their settlement sites. All three respondents accuse the government of misleading them by deliberately excluding the dense forests and hills of the Andamans from the frame. While Sukharanjan reasoned that the 'bioscope' must have shown the better lands in South Andaman, his wife accused the government of outright fraud. 'From where they showed us such sights I do not know- I have not seen anything like it since I have come to Andamans.'[83]

For the vast majority of refugees who opted to settle in the Andamans, the primary attraction was the possibility of obtaining ten acres of good land free of cost. Added to this were the other 'facilities' promised by the government: plough cattle and a milk cow, seeds and agricultural implements, aid in constructing houses, and a maintenance allowance to tide the settlers over until the first harvest.[84] These were extraordinarily generous terms, especially when measured against the contemporary reluctance to provide any rehabilitation to East Bengali refugees within West Bengal. It was not until 1951 that the authorities were forced to concede that the thousands of Bengali refugees had no intentions of returning. Belatedly, and often reluctantly, the authorities started formulating rehabilitation schemes. Besides the negotiated dispersal of refugees to neighbouring states, authored by Dr B. C. Roy, there were also some attempts at rehabilitation of refugees within West Bengal, on 'empty lands'. However, the amount of government aid offered in most of these schemes compared poorly with the Andamans. Many more asked the

---

[81] Interview with Sujata Mandal, 4 February 2007.

[82] Interview with Mrs Sukharanjan Mridha, Kalsi village, Middle Andamans, 4 February 2007

[83] Ibid.

[84] 'Summary of the Colonisation Scheme', File No: 8/8/53- AN, Andaman Files, 1953, NAI.

impossible of refugees by expecting them to resettle successfully in patently uninhabitable tracts of land.[85] Therefore, the attraction to avail of 'facilities' provided in the Andamans continued to be a major pull factor for later settlers in the Middle and North Andamans.

The government of West Bengal sought help from pro-government Bengali dailies to publicise the success of refugee resettlement in the Andamans. During the early years of the scheme, there were regular reports in the *Anandabazar Patrika* describing the success of the project. In 1949, an elaborate report described the 'effusive welcome' accorded to the first batch of refugees in Port Blair. Careful to omit the opposition of the Local Born population to large-scale refugee resettlement, the report instead focused on the 'commendable' support of the local Bengali club and described the 'beautiful' location of the refugee camps.[86] In 1951, a special correspondent reported that even if the Andaman Islands had not become '*bhusvarga*' or 'heaven on earth' for the Bengali refugees, for those who had gone there 'life had once more found its normal course and rhythm'.[87] Besides sections of the vernacular press, the government of West Bengal found an unexpected ally in its attempts at publicity – the refugees themselves. Among the camp refugees, information travelling by word of mouth and positive reports from friends, family and acquaintances had far greater credibility and reach than government propaganda. A potent mix of press reports, letters from friends and relatives, hearsay and rumours carried information regarding various rehabilitation schemes from camp to camp. For example, refugee settlers in the Andamans frequently referred to Dandakaranya as a 'desert land,' indicating their knowledge of the scarcity of water which plagued the scheme in its early years. In contrast, the reports regarding the Andaman Islands that trickled into the camps in West Bengal were largely positive.

Many among the 1949 batch wrote letters to their friends and relatives to come and join them.[88] As a result, by October 1949, the Chief Commissioner received fifty-three applications from refugees requesting permission to come to South Andamans.[89] Sukharanjan Mridha

---

[85] For a case study of an early scheme of dispersal within West Bengal see Chatterji, 'Dispersal and the Failure of Rehabilitation, (2007) 995–1032. Also see B. S Guha, *Memoir No. 1, 1954, Studies in Social Tensions Among the Refugees from Eastern Pakistan* (Calcutta, 1959).

[86] *Anandabazar Patrika*, 16 April 1949.   [87] *Anandabazar Patrika*, 16 March 1951.

[88] Ironically, it was the 'unsuitable' nature of this batch of refugees including middle-class and educated individuals, which enabled them to write these letters.

[89] 'Administrative Report on the Andaman and Nicobar Islands for the Period ending 15/10/49', in File No. 53/10/49-AN, Andaman Files, 1947, NAI.

described how later settlers, including himself, drew courage from the example of the 1949 batch.

They had relatives in West Bengal. They used to go and say that the land is good, there are no problems. They did say; there is the problem of Jarawas, but no other problems were there. There's plenty of fish and vegetables, soil is good, paddy can be grown ...[90]

Jagabandhu Das of Rangat encouraged his younger brother to join him in Rangat. Lalitmohan Pal provided a detailed and fascinating account of how a combination of caste and kinship ties and an informal network of communication drew more refugees to the Andamans.

I decided upon Andamans because the year before in Nabagram several families had been settled. Amongst them there were two families from of our Pal clan. They were our relatives .... They wrote letters to us. They wrote in these letters that for next year, a new area called Diglipur is being cleared. That is a very big settlement area. The land there is also very good. You get your names enrolled and come .... Hearing all this, our family took a decision. Our relatives were attracted (to the scheme) ... Hearing all this, we enrolled our names.[91]

Lalitmohan Pal's account suggests that the refugees who entered government camps were not necessarily reduced to isolated family units, subject to the will of the state. They could retain a rich network of friends and relations spread across camps and various sites of rehabilitation that enabled them to make informed choices.

The government treated the patriarchal nuclear family or household as the unit of rehabilitation. However, as these narratives from the Andamans reveal, displaced families seldom functioned as discrete units. Having already lost their property and livelihoods, the refugees in camps often sought strength in numbers. The men formed groups consisting of an extended circle of relatives, past acquaintances and friendships born of a shared life in camps. Decisions regarding rehabilitation were often taken jointly. These organic associations were similar to the celebrated committees of the squatters' colonies in as much as they gave the refugees greater bargaining power with the authorities. By acting in groups, many refugees managed to foil the cynical selection process designed to pick out the 'right type' of settlers. Many first-generation refugees recounted how they had forced their way into the group selected for resettlement despite being deemed unsuitable. Naren Haldar of Nimbutala vividly recalled how he had formed a *dal* or group with Dhiren Boral and Hemanta Ray, fellow refugees he got to know at Bagjola camp. They had decided to travel

[90] Interview with Sukharanjan Mridha, 4 February 2007.
[91] Interview with Lalitmohan Pal, Madhupur village, North Andaman, 6 February 2007.

together to the Andamans. But problems arose when *Rahababu* refused to include Mr Haldar in the list of settlers.

> He wouldn't bring me because how would I manage alone in the Andamans? I would be given 30 *bigha* of land; I would have to plough the land. Back in my *desh* I had never ploughed land- workers used to do it. So he said- you won't be able to cope. I said, why wouldn't I? If everyone can do it, so can I.[92]

Naren Haldar failed every single test of a suitable settler for the Andamans. Yet, he managed to enrol his name by persisting in a group of three families. Ultimately all three men managed to procure settlements in the Middle Andamans. Lalitmohan Pal's account illustrates, with much greater clarity, how negotiating in a group enabled the refugees to subvert official selection procedure. At Supur Ambagan camp, near Birbhum, Lalitmohan banded together with six of his relatives, each 'heads' of their respective households. Determined to go to the Andamans, they turned down all other offers of rehabilitation and enrolled for the colonisation scheme. All of them had to pass the screening process, conducted by Sadhan Raha and an official of the Rehabilitation Ministry of West Bengal, for their plan to work. One by one the refugees were called into a tent set up for selection purposes within the camp and questioned. Five of the seven Pals were turned down for being too old. 'I could figure out some of what they were saying to each other. 'Old man, old man', they muttered.'[93] When Lalitmohan Pal's name was called, he and Atul Pal refused to go, though they were young and fit the desired profile. Lalitmohan explained to the officials that the seven families had decided to take rehabilitation together. At this, the earlier disqualifications were reversed and all seven families were included for resettlement in Diglipur. Through collective bargaining, the camp refugees protected their weaker or older friends and relatives from exclusion. It substantially eroded the power of the state to micro-manage the 'type' of settlers.

Despite these petty acts of subversion, it must be admitted that the scope of refugee agency remained severely constrained by the circumstances of refugee life. Though all the respondents insisted on their 'choice' to come to the Andamans, many also referred to the constrained nature of this choice. Several settlers explained how given their circumstances, the Andamans had emerged as their only viable option for rehabilitation. However, the reasons which informed this perception varied widely from one individual to the other. Lakshmikanta Ray of Sabari village had enrolled for the colonisation scheme going against the

[92] Interview with Naren Haldar, 1 February 2007.
[93] Interview with Lalitmohan Pal, 6 February 2007.

advice of Manoranjan Ray, the superintendent of his camp. When pressed
to explain his behaviour, he could do little more than recount his sense of
helplessness. 'What could I do? All the people who were staying with me
were going off (to the Andamans).'[94] Manipada Bairagi of Ghusuri camp
enrolled for the Andamans simply because most other refugees in his
camp did the same. Not all the camp refugees were equally resourceful, or
equally aware of the choices available. Many blindly followed their more
capable neighbours. Many more were driven to the Andamans by the
subhuman conditions of life in refugee camps. Sujata Mandal feared that
a prolonged stay in refugee camps would prove fatal for her children:

We had two children- they were constantly ill. Then I saw that people were dying
daily- they removed a car-load (of the dead) every morning and evening ... Seeing
all this we thought that we have come away with our children, what if we were to
lose them sitting in a refugee camp?[95]

The call to enrol for rehabilitation in Andaman Islands provided the first
opportunity to escape what appeared to be a death trap for her children.
In the ultimate analysis, Sujata's fear of losing her children outweighed
her fear of *kalapani*.

Others, like Gokul Biswas of Havelock Island, came to the conclusion
that Andamans was their only real chance of rehabilitation based on an
astute evaluation of changing circumstances. For six and a half years,
Biswas had waited for rehabilitation in Ashoknagar camp, where he had
also joined the communist-led movement demanding rehabilitation
within West Bengal. By enrolling for rehabilitation in the Andamans,
he betrayed his comrades. This perhaps can also explain his feeling of
being 'branded' for his decision, which has been discussed earlier.
Pushed to explain his change of heart, Gokul Biswas suggested that he
had run out of options, and of hope that he would ever obtain agricultural land in West Bengal. 'There was no shelter there (in West Bengal).
I didn't have money or resources, knew neither to write nor to read. How
would I survive there? So I came.'[96] The timing of his change of heart
suggests possible reasons for it. In 1958, the Government of India
launched the Dandakaranya scheme, designed to absorb the entire
population of camp refugees in West Bengal. This was followed by the
decision to close all refugee camps in the eastern sector by July 1959.
The government also decided to wash its hands of all those who refused
rehabilitation in Dandakaranya. Despite its opposition to the dispersal
of refugees outside West Bengal, the CPI-led UCRC refused to launch a

[94] Interview with Lakshmikanta Ray, 1 February 2007.
[95] Interview with Sujata Mandal, 4 February 2007.
[96] Interview with Gokul Biswas, 29 January 2007.

movement opposing dispersal. Gokul Biswas enlisted for the colonisation scheme in 1961. Biswas was lucky to get out in time. After 1961, no Bengali refugees were brought to the Andamans. His two older brothers eventually chose to go to Dandakaranya and Madhya Pradesh, while those who clung on to Ashoknagar were, according to him, still 'drifting'.[97]

The above account by no means exhausts the variety of factors which informed the choices made by the refugee-settlers of the Andamans. Several respondents cited reasons that ranged from the unexpected to the eccentric. Dasharath Barui of Havelock Island opted for the Andamans because his father, while serving in the Indian National Army under Subhash Chandra Bose, had visited the Andamans and used to speak positively of it.[98] Manoranjan Sutar of Billiground was a survivor of tuberculosis. He opted for the Andamans in the hope that exposure to the salty air of the sea would cure the last traces of the disease from his body.[99] This wide variety of reasons demonstrates the difficulty of any simplistic reading of limited choice as compulsion. It also challenges the tendency within current historiography to dismiss the displaced persons, who enrolled in government camps and eventually accessed various rehabilitation schemes, as bereft of all agency – passive victims of ill-conceived policy. There is also the opposite trend of celebrating the initiative and resourcefulness of refugees who took the path of aggressive land-grabbing and illegal construction of refugee colonies. In sum, lived experiences of Bengali refugees have more often than not been framed within the binary of agency and victimhood. In the narratives of refugee life and rehabilitation that emerge from these interviews, this binary opposition breaks down completely. Instead, there are richly textured narratives of rebuilding lives, of complex choices faced and negotiated within severely restrictive circumstances.

Landscape of Memory: Primal Forests, Remote Villages and Encounters with Jarawas

'Sei rakam to roop nai ... kothao nai je ami ekta bolbo'
'Landscape of that type no longer exists ... it exists nowhere- I can't even give you an example'

Rajlakshmi Biswas, settler[100]

---

[97] Ibid.   [98] Interview with Dasharath Barui, Havelock Island, 28 January 2007.
[99] Interview with Manoranjan Sutar, Billiground, 15 January 2007.
[100] Interview with Rajlakshmi Biswas, Sabari Village, Middle Andaman, 1 February 2007.

By 2007, when the interviews were conducted, the Andaman Islands had been radically transformed by decades of developmental activity. The population had crossed 356,152, while illegal encroachments into reserve forests raised serious concerns of environmental degradation.[101] Villagers who had once lived in fear of raids by the 'hostile' Jarawas were eager to direct tourists towards 'sighting' a member of the now 'friendly' tribe.[102] Nevertheless, every single respondent described in great detail harsher conditions of life in a very different past. For the first-generation refugees, the landscape of memories was constituted by dense forests, virgin agricultural land studded with tree trunks, and isolated nascent settlements. The familiar themes of longing for a lost homeland, trauma of displacement and nostalgia for 'remembered villages' are conspicuous by their absence.[103] Most first-generation refugees ran through the details of their displacement from East Bengal readily but dispassionately, as a necessary prologue to their lived experience of rehabilitation in the Andamans. Moulded by the landscape they gained through resettlement, instead of the landscape they left behind, the reminiscences of refugees from the Andamans strike a discordant note within the scholarship on memory and identity of Hindu Bengali refugees.[104]

When encouraged to speak about their past experiences, first-generation refugees spoke anecdotally about 'how things were' in their villages or settlement areas. Vivid, perhaps exaggerated, descriptions of the density of the forests which surrounded the settlements were by far the most common theme. The preponderance of the forests in refugee memory is unsurprising given the degree to which it dominated the landscape and dictated conditions of life during the early years of colonisation. Absence of roads or transport, and dejection born of isolation were frequently mentioned as related difficulties. The forests and the isolation of the new villages initially had a negative impact on a majority of the settlers.

---

[101] The population total has been taken from *Census of India 2001, Series 36, Andaman & Nicobar Islands. Final Population Totals: State, District, Tehsil and Town* (Republic of India, 2004)

[102] The Jarawas, long denigrated as a 'hostile' tribe, chose to initiate friendly contact with their neighbouring villages of settlers in 1997. Since then, members of the tribe, especially young men and boys, have frequently interacted with locals and tourists in order to procure food, gifts and medical care. See Report of the Expert Committee on Jarawas of Andaman Islands, June 2003, (http://www.and.nic.in/C_charter/Dir_tw/ecr/contents .htm), accessed on 14 July 2015.

[103] Dipesh Chakrabarty, 'Remembered Villages: Representations of Hindu Bengali Memories in the Aftermath of Partition', *Economic and Political Weekly*, 31:32 (1996) 2143–51.

[104] See Sandip Bandyopadhyay, 'The Riddles of Partition: Memories of the Bengali Hindus', and Pradip Kumar Bose, 'Partition – Memory Begins Where History Ends', Ranabir Samaddar (ed.), *Reflections on Partition in the East* (Calcutta: Calcutta Research Group, 1997), pp. 59–86.

The refugees from East Bengal were ill-prepared for the landscape that greeted them. As Sukharanjan Mridha of Kalsi village explained, being told in advance that they were being given lands in forested areas did little to mitigate their shock. 'It was not possible for us to even imagine jungle this dense. We had never seen forests like these ... (It was) beyond our imagination!'[105] Though the jungles which ringed the settlements were strange and unfamiliar, they provoked familiar fears. Kalipada Shikdar of Urmilapur confessed that, 'Most of us, those who were heads of the families, adults, we thought – it won't be possible to live in this country. There will certainly be tigers.'[106] The settlers had to rapidly master their fear of the jungle. Leech-infested jungle paths, which turned into chan-nels of knee-deep sludge when it rained, were the only links between refugee settlements and the nearby jetties, the local grocery store and even the streams and creeks that provided drinking water. During the early years of colonisation, an entire settlement area would be supplied by a single grocery store, located at the local jetty. For the settlers of Rangat region, buying provisions entailed a day-long trek through the jungle to the store at Kadamtala. Those settled around Diglipur faced a similar journey on foot to Kanaibabu's shop at Ariel Bay jetty. Though the forests were free of predators, fear of the Jarawas, wild boars and elephants made the men travel in groups for safety.

All the respondents stressed the 'koshto' or hardship involved in establishing new settlements. Here, narratives were often gendered. The men mostly spoke of their back-breaking labour to make the allotted land fit for cultivation. The women stressed the hardship endured in trudging long distances to fetch water through knee-deep mud. Wide variations in the readiness of the land allotted meant that some refugees had to put in more work than others. While the first batch of refugees resettled in the South Andamans were allotted fallow fields which needed very little work, the first refugees resettled in the Middle Andamans were given land which had been cleared years ago, in 1949. By 1953, when settlement began at Rangat, the forest had largely reclaimed these lands. The refugees who were settled in the region complained bitterly regarding the condition of the lands allotted to them. Jagabandhu Das of Dasarathpur claimed that in the early years of settlement, it was impossible for human beings to even set foot on the land.[107] It took him years of hard labour to bring his plot under the plough. According to Lakshmikanta Ray, the overgrowth in his

---

[105] Interview with Sukharanjan Mridha, 4 February 2007.
[106] Interview with Kalipada Shikdar, Urmilapur Village, Middle Andaman, 3 February 2007.
[107] Interview with Jagabandhu Das, 1 February 2007.

allotment was dense enough to hinder elephants.[108] Even recently 'cleared' lands were riddled with tree stumps and roots. It was a tall order for nuclear families of one or two able-bodied men to clear and cultivate five acres within the stipulated time of six months. The men often formed groups of eight to ten and took turns in clearing individual plots. At times, the women had to pitch in. Rajlakshmi Biswas recalled helping her husband to clear fields.[109] The exigencies of survival in a semi-wild terrain saw women who had led relatively cloistered lives in East Bengal take on a variety of roles. Besides collecting drinking water, Saralabala Pal of Madhupur grew vegetables, collected firewood, fished in the creeks and threshed paddy.[110]

The difficult terrain and alien conditions of the Andaman Islands forced men, women and children of the refugee families to adapt. Though this led to greater mobility for refugee women, it did not significantly challenge gender roles. Not all families allowed the women of the house to work in the fields. Mohanlan Majumdar of Sitanagar rejected even the possibility of his wife helping in agricultural work on the grounds that 'women of our family do not work.'[111] It is significant that Mr Majumdar was the eldest of three brothers when he came to the Andamans and therefore his family could afford to maintain traditional gender roles. Though many women might have taken up a variety of chores traditionally reserved for men during the early years of settlement, this was viewed as an aberration born of exigency. It did little to destabilise gendered division of labour within households in the long run. The stress on selecting able-bodied men for resettlement led to a shortage of marriageable women during the early years of colonisation. According to Surajit Sinha's survey, conducted in 1951, marriageable women came to be viewed as a valuable and scarce resource. It was the bride's father who reaped the benefits of this situation by demanding bride price instead of paying dowry.[112] By 2007, not only had this practice disappeared completely, but it was also passed over in embarrassed silence by the respondents as it ran counter to notions of social respectability. Instead, the respondents commented adversely on the greater incidence of remarriage of women and love marriages across caste or linguistic barriers. Clearly, even in 2007, the refugee settlements of the Andaman Islands retained the flavour of being a frontier where social taboos carried less weight.

---

[108] Interview with Lakshmikanta Ray, 1 February 2007.
[109] Interview with Rajlakshmi Biswas, 1 February 2007.
[110] Interview with Saralabala Pal, Madhupur Village, North Andaman, 6 February 2007.
[111] Interview with Makhanlal Majumdar, Sitanagar Village, North Andaman, 7 February 2007.
[112] Sinha, *Report on East Pakistan Refugees in Andaman Islands* (1952).

While remembering 'those days', first-generation refugees interwove tales of their myriad strategies of protecting nascent villages and cultivated fields from the surrounding wilderness, with repeated assertions of the fear that the forest evoked. For those settled close to Jarawa territory, this fear was compounded by rumours of their ferocity. Government policy of maintaining bush police camps, ostensibly to protect the settlers from the Jarawas, further encouraged this dehumanised image of hostile and murderous *janglis* or wild men. Far more real threats to agricultural expansion were posed by wild pigs, deer and rats, which regularly destroyed crops. Added to these regular pests were the occasional deadly rampages by '*mast*' elephants.[113] The refugee-settlers often lived in close proximity to twenty to thirty trained elephants used by the Forest Department for transporting timber. Occasionally, the *mahouts* or elephant handlers would lose control over a *mast* elephant, which would then run amok in the refugee settlements. The Bengali settlers saw the jungle and wild animals as adversaries in rebuilding their lives. Their accounts betray great ingenuity in overcoming these obstacles.

The biggest threat to agriculture was posed by wild deer.[114] In the villages of the Middle and North Andamans, herds of deer could ruin the entire crop of paddy in a single night. The refugees built fences around their fields to protect their crops. During the harvest season they stood guard at night in makeshift watchtowers built from foraged materials, such as wild cane, leaves and wood. In order to collect building materials, the settlers ventured into the forest, often under the protection of the bush police. Thus began the unequal competition between the settlers and the Jarawas over forest resources. The refugees also hunted deer for food. A number of respondents suggested that they had learnt to hunt from the Burmese settlers, who used trained dogs to hunt deer and wild pigs. Some refugees also bought trained dogs from the Burmese. In the early years of colonisation, trained dogs were valued more highly than cows.[115] However, food was not the primary reason for hunting deer. The refugees primarily treated deer as pests which threatened their livelihood and killed

---

[113] *Mast*, alternatively spelt as *must* or *musht*, is a periodic condition in bull elephants characterised by highly aggressive behaviour linked to sexual arousal or dominance. The word is derived from Persian and literally means intoxicated.

[114] Deer were alien to the ecosystem of the Andamans. Various species including the spotted deer, barking deer, hog deer and sambar had been introduced by the British in the 1920s. The spotted deer thrived beyond expectations, largely because they developed an uncanny ability to swim, along with the tides and currents, from one island to the other. The Jarawas of Great Andaman did not hunt deer for food and in the absence of any natural predators, their numbers exploded. These were the deer which the refugees battled. See V. K. Prabhakar, *Encyclopaedia of Environmental Pollution and Awareness in the 21st Century* (New Delhi: Anmol Publications, 2000), p. 92.

[115] Interview with Narayan Dutta, Havelock Island, 28 January 2007.

the animals indiscriminately. Second-generation settlers, who were either born in the Andamans or came there as young boys, were more adept at hunting. 'Living in jungles habituated us to the wilderness. We had gone wild along with them (the Jarawas)'; admits Goswami, who had come to the Andamans when he was five.[116] Kalipada Mandal of Kalipur confessed to killing deer in sheer anger. After a herd had ruined his father's crops, he claimed to have killed at least five every day after returning from school![117] From the abundance of wild deer in the remembered landscape and their complete absence in the settlement area today; it is clear that the refugee settlers succeeded in ridding their fields of this pest.

In sharp contrast to the policy of zero tolerance adopted towards deer, the refugees had little choice but to weather the depredations of the elephants owned by the Forest Department. The early settlers of Middle Andaman were the worst sufferers. Many were settled close to the forest camps, and their huts and fields were easy targets for aggressive elephants. Kalipada Mandal of Kalsi recalled how elephants frequently destroyed crops.[118] Though the Forest Department was directly responsible for these animals, the authorities offered little protection or compensation. According to Sujata Mandal, 'when an elephant went mad, they would come and warn us. They would visit every household saying, turn off all lights and be quiet'.[119] Prior warning offered no protection for the houses and fields of the refugees. At times, it also failed to prevent casualties among refugees. The villagers of Urmilapur vividly described how Upen Byapari, the head of his family, had been killed by a rampaging elephant while guarding his field at night.

Refugee reminiscences regarding the Jarawas were complicated by a recent turnaround in the latter's behaviour. A group led by a boy named Enmei, who had been treated for a fractured leg and sent back with gifts the previous year, emerged unarmed from the forest and initiated peaceful interactions with the villagers of Kadamtala in October 1997. Arguably, this signalled the end of 150 years of unequal guerrilla warfare waged by the Jarwas against the encroachment of outsiders. As a result, government policy of containing and policing the 'hostile' tribe became redundant overnight.[120] Most respondents spoke excitedly of how the Jarawas were

---

[116] Interview with Mr. Goswami, Rangat, Middle Andaman, 1 February 2007.
[117] Interview with Kalipada Mandal, Kalipur Village, North Andaman, 5 February 2007.
[118] Interview with Kalipada Mandal of Kalsi Village, 3 February 2007.
[119] Interview with Sujata Mandal, 4 February 2007.
[120] For an astute analysis of the academic and historical conjunctures that shape the current understanding of the status and identity of Jarawas see Vishvajit Pandya and Madhumita Mazumdar, 'Making Sense of the Andaman Islanders: Reflections on a New Conjuncture', *Economic and Political Weekly*, 47: 44 (2012), 51–8. For an official version of this turn-around in Jarawa behaviour and the consequent crisis of policy, see *Report of*

now 'civilised'. By 2007, the memory of the fear they had once evoked had largely been displaced by excitement regarding their exoticism. A deep-seated racism against the Jarawas was nevertheless discernable. Much of the excitement revolved around the recent 'discovery' that the Jarawas were human. Sujata Mandal believed that 'after they were caught, the government tested their blood. Then they realised that they were humans. Then the government adopted policies to civilise them.'[121] Among refugees who had lived in close proximity to the Jarawas in the Middle Andamans, the signs of entrenched prejudice were still evident. Most described them as indiscriminate killers, who 'killed whatever crossed their path, man or beast'.[122] Yet, upon further questions, it became evident that the actual experience of this 'hostility' was more often than not confined to overnight raids, during which the raiding party made off with iron implements and fruits. Despite their depiction as wild and irrational killers, there was a clear pattern to the Jarawas' violence. Their victims were usually those who entered the jungle and could have been seen as trespassers or aggressors. They seldom actually attacked the refugees within their settlements; and most settlers were aware of this.

Sukharanjan Mridha of Kalsi village[123] attempted to rationalise the 'hostile' behaviour of the Jarawa. He was resettled at Kalsi in 1955, along with twenty-four other refugee families. According to him, the area was frequently raided by Jarawas; so much so that fifteen refugee families had to be relocated to a different region. 'The fear was real. The Jarawas frequented the area, killed people'. He spoke of how there had been a fierce battle between the bush police and Jarawas at a police outpost near Kalsi.[124] Yet, Sukharanjan exhibited rare empathy.

The Jarawas were such that initially they did not kill. But they had also been subjected to maltreatment. For example, their roads got blocked. For example, from that hillock down through here the Jarawas could travel to Rangat- through the forests. There were no settlements here... the entirety, the jungle was theirs. Now, the settlement was built in their areas, we were brought over and settled. It would automatically cause them inconvenience. They hunt for food- deer, wild

the Expert Committee on Jarawas of Andaman Islands, July 2003, <http://www.and.nic.in/C_charter/Dir_tw/ecr/>, Last accessed 5 May 2009.

[121] Interview with Sujata Mandal, 4 February 2007.

[122] Interview with Kalipada Shikdar, 3 February 2007.

[123] Kalsi is the westernmost village in the Bakultala region of Middle Andamans. It is located on the border of the Jarawa reserve. During the colonisation period, it suffered from regular Jarawa raids.

[124] There is corroborating evidence of this battle in local records, according to which on 23 February 1959, fifty Jarawas surrounded the No. 5 police outpost at Kalsi. Mentioned in 'Annexure 2: Some Major Incidents of Conflicts, 1946–1998', in K. Mukhopadhay, P. K. Bhattacharya and B.N. Sarkar (eds) Jarawa Contact: Ours with Them, Theirs With Us (Calcutta: Anthropological Survey of India, 2002), p. 225.

pigs. No, they don't eat deer; but they eat wild pigs etc. Now taking their land, the government built settlements. Their area decreased. They had to go around us—they became angry. Then, if they got a chance, they killed. And they beat *pankha* ... This is something worth knowing. Many of our children who have been born here, even they will not know of this. Maybe a few will know. Imagine there are three-four of us here, walking along the creek; and that there are a group of them too. Once they sensed our presence, they would move off a bit and beat *pankha* on the trees. By beating *pankha* I mean they would make a loud noise. On *pankha* of some trees, if you hit, especially on pephak [sic] tree – with the *pankha* of pephak the sound is the loudest. That was letting us know, that 'we are here'. At that we would run away in fear. They were scared, and so were we. This was the situation earlier ... Some days later they stopped beating *pankha*. After that, a few people died.[125]

It is likely that the 'pephak' tree of Sukharanjan's account is a corruption of *padauk*, a tree highly valued for timber in the Andamans. *Pankha* is the colloquial name for the tree burrs or buttresses, a common feature in the variety of *padouk* found in Andamans. Buttress beating was the Jarawas' method of warning off intruders.[126]

Sukharanjan's account suggests that fear dominated the uneasy co-existence between the refugee-settlers and the Jarawa. It also suggests that the Bengali refugees were not entirely unaware of the negative impact their new settlements had on the hunting and foraging habits of the original inhabitants of the forests. Despite his professed empathy, Sukharanjan places the blame for the marginalisation of the Jarawa squarely on the government. He omits the fact that poaching and encroachment into the Jarawa reserve had become common practice among the settlers. This naturally increased the number of 'encounters' and escalated conflict between the two groups.[127] As the population increased, so did the demand for more land among the descendants of the settlers, and among new migrants from Bangladesh. Many 'Ranchi' labourers[128] built illegal settlements within the forest, while the temporary construction sites set up during the construction of the Andaman Trunk Road, which cut through the Jarawa reserve, invariably grew into permanent settlements. Today, there are numerous villages of Bengalis and Ranchis, within the reserved area, such as Hanspuri. Jarawas are seldom seen in the area around Kalsi. 'As the population kept increasing,

---

[125] Interview with Sukharanjan Mridha, 4 February 2007.
[126] Mukhopadhay et al. (eds), *Jarawa Contact* (2002).
[127] While mortality among poachers was often meticulously recorded, the actual number of the Jarawa killed might never actually be known.
[128] The Ranchis or Ranchiwallahs were labourers recruited from Oraon, Munda and Kharia tribes of the Chotonagpur region, who were brought to the Andaman Islands by the Forest Department or the Department of Public Works on short term contracts.

they gradually moved off,' says Shukharanjan,[129] in effect acknowledging that the Jarawa ultimately lost their unequal battle with the new settlers over forest resources.

While remembering their pasts, the first-generation refugees privileged certain aspects over others. The striking absence of nostalgia for their ancestral villages was paralleled by a reluctance to describe more recent developments. Vivid descriptions of the challenges faced and overcome 'in those days' petered out into short, disinterested, and often dismissive summaries of more recent developments. Narayan Dutta of Havelock summarised the transformation of the island into a popular and well-connected tourist destination in one sentence. 'Now many things have developed – houses, vehicles and transport, roads, vote, etc. – so many people ... In those days, there were hardly any people; it was difficult to form an attachment (to the land)'.[130] Yet, this very period of struggle, when the refugees from East Bengal had found it hard to reconcile themselves to their forested and isolated new homes, is repeatedly narrated as the relevant past in the interviews. This selective remembering can be read as part of a process of developing and projecting a specific identity.

Memories and anecdotes recounted by the respondents not only privileged the early years of colonisation, but also highlighted their interaction with the wild terrain. The jungle, wild animals and the Jarawas are all portrayed as part of the landscape, which the refugees successfully colonised. In these narratives, the refugees appear repeatedly as solitary pioneers, struggling against and prevailing over the obstacles thrown up by the wild terrain. The role of the government in clearing the forests is trivialised, as most respondents described how it had taken them years of work to make the land fit for cultivation. The refugees seldom attributed any active role to the substantial population of migrant workers present at the colonisation sites. This included the *mahouts*, Ranchi labourers and Burmese forest workers. This omission is significant as the refugees not only shared the wild landscape with them, but also benefitted from their presence. The East Bengalis learnt hunting from the Burmese and at times employed Ranchis as *kisans* or day labourers in their fields. Jagabandhu Das of Dasarathpur admitted with great reluctance, and only at the insistence of his wife, that he had indeed employed Ranchis to help clear his fields.[131] The refugees spoke exclusively of the hardships they had endured during the first few years of colonisation precisely

---

[129] Interview with Sukharanjan Mridha, 4 February 2007.
[130] Interview with Narayan Dutta, 28 January 2007.
[131] Interview with Jagabandhu Das, 1 February 2007.

because it bolstered their collective identity as pioneering agriculturists and settlers of Andaman Islands. 'The hardship that had to be endured, was endured by us,' said Saralabala Pal of Madhupur village. 'Now there is comfort.'[132]

This self-image of the refugees as pioneers of colonisation in Andamans might also explain their reluctance to talk about later developments. A programme of 'accelerated development' for the Andaman Islands was adopted in 1965, which treated population as the main 'engine' promoting growth in the Andamans. The programme envisioned doubling the population of the islands by 1970. However, in order to diversify this increased population, it excluded Bengali refugees.[133] Though the refugees were not aware of this shift in policy, they nevertheless felt its impact. Most respondents complained of being swamped by a veritable flood of 'outsiders' in later years. Ananta Kumar Biswas, in his amateur history of Manglutan village in South Andaman, blames the large-scale influx of Tamils, Telegus and Ranchi labourers employed in new projects of development, for severely disrupting familiar and 'traditional' patterns of life. The folk traditions of East Bengal which had hitherto marked the rhythm of village life were marginalised and Hindi started replacing Bengali as the lingua franca of an ethnically mixed rural population. In fact, he blames the 'outsiders' for every woe of Manglutan and the Andamans, ranging from increasing addiction among Bengali settlers to deforestation, soil erosion and decline in wildlife.[134] The period after 1965 saw the rapid growth of new trade, transport and businesses in the Andamans. But the refugee-settlers were unable to compete with the new migrants in reaping the benefits of the new developments. The detachment of the refugees from more recent developments, evident in their reminiscences, was perhaps born of this sense of marginalisation.

Since the recent history of development in the Anadamans coincided with the growing marginalisation of the refugee-settlers, all the respondents chose to privilege an earlier period of their pasts, when they were the only inhabitants of nascent villages. In doing so, they were staking a primary claim upon the land and resources of Andamans by virtue of having pioneered agriculture in the islands. They project themselves as settlers and colonisers despite being, quite

---

[132] Interview with Saralabala Pal, 6 February 2007.
[133] Inter-Departmental Team on Accelerated Development Programme for Andaman and Nicobar Islands, Ministry of Rehabilitation, Government of India, *Report by the Inter-Departmental Team on Accelerated Development Programme for Andaman and Nicobar Islands*, Delhi, December 1966.
[134] A. K. Biswas, *Manglutan: Birth and Upbringing of a Refugee Settlement in the Isles*, unpublished essay, n.d.

literally, card-carrying refugees. The refugee-settlers in the Andamans had often spent years in refugee camps. Many, as discussed above, had even participated in refugee politics. Yet, they had no investment in a refugee identity. By 2007, the identity of the Bengali refugees settled in the Andamans had become inextricably linked to the land-scape they had inhabited since resettlement. Their primary identity was that of agricultural colonisers and they called themselves 'settlers'. Though none had forgotten their erstwhile homes, none longed for it either. Many confessed that there had been a time when they had pined for their ancestral villages. However, by 2007 the refugees had re-imagined this period of hardship and struggle as a golden period of cultural unity and social amity within homogenous refugee settle-ments. Many were nostalgic about selective elements of the colonisa-tion period. Life had been harsh, but simple and inexpensive. Sumana Majumdar rattled off the prices at which she used to buy provisions while her husband, Makhanlal, compared the easy availability of building materials in 'those days' with the hassles of buying and trans-porting wood 'now'.[135] There were no diseases other than malaria while the virgin soil ensured large harvests. Thus, among the refu-gee-settlers of the Andamans, nostalgia for a more recent past had displaced an earlier experience of loss.

The memories of the refugees settled in the Andaman Islands challenge received wisdom on memory and identity of Hindu Bengali refugees. The familiar themes of refugee memory, such as displacement, violence, trauma and nostalgia, are conspicuous by their absence. Historians, especially the practitioners of oral history, have repeatedly identified the loss of homeland or *desh* and the trauma associated with it as the core ingredient structuring the Bengali refugees' memory, and therefore, the selfhood which is constructed through such remembering.[136] In striking contrast, the first-generation refugees settled in the Andaman Islands had little interest in reminiscing about their lost homes in East Bengal. Though they had not forgotten the villages they came from, among them, the memories of their homeland had lost both relevance and poignancy. Several studies have shown that many who continued to identify as refugees decades after partition, and well into the second or even third generation, often do so for diametrically opposite reasons. For those bypassed by the regime of rehabilitation, such as the landless and urban poor among Punjabi refugees who got no compensation, the

---

[135] Interview with Sumana and Makhanlal Majumdar, Sitanagar Village, North Andaman, 7 February 2007.

[136] There is a vast, but largely repetitive literature on this topic. For an example, see Bose, 'Partition – Memory Begins Where History Ends' (1997), pp. 72–86.

families living in poverty in ex-campsites of West Bengal, and the squatters in Calcutta who still await regularisation, self-identifying as refugees, serves as a reminder to the state of dues still owed. Conversely, for the well-settled displaced families, the sentimental reiteration of loss of land and nostalgia of past status, reinforced present claims to social status and respectability.[137] For the illiterate *Namasudra* peasants who were 'selected' for colonising the Andamans, neither project was relevant. They could stake claims upon the resources of the state much more effectively as settlers. However, instrumental factors cannot fully explain the enthusiastic adoption of the identity of settlers and agricultural pioneers among Andaman Islands' Bengali refugees. The act of remembering is always a dialogue between the past and the present, informed by both past experiences and present locations and priorities. Identities, as reflected in memory, are therefore seldom static. They are constantly refigured by lived experiences. The reminiscences of refugees settled in the Andamans illustrate one such radical reconfiguration of memory, and along with it, of identity. It is possible that their struggle to live up to their ascribed role of pioneers and colonisers and the richness and novelty of the settler experience in the Andaman Islands had overwritten earlier experiences of displacement. Madhumita Mazumdar's ethnographic exploration of Bengali settler identity in the Andaman Islands confirms this absence of nostalgia for lost homes amongst first and second-generation refugee-settlers. However, she offers a different explanation for it. Mazumdar argues that fluid and spiritual notions of home and dwelling, derived from the teachings of the Matua sect, played a dominant role in forging a distinctive identity amongst Andaman Island's Bengali settlers.[138] While Mazumdar's work is significant in highlighting the need to pay more attention to the role of religion in the Andaman Islands, she does not attempt to explain how Matua notions of home and dwelling could translate into the adoption of a settler identity by erstwhile refugees. While the teachings of the Matua sect might well have aided in the marginalisation of narratives of displacement, it cannot explain the parallel adoption of a new identity of 'settlers' and agricultural pioneers. Intimate and everyday negotiations of the landscape of the Andaman

---

[137] This aspect of nostalgia and reiteration of loss is fleshed out by Ravinder Kaur in 'Distinctive Citizenship: Refugees, Subjects and Post-colonial State in India's Partition', *Cultural and Social History*, 6: 4 (2009), 429–46.

[138] Madhumita Mazumdar, 'Dwelling in Fluid Spaces: The Matuas of the Andaman Islands' in Clare Anderson, Madhumita Mazumdar and Vishvajit Pandya, *New Histories of the Andaman Islands: Landscape, Place and Identity in the Bay of Bengal, 1790–2012*, (Cambridge and New York: Cambridge University Press, 2015), pp. 170–200.

Islands and the socio-economic context of remembering no doubt played a crucial role in this re-figuration of identity.

Conclusion

The Andaman Islands was both the earliest site identified for the dispersal of refugees and the longest-running scheme of dispersal and resettlement of East Bengali refugees outside West Bengal. It took in refugees continuously, albeit in small numbers, between 1949 and 1961. Despite an official decision to discontinue colonisation using Bengali refugees in 1965, the islands continued to take in refugees through isolated resettlement schemes, which reflected spikes in the influx of refugees from East Bengal. Some of the refugee families who had fled the riots triggered by the Hazratbal incident of 1964 found their way to North Andaman Island as part of a labour corps. They were eventually settled on the land they cleared. The years between 1969 and 1971 saw new settlements established at Neil Island to make room for Bengali Hindus fleeing the escalation of hostilities in East Pakistan. In other words, the Andaman Islands is unique in providing a home to a cross-section of East Bengali refugees who migrated for different reasons and entered different government camps over a period of twenty-six years, in one concentrated geography. Their memories are therefore not only useful in understanding the growth of refugee settlements in the Andaman Islands, but also have a wider relevance in understanding how East Bengali refugees negotiated displacement, life in camps and dispersal.

For the refugee-settlers of the Andaman Islands, experience of camp life ranged from a few months in a single camp to years spent on rudimentary dole, while the government of West Bengal moved them around from one camp to the other. Among them I encountered an erstwhile agitator of the anti-dispersal movement, who had changed his mind, as well as a couple who had spent two years on the platform of the Sealdah station in utter destitution. There were refugees who had fled the horror of an epidemic of smallpox in a crowded camp, as well as a survivor of tuberculosis. Some confessed to a reasonably comfortable life in camps, either because no real work was required in work-site camps or because they could supplement the meagre dole with casual employment in the surrounding areas. The glimpses we glean of life in camps, albeit from a self-selected group who took the risk of travelling to the remotest end of India to build a new life, is not one of unmitigated misery or flattened victimhood. What emerges instead is a window into a world of active and informed negotiations of the regime of rehabilitation. The refugee-settlers of the Andaman Islands displayed little of the 'demoralisation', 'dependence' and loss of enterprise attributed to East Bengali refugees due to their long wait for rehabilitation. The remarkable resourcefulness and fortitude of the refugees in rebuilding their lives in the Andaman Islands lays to rest the most popular official explanation provided for the failure of rehabilitation of refugees from East Bengal – the flawed character of the refugees.

There is little doubt that in numerical terms, the refugee-settlers of the Andaman Islands constitute a minority of those dispersed outside West Bengal. Considerable numbers were dispatched to cultivable 'waste' lands and forested lands in locations as diverse as Orissa, Bihar, Andhra Pradesh, Uttar Pradesh or present day Uttaranchal, and even Rajasthan. The largest rehabilitation site by far was the Dandakaranya Development Project that spanned the contiguous districts of Bastar in Madhya Pradesh or present-day Chhattisgarh, and Koraput and Kalahandi in Orissa. According to official estimates, by 1971, 44,000 refugee families had been rehabilitated while an equal number were still awaiting final settlement in various sites outside West Bengal.[139] Within received wisdom, these projects of dispersal are frequently represented as a flattened geographies of exile. Locations outside West Bengal are uniformly described as 'remote and unwelcoming', without any attempt to explore the specific histories of diverse settlements. This propensity to tar all projects of dispersal of refugees outside West Bengal with the same brush of misery and failure is largely born of a tendency to generalise from the well-publicised failures of the Dandakaranya project. Ill-planned and burdened with a top-heavy and divided administration, it suffered from lack of water, inadequate employment opportunities and land that was in large parts unsuitable for agriculture. The mass desertion of refugees from Dandakaranya, who attempted to return to West Bengal in 1978, and were brutally evicted from Morichjhanpi, is perhaps the most notorious episode in the long history of official neglect of East Bengali refugees. However, there is no evidence to suggest that all refugees dispersed from West Bengal were thrown into a life of exile and misery. Even in Dandakaranya, there was considerable internal variation in levels of irrigation and quality of land allotted, leading to 'thriving peasant villages' in Paralkote.[140] These nuances are largely lost in a historiography of the Dandakaranya project that is firstly, slim, and secondly, overtly

---

[139] P. N. Luthra, *Rehabilitation* (New Delhi: Ministry of Information and Broadcasting, Publications Division, 1972), pp. 21–3, also cited in Chatterji, *Spoils of Partition*, (2007), p. 136.

[140] Prafulla K. Chakrabarti, *The Marginal Men: The Refugees and the Left Political Syndrome in West Bengal* (Calcutta: Naya Udyog, 1999), p. 435.

reliant on the evidence provided by deserters and the politically charged debates and reports that followed.[141] These debates analyse projects of dispersal of camp refugees solely in terms of success or failure, which leaves little room for internal complexity. More importantly, it fails to do justice to the myriad struggles and complex negotiations of the thousands of refugees settled beyond the borders of West Bengal. If the reminiscences of refugees resettled in the Andaman Islands are any indication, the experiences of dispersed refugees might well exceed the current portrayal of dispersal as exile, tragedy, or abject victimhood.

---

[141] K. Maudood Elahi, 'Refugees in Dandakaranya', *International Migration Review*, 15:1/2 (1981); Alok Kumar Ghosh, 'Bengali Refugees at Dandakaranya: A Tragedy of Rehabilitation', in Pradip Kumar Bose (ed.), *Refugees in West Bengal: Institutional Practices and Contested Identities* (Calcutta: Calcutta Research Group, 2000), pp. 106–29; Debjani Sengupta, 'From Dandakaranya to Marichjhapi: Rehabilitation, Representation and the Partition of Bengal', *Social Semiotics*, 21: 1 (2011), 101–23. A notable exception to this trend is Babul Kumar Pal, *Barishal theke Dandakaranya: Purbabanger krishijibi udvastu-r punarbasan itihas (From Barishal to Dandakaranya: The History of Rehabilitation of East Bengal's Refugee Agriculturists)* (Calcutta: Granthamitra, 2010).

4   Unruly Citizens

Memory, Identity and the Anatomy of Squatting in Calcutta

Introduction

In February 1948, as India struggled to cope with the massive and unanticipated displacement of minorities that followed in the wake of partition, Prime Minister Jawaharlal Nehru expressed his dismay at the state of affairs in the capital city of Delhi. Large numbers of refugees from various parts of Pakistan, particularly Punjab, flocked to Delhi. Nehru despaired at finding an 'effective method' to 'stop more refugees from coming into Delhi'.[1] Though otherwise sympathetic to the plight of Hindu minorities in West Pakistan and willing to mobilise vast resources for their evacuation, relief, and rehabilitation, the methods Nehru suggested to protect the capital city of Delhi from a continuing influx of refugees amounted to deliberate misinformation. He urged the Union Minister of Rehabilitation, K. C. Neogy, to publicly announce 'that no arrangements will be made in Delhi for newcomers and that these will be sent off immediately to camps in Bihar or elsewhere'.[2] The use of immediate dispersal to 'Bihar or elsewhere' as a deterrent is extremely revealing as it inadvertently acknowledges refugee agency in patterns of migration. Despite overcrowding, Delhi was clearly a preferred destination for many refugees, especially urban and educated ones. They quite rightly calculated that they stood a better chance of finding employment and receiving government aid as a visible problem in the capital city, as opposed to being forgotten in a remote camp. The situation in Delhi was far from unique. The impetus to preserve civic order in capital cities put the governments of India and Pakistan on a collision course with refugees who flocked to the cities in general, and the capital cities in particular, to stake their claim to belong to their putative homelands.

---

[1] Jawaharlal Nehru, Prime Minister of India, to K. C. Neogy, Minister of Relief and Rehabilitation, 20 February 1948, in S. Gopal (ed.), *Selected Works of Jawaharlal Nehru, Second Series, Vol. 5* (New Delhi: Jawaharlal Nehru Memorial Fund, 1984), p. 156.

[2] Ibid.

The demographic impact of partition was felt acutely in the capital cities. This included not just Delhi, but also the administrative capitals of the divided provinces, namely Lahore in Eastern Punjab and Calcutta in West Bengal, and the trading towns of Karachi and Dhaka, which were elevated overnight to the status of capital cities. Besides a massive rise in population and rapid expansion of area, these cities also witnessed significant transformations in their urban cultures in the decades following partition. These changes were wrought partly by the disappearance of established minority communities who either left or were forced to leave for their putative homelands on the 'other side', and partly by the new dialects, languages, political cultures and cuisines brought in by the refugees. The broad patterns of these transformations are well documented in existing scholarship.[3] These changes are also frequently evoked in everyday negotiations of urban space in India. Take, for example, the celebration or lament, depending on one's perspective, about the 'Punjabification' of Delhi and the largely benign rivalry between *ghotis*, or residents of West Bengal, and *bangals* or East Bengalis that permeates various aspects of urban culture in Calcutta, from cuisine to sports. These everyday affirmations of the transformation of capital cities wrought by partition refugees provide little evidence of how refugees were deeply unwelcome in capital cities in the immediate aftermath of partition. In Delhi, Calcutta and Karachi, overcrowding, unsanitary conditions, public disorder, soaring property prices, rising corruption and immorality in civic life were all linked to the presence of too many refugees. The authorities, in both India and Pakistan, responded by attempting to preserve civic order by excluding refugees from capital landscapes. The refugees who succeeded in carving out space for themselves in and around these cities often swam against the current of official policy. This chapter uses the alternative archive of memory and oral history to explore what enabled these new citizens of India to carve out space for themselves in and around capital cities. It focuses particularly on Calcutta, which by

---

[3] For a general survey of changing 'capitol landscapes', see Gyanesh Kudaisya and Tan Tai Yong, *The Aftermath of Partition in South Asia* (London and New York: Routledge, 2004), pp. 159–98. For Delhi, see Ravinder Kaur, *Since 1947: Partition Narratives among Punjabi Migrants of Delhi* (New Delhi: Oxford University Press, 2007), and for Karachi, see Sarah Ansari, *Life after Partition: Migration, Community and Strife in Sindh, 1947–1962* (Oxford: Oxford University Press, 2005). For a comparative study of Karachi and Delhi, see V. F. Zamindar, *The Long Partition and the Making of Modern South Asia*. For Calcutta, see Mushirul Hasan and Asim Roy (eds.), *Living Together Separately: Cultural India in History and Politics* (New Delhi; New York: Oxford University Press, 2005), Pranati Chaudhuri, *Refugees in West Bengal: A Study of the Growth and Distribution of Refugee Settlements within the CMD*, CSSS Occasional Paper (Calcutta: Centre for Studies in Social Sciences, 1983) and Romola Sanyal, 'Contesting Refugeehood: Squatting as Survival in Post-Partition Calcutta', *Social Identities*, 15: 1 (2009), 67–84.

1951 had an official refugee population of 433,000.[4] This figure excludes an estimated 50,000 families living in the illegal refugee settlements that had sprung up in the fringes of the city between 1949 and 1950.[5] Though these refugees were technically not residents of Calcutta city, they nevertheless looked to the city for work, social acceptance, and political belonging.

Calcutta's Deus ex Machina: Refugee Agency and Squatters' Colonies

In the immediate aftermath of partition, the government response to the refugee crisis lagged far behind the actual needs of refugees. In the cities of Karachi, Delhi and Calcutta, an acute shortage of housing was soon evident. Rising prices of property and rent, aided in no small measure by unscrupulous middle-men keen to make a profit off the misfortune of refugees, soon pushed all but the richest refugees out of the housing market. As a result, unauthorised occupation of abandoned houses, military structures, warehouses or closed factories became standard practice amongst displaced persons in the large cities of India and Pakistan. Refugees everywhere felt entitled to abandoned and partially occupied houses of the 'other' community and resisted any attempts of eviction. Both India and Pakistan responded with a series of legislation around 'evacuee' property that effectively legalised this de facto transfer of property from minorities to refugees as part of the solution to the crisis of accommodation.[6] In this era of forced occupation and illegal squatting, the pattern that evolved in Calcutta was somewhat distinct. The policy of encouraging the repatriation of refugees from East Bengal meant that the provisions of the Evacuee Property Act that allowed such properties to be unilaterally requisitioned by the government and used for 'public purposes', which included the rehabilitation of refugees, were not extended to West Bengal, Tripura and Assam. While Hindu refugees in Calcutta were no less proactive in occupying Muslim houses and mosques, official policy moved in the opposite direction. During

---

[4] See West Bengal Census Office, *Census of 1951, West Bengal. (Sikkim and Chandernagore.). pt. III. Calcutta City. [by] A. Mitra* (New Delhi: Manager of Publications, 1994), p. 305.

[5] Based on the figures provided in Committee of Review of Rehabilitation Work in West Bengal, *Report on Development of Colonies of Displaced Persons from Erstwhile East Pakistan in West Bengal* (New Delhi: Ministry of Supply and Rehabilitation, 1974); Prafulla K. Chakrabarti, *The Marginal Men: The Refugees and the Left Political Syndrome in West Bengal* (Calcutta: Naya Udyog, 1999), pp. 109–55.

[6] For details of evacuee property legislation, see Joya Chatterji, 'South Asian Histories of Citizenship, 1946–1970', *The Historical Journal*, 55:4 (2012): 1049–71 and Vazira Zamindar, *The Long Partition* (2010).

the early 1950s, the government of West Bengal actively sought to restore evacuee property to returning Muslims in order to demonstrate their commitment to the Nehru-Liaquat Ali Pact of 1950. While this did not necessarily prevent the de facto dispossession of Muslims by belligerent squatters,[7] it did deprive the government of West Bengal of the primary resource utilised by the authorities in Delhi and Karachi to alleviate the crisis of providing accommodation to refugees. At the height of the refugee crisis in Calcutta, the Congress government under the leadership of Dr B. C. Roy was unable to either legally transfer evacuee property to refugees, or use it as a 'compensation pool' to defray the costs of rehabilitation.

The crisis in Calcutta was further deepened by the theory of saturation that had gained currency in West Bengal as early as 1948. Convinced that West Bengal in general and Calcutta in particular was already saturated, the Congress government stubbornly refused to make any arrangements for refugees within Calcutta. Unlike Delhi, which had four refugee camps within the city, Calcutta had none.[8] Moreover, in both Delhi and Karachi, the authorities launched large-scale construction of housing designed primarily to provide accommodation to displaced persons. In Delhi, the Ministry of Relief and Rehabilitation directly took charge of construction of houses,[9] while in Karachi, the government preferred to distribute land for construction of houses to the Karachi Co-operative Housing Society Union, an umbrella organisation that brought together various refugee associations.[10] Calcutta rapidly gained the dubious distinction of being the only metropolis in post-partition India that received a large number of partition refugees, but had no real plan for their rehabilitation. This combination of circumstances led to the emergence of a veritable movement of unauthorised occupation not only of abandoned buildings, but also of all available fallow land in and around Calcutta. Groups of refugees got together to form *dals* or associations. Familial ties, connections from a past life in East Bengal and political contacts formed the basis of these initiatives. After suitable fallow land was identified, its occupation followed a standard pattern. The land was measured, divided into plots and parcelled out amongst refugee families. The occupiers of each plot had to erect a thatched shelter overnight and

---

[7] See Joya Chatterji, *The Spoils of Partition: Bengal and India, 1947–67* (Cambridge and New York: Cambridge University Press, 2007), pp. 159–208.

[8] Kaur, *Since 1947*, p. 99.

[9] Committee of Review of Rehabilitation Work in West Bengal, *Report on Rehabilitation Loans to the Displaced Persons from Erstwhile East Pakistan in West Bengal* (New Delhi: Ministry of Supply and Rehabilitation, 1974), p. 8.

[10] Sarah Ansari, *Life after Partition* (2005), pp. 139–44.

move into it. By the time the landlords or the authorities arrived on the scene, they had to contend with a fully fledged illegal settlement. These overnight occupations of land more often than not managed to survive as refugee colonies and were eventually enumerated by the government as 'squatters' colonies'.

During the first few years of their existence, the government of West Bengal refused to acknowledge these settlements as colonies, instead referring to them as 'unauthorised occupations'. The official inclusion of squatters' colonies within schemes of rehabilitation can be dated to 1955, when a Development Committee was appointed by the government of West Bengal to review the condition of refugee colonies in West Bengal and suggest recommendations for their future development.[11] In this report, the 149 illegal refugee settlements that had sprung up in and around Calcutta by the end of 1950 were treated at par with government-sponsored and private refugee colonies in urban areas. The Committee recommended the development of civic amenities in these colonies to bring them up to the same level as other settlements within the city. The government of India generally accepted these recommendations, and the development of squatters' colonies was included within the project of 'residual rehabilitation' in West Bengal after 1957.

This laid to rest any threat of eviction for the residents of these colonies and amounted to an official acknowledgement of the moral legitimacy of the patently illegal actions of the refugees. However, the initial response of the government of West Bengal to this epidemic of squatting had been the exact opposite of later policy. Dr B. C. Roy treated the squatters as a law and order problem. Between 1949 and 1951, his government attempted to evict and disperse the squatters. When the brute force of the police and *goondas*, or hired muscle of the landlords, did not succeed in ousting the squatters, the government resorted to drafting an Eviction Bill. This Bill sought to strengthen the hands of the landlords by making the legal process of evicting squatters both simpler and cheaper. An organised upsurge of refugees, under the leadership of the United Central Refugee Council (UCRC) and championed by a vocal Left opposition, forced the government to backtrack. In its final form, The Rehabilitation of Displaced Persons and Eviction of Persons in Unauthorised Occupation of Land Act conceded the need to provide alternative accommodation to squatters as a precondition of eviction.[12] In sum, refugees wrested the right to remain in their improvised one-room shelters, which used *bansher bera* or sheets of woven bamboo strips for walls, and *hogla* leaves for a

[11] Committee of Review, *Report on Development of Colonies* (1974), p. 3.
[12] Chakrabarti, *The Marginal Men* (1999), pp. 109–55.

thatched roof, from the state through organised resistance. This has since become the stuff of urban legend in Calcutta.

Within existing historical scholarship, autobiographical texts and fictional representations of the post-partition refugee crisis, the architects of the squatters' colonies are celebrated for their resilience and resourcefulness.[13] While the squatters' ability to resist eviction was a significant victory against overwhelming odds, the literature celebrating this achievement obscures more than it reveals of the nature of refugee agency and the history of refugee squats in post-partition Calcutta. Contemporary accounts frequently resort to a celebration of the character or resolve of the refugees in lieu of an explanation. Hiranmoy Bandyopadhyay's narrative of rehabilitation in West Bengal, which draws upon his experience as the Rehabilitation Commissioner, betrays an admiration for the squatters. He indulges in a threefold categorisation of displaced persons based on the reserves of money and willpower they could command. The squatters occupy a middle ground between those who were relatively well-off and did not require government help, and the poor refugees who 'lacked the will to stand on their own two feet' and ended up in government camps.[14] The architects of the squatters' colonies represent the official ideal of the self-sufficient refugee, who despite limited means refused to enter government camps. Bandyopadhyay clearly approved of their occupation of abandoned houses and fallow land since by doing so, they shouldered the responsibility of earning their own living. In this curious psychological-economic taxonomy of refugees, the celebration of the resolve and initiative of squatters serves a statist narrative where the responsibility for the success or failure of policies of rehabilitation is transferred onto the refugees. Privileging the character of refugees as the determining factor in patterns of rehabilitation allowed the state to shame poor refugees for their supposed lack of initiative. Moreover, the failure of ill-planned rehabilitation schemes could be blamed upon the dependent nature of camp refugees.

The official discourse of rehabilitation is replete with this strategy of splitting the figure of the partition refugee into binary opposites: the self-settled refugee and the childlike, dependent refugee who fails to achieve self-sufficiency. In U. Bhaskar Rao's propagandist narrative of rehabilitation, this split manifests itself as ethnic difference, with the hard-working Punjabi refugees held up in contrast to the 'rebellious and obstructive'

---

[13] See Sabitri Roy, *Bwadwip (The Delta)* (Calcutta, 1972); Sunil Gangopadhyay, *Arjun* (Delhi: Penguin, 1990); and Debjani Sengupta, *The Partition of Bengal: Fragile Borders and New Identities* (New Delhi: Cambridge University Press, 2016).

[14] Hiranmoy Bandypadhyay, *Udvastu (Refugee)* (Calcutta: Sahitya Samsad, 1970), p. 3.

refugees from East Bengal.[15] This stark contrast is achieved through the deliberate erasure of the experience of Punjabi refugees of lesser means who were entitled to little or no compensation and struggled for years to rebuild their lives,[16] and the complete omission of the belligerent squatters of West Bengal. The latter's self-sufficiency was premised upon breaking the law, which made them a difficult example to celebrate. Within studies that focus on West Bengal alone, the quest for a success story led even state-sponsored studies, such as B. S. Guha's study of social tensions amongst East Bengali refugees, to highlight the achievements of the squatters.[17] This study was conducted by a team of anthropologists from the Anthropological Survey of India who compared the pattern of settlement of refugees at the Azadgarh squatters' colony with that of 500 families resettled by the government at Jirat. Joya Chatterji's detailed analysis of this report provides a damning indictment of scholarly complicity with the official tendency to blame East Bengali refugees for the failure of fundamentally flawed schemes of rehabilitation.[18] She demonstrates how the 'experts' swept aside obvious reasons for the failure of the colony at Jirat, such as the lack of employment opportunities, unsanitary and malarial conditions and poor quality of agricultural land as mere whingeing. Instead, the inferior character of the refugees sent to Jirat, who were 'childishly dependant [sic]' on the government, is highlighted as the main reason for the failure of the scheme. The contrast afforded by the high morale and impressive organisation of the self-settled refugees at Azadgarh served to deepen this strange reasoning where the success or failure of rehabilitation is reduced to an outward manifestation of the inherent character of the refugees involved. Chatterji aptly illustrates how the greater means of the squatters at Azadgarh coupled with the widely divergent potential of the two locations of rehabilitation in terms of employment generation offers a far better explanation for the divergent fate of the two groups of refugees. While this effectively lays to rest pseudo-scientific pronouncements regarding the flawed character of the refugees settled at Jirat, the heroism of the squatters is largely taken at face value. Guha's eulogy of the squatters, as 'a people who met sword

[15] U. Bhaskar Rao, *The Story of Rehabilitation* (Ministry of Labour, Employment and Rehabilitation, Government of India, 1967), p. 141.

[16] For a critical exploration of class difference and its impact on rehabilitation of refugees from Punjab, see Ravinder Kaur, 'The Last Journey', *Economic and Political Weekly*, 41: 22 (2006), 2221–8; and 'Distinctive Citizenship: Refugees, Citizens and Postcolonial State in India's Partition', *Cultural & Social History*, 6: 4 (2009), 429–46.

[17] B. S. Guha, *Memoir No. 1, 1954. Studies in Social Tension Among the Refugees from Eastern Pakistan* (Calcutta: Department of Anthropology, Government of India, 1959).

[18] Joya Chatterji, 'Dispersal and the Failure of Rehabilitation: Refugee Camp-Dwellers and Squatters in West Bengal', *Modern Asian Studies*, 41:5 (2007): 995–1032.

with sword' in resisting eviction, and 'joined their heads and hands together' in setting up a self-sufficient colony, is repeated without any attempt to complicate what is, in effect, a continuation of the same official rhetoric that privileges the character of refugees as the main explanatory factor behind the success or failure of rehabilitation.[19] However, if lack of resolve is an inadequate explanation for the failure of rehabilitation, the opposite is also true. Resolve and willpower alone, no matter how heroic, cannot explain the ability of the squatters to successfully resist the combined might of the state and landlords, while also setting up schools and marketplaces on illegally occupied land.

This praise for the refugee squatters reaches its highest pitch in Prafulla Chakrabarti's account of the development of the squatters' colonies and their success in resisting eviction. To him, the squatters were no less than post-partition West Bengal's *deus ex machina*, who through an organised movement of squatting on fallow land solved the apparently insoluble problem of providing shelter to thousands of impoverished refugee families.[20] Chakrabarti singles them out as a category of refugees who 'lacked the resources but not the will' and were 'determined to carve out their own place in West Bengal'.[21] By praising the squatters for their refusal to enter government camps, Chakrabarti in effect endorses the official stereotyping of those who entered camps as refugees of lesser resolve. More importantly, Chakrabarti's account presents an incomplete and selective view of the incidence and significance of squatting in Calcutta. Though illegal construction on fallow land became a widespread tactic used by displaced persons from East Bengal in post-partition Calcutta, it actually had a longer history amongst the urban poor of the city.[22] Moreover, Chakrabarti's account celebrates only one aspect of refugee squatting – the organised forced seizure or *jabardakhal* of empty land. He has little to say about other forms of squatting, such as the occupation of a range of empty buildings in and around Calcutta. This included properties owned or requisitioned by the government, factories, warehouses, military barracks, and the suburban *bagan baris* or spacious villas with gardens that functioned as second homes of the city's rich. Last, but not least, in this list of omissions are the abandoned land and properties

---

[19] Ibid, p. 1020.   [20] Chakrabarti, *The Marginal Men* (1999), p. 33.   [21] Ibid.

[22] There is a vast literature on this topic, usually focusing on case studies or shifting patterns of slum improvement. For the history of slums in Calcutta and general patterns, see M. K. A. Siddiqui, 'Life in the Slums of Calcutta: Some Aspects', *Economic and Political Weekly*, 4:50 (1969): 1917–21; Collin W. Schenk, 'Slum Diversity in Kolkata', *Columbia Undergraduate Journal of South Asian Studies*, 1:2 (2010), 91–108; Frederic C. Thomas, *Calcutta Poor: Elegies on a City above Pretense* (New York: M. E. Sharpe, 1997); and Maitreyi Bardhan Roy, *Calcutta Slums: Public Policy in Retrospect* (Calcutta: Minerva, 1994).

of Muslim 'evacuees'. While these squats preceded or developed in parallel with the *jabardakhal* movement, there was another form of squatting that took roots in West Bengal between 1959 and 1961, as a direct consequence of the closure of all refugee camps. The vast majority of the 25,000 families who were served notices to proceed to Dandakaranya refused to leave West Bengal.[23] The authorities hoped to disperse them from the camps with six month's maintenance allowance. While refugees accepted this payment, most stayed on in the closed camps despite the withdrawal of basic amenities, such as water supply and electricity. By 1962, many of these camps had turned into squats with a self-supporting population of refugees.[24]

Squatting, as a strategy of survival, was not exclusive to the refugees who built the squatters' colonies. By 1970, an estimated 10,000 refugee families lived in 75 ex-campsites spread across different districts of West Bengal.[25] An additional 8,930 families had illegally constructed homes on vacant plots within government-sponsored colonies.[26] These squats were located outside Calcutta and had little or no links to the Left-led movement of squatting that swept the city between 1949 and 1951. Within Calcutta, six properties requisitioned by the state government were illegally occupied by refugees well into the 1960s. These properties were originally requisitioned for military needs during the Second World War and eventually taken over by the Department of Relief and Rehabilitation for the explicit purpose of providing rental accommodation to refugees. These turned into squats when the refugee families were unable to pay rent, but resisted eviction. Only two of these properties, namely the B.R.O. Camp and USAF Camp in the Tollygunge region, became the nucleus of squatters' colonies.[27] To sum up, squatters and camp inhabitants were not mutually exclusive categories of refugees in West Bengal. More importantly, the Left-led movement of squatting

---

[23] For details, see chapter 1.

[24] For details, see Committee of Review of Rehabilitation Work in West Bengal, *Report on Rehabilitation of Displaced Persons from East Pakistan at Ex-Camp-Sites in West Bengal* (New Delhi: Ministry of Supply and Rehabilitation, Department of Rehabilitation, 1969).

[25] Figures compiled from Committee of Review, Report on Ex-Camp-Sites in West Bengal (1969) and Committee of Review of Rehabilitation Work in West Bengal, *Report on Rehabilitation of Displaced Persons from East Pakistan Living at Bagjola Group of Ex-Camp-Sites in West Bengal* (New Delhi: Ministry of Supply and Rehabilitation, Department of Rehabilitation, 1970).

[26] Committee of Review of Rehabilitation Work in West Bengal, *Report on Rehabilitation of Displaced Persons from East Pakistan Squatting on Government and Requisitioned Properties in West Bengal* (New Delhi: Ministry of Supply and Rehabilitation, Department of Rehabilitation, 1970), p. 55.

[27] Ibid, pp. 15–54.

represents only one aspect of the practice of squatting amongst refugees. Locating the celebrated squatters' colonies within a more diverse practice of refugee squatting in post-partition West Bengal is helpful in identifying possible reasons for the disproportionate focus on this particular group.

The emphasis on celebrating the achievements of the residents of the squatters' colonies derives partly from the Calcutta-centrism of existing scholarship, and partly from an inherent class bias. While refugees in Nadia fought pitched battles with local landlords and farmers in their quest to carve out space in West Bengal, such acts of defiance did not enjoy the same level of press coverage as disturbances in Calcutta.[28] The greater visibility of Calcutta's refugees within contemporary reports and political debates has in some ways translated into their greater visibility within histories of partition. However, this by itself does not explain the often uncritical celebration of the agency and resolve of the squatters. Three interrelated features distinguished the residents of *jabardakhal* colonies from the urban poor of Calcutta,[29] and from other refugees who squatted on pavements or platforms of railway stations. First, a significant number of the residents of the squatters' colonies were educated and middle-class refugees who belonged to the three dominant castes of Bengal – *brahman, baidya* and *kayastha*. A second and related feature was their ability to inform history through the production of a range of autobiographical narratives that highlighted their achievements. Last, but not least, was the content of their achievement. This was not limited to successful resistance of eviction. Many of the squatters' colonies, despite their patent illegality, betrayed signs of civic planning. Houses were organised into neat blocks, with spaces left for roads, markets and playgrounds.[30] A large number of these colonies established officially recognised primary schools, while others managed to set up secondary schools and even colleges and hospitals within a decade of their existence. These markers of urban culture and middle-class life distinguished the squatters' colonies from both the slums of Calcutta and the squats on ex-campsites. It was this aspect of squatting that won

---

[28] Subhasri Ghosh, *The Impact of Immigration on West Bengal, 1947–71*, unpublished Phd thesis, Jawaharlal Nehru University, 2006.

[29] Constructing illegal settlements along roads and canals or *khalerdhar*, colloquially referred to as *jhupri* or *basti*, was a common practice of the urban poor in Calcutta that dated back to the nineteenth century. See Christine Furedy, 'Whose Responsibility? Dilemmas of Calcutta's Bustee Policy in the Nineteenth Century', *Journal of South Asian Studies*, 5:2 (1982), 24–46.

[30] This aspect of the squatters' colonies impressed a range of contemporary observers. For example, see A Calcutta Correspondent, 'Squatters' Colonies' *The Economic Weekly*, 6:23 (1954), 631–4; and B. S. Guha, *Studies in Social Tension among the Refugees from Eastern Pakistan* (1959).

the grudging respect of contemporaries, including government officials such as Hiranmoy Bandyopahyay, and marked the architects of the squatters' colonies as subjects worthy of celebration. Yet, this constructive aspect of the initiative of the squatters remains largely unexplained.

In all existing scholarship, the architects of the squatters' colonies are consistently portrayed as quintessential underdogs, who relied on nothing but mental determination and physical valour to first seize land and then resist eviction. This is particularly true of Prafulla Chakrabarti's narrative of the *jabardakhal andolan* or movement of forced seizure of land. His account focuses on the emergence of a series of squatters' colonies in the northern and southern fringes of Calcutta between 1949 and 1950.[31] He consistently highlights direct action and political agitation as the main weapons of the squatters. According to Chakrabarti, 'bitter struggles' of unarmed refugee men and women who stood firm against the onslaught of the police, and pitched battles with *goondas* hired by landlords enabled the foundation of these colonies. He credits their eventual survival to the successful agitation of refugees under the leadership of the UCRC against the Eviction Bill. Chakrabarti's account has largely been accepted as the authoritative narrative of refugee squatting in post-partition Calcutta. As a result, protest meetings, processions, and demonstrations against government policy have become the hallmarks of refugee agency. Subsequent scholarship reiterates his emphasis on direct action and political agitation as the main explanations for the success of the squatters.[32]

The inadequacy of this narrative in explaining the constructive aspect of squatting becomes particularly evident when one looks at the history of individual colonies, such as Bijoygarh. It was the earliest refugee colony established through illegal occupation of land on the margins of Calcutta. By 1954, it had already gained a reputation for being not only the 'biggest of them all' but also the only colony with a college. A contemporary viewed it as an 'impressive' undertaking with influential people in residence.[33] The rest of this chapter draws upon refugee reminiscences, popular history and a range of autobiographical narratives to explore the foundation and growth of Bijoygarh colony. Through the detailed

---

[31] Chakrabarti, *The Marginal Men* (1999), pp. 33–66.

[32] See, for example, Pradip Kumar Bose (ed.), *Refugees in West Bengal: Institutional Practices and Contested Identities* (Calcutta: Calcutta Research Group, 2000), Romola Sanyal, 'Contesting Refugeehood: Squatting as Survival in Post-Partition Calcutta', *Social Identities*, 15:1 (2009), 67–84 and Subhasri Ghosh, 'The Refugee and the Government: A Saga of Self-Rehabilitation in West Bengal' in (Daniel Coleman et al. eds.) *Countering Displacements: The Creativity and Resilience of Indigenous and Refugee-ed People* (Alberta: University of Alberta Press, 2012), pp. 151–76.

[33] A Calcutta Correspondent, 'Squatters' Colonies' *The Economic Weekly*, 6:23 (1954), 631.

exploration of a single colony it illuminates hitherto unexplored aspects of refugee agency and argues for a more nuanced understanding of the dynamics of refugee-led squatting in post-partition Calcutta.

Locating Bijoygarh: History, Memory and Foundation Myth

The archives of the state yield little or no information on the genesis and survival of Bijoygarh colony. It is merely enumerated as one of the 149 'pre-1950 colonies' that was approved for regularisation but was still awaiting it, as of 1974.[34] By contrast, on account of being the first of its kind, Bijoygarh features prominently not only in several histories of rehabilitation, but also in a range of popular narratives that include autobiographies, amateur histories and published collections of refugee reminiscences. However, the scope of these accounts and the location of Bijoygarh colony within them vary widely. In Hiramnoy Bandyopadhay's *Udvastu* and Prafulla Chakrabarti's *Marginal Men*, Bijoygarh is mentioned as one of many squatters' colonies. Though an important detail, it is not central to the narrative.[35] In contrast, Kaliprasad Mukhopadhyay's *Shikorer Sandhane (Quest for Roots)*[36] and an edited volume entitled *Dhangsa-o-Nirman (Destruction and Creation)*[37] devote large sections to interviews of refugees who built the Bijoygarh colony. Both Mukhopadhyay and the editors and interviewers of *Dhangsa-o-Nirman (Destruction and Creation)* have strong affinity and empathy for their respondents, but are not refugees themselves. While Mukhopadhyay's book is a work of amateur history, the edited volume aspires to narrate the history of Bengali refugees in 'their own voices', unmediated by analysis. This is an impossible ambition as oral history interviews, by their very nature, are co-authored by the interviewer and the interviewee. Nevertheless, when subjected to reflexive analysis, this collection of interviews provides valuable insight on the early history of Bijoygarh. In contrast, *Bijoygarh: Ekti Udvastu Upanibesh (A Refugee Colony)*[38] deals exclusively with Bijoygarh's history and is authored by

---

[34] Committee of Review, *Report on Development of Colonies* (1974).

[35] Chakrabarti, *The Marginal Men* (1999), pp. 33–66 and Bandyopadhyay, *Udvastu (Refugee)*, p. 23.

[36] Kaliprasad Mukhopadhyay, *Shikorer Sandhane (Quest for Roots)* (Calcutta: Bhasa o Sahitya, 2002).

[37] Tridib Chakrabarti, Nirupama Ray Mandal, and Paulami Ghoshal (compiled and eds.) *Dhangsa-o-Nirman: Bangiya Udbastu Samajer Svakathita Bibaran (Destruction and Creation: Self-Descriptive Accounts of Bengali Refugee Society)* (Calcutta: Seriban, 2007).

[38] Debabrata Datta, *Bijoygarh: Ekti Udvastu Upanibesh (A Refugee Colony)* (Calcutta: Progressive Publishers, 2001).

the son of Santosh Dutta, the veteran freedom fighter, who is at times described as Bijoygarh's founder. Indubaran Ganguly's eyewitness account of the proliferation of colonies in the area surrounding Bijoygarh, between 1948 and 1954, offers an onlooker's perspective on the influence of Bijoygarh in the neighbourhood.[39] This multiplicity of accounts and the diversity in authorial intentions and contexts of production facilitate the attempt to recover, from largely oral and inevitably subjective accounts, a coherent, albeit incomplete, narrative of the genesis of Bijoygarh. Through comparisons and cross-referencing, it is possible to arrive at the bare bones of a historical narrative which is common to these diverse texts.

Bijoygarh colony began as a squat of twelve refugee families in an abandoned military camp at Jadavpur. In November 1947, they travelled ticketless from Sealdah to Jadavpur station under the leadership of a group of local residents who hailed from East Bengal but had either migrated earlier, or had managed to find jobs and housing in Calcutta after partition. Shombhu Guha Thakurta, Kalu Sen, Ashish Debray and Shantiranjan Sen were a close-knit group of young East Bengali men who decided to help their less fortunate brethren stranded on railway platforms. The refugees transported their meagre belongings, such as utensils and sleeping mats, by hand-drawn carts from the railway station to the abandoned huts. As news of the squat spread through word-of-mouth amongst the thousands of displaced families pouring into Calcutta, a steady stream of refugees started trickling in to the military camp. The founders and residents formed the *Jadavpur Bastuhara Samiti* or Jadavpur Refugee Camp Association to promote co-operation amongst the refugees and to work towards providing basic amenities. As the military barracks filled to capacity, latecomers started building thatched shelters on neighbouring fallow land. There seems to have been little organisation or co-ordination behind this first phase of squatting. Shanti Sen, the general secretary of the refugee association, stressed its spontaneous nature. 'At that time, none heeded the other. People squatted wherever they could.'[40] Nevertheless, the association attempted to preserve a modicum of order, demarcating household plots measuring up to a maximum of 4 *kottahs*[41] for each family and registering them in lieu of a contribution of two rupees.

---

[39] Indu Baran Ganguly, *Colonysmriti (Memories of Colonies)* (Calcutta: InduBaran Ganguly, 1997).

[40] Interview with Shantiranjan Sen, Mukhopadhyay, *Shikorer Sandhane (Quest for Roots)* (2002), p. 48.

[41] *Kottah* is a popular unit of measuring land in Bengal. One *kottah* roughly equals 720 square feet.

The squatters were acutely aware of the vulnerability of their position and resorted to various strategies to gain legitimacy and government aid. A common practice was to invite leading scions of Calcutta society, especially those who enjoyed close ties with the Congress in West Bengal, to be the president of their refugee association. Thus, Basanti Debi, the widow of the veteran Congress leader Chittaranjan Das, was president of Jadavpur Refugee Association for a few months.[42] Following this pattern, leadership passed to freedom fighter Santosh Datta in 1948. The residents of the growing refugee settlement had hoped to gain the favour of the Congress government of Dr B. C. Roy through Datta's political connections. Though the exact date is not recorded, there is little doubt that this change in leadership was the driving force behind the transformation of a sprawling refugee squat into a planned settlement. The period from late 1948 to late 1949 marked a crucial period in the history of Bijoygarh. In the middle of 1949, the landlord, Layalka, hired goons to evict the refugees. This erupted into a pitched battle, which the refugees won. To commemorate this victory, the residents renamed their refugee camp as Bijoygarh colony. The transformation from camp to colony indicated the determination of the refugees to build a permanent settlement in the area, while the name, literally meaning fort of victory, evoked a militant spirit as the driving force behind the establishment of the colony.

The subsequent history of the colony is an impressive litany of the rapid proliferation of institutions. By 1952, Bijoygarh could boast four schools, one college, a market, a post office, a temple and even a hospital. Certain philanthropists, residents or groups of residents are credited with the foundation of specific institutions. For example, Nalinimohan Dasgupta is credited with establishing the first school in the colony, the *Jadavpur Bastuhara Bidyapith* (Jadavpur Refugee School), while Dr Aparnacharan Dutta is remembered as the driving force behind the establishment of *Prasuti Sadan* (Maternity Home), a maternity hospital.[43] Though the vicissitudes of memory coupled with different political affiliations of respondents and authors often lead to contradictory accounts, this rudimentary outline of Bijoygarh's genesis holds water across party lines and perspectives. The consensus breaks down over the nature of the colony,

---

[42] Despite retiring from active politics after the death of C. R. Das, Basanti Devi continued to be associated with Gandhian social reconstruction in East Bengal. She commanded great respect amongst politicians and social workers in Calcutta.

[43] Datta, *Bijoygarh* (2001), p. 28. Also see interview of Shanti Ranjan Sen and Gouranga De Chowdhury in Mukhopadhyay's *Shikorer Sandhane* (*Quest for Roots*)(2002), pp. 46–66; and interview with Manindra Pal in *Dhangsa-o-Nirman* (*Destruction and Creation*) (2007), pp. 123–4.

with popular myths, perceptions and perspectives beginning to inform its inclusion within or exclusion from the category of *jabardakhal* colony.

Hiranmoy Bandyopadhyay first mentions Bijoygarh while speaking of the tendency amongst refugees to occupy abandoned Allied military barracks in the southern suburbs of Calcutta. Initially, the squat at Jadavpur camp was one of many contemporary refugee squats on abandoned military facilities in and around Calcutta. However, the sheer scale of the occupation and the fact that a permanent refugee settlement emerged from it set Bijoygarh colony apart.[44] Bandyopadhyay credits the residents of Bijoygarh with a high degree of organisation and foresight. Planned initiatives, such as reserving open areas for parks and playgrounds, won his respect despite their patent illegality. He nevertheless insisted that Bijoygarh was far from an ordinary *jabardakhal* colony because 'evidence can be found suggesting that they received some indications of consent from the authorities'.[45] Prafulla Chakrabarti seconds this characterisation of Bijoygarh as being in a class by itself. He too speaks of 'evidence' of verbal consent by the government.[46] Neither Bandyopadhyay nor Chakrabarti provide any details regarding the nature or content of this evidence. Chakrabarti nevertheless points to the crucial role played by Bijoygarh in the *jabardakhal* movement. According to him, since only a select few were privy to Santosh Datta's success in obtaining government approval, contemporaries saw the emergence of Bijoygarh as a success story which could be replicated. 'When the colony, which apparently sprang out of unauthorised occupation of land was allowed to exist, there were many amongst the refugees who believed that if only they could take an organised plunge, they could easily get away with the land.'[47] In other words, the real significance of Bijoygarh colony lay in the inspiration it provided to refugees. The refusal to describe Bijoygarh as a true *jabardakhal* colony is taken one step further by Indubaran Ganguly. He claims that far from being a squatters' colony, Bijoygarh actually approximated to a government-sponsored one. He claimed that Bijoygarh enjoyed covert official support, with Santosh Datta providing the vital link between the residents of Bijoygarh and the Chief Minister of West Bengal, Dr B. C. Roy.[48]

Ganguly's explanation of the reasons compelling Dr Roy to keep his support secret are worth quoting at some length as they provide an insight into the contemporary world of rumours and hearsay which coloured the actions of refugees.

---

[44] Bandyopadhyay, *Udvastu (Refugee)*(1970), p. 23.   [45] Ibid, p. 35.
[46] Chakrabarti, *The Marginal Men* (1999), p. 36.   [47] Ibid., p. 37.
[48] Ganguly, *Colonysmriti (Memories of Colonies)*(1997), p. 28.

Dr Bidhan Chandra Roy had started trying to change official policy towards the East Bengali refugees. The land on which the Jadavpur military camp stood belonged to the government of India. So, until and unless the central government changed its policy towards refugees, it was not possible for the state government to openly support an initiative of building a refugee colony on this land. Yet, he was unshaken in his belief that he would eventually be able to change the Nehru administration's policy towards refugees. That's why he remained in the background and provided patronage to Santoshbabu in his initiative to establish Bijoygarh. It's a matter of note that Santoshbabu too was careful to keep this matter of patronage from Dr Roy a secret.[49]

It is unlikely that Indubaran Ganguly, a dissident member of the Communist Party of India and the founder of Azadgarh colony, actually enjoyed the confidence of the Chief Minister of West Bengal. A careful reading of his account betrays his claim as little more than imaginative speculation. In an account based entirely on personal memory, while speaking about Bijoygarh's origins, he falls back upon citing texts.[50] He had clearly not witnessed the establishment of Bijoygarh, and was not acquainted with the leaders, whose intentions he expounded on with such confidence. Nevertheless, his speculation on Santosh Datta's secret pact with Dr B. C. Roy is significant as it reflects the general belief amongst the residents of neighbouring refugee colonies regarding the special status of Bijoygarh. This belief was born of the respect Santosh Datta commanded within the Bengal Congress and in wider political circles of West Bengal. He was famous for his exploits as the second-in-command of Faridpur district's Jugantar cell, one of colonial Bengal's famous revolutionary terrorist organisations.[51] On the one hand, his celebrated status as a national hero gave him access to the contemporary luminaries of West Bengal. On the other hand, he was a refugee and a squatter. This no doubt enabled him to champion the cause of Bijoygarh amongst bureaucrats and politicians. However, his methods were not of open confrontation or political agitation against the government, but of negotiation and judicious exploitation of influence. It seems that these differences in method as well as in political allegiance lay at the core of Bijoygarh, under the

---

[49] Ibid.

[50] Indu Baran Ganguly quotes entire sections of Hiranmoy Bandyopadhyay's *Udvastu (Refugee)* (1970) and verbatim summarises Prafulla Chakrabarti's *The Marginal Men* (1999).

[51] A scattered group of revolutionary terrorists who joined the Indo-German Conspiracy came to be known as the Jugantar group. For a history of Jugantar, see Arun Chandra Guha, *Aurobindo and Jugantar* (Calcutta: Sahitya Sansad, n.d.). Also see David M. Laushley, *Bengal Terrorism and the Marxist Left: Aspects of Regional Nationalism in India, 1905–42* (Calcutta: K. L. Mukhopadhyay, 1975).

leadership of Santosh Datta, falling foul of being a 'true' squatters' colony.

The need for associative politics was urgently felt by the refugees of squatters' colonies. The early leaders had largely been supporters of the Congress or of the various socialist parties, such as Revolutionary Socialist Party and the Praja Socialist Party. However, the obduracy of the authorities in upholding public order and property ownership in the face of an unprecedented crisis forced the squatters to take up a more radical anti-establishment stand. This radicalisation of refugee organisations was coupled by a shift in leadership to the Communists and other Left parties. As a result, particular attributes were associated with the typical squatters' colony of Calcutta. It was seen as a hotbed of anti-establishment agitation and a fertile recruiting ground for the Communist Party. In this respect, Bijoygarh colony was indeed an exception. In the 1950s, when increasing militancy amongst the residents of squatters' colonies led to the emergence of 'refugee power' as a new player in the complex political milieu of post-partition West Bengal, Bijoygarh, under Santosh Datta's guidance, held back from overt opposition to the Congress. Indubaran Ganguly has described this rift vividly.

In April 1950, a conference of refugee leaders from all the squatters' colonies in the southern suburbs of Calcutta was organised with the express purpose of launching a new umbrella organisation, the *Dakshin Kalikata Sahartali Bastuhara Samhati* (DKSBS), or the South Suburban Calcutta Refugee Association.[52] Though the representatives of Bijoygarh colony attended the conference, they refused to be a part of the organisation. Santosh Datta supported the cause of regularisation of the squatters' colonies, but voiced his inability to participate in the methods of agitation which were likely to be adopted by the DKSBS.[53] Bijoygarh colony thus occupied a contradictory position within the history of the *jabardakhal* movement. On the one hand, by virtue of being the first colony born of illegal squatting, it provided a model to be mimicked by refugee colonies subsequently set up in the area. These colonies not only looked to Bijoygarh for inspiration, but also benefitted from the institutions and amenities developed by its residents, such as schools and markets. Nevertheless, Bijoygarh's leaders held themselves aloof from contemporary refugee organisations and refused to participate in the growing

---

[52] Chakrabarti, *The Marginal Men* (1999), p. 66; and Ganguly, *Colonysmriti* (*Memories of Colonies*)(1997), pp. 28–9.

[53] Ganguly, *Colonysmriti* (*Memories of Colonies*)(1997), pp. 28–9.

movement for the regularisation of squatters' colonies. This soured its relations with other squatters' colonies and fed rumours of a 'secret pact'.[54]

The relevance of this contradictory position of Bijoygarh can only be understood within the context of contemporaneous refugee politics. The ill-devised Eviction of Persons in Unauthorised Occupation of Land Bill, drafted by the government of West Bengal in 1951 to 'reconcile the demands of the law with the needs of the refugees',[55] was viewed by the refugees as an elaborate scheme to demolish the squatters' colonies. It provided the catalyst for the heydays of belligerent refugee politics under the leadership of the UCRC. As meetings, processions and often violent demonstrations drove protesting refugees into a collision course with the authorities, the government of West Bengal increasingly saw the refugees as a political 'problem'. The typical squatters' colony in Congress-ruled West Bengal was reconfigured as a settlement of militant underdogs. There is little doubt that the inhabitants of squatters' colonies led a severely marginalised life. Besides having no access to the basic amenities of urban life, such as water and electricity, the squatters also had to combat repeated police raids and private eviction operations of landlords using hired muscle. The target of these operations would often be the shanties built by the refugees rather than the refugees themselves. Nevertheless, these clashes frequently involved violence and at times, refugees died defending their new homes.[56] However, far more significant than the actual details of these clashes was their representation in the public sphere of refugee politics.

---

[54] In the absence of any documentary evidence, it is impossible to conclusively prove or disprove this theory of a 'secret pact'. Besides rumours and speculation, later accounts faithfully reproduce Hiranmoy Bandyopadhyay's unsubstantiated reference to evidence of government consent (*Udvastu* [*Refugee*], 1970, p. 23). However, taking into account all the available interviews of the residents of Bijoygarh, it is clear that Dr B. C. Roy was far from pleased with the actions of the refugees at Bijoygarh. The unofficial support might have come from lower down, i.e. from the Rehabilitation Commissioner and Secretary of Rehabilitation in Dr Roy's government, Hiranmoy Bandyopadhyay himself. Dhirendranath Raychowdhury, alias *Kalabhai*, and Shantiranjan Sen repeatedly allude to the sympathetic response of Bandyopadhyay in their interviews (*Dhangsa-o-Nirman* [*Destruction and Creation*], 2007 and Mukhopadhyay, *Shikorer Sandhane* [*Quest for Roots*], 2002). Kalabhai claims that Hiranmoy Bandyopadhyay, in response to a memorandum submitted by the refugees, had promised to legally acquire the colony's lands for regularisation if he ever became the Rehabilitation Commissioner. He had apparently kept his word, though given the proliferation of colonies by 1950, Bijoygarh's claim for special consideration had become impossible to implement (Mukhopadhyay, *Shikorer Sandhane* [*Quest for Roots*], p. 90). If this is true, then it could also explain Bandyopadhyay's uncharacteristically vague allusion to 'evidence'.
[55] *Amrita Bazar Patrika*, 21 March 1951.
[56] For details, see Chakrabarti, *The Marginal Men* (1999), pp. 80–1.

As local leaders inspired by the revolutionary ideology of the Left sought to organise the refugees and champion their cause, the brutality of the police in evicting refugees became the standard rhetoric of anti-establishment speeches. Every single clash between the refugees and the police was portrayed as an organised campaign. Repeated evocation of unity and militancy amongst the refugees in fiery speeches, pro-refugee editorials, pamphlets and public meetings gradually produced a standardised mythic narrative of the battle between the refugees and the establishment. For example, at mass public meetings organised by the UCRC, local refugee leaders such as Madhu Bannerji of Jadavpur colony urged refugees to establish armies of volunteers in all colonies and convert them into 'impregnable fortresses'.[57] Editorials in the *Swadhinata*[58] catalogued these battles and the price paid by refugees in terms of loss of shelter, injuries, imprisonment and death.[59] In the public theatre of refugee politics, those who fell to police bullets were memorialised as martyrs and heroes of the refugee movement. For example, Binapani Mitra, a pregnant woman killed by the police in their attempt to clear Jadabgarh squatters' colony was mentioned repeatedly in the public meetings of refugees. Her death became a symbol of the suffering and fortitude of the refugee squatters. The *Sanjukta Bastuhara Sammelan* (Joint Meeting of Refugees) of Hooghly district, organised by the Communist Party of India and the Forward Block on 28 January 1951, named one of the main gates for the open-air event Binapani *toran* (gate), thus memorialising her death as martyrdom.[60] As a result, chronicles of anti-establishment politics and direct clashes with the police were privileged over all other aspects of the lived experience of refugees. While remembering their pasts, the residents of the squatters' colonies frequently fall back upon the tropes of struggle, martyrdom and sacrifice. In history and memory, this standardised narrative plays the role of a foundation myth, which both explains and legitimises the origin of squatters' colonies. Bijoygarh colony was dismissed from the ranks of squatters' colonies on account of its leaders' proximity to the Congress government and their refusal to

---

[57] Extract of the report by the commissioner of police, Calcutta, for the week ending 7/4/51, File no:- 321/22 (KW), Sl No: 46/1922, Government of Bengal, Intelligence Bureau, henceforth GB IB.

[58] The Bengali daily, *Swadhinata* (Independence), was first published in 1946 as the mouthpiece of the Bengal Provincial Committee of the Communist Party of India. It fell victim to the severe factional fights within the Communist Party during the early sixties and ceased publication by 1965.

[59] For example, see *Swadhinata*, 22 February 1951.

[60] Report on the Proceedings of the Hooghly District *Sanjukta Bastuhara Sammelan* (Joint Meeting of Refugees) held at Masirbari Maidan, Mahesh, P. S. Serampur on 28 January 1951, File no:- 321/22 (KW), Sl No: 46/1922, GB IB.

engage in stereotypically militant struggle. Yet, the residents of Bijoygarh rely on a similar myth of origin to lay claim to the radical identity of self-settled refugees.

The standardised model of refugee resistance, which coalesced out of the multiple representations of refugees as militant underdogs, envisions the entire refugee colony as a mobilised machine of war against the establishment. In uncertain times, all colony residents had the responsibility of keeping watch. At any sign of the police or suspicious outsiders, the women raised an alarm by blowing on conch shells and by beating steel utensils together. This was the signal for every able-bodied man present to rush out to battle, armed, literally, with sticks and stones. Children also played a vital role in this idealised armed community. 'There was an informal information network in place, which signalled their arrival (mostly done by young boys). Men resisted as women blew conch.'[61] Thus, within moments, a settlement of respectable refugees would be transformed into a militant army of resistance. Anecdotes regarding the bravery of refugee women, who fought at the vanguard,[62] or the strategic use of women and children as shields against the police,[63] would frequently be used to embellish these accounts. These battles, more often than not, ended in refugee victory, though the invaders did manage to destroy a few shanties before they left. With exemplary fortitude, the refugees rebuilt their shelters and continued their struggle for rehabilitation and legitimacy within the socio-economic and political milieu of West Bengal. This standardised origin myth of squatters' colonies dominates popular imagination in West Bengal. It not only moulds the way in which refugees remember and represent their past, but also the production of refugee histories. Kaliprasad Mukhopadhyay's *Shikarer Sandhane* illustrates this starkly when the author asks Shantiranjan Sen:

So there had not been any clashes over the land? Then why did the people live in terror? The women were instructed to raise an alarm blowing conch shells and beating upon tin, etc. – why had these precautionary measures been taken?[64]

---

[61] Manas Ray, 'Growing Up Refugee: On Memory and Locality', in Bose (ed.), *Refugees in West Bengal* (2000), p. 166.

[62] The first attempt at establishing a squatters' colony under NVBKP leadership in south Calcutta, though a failure, was made memorable by the dogged fight put up by refugee women against the police. For details, see Chakrabarti, *The Marginal Men* (1999), p. 65.

[63] The suburban squatters' colony at Mahesh evolved this strategy under the leadership of a local CPI student activist. For details, see Chakrabarti, *The Marginal Men* (1999), pp. 81–2.

[64] Mukhopadhyay, *Shikorer Sandhane* (*Quest for Roots*)(2002), p. 54.

Having immersed himself in refugee folklore, Kaliprasad aggressively sought confirmation of his preconceived notions from his respondents, once he set out to interview the residents of Bijoygarh.

For Bijoygarh, this standardised folklore was combined with the memories of an actual clash between the residents and hired goons sent by Layalka, the landlord, to produce the foundation myth of the colony. However, Manindra Pal,[65] Shantiranjan Sen and Dhirendranath Ray Chowdhury's[66] memories of this clash do not fit the mythologised pattern of refugee warfare. The residents of Bijoygarh colony were largely taken by surprise by truckloads of hired musclemen who drove into the area. They strategically chose to attack in the afternoon, hoping that the men of the colony would be away at work. This strategy paid off, as initially the refugees were heavily outnumbered and several sustained injuries. According to Manindra Pal, a resident named Badal had been given the responsibility of keeping watch with a bugle at hand for raising the alarm.[67] Of the crowd which assembled in response, a fraction actually offered resistance. The students of Jadavpur Engineering College, who shared close ties with the founding members of Bijoygarh due to their common socialist affiliations, came to the rescue of the colony. However, in 1950, when the residents commemorated this victory by renaming Jadavpur Refugee camp as Bijoygarh, or victory fort, few chose to credit the role played by 'outsiders'. By suggesting the new name, Shombhu Guha, who was a member of the Congress Socialist Party and played an active role in various constructive ventures within the colony, claimed this victory and its attendant self-image of victorious underdogs for all the residents of the colony.[68] It fed into the squatters' self-image of proud and independent East Bengalis, who relied on a combination of wit and physical valour to wrest rehabilitation from an unsympathetic state. With the proliferation of popular and autobiographical accounts in Bengali from the mid-nineties, these themes of physical courage, militant organisation and struggle against the establishment have found their way into refugee histories.

The stereotype of the militant refugee obscures more than it reveals of the micro-history of the squatters' colonies. As mentioned earlier, the community leaders of Bijoygarh colony had close ties with the Congress

---

[65] For the full text of Manindra Pal's interviews, see ibid., pp. 112–5 and *Dhangsa-o-Nirman* (*Destruction and Creation*)(2007), pp. 117–34.

[66] For the full text of Shantiranjan Sen and Dhirendranath Roy Chowdhury's interviews, see Mukhopadhyay, *Shikorer Sandhane* (*Quest for Roots*)(2002), pp. 46–93.

[67] Ibid., p. 114.

[68] Interview with Manindra Pal, *Dhangsa-o-Nirman* (*Destruction and Creation*)(2007), p. 123.

party. Their reminiscences are littered with numerous incidents of non-confrontational interaction with the authorities, such as memorandums, deputations, appeals and unofficial conversations leading to equally unofficial understandings with members of the police and the bureaucracy. Such negotiations were by no means unique to Bijoygarh. In other words, confrontation, especially violent confrontation with the authorities, was only one of the many modes in which the refugees dealt with the state. The significance of the mythic battle waged by refugees lay in its ability to produce a homogenised refugee identity in opposition to the external 'other', i.e. the state and the host society, as embodied in ruthless landlords. It papered over differences in caste, class and cultural capital, which not only divided the refugees from East Bengal, but also moulded the kind of rehabilitation which particular refugee families had access to.

Deciphering 'Refugee Power': Networks and Knowhow

Large numbers of refugees took to political agitation in their quest for rehabilitation, signalling their presence and predicament with slogans of *'Amra kara? Bastuhara!'* ('Who are we? The refugees!').[69] Numerous scholars have read their processions and slogans as the sign of the arrival of a new 'power in the land', who derived political clout from 'their number, their completely expropriated condition and rootlessness, their poverty and hunger'.[70] There is little doubt that the radicalisation of refugees irretrievably altered the political balance in West Bengal.[71] However, the brute force and determination of desperate men, which is the most common understanding of 'refugee power', is a poor explanation for the resilience of refugees. The reminiscences of the founders of Bijoygarh colony suggest an alternative explanation of the roots of refugee power. Scattered throughout the reminiscences of the squatters are anecdotes of everyday resistance, negotiation and accommodation, which together provide a more complex and nuanced explanation of the ability of refugees to challenge government policies.

Constant attempts by the refugees to obtain government aid or legal recognition characterised the foundation of Jadavpur Refugee camp and

---

[69] See Nilanjana Chatterjee, 'Interrogating Victimhood: East Bengali Refugee Narratives of Communal Violence' (http://www.swadhinata.org.uk/document/chatterjeeEastBengal%20Refugee.pdf, accessed 18 August 2015).

[70] Chakrabarti, *The Marginal Men* (1999), p. 48. He equates the first refugee rally in Calcutta, organised on 14 January 1949, as the city's 'first taste of a new power in the land' (p. 53).

[71] For a detailed analysis of the political fallout of partition and the role played by refugees in changing political calculations in West Bengal, see Chatterji, *Spoils of Partition* (2007), pp. 209–309.

its eventual transformation into Bijoygarh colony. The reminiscences of the residents suggest that far from being marginal to the political and bureaucratic order of West Bengal, it was their familiarity with the 'system' which enabled the founders of Bijoygarh to give permanence to an illegal settlement. Old ties of caste, class and locality often aided the quest for new roots in an alien milieu. The affinity born of a shared past, of living in the same district in East Bengal, of belonging to particular educational institutions, political parties or cultural movements, provided not only the building blocks of new communities but also markers for identifying potential sympathisers within the government and the bureaucracy. Though illegal, the initial occupation of the Jadavpur military camp met with little opposition from the government. According to Indubaran Ganguly, Kamalkrishna Ray, who was West Bengal's relief minister during Dr P. C. Ghosh's brief tenure as chief minister, opened all the abandoned military camps and barracks in and around Calcutta for the refugees. Ganguly suggests that since Kamalkrishna Ray came from Myemensingh in East Bengal, his actions were impelled by his empathy for fellow East Bengalis.[72] While it is not possible to verify Ganguly's claim, it would be a mistake to underestimate the role played by East Bengali solidarity, born quite recently of a shared displacement wrought by partition, in moulding the course of rehabilitation in West Bengal.

Some of the earliest migrants from East Bengal and the only ones encouraged, even welcomed, by the Indian state, were the 'optees'. They were government employees, including the educated middle-class Hindus who had staffed the vast majority of posts at various levels of administration in East Bengal. With partition, they availed of special provisions made for government servants and 'opted' for India. Though assured an income, most were forced to abandon their ancestral homes and property in East Bengal. Most optees had to negotiate a sharp drop in their standard of living, though few claimed refugee status. In the years after partition, the East Bengali optees maintained a conscious social distance from the squalor and desperation of the refugee colonies and camps.[73] Nevertheless, the reminiscences of refugees suggest that post-partition West Bengal also saw the affirmation, perhaps even the creation, of bonds of empathy between optees and refugees who hailed roughly

[72] Ganguly, *Colonysmriti* (*Memories of Colonies*)(1997), pp. 25–6.
[73] For a literary representation of this social distance, see Amitav Ghosh, *The Shadow Lines* (London: Bloomsbury, 1988). Also see Md. Mahbubar Rahman and Willem Van Schendel, 'I Am Not a Refugee': Rethinking Partition Migration', *Modern Asian Studies*, 37:3 (2003), 551–84. It is only of late that the popularisation of the heroic trope of the self-settled Bengali refugee has made refugee identity a mantle worth wearing amongst the *bhadraloks* of Calcutta.

from the same sociocultural milieu, and often from the same district or town. The bureaucrats and officials who served the cause of rehabilitation beyond the call of duty were often from East Bengal. Hiranmoy Bandyopadhay and Jashoda Kanta Ray[74] are two such individuals who feature prominently in refugee narratives, though no special credit is reserved for them in the state's archives. The more enterprising amongst the refugees specifically appealed to bureaucrats, administrators and lawyers from East Bengal for help, hoping to exploit these affective ties. The middle-class refugees of the squatters' colonies viewed optees within the administration of West Bengal as possible allies in their quest for rehabilitation. It is possible that for the elite amongst the optees, who were also dealing with loss and dislocation, patronage of destitute East Bengalis offered a means of rebuilding social status and influence in West Bengal.

Several references to such interactions with authorities and appeals to individual bureaucrats or government officials can be found in the reminiscences of the leaders of Bijoygarh. This strategy became particularly relevant in the immediate aftermath of the 'battle' with Layalka's hired muscle. Though in the skirmish the residents of Bijoygarh came out on top, it was, in fact, only the beginning of their troubles. The police swiftly issued warrants for the arrest of all the refugees involved in the fight and for all the committee members. Moreover, Layalka, unwilling to give up his land, took the Jadavpur Refugee Camp Association to court. Desperate to avoid imprisonment and conviction for activities which were patently illegal, Santosh Datta and his cohort, Dhirendranath Ray Chowdhury, alias Kalabhai, sought a meeting with Hiranmoy Bandyopadhyay. The latter was then the District Magistrate of 24 Parganas, but had been a *khashmahal* officer in Barisal district of East Bengal before partition. As a result he was not a complete stranger to Kalabhai, who had been a local celebrity of sorts in Barisal on account of his participation in revolutionary terrorism and his role as the editor of a literary journal called *Sarathi*.[75] Kalabhai had met Bandyopadhyay at a cultural function organised by the Brahmo Samaj in Barisal, where he had been extremely impressed by the latter's lecture on Vedic philosophy. Subsequently, he had invited Hiranmoy Bandyopadhyay to be the chief

---

[74] Jashoda Kanta Ray was the Deputy Commissioner of Relief and Rehabilitation with the Government of West Bengal.

[75] *Sarathi* literally means the charioteer, but in this context clearly evoked the role played by Krishna in the epic battle of *Mahabharata* where he had guided the mythical Pandava brothers to victory as the charioteer of Arjun.

priest at a cultural festival, *Kalidas Janmajayanti*,[76] at the town hall of Barisal. Kalabhai did not hesitate to remind the District Magistrate of their previous acquaintance, no doubt in the hope of eliciting sympathy for the squatters.[77]

Bandyopadhyay directed the refugees to seek the help of yet another optee: the officer-in-chief of Tollygunj police station, Amulya Bannerjee. He had been a police officer at Keraniganj police station of Dhaka district before partition.[78] The vast majority of the squatters' colonies of south Calcutta, including Bijoygarh, came under his jurisdiction. Refugee reminiscences from Bijoygarh suggest that Amulya Bannerjee secretly helped them to exploit every possible loophole of the criminal procedure code, while publicly continuing to carry out his duty of evicting illegal squatters.[79] If Kalabhai's account is to be believed, Amulya Bannerjee came to a mutually beneficial compromise with the refugees. He agreed to allow the named refugees to surrender at a predetermined spot, and to immediately grant them bail. Thus, the refugee leaders were spared the ignominy of being locked up. Mr Bannerjee, in return for his co-operation, was promised a plot or two of the illegally occupied land.[80]

Though the threat of harassment from the police had been averted, the case still had to be fought in court. As the hearing dragged on, the refugees again turned to their more accomplished East Bengali brethren for support. Girin Ray Chowdhury, the lawyer representing the refugees, was from Faridpur district.[81] However, defeat and conviction seemed imminent until the refugees requested Chinta Haran Ray, a famous criminal lawyer from Subidda in Dhaka, to argue on their behalf. The colony dwellers could not afford the services of a renowned lawyer. It seems that ties of a lost homeland, coupled with a sense of obligation arising from personal familiarity with one of the refugees, prompted Ray to take up their case free of charge. 'He knew me', explained Manindra Pal, one of the many leaders of colony construction. 'I used to be his brother's

---

[76] Literally, this means the birth anniversary of the Sanskrit composer Kalidasa. However, it was more likely to be the opening ceremony of a literary and cultural festival.

[77] Interview with Dhirendranath Ray Chowdhury, Mukhopadhyay, *Shikorer Sandhane* (*Quest for Roots*)(2002), p. 77.

[78] Interview with Mani Pal, Ibid, p. 113.

[79] Himanghsu Majumdar, a member of the central committee of Bijoygarh colony and its resident since December 1947, makes special mention of his aid. For details, see Interview with Himangshu Majumdar in Mukhopadhyay, *Shikorer Sandhane* (*Quest for Roots*)(2002), p. 103.

[80] Interview with Kalabhai, ibid., pp. 79–80.

[81] Interview of Manindra Pal, ibid., p. 115.

classmate at Jagannath Hall in Dhaka.'[82] Chinta Haran Ray's legal intervention finally forced Layalka to drop charges.[83] Thus, the battle with
Layalka, which has been mythologised as a militant conflict won by the
sheer muscle and grit of desperate refugees, was actually won in court.

This was followed by another coup based on East Bengali solidarity
orchestrated by the colony committee. According to Kalabhai, the military camp at Jadavpur was the property of the army and in 1950 plans
were afoot to auction it off. This precipitated a meeting between the
leaders of Bijoygarh and the GOC Eastern Command, Satya Brata
Sinha Roy, or S. B. S. Roy.[84] Debabrata Datta provides a slightly different
context for the meeting. According to him, the colony committee wanted
to use the last extant military barrack, still controlled by the army, to
establish a college. They requested Hiranmoy Bandyopadhyay's help in
the matter, who directed them to meet S. B. S. Roy.[85] However, both
accounts place equal emphasis on the General's East Bengali origin.
Kalabhai requested him to visit the colony in order to understand the
compulsion of the refugees. 'You are after all from East Bengal', he
implored, once more hoping to exploit the sentiments of East Bengali
sub-nationalism.[86] Datta's narrative underlines this factor. 'He too was
from East Bengal. Therefore, realising the difficulty of the refugees, he did
not hold back in expressing a spirit of cooperation.'[87] The commander-
in-chief visited Bijoygarh on 21 August 1950 and officially handed over
the military barrack of Bijoygarh to the colony committee, to be used for
'educational purposes'.[88]

The success of the refugees in negotiating the bureaucratic and legal
maze of partitioned Bengal cannot be attributed to successful appeals to
well-placed East Bengalis alone. To the colonies they inhabited, many
refugees brought a measure of familiarity with associative politics. The
founders of the Jadavpur Refugee camp, Shombhu Guha Thakurta,
Sushil Sengupta and Ashish Deb Ray, besides being East Bengalis and
residents of the small residential complex around Jadavpur University,

---

[82] Interview with Manindra Pal, *Dhangsa-o-Nirman* (*Destruction and Creation*)(2007),
p. 120–1. Also see interview with Manindra Pal in Mukhopadhyay, *Shikorer Sandhane*
(*Quest for Roots*)(2002), p. 115.

[83] Since the records of criminal cases which do not reach the higher courts are routinely
destroyed every ten years, the records of this case have not survived.

[84] Interview with Dhirendranath Roy Chowdhury, Mukhopadhyay, *Shikorer Sandhane*
(*Quest for Roots*)(2002), p. 81.

[85] Datta, *Bijoygarh* (2001), p. 59.

[86] Interview with Dhirendranath Roy Chowdhury, Mukhopadhyay, *Shikorer Sandhane*
(*Quest for Roots*)(2002), p. 81.

[87] Datta, *Bijoygarh* (2001), p. 59.

[88] The details of this visit are roughly the same in Debabrata Datta, Ibid., and Kalabhai's
interview in Mukhopadhyay, *Shikorer Sandhane* (*Quest for Roots*)(2002), pp. 80–2.

shared in common their membership of the Jayprakash faction of the Congress Socialist Party.[89] The refugees who took the lead in establishing squatters' colonies usually proceeded only after forming an association or a committee.[90] These committees and associations were spontaneously formed through mutual consent. But they were invariably registered with the Registrar of Firms, Societies and Non-trading Corporations of West Bengal under the Society Act of 1886. They conformed to the institutional structure required of registered societies, framing a constitution and electing or nominating an executive committee consisting of a president, treasurer and secretary. This indicated not only a high degree of literacy, but also organisational skills typical to a bourgeois public sphere. This knowhow of popular associations provides a far more convincing explanation than mere willpower or enterprise, for the ability of a certain section of the refugees to resist official policies of eviction and dispersal.

A significant number amongst the squatters worked as clerks or lower-level officials in the various departments of the government of West Bengal.[91] This made the colony committees privy to an 'insider's' knowledge of bureaucracy. Often, these contacts succeeded in obtaining government aid for particular projects. A number of Bijoygarh's constructive initiatives derived support and stability from such linkages. Shanti Sen worked at Writers' Building, possibly as one of the many clerks employed at the seat of government in West Bengal. He saw himself as a facilitator of the first meeting between the refugees of the Jadavpur camp and the authorities at Writers' Building. 'I had gone with them (the refugee leaders) since they had never seen Writers' Building before. I guided them and we met the Relief Minister.'[92] Familiar with the idiosyncrasies of bureaucracy, Shantiranjan came up with an ingenious plan of exploiting the loopholes in administrative procedure in order to derive some official recognition for Bijoygarh.

[89] Interview with Dr Subratesh Ghosh, *Dhangsa-o-Nirman (Destruction and Creation)* (2007), pp. 97–8.

[90] Here, Bijoygarh was the exception rather than the rule, as a committee to regulate the day-to-day life of the Jadavpur Refugee Camp took shape after the abandoned military barracks had already been occupied.

[91] The East Bengali migrants' ability to secure white-collar jobs has been highlighted by Chatterji in *Spoils of Partition* (2007), pp. 141–50. Also see Nirmal Kumar Bose, *Calcutta: 1964, A Social Survey* (Bombay: Lalvani Publishing House, 1968), p. 34. According to Bose, refugees from East Bengal tended to avoid manual labour and most found jobs as clerks. A statistical survey of refugees in West Bengal conducted in 1955 noted with alarm their high rates of employment in government and other services. For details, see Government of West Bengal Statistical Bureau, *Rehabilitation of Refugees: A Statistical Survey, 1955* (Alipore: Government of West Bengal, 1956), pp. 5–9.

[92] Interview of Shanti Ranjan Sen, Mukhopadhyay, *Shikorer Sandhane* (Quest for Roots) (2002), pp. 46–7.

There were several government employees amongst the refugees at Jadavpur camp who had 'opted' for government service in West Bengal. Sen instructed these men to address an official letter to their respective departments, asking for some land for resettlement. The letters further requested that if the authorities could not provide land, could they at least forward the application to the Jadavpur Refugee Association, along with a request for land for the applicant. The point of the exercise was not to actually obtain land, but to trick government departments into indirectly endorsing an illegal seizure of land.

This strategy of ours paid off. Every department approached in this manner forwarded the applications to our association. They did not know what value these had ... Later on, we could tell the government that they could not deem us to be trespassers, since their administrative departments had forwarded applications to the secretary of our association. This was a great safeguard for us in legal terms. Ten or twelve such applications were forwarded to us.[93]

At other times, Bijoygarh colony enjoyed more direct benefits of having government employees amongst its residents. All respondents acknowledged Nalini Mohan Dasgupta as the driving force behind the establishment of the first secondary school for the children of Jadavpur camp. Local refugee leaders founded a school named *Jadavpur Bastuhara Banipeeth* on 6 January 1949. It was later renamed *Jadavpur Bastuhara Vidyapeeth* and with the rechristening of the camp as Bijoygarh colony, came to be known as *Bijoygarh Vidyapeeth*. At this stage, a permanent committee took over the administration of the boys' section of the school and Nalini Mohan Dasgupta became the secretary of this committee.[94] Dasgupta earned his living as an employee of the Refugee Relief and Rehabilitation Department of West Bengal and was, therefore, uniquely placed to obtain government recognition for the school, as well as the full package of benefits that refugee students were entitled to.[95] While writing the history of Bijoygarh, Debabrata Dutta made a direct connection between education and influence.

Through untiring efforts of Nalini Mohan Dasgupta and Santosh Dutta's influence in circles of governance it was possible to obtain government aid for every single refugee student. This is what enabled the refugee children of this area to continue their education.[96]

[93] Ibid., p. 52.   [94] Datta, *Bijoygarh* (2001), p. 28.
[95] According to Gouranga De Chowdhury, he was employed as the office superintendent in the Ministry of Relief and Rehabilitation. See interview with Gouranga De Chowdhury, Mukhopadhyay, *Shikorer Sandhane (Quest for Roots)*(2002), p. 61.
[96] Datta, *Bijoygarh* (2001), p. 29.

Despite high aspirations, most refugees in squatters' colonies did not have the means to educate their children. Education and therefore, social mobility amongst refugees, depended upon the ability to obtain concessions from the government.

The importance of education in the social geography of the squatters' colonies cannot be overstated.[97] Almost every colony boasted of at least one secondary school and several primary schools. These schools were not only vital to refugee aspirations of economic rehabilitation through training the next generation for employment; they also embodied the educated and cultured *bhadralok* identity the middle-class squatters clung to.[98] According to Manas Ray, the refugees believed that *shiksha* (education) would enable them to gain recognition as *bhadraloks* from Calcutta society, 'something we thought we rightfully deserved, but were deprived of'.[99] These schools also bound the refugee community together at a more practical level. Almost all the teachers of the schools were drawn from amongst local refugees. Manas Ray, in his autobiographical account, noted large numbers of schoolteachers among the early migrants to West Bengal.[100] Schools were popular as they provided local employment. Most schools were started by pooling together meagre funds. The teachers depended upon *chanda*, or donations, for their salary, which was paid irregularly, if at all.[101] Yet, given the high levels of unemployment in contemporary Calcutta, the colony's schools seldom suffered from a dearth of teachers. Moreover, compared to regularisation of land ownership, which still awaits many refugees, it was comparatively easy to obtain government recognition for the schools. Once a school was registered, which the refugees were quick to organise through their network of connections, it provided regular government jobs to a significant number

---

[97] For an analysis of the significance of education in the mind-set of the residents of refugee colonies, see Dipankar Sinha's 'Adjustment and Transition in a Bengali Refugee Settlement: 1950-1999' in Bose (ed.), *Refugees in West Bengal* (2000), pp. 147–51.

[98] Literally meaning 'decent people', the term was originally used to describe the landed and educated Hindu middle class of Bengal. However, with the radical decline of the *bhadralok* in the first half of the twentieth century, the term had increasingly come to represent a claim towards social respectability, bolstered by superior educational qualifications, lineage and cultural pursuits, which may or may not be reflected in economic status. For an exploratory survey of the decline of the Bengali *bhadralok* and their attempts to stem the rot, see Joya Chatterji, 'The Decline, Revival and Fall of Bhadralok Influence in the 1940s: A Historiographic Review', in Sekhar Bandyopadhyay (ed.), *Bengal: Rethinking History, Essays in Historiography* (Delhi: Manohar, 2001), pp. 297–315.

[99] Ray, 'Growing Up Refugee', in ibid., p.173.

[100] Manas Ray, '*Kata Deshe Ghorer Khonj*' (*The Quest for Home in a Divided Land*), in Chakrabarti et al. (eds) *Dhangsa-o-Nirman (Destruction and Creation)* (2007), p. 254.

[101] For a descriptive account of the foundation of numerous schools in Bijoygarh see Datta, *Bijoygarh* (2001), pp. 27–31.

of refugees. It also became the first step towards gaining legitimacy from the authorities and recognition from the host society of Calcutta.

Not all the residents of the squatters' colonies were middle class or educated. However, the self-image of the squatters was without an exception of the educated *bhadralok*. Their leaders, irrespective of political affiliations, represented the colonies as *bhadralok* communities, repeatedly stressing education and pursuit of bourgeois culture as markers which set them apart from the urban poor of Calcutta. Kalabhai's attempt to elicit support for the regularisation of Bijoygarh colony from the District Magistrate of 24 Parganas, discussed above, provides a relevant example.[102] In this meeting, he described the squatters of Bijoygarh as 'members of that (East Bengali) erudite society'.[103] Sailen Chowdhury chose a more dramatic way to highlight the cultured identity of the squatters. Previously the chairman of Sherpur Municipality of Mymensingh in East Bengal, Sailen had joined the ranks of squatters in West Bengal and had helped to found Deshbandhu colony.[104] He succeeded in eliciting an impromptu meeting with the Governor of West Bengal, Dr Katju, through a calculated display of cultural affinity. Young refugee girls dressed in saris, blowing conch shells and scattering flowers upon the governor's car as he travelled along the main road bordering the colony, proved to be far more effective than a roadblock. The governor was ushered into a squatter's shack and felicitated with garlands, accompanied by songs and recitations by refugee children. Sailen Chowdhury wrapped up the session with an appeal for help.[105] This display had the desired effect upon Dr Katju. According to Hiranmoy Bandyopadhyay, who was his companion on this tour, the governor was extremely impressed by the refugees' commitment towards preserving their cultural heritage despite poverty. He showed his appreciation by arranging for the resettlement of Deshbandhu colony on land legally requisitioned nearby. Naktala No. 1 colony, an island of legal settlement within the expanding mosaic of squats in south Calcutta, emerged as a result of Dr Katju's determination to rescue these cultured families from a life of illegality.[106]

Much of the enterprise and initiative of the squatters in rehabilitating themselves derived from their social and cultural antecedents. The refugees who built the squatters' colonies came from a sociocultural milieu where education and white-collar jobs were highly valued. The East

---

[102] Ibid., p 24.
[103] Interview of Dhirendranath Ray Chowdhury, alias, Kalabhai, Mukhopadhyay, *Shikorer Sandhane (Quest for Roots)* (2002), p. 78.
[104] Ganguly, *Colonysmriti (Memories of Colonies)* (1997), pp. 36–9.   [105] Ibid., pp. 39–41.
[106] Bandyopadhyay, *Udvastu (Refugee)* (1970), p. 39. Also described in Ganguly, *Colonysmriti (Memories of Colonies)* (1997), pp. 36–9.

Bengali migrants who succeeded in rebuilding reasonably prosperous lives in West Bengal, either as well-paid professionals or as officials in the national administration, remained connected to their poorer 'country cousins' through social ties born of common schools, colleges, sociocultural forums, or through familial ties perpetuated by marriage. What the squatters around Calcutta lacked in economic means and urban sophistication, they sought to make up through judicious exploitation of social networks and familial ties.[107] However, cultural capital alone was not sufficient to see the refugees through. They turned to politics in order to combat the might of the state, which remained stubborn in its attachment to 'law and order' and reluctant to concede space to the refugees. The 'infiltration' of refugee associations by the Communist Party of India, the relationship between refugee politics and the electoral success of Left parties in West Bengal, as well as the limits of CPI's commitment to the refugee cause have been discussed in vivid detail by Prafulla Chakrabarti.[108] It cannot be denied that Communist support played a crucial role in bolstering the refugees' demand for rehabilitation. But an overt emphasis on confrontational politics obscures the diverse strategies employed by refugees to find a foothold in Calcutta. The vast majority of the refugee families who unleashed the veritable movement of land-grabbing upon Calcutta had been reduced to bare subsistence levels by circumstances. Desperate to better their lot, they used every possible means, whether legal or illegal. At the micro-historical level, political agitation is revealed to be the most visible of the many strategies of wresting rehabilitation from a reluctant state – not the only, or even the most effective one.

The *Bhadralok* Refugee and Paradoxes of Refugee Identity

The pattern of refugee experiences that comes to light from the above discussion suffers from a near-exclusive focus on the squatters' colonies and their *bhadralok* residents. The stereotypical Bengali refugee delineated in these narratives is both a victim and a survivor. Despite state apathy and abysmal conditions in government camps, they emerge triumphant in their

---

[107] In 'Dispositions and Destinations: Refugee Agency and "*Mobility Capital*" in the Bengal Diaspora, 1947–2007', *Comparative Studies in Society and History*, 55:2, (2013), 273–304, Joya Chatterji demonstrates how the patterns of migration of the Bengali Muslim diaspora were determined by a similar cluster attributes and resources, where networks, information and knowhow played a more definitive role than economic means. She conceptualizes this as 'mobility capital'.

[108] Chakrabarti, *The Marginal Men* (1999).

quest for social and economic rehabilitation through the establishment of the squatters' colonies. Commemorative booklets, memoirs and popular histories are crowded with the names of leaders and pioneers, and descriptions of their achievements.[109] No such popular accounts exist regarding the residents of government camps. Their voices and lived experiences of rehabilitation are conspicuously absent.[110] Yet, the reminiscences, amateur histories and autobiographies authored by squatters are haunted by the spectre of government camps. The dehumanising conditions of government camps combined with the failure of the authorities to provide any shelter to the swelling tide of refugees provide the moral justification for illegal occupation of land. Despite the pervasive horror of a prolonged stay on railway platforms or in government camps, a lived experience of either site is completely absent in the reminiscences of squatters.[111] In order to understand this paradoxical feature of refugee reminiscences, it is necessary to take into account the squatters' attachment to respectability and its divisive impact on colony life.

All accounts of Bijoygarh's history mention a handful of refugee families from Sealdah Station as the colony's earliest residents. However, none of the respondents selected by three separate oral history initiatives fit this profile.[112] Even the names of these early settlers elude most respondents. Dr Subratesh Ghosh could barely recall the name of one such family.[113] Bharat Chandra Debnath's childhood memory of accompanying Shombu Guha to bring refugees from the railway station

---

[109] Though the majority of the refugee colonies in Jadavpur and Tollygunj regions have been regularised and integrated into the urban sprawl of greater Calcutta, most have retained the colony committees and membership of the UCRC. While the latter continues to highlight outstanding issues and grievances of refugee colonies, most colony committees now concentrate on organising communal yearly festivals, especially the *Durga Puja*. Between 1998 and 2000, the fiftieth anniversary was celebrated by a number of colonies, their schools or by the local *Durga Puja*. Most commemorated the occasion by printing a booklet which included a section on the foundation and history of the particular colony and its institutions. One such example is *Regent Colony Bastuhara Samiti, Subarna Jayanti Utsab (Regent Colony Refugee Association, Golden Jubilee Celebrations), 1999–2000* (Calcutta, n.p., 2000).

[110] A handful of studies which have explored the lived experience of refugees in the various government camps and colonies reveal a far more complex world of everyday resistance and negotiations. See Kaur, *Since 1947* and Kathinka Sinha-Kerkhoff, 'Permanent Refugees: Female Camp Inhabitant in Bihar', Philomena Essed, Georg Frerks and Joke Schrijvers (eds), *Refugees and the Transformation of Societies: Agency, Policies, Ethics and Politics* (New York, Oxford: Berghahn, 2004).

[111] Of the fifteen interviews published in *Dhangsa-o-Nirman (Destruction and Creation)*, none confess to the experience of living in government camps or on railway platforms.

[112] These include the fifteen interviews published in *Dhangsa-o-Nirman (Destruction and Creation)*; five respondents of Mukhopadhyay in *Shikorer Sandhane (Quest for Roots)*, and the various informants consulted by Datta in *Bijoygarh*, 2007.

[113] Interview with Dr Subratesh Ghosh, *Dhangsa-o-Nirman (Destruction and Creation)* (2007), pp. 98–9.

did not extend to actual familiarity with these families, or any concrete memory of them. 'But I don't remember their names', he said. 'They are dead ... There was one who was a contractor – he lived in number one [ward].'[114] While collective memory in Bijoygarh had forgotten the first squatters who had come from Sealdah station, the popular histories of other colonies seldom mentioned any resident fleeing the squalor of railway platforms. In a booklet commemorating the fiftieth anniversary of Regent colony, the customary summary of the horrors of the camps and platforms is followed by an explanation of the crisis of housing faced by displaced persons who already held jobs in Calcutta, but could not afford shelters for their uprooted families.[115] Indubaran Ganguly's description of the genesis of Deshbandhu colony openly admits that all the names included in the list of plot holders were the friends and relatives of the members of the founding committee.[116] This committee consisted of prominent refugee leaders living in neighbouring *jabardakhal* colonies and their confidants, such as the author himself, who at that time lived in a rented house nearby. Similarly, Manas Ray's account of the origins of Netaji Nagar colony identifies teachers and lawyers as members of the founding committee, and refugees 'known to the committee members' as the eventual residents.[117]

Thus, the stereotypical refugee, driven to illegally occupy land to escape the degradation of living on pavements and railway stations, was historically a marginal figure in the squatters' colonies. The vast majority of the squatters either left rented accommodation, or the temporary shelter of friends and relatives, to lay claim to their own plot of land in the outskirts of Calcutta. None of the middle-class refugees, who waxed eloquent on the dehumanising congestion of camp life and the ignominy of weeks spent on the platform, had actually experienced either. The very real fear of being reduced to such destitution acted as a powerful motive for *jabardakhal* among refugees who had limited means. The actual experience of camps and platforms was reserved for the poorer refugees who lacked the cultural capital, education and bureaucratic knowhow that characterised the colony dwellers. The inmates of government camps, especially those who arrived after 1950, tended to belong to the subaltern castes of East Bengal, especially the *Namasudras*.[118] There is

---

[114] Interview with Bharat Chandra Debnath, ibid., p. 156.
[115] *Regent Colony Subarna Jayanti Utsab (Regent Colony Golden Jubilee Celebrations), 1999–2000*, 2000.
[116] Ganguly, *Colonysmriti (Memories of Colonies)* (1997), pp. 36–9.
[117] Ray, 'Growing up Refugee', 149–79.
[118] For the changing socio-economic character of East Bengali refugees, see Chatterji, *Spoils of Partition* (2007), pp. 105–58.

evidence to suggest that the *bhadraloks* of the colony were not only desperate to avoid entering government camps, but also eager to maintain a social distance from the refugees who did not live up to their standards of respectability.

The *bhadralok* identity of squatters' colonies was not limited to benign performances of culture. It was also used to justify the replication of social hierarchies within colonies. Indubaran Ganguly's account faithfully reproduces contemporary rumours of social segregation within colonies, such as the rumour of an 'exclusive' enclave of larger plots reserved for the founders of Gandhi colony. Jadavpur Association[119] went one step further to announce that only *bhadraloks* would be allotted plots in the colony. An 'action squad' implemented this diktat by displacing refugees deemed to be '*chotolok*' or of low status to make room for suitably cultured, and substantially better-off *bhadraloks* of East Bengal.[120] If there is truth in this allegation, it might explain the complete disappearance of the families who had been brought over from railway platforms by Shombhu Guha and his cohorts from the geography and collective memory of Bijoygarh colony. Dr Ghosh struggled to explain the absence of these families, vaguely alluding to a second displacement. 'Don't know if they are still here, as later they were displaced all over again. Either they sold off the place, or gave it away – I do not know. Except one or two, all the families left.'[121]

Manas Ray's autobiographical account of growing up in Netaji Nagar colony speaks at some length of these internal divides, and is worth quoting at some length.

The vast majority of those who came were middle-class people with some urban exposure. Those who did not fall in this bracket – fishermen, carpenters, hut-builders, masons, barbers – tended to concentrate in two adjacent wards lying at one end of the locality . . . In retrospect, it seems amazing how little I knew of that world, how subtle and comprehensive was the process of normalization of divisions.[122]

Thus, the refugees of the squatters' colonies, who have long been feted as the sheet anchor of left-wing politics in Calcutta, were at best partial towards including friends, relatives and acquaintances in their constructive ventures, and at worst, practised active social segregation in order to

---

[119] By Jadavpur Association reference must have been made to the Jadavpur Refugee Camp Association – the Committee which established the squat which was renamed Bijoygarh Colony in 1950.

[120] Ganguly, *Colonysmriti* (*Memories of Colonies*)(1997), p. 35.

[121] Interview with Dr Subratesh Ghosh, *Dhangsa-o-Nirman* (*Destruction and Creation*) (2007), p. 99.

[122] Ray, 'Growing Up Refugee', 149–79.

maintain social respectability. Caste was the most visible marker of respect among the refugees. The refugees marginalised within the social geography of Netaji Nagar, as well as the unfortunates who stagnated in camps or were dispersed to distant inhospitable lands, shared one thing in common – they inevitably belonged to the subaltern castes of rural East Bengal. The fishermen, carpenters, hut-builders, masons and barbers mentioned by Manas Ray are not merely names of occupations lacking social status, but also indicative of caste identities. This caste-based segregation also divided the refugee agitation for rehabilitation in West Bengal. When the UCRC attempted to take up the cause of the camp refugees who had deserted the Bettiah camp of Bihar, they ran up against the age-old distrust of upper-caste Hindus among the *Namasudras* of East Bengal. Ninety per cent of the deserters were *Namasudras* and were open only to the leadership of a certain Apurbalal Mazumdar. The latter had little say within the various refugee organisations of Calcutta, but exerted tremendous influence amongst the Bettiah deserters due to his *Namasudra* background.[123] While highlighting the caste-based affiliations of the camp refugees, Chakrabarti fails to comment upon the absence of refugees from humbler caste backgrounds in the various democratic refugee organisations that emerged in West Bengal during the 1950s.[124]

The movement demanding rehabilitation for Bettiah deserters failed, despite the support of all the Left-led refugee organisations.[125] The primary reason for its failure was the lack of active public support. Tellingly, the people of the squatters' colonies could not be moved to participate in the movement. This was not for want of trying on the part of refugee organisations, which had organically grown out of these very colonies. This prompted Chakrabarti to move away from his celebratory narrative of the *jabardakhal* movement and speculate that 'the petty bourgeoisie squatters who had very little relationship with the lowly *Namasudra* peasant before migration felt no real concern for the fate of these agriculturists'.[126] In other words, in the absence of social and cultural ties, an inclusive refugee identity did not emerge in West Bengal. Nor did any semblance of solidarity bind the refugees together.

---

[123] Chakrabarti, *The Marginal Men* (1999), p. 171.

[124] Recent research has brought to light a sense of persecution amongst Namasudra refugees who clearly flag their low-caste identity as the basis of their marginalisation. For details, see Annu Jalais, 'Dwelling on Morichjhanpi: When Tigers Become "Citizens" and Refugees "Tigerfood"', *Economic and Political Weekly*, 40:17 (2005), 1757–62. Also see Ross Mallik, 'Refugee Resettlement in Forest Reserves: West Bengal Policy Reversal and the Marichjhapi Massacre', *Journal of Asian Studies*, 58: 1 (1999), 104–21.

[125] For details of this agitation, see Chakrabarti, *The Marginal Men* (1999), pp. 162–207.

[126] Ibid., pp. 178–9.

The discourse of respectability running through the refugee narratives and the emphasis on culture and education served to naturalise the recreation of caste and class hierarchies of rural East Bengal amongst the displaced Hindu population in West Bengal.

Refugee narratives regarding the genesis of squatters' colonies harp on the self-respect of middle-class refugees, which made it difficult for them to accept 'charity' from the government. This, coupled with a refusal to resign themselves to a life of dependence on state munificence, is presented as the driving force behind the East Bengali *bhadralok's* planned illegal seizure of land. For Indubaran Ganguly, living in camps and accepting the so-called government largesse was no different from begging. By explaining the reluctance of colony dwellers to accept government dole in terms of their middle-class sensibilities, Ganguly introduces class background as the main distinguishing feature between camp refugees and colony dwellers.

[I]t hurt the self-respect of many middle-class and lower middle-class refugee families. To make the future of their children so dependent on others also jarred the sensibility of many guardians. It can be said, that it was the force of such circumstances that made the desperate refugees take the historic step towards authoring their own rehabilitation in fallow land. The result was the *jabardakhal* colony.[127]

A similar passage or sentiment can be discerned in every single refugee narrative emerging from the squatters' colonies, whether textual or oral. The cultural arrogance of a middle-class identity is clearly visible in these narratives. Squatters' colonies, besides providing their residents with shelter, also enabled middle-class Bengalis to maintain a clear social distance from the camp refugees, who by implication were seen to lack respectability and self-respect.

The self-sufficient refugee who scorned government charity and rehabilitated himself is a carefully constructed cultural identity. It draws its strength from the origin myth of the refugee colonies, which runs through both refugee histories and reminiscences. However, it does not hold up to closer scrutiny. Reading between the lines of refugee narratives, it becomes evident that far from being averse to government aid, the squatters were adept at obtaining concessions and exemptions from the authorities. Even as the colony committees were caught up in a movement against the government to stall eviction, there were many amongst the residents who benefitted from the loans being distributed by the Ministry of Rehabilitation. Jatindranath Das of Bijoygarh colony obtained a loan of

---

[127] Ganguly, *Colonysmriti (Memories of Colonies)*(1997), p. 25.

Rs 8,000 from the government, which he used to start a business.[128] Jiten Datta of Bijoygarh set up a grocery shop in Bijoygarh's refugee market with a similar loan.[129] Official records suggest that their experience was far from exceptional. In 1960, Morarji Desai, the Finance Minister of India, wrote to Renuka Ray, the erstwhile Minister of Relief and Rehabilitation of West Bengal (1952–7), citing a comprehensive set of figures, which were designed to refute her allegation of state apathy towards the non-camp refugees in West Bengal.[130] These figures suggest that contrary to their professed identity of 'self-settled' refugee, the residents of squatters' colonies benefitted significantly from a variety of government aid.

Renuka Ray sought to use her influence as an elected Member of Parliament to remedy what in her opinion were the ills that plagued the rehabilitation of Bengali refugees.[131] Based on her experience as the Minister of Rehabilitation, she criticised as flawed and unfair the central government's policy of prioritising the resettlement of refugees living in various government camps over and above the work of regularising and developing the squatters' colonies. Her repeated letters to Morarji Desai, insisting that the government of India had given little or nothing to non-camp refugees, were eventually silenced by a detailed response from the Finance Minister, marshalling facts and figures to prove that Ray's allegations had little basis.[132] According to the Minister of Finance, by August 1960, 21 lakh refugees had received a total sum of Rs 66.5 crores as rehabilitation assistance. Not only were the majority of the recipients, an estimated 15 lakhs, from 'outside camps' but also their share of government grants amounted to 48.5 crores. Desai proceeded to break up this total into its constituent types of rehabilitation benefits, illustrating that in each category, the 'non-campers' received a significantly larger proportion of government aid.

Out of 92,000 displaced families to whom rehabilitation loans have been advanced, 17,000 are campers and 75,000 non campers; all the 15,000 families to whom trade loans have been advanced by the Refugee Businessmen Rehabilitation Board and by the Rehabilitation Finance Administration are

---

[128] Interview with Jatindranath Das, *Dhangsa-o-Nirman* (*Destruction and Creation*)(2007), p. 206.
[129] Interview with Jiten Datta, ibid., p.145.
[130] Morarji Desai, Finance Minister, Government of India to Renuka Ray, MP, 15 August 1960, *Renuka Ray Papers*, Subject File No 5, Nehru Memorial Museum and Library (henceforth NMML).
[131] Renuka Ray, *My Reminiscences: Social Development During the Gandhian Era and After* (Calcutta: Stree, 2005), p. 189.
[132] Morarji Desai to Renuka Ray, 1960, Renuka Ray Papers, NMML.

non-campers, out of 36,000 persons who have been given training under the Technical and Vocational Training Schemes, 3,500 are campers and 32,500 are non campers; practically all the displaced persons employed in the 300 sanctioned schemes of medium, small scale and cottage industries are non-campers; and almost all the 22,000 displaced families who have been given house-building loans (including the Contributory scheme) or accommodated in government built houses in West Bengal are non-campers.[133]

These non-campers were none other than the 'self-settled' refugees of West Bengal, the vast majority of whom lived in the various squatters' colonies. In other words, the avowedly self-sufficient squatters actually enjoyed the lion's share of the admittedly inadequate rehabilitation loans and grants in West Bengal.

Conclusion

A critical exploration of the genesis and development of Bijoygarh colony challenges received wisdom on the nature of refugee agency. Though the residents of squatters' colonies have been treated as a separate category of refugees within existing scholarship, what distinguished them from the refugees who entered camps was neither an inherently superior character, nor a refusal to accept government aid. The difference in the behaviour of the refugees derived from their disparate socio-economic backgrounds. The pioneers of the *jabardakhal* colonies were those who had the requisite skills for such an enterprise – education, familiarity with the urban geography of Calcutta and social and cultural capital. The refugees who lacked this crucial set of attributes were either physically excluded from the colonies or, as Manas Ray suggests, segregated within them. In other words, the refugees who were able to carve out a permanent place for themselves within the urban geography of Calcutta were not militant underdogs, but those who came from relatively privileged backgrounds.

This is not to suggest that poorer refugees who lacked both capital and social connections did not also attempt to gain a foothold in Calcutta. The quest for employment and the persistent hope of obtaining rehabilitation benefits drew poor and destitute refugees to Calcutta in the thousands. By the mid-1950s, their ranks were swelled by 'deserters' or refugees who returned to Calcutta from various marginal rehabilitation sites in Bihar and Orissa.[134] Few amongst them had the necessary know-how for building squatters' colonies, or the necessary social connections

---

[133] Ibid.
[134] For a contemporary account, see 'East Bengal Refugees' *The Economic Weekly*, 6:43–44 (1954), 1173–5.

to belong to middle-class *dals*, or associations of refugees. It is likely that the poorer refugees simply joined the ranks of Calcutta's poor, increasing the population of existing slums and leading to the emergence of new ones. For example, a series of settlements consisting of both refugees and non-refugees emerged all along the railway tracks between Ballygunje and Tollygunge railway stations in south Calcutta.[135] While Sealdah station and its environs turned into a refugee slum of families who quite simply had nowhere else to go, the 'deserters' were found to 'naturally cluster' on the pavements around Auckland House, the headquarters of the government's rehabilitation department in Alipore.[136] None of these desperate attempts to cling on to a hostile city measured up to the success story of the squatters' colonies. Those who squatted on pavements and railway platforms were either moved to refugee camps or quite simply evicted from their temporary shelters. The most stubborn amongst the refugee residents of Sealdah and Howrah stations were summarily declared to be vagrants and locked away in vagrant homes in 1958.[137] The railway colonies, with their mixed population of refugees and the migrant poor, failed to qualify for 'regularisation' that was reserved for illegal settlements of bona fide refugees. Despite years of organised agitation, by 2005, the squatters of the railway colonies had been evicted to make room for the development of the city. Amongst them were refugees like octogenarian Nanigopal Sinha, who confessed to no longer having any fight left in him.[138] Unlike the architects of the squatters' colonies, the thousands of destitute refugees who squatted on pavements, platforms and the slums of Calcutta left no permanent mark upon the geography of the city.

The *bhadralok* refugees who shunned camps not only succeeded in aggressively carving out a space for themselves in the society and politics of West Bengal, but also monopolised government schemes offering training, employment and loans to refugees. Yet, it is their self-image as 'self-settled' refugees and radical underdogs that has been replicated within existing scholarship. This is partly due to the ability of the educated and middle-class refugees to quite literally write their way into history. Popular histories of refugee rehabilitation in West Bengal have

---

[135] Asok Sen, *Life and Labour in a Squatters' Colony, Occasional Paper No. 18* (Calcutta: Centre for Studies in Social Sciences, 1992).

[136] 'East Bengal Refugees', 1173.

[137] Committee of Review of Rehabilitation Work in West Bengal, *Interim Report on Rehabilitation of Displaced Persons from East Pakistan Living at Asrafabad Ex-Campsite and Vagrant's Homes* (New Delhi: Ministry of Supply and Rehabilitation, Department of Rehabilitation, 1969).

[138] Sanjay Mandal, 'Self-eviction, Silently: 60-Year Homes Dismantled Amidst Dread of Future', *The Telegraph*, 16 December 2005.

proliferated in the last two decades and these accounts are usually Calcutta-centric narratives that privilege the perspective of middle-class refugees from dominant castes. The replication of this self-aggrandising narrative within existing scholarship has led to a gross overestimation of the incidence of radicalism amongst the East Bengali refugees. The unruly citizens of the squatters' colonies have been portrayed as agents of political change, whether as the Left's 'footstool' to power,[139] or as the 'Trojan horse' of the Left's siege on the Congress' bastion.[140] Though there is little doubt that partition migration had a transformative impact on the society, politics and economy of West Bengal, the refugees tended to make conservative choices when it came to rebuilding their lives. The *bhadraloks* amongst the refugees chose to recreate the caste distinctions, class differences and district-based rivalries and solidarities of East Bengal, within the microcosm of the squatters' colonies. A more serious consequence of the complicity between *bhadralok* memories and histories of rehabilitation is the active marginalisation of the experiences of the refugees who had to enter government camps and were subjected to the official policy of dispersal.

[139] Chakrabarti, *The Marginal Men* (1999), p. 433.
[140] Joya Chatterji, 'Right or Charity?' *Partitions of Memory* (2001), p. 102.

5   Gendered Belongings
State, Social Workers and the 'Unattached' Refugee Woman

Introduction

Refugee women occupy a contradictory position within partition history. On one hand, they are hyper-visible as the 'chief sufferers' of gendered violence, including mass rapes and abductions, that accompanied and followed the partition of India.[1] On the other hand, as soon as the focus shifts from the extraordinary and traumatic events of partition to the mundane and prolonged affair of rehabilitation, women all but disappear from the archives of the state. The government of India privileged the patrilineal nuclear family as the relevant unit for the enumeration of refugees and the disbursement of relief and rehabilitation. As a result, the male head of the family emerged as the generic refugee with whom the state interacted. Refugee women were expected to gain access to relief and rehabilitation through their male family members. However, not all refugee women could fit this ideal. There were a large number of single and widowed women in refugee camps. They entered official records as 'unattached women', or women who quite literally were not attached by familial ties to an adult male. Significant numbers of unattached women were enumerated by officials in the refugee camps of Punjab and West Bengal. They were, along with abducted women, the only refugee women starkly visible within official records. However, unlike abducted women who were 'recovered', frequently by force, and returned to their original community and families, unattached women could not be subsumed within the structures of the patriarchal family. They could not be treated as the property of men, simply because they had neither husbands nor fathers laying claims upon them. This proved to be a significant challenge for a regime of rehabilitation that imagined the generic refugee to be male. The presence of single and widowed women within various refugee camps forced the authorities to directly address refugee women. The separate

---

[1] Andrew J. Major, '"The Chief Sufferers": Abduction of Women during the Partition of the Punjab,' *South Asia: Journal of South Asian Studies XVIII* (2007): 57–72.

policies designed to care for 'unattached women' provides valuable insight into how the state conceptualised their needs and the place assigned to women within the regime of rehabilitation.

By 1950, the Indian nation-state had decided to step in as the missing patriarch or male provider for *all* 'unattached women', irrespective of their locations. This was a significant departure in an otherwise split regime of rehabilitation that advocated compensation and rehabilitation for refugees from Punjab, and repatriation for East Bengali refugees. Despite the aggressive nationalist ideology driving forward the hetero-patriarchal project of 'recovery' of abducted women, it remained largely confined to the western region. The exclusion of West Bengal, Assam, Tripura and eastern Pakistan from the purview of this policy was not entirely surprising given the qualitatively different texture of gendered violence in these regions. In partitioned Bengal, reports of rape and abduction of women were largely confined to the Noakhali riots of 1946.[2] Hindu refugees who migrated after 1947 from East Bengal mostly recounted taunts and petty incidents of sexual harassment, inappropriate marriage proposals from Muslim men and threats of abduction.[3] Even if allowance is made for the reluctance to report crimes against women, it cannot be denied that Bengal witnessed nothing like the turf war over women's bodies that characterised partition violence in Punjab.[4] As a result, the analogy with war widows, which was liberally used to justify the official decision to provide for widowed refugee women who were displaced from western Pakistan, was never evoked in the eastern sector.[5] Yet, the government of India was willing to bear the everyday costs of food

[2] For anecdotal evidence of rape and abduction of women during the Noakhali riots see Ashoka Gupta, *In the Path of Service: A Memoir of a Social Worker* (Calcutta: Popular Prakashan, 2005).

[3] For examples of such everyday harassments, see Hiranmoy Bandyopadhyay, *Udvastu (Refugee)* (Calcutta: Sahitya Samsad, 1970), pp. 15–16.

[4] The different experience of Bengali women largely derived from the different patterns of violence in Bengal and Punjab. Although there were periodic outbursts of violence against the non-Muslim minorities of East Bengal, when houses were burnt, families were butchered and property was looted, the vast majority of the migrants who left for West Bengal did not experience these horrors. The nature of oppression of minorities in the eastern region was far more insidious. Intimidation, threats, illegal confiscation of property and means of livelihood, especially houses, paddy fields and fish ponds, and increasing economic and political marginalisation of Hindus set the pattern. See Nilanjana Chatterjee, 'Interrogating Victimhood: East Bengali Refugee Narratives of Communal Violence', Department of Anthropology, University of North Carolina-Chapel Hill, n.d. <www.swadhinata.org.uk/misc/chatterjeeEastBengal%20Refugee.pdf>. Last accessed 18 July 2009.

[5] This is true only of the period before 1971, as the Liberation War of 1971 gave rise to the nationalist veneration of thousands of women who survived rape by the Pakistani military and their collaborators as *birangonas* (brave women). See Nayanika Mookherjee, *The Spectral Wound: Sexual Violence, Public Memories, and the Bangladesh War of 1971*, (Durham: Duke University Press, 2015).

and accommodation of all 'unattached women' living in refugee camps of West Bengal, Tripura and Assam.

It is tempting to read the pan-Indian remit of the policy of providing for 'unattached' refugee women as a pledge to support the welfare of vulnerable women that had no precedence in colonial India. Historians have read this promise of financial support for single and widowed women, in diametrically opposite ways. They have either congratulated the post-colonial state for acting in the interest of vulnerable widows, or indicted it for discriminating against women and reducing them to abject victimhood.[6] A closer look at the evolution of official policy towards 'unattached women' suggests a complex sphere of governance that cannot be adequately captured through binary narratives of welfare or abjection. This chapter begins with an exploration of the evolution of official policy towards 'unattached women' between 1947 and 1950. It illustrates how, contrary to the later self-serving propaganda by the Ministry of Rehabilitation, this formative period yields little evidence of any genuine concern regarding the welfare of refugee women. However, tracing the official motivations behind the formulation of policy offers a poor guide to its actual impact. This is partly because a large number of unofficial organisations and prominent social workers got involved in various schemes designed to train and rehabilitate refugee women; and partly because 'unattached women' were far from passive recipients of state largesse. Using archival records, autobiographical narratives and oral history, this chapter explores the fraught and unequal partnership between the post-colonial state and social workers; and the lived experience of 'unattached women'. It draws upon thirty-one interviews with refugee women living in four different camps in West Bengal, at Champta, Bhadrakali, Dhubulia and Bansberia. These interviews provide an insight into how women negotiated their position within a gendered regime of rehabilitation, and through it, their relationship with the Indian nation-state.[7]

A Sphere of Feminine Intervention: The Women's Section and Social Workers

The scale of the refugee crisis in post-partition India and the extent of state intervention that was required to manage it had no precedent. The

---

[6] See Ritu Menon and Kamla Bhasin, Borders and Boundaries: Women in India's Partition (New Delhi: Kali for Women, 1998) and Ravinder Kaur, 'Bodies of Partition: Of Widows, Residue, and Other Historical Waste', in S Jensen and H Ronsbo (eds.), *Histories of Victimhood*, (Philadelphia: University of Pennsylvania Press, 2014), pp. 44–63.

[7] The interviews were conducted by Subhasri Ghosh and Debjani Datta in 2002, as part of a larger research project on gendered aspects of partition in the East under the direction of Subhoranjan Dasgupta, faculty of Institute of Development Studies Kolkata. The interviews are stored in the Personal Collection of Subhoranjan Dasgupta, henceforth PCSD.

project to provide relief and rehabilitation to several million refugees necessitated the creation of new ministries at the central and provincial levels of governance, and a veritable army of administrators that ranged from senior civil servants attached to the new ministries to the humble officer on the spot.[8] However, emergency provision of relief to the distressed and destitute was not entirely new in India. The frequency of famines in India had led the colonial government to develop a standard set of measures to provide relief. This was initially provided solely in the form of subsistence wages in lieu of manual labour performed by men, women and children. No provisions were made for those unable to work. The Famine Code of 1880 recommended gratuitous relief for those unable to work, though this was more often than not withheld in the name of economy.[9] Women often constituted a large number of the able-bodied poor who were expected to work for subsistence. A high number of single or 'unattached women' among the destitute is particularly well documented for the Bengal famine of 1943.[10] However, the colonial state did not make any special provisions for destitute women, or keep track of their familial ties. Women joined the ranks of the starving poor who flocked to the gruel kitchens and were expected to work to earn subsistence wages at the temporary workhouses and sites of 'test relief.'[11] Thus, the presence of a significant number of 'unattached women' among those who sought state aid was not an entirely novel phenomenon in Bengal. What was new was the official response to it.

The official understanding of the unique needs of refugee women was born in the context of the deeply gendered patterns of violence that led up to and accompanied the decision to partition India. A special Women's Section of the Ministry of Relief and Rehabilitation was set up under Rameshwari Nehru[12] in November 1947, in order to handle the 'delicacy' and 'magnitude' of the problem posed by refugee women, many of whom

---

[8] For details, see Ravinder Kaur, *Since 1947: Partition Narratives Among Punjabi Migrants of Delhi* (New Delhi: Oxford University Press, 2007).

[9] Sanjay Sharma, *Famine, Philanthropy, and the Colonial State: North India in the Early Nineteenth Century* (Delhi: Oxford University Press, 2001) and L. Breannan, 'The Development of the Indian Famine Codes: Personalities, Politics and Policies', in B Currey and G. Hugo (eds), *Famine as a Geographical Phenomenon* (Riedel: Dotre, n.d.).

[10] For descriptions and representations see Ela Sen, *Darkening Days, Being a Narrative of Famine-stricken Bengal, with Drawings From Life* by Zainul Abedin, (Calcutta: Susil Gupta, 1944) and Karunamoy Mukerji, *Agriculture, Famine and Rehabilitation in South Asia: A Regional Approach* (Calcutta: Visva-Bharati, 1965).

[11] For a summary of the logic and implementation of 'test' reliefs see Jean Drèze, *Famine Prevention in India*, DEP Paper (London: Development Economics Research Programme, Suntory-Toyota International Centre for Economics and Related Disciplines, 1988).

[12] Rameshwari Nehru was the founder and editor of the women's periodical *Stri Darpan* (1909–24), a Gandhian nationalist and a founding member of the All India Women's Conference. She was married to Brij Lal Nehru, who was Motilal Nehru's nephew and a

were survivors of rape and ethnic cleansing. Established at a time when the government of India was preoccupied with the crisis in Punjab, it initially confined its activities to ameliorating the lot of Hindu and Sikh women displaced from West Pakistan.[13] But not all refugee women came under the purview of this section. It focused on those who had been wrenched out of their familial moorings, i.e., victims of rape, 'recovered' abducted women, widows, women who had lost their male family members in riots, or those who had been simply abandoned by their fleeing families. In other words, refugee women made their way into the official discourse of rehabilitation only through social rupture. The official term for such women, who were regarded as exceptional cases requiring special care, was 'unattached women'. While the term itself was not new, it took on new meanings within a regime of rehabilitation that treated households and not individuals as the relevant unit of governance. The post-colonial state privileged men, who were the heads of their respective households, as the recipients of relief and rehabilitation on behalf of their entire family. By implication, the state decreed that the normative position of women within the regime of rehabilitation was to be *attached to* adult male relatives. As a result, the majority of refugee women remained outside the purview of the Women's Section and were subsumed within the patriarchal family. Thus, the state reinforced men's control over female family members, reproducing within the regime of rehabilitation the 'new patriarchy' of nuclear families.[14] In this formulation women could access rehabilitation schemes only by virtue of their *attachment* to male family members. It follows that though 'refugee' is a gender-neutral term, in independent India the generic refugee was male. The state dealt directly with refugee women only in the absence of adult male family members. This became the purview of the Women's Section.

The Women's Section was designed to provide relief and where possible, rehabilitation, to unattended women and children and to help in the

cousin of Jawaharlal Nehru. Besides her own considerable talents, her prominence in post-colonial India derived in no small measure from her location within the Nehru family. For details see Rameshwari Nehru, *'Gandhi is My Star': Speeches and Writings* (Delhi: Pustakbhandar, 1950) and Om Prakash Paliwal, *Rameshwari Nehru, Patriot and Internationalist* (New Delhi: National Book Trust, 1986).

[13] See U. Bhaskar Rao, *The Story of Rehabilitation* (Labour, Employment and Rehabilitation, Government of India, 1967), p. 78.

[14] For an evaluation of how reform served 'new patriarchies' Kumkum Sangari and Sudesh Vaid (eds) *Recasting Women: Essays in Indian Colonial History* (New Brunswick: Rutgers University Press, 1990). For a study focusing on the late colonial and the post-colonial period, see Eleanor Newbigin, *The Hindu Family and the Emergence of Modern India: Law, Citizenship and Community* (Cambridge and New York: Cambridge University Press, 2013).

recovery of abducted women.[15] The new rulers in Delhi advocated a policy of compulsory recovery of all abducted women and provided for their eventual care in special homes. However, it was reluctant to directly implement either aspect of this policy. Instead, it delegated the work to various non-official and charitable organisations and individual women who were active as social workers, on the grounds that 'ameliorative work among women and children was their forte.'[16] The nationalist imagination of the ideal Indian woman as a sacrificing and nurturing mother figure thus found its way into the allocation of administrative responsibility in independent India.[17] The care of vulnerable citizens, in this case, unattached refugee women, was demarcated as a sphere of feminine intervention, which could be delegated to social workers and philanthropic organisations. This delegation took different forms. At the highest level, it involved prominent social workers and nationalists, who had a history of working for women's rights and education. They were either attached to the Ministry of Relief and Rehabilitation in an advisory capacity, or appointed as the executive heads of specific official bodies designed to serve women and children. Rameshwari Nehru, Mridula Sarabhai[18] and Durgabai Deshmukh[19] fitted this profile. While Sarabhai headed the state-led operation of recovery of abducted Hindu women from Pakistan, Deshmukh was appointed the chairman of the Central Social Welfare Board, established in 1953 to coordinate the collaboration between the post-colonial state and various non-official

[15] *Displaced Women and Children from Pakistan, Constitution and Function of the Women's Section*, File No. 453/47, Public, Ministry of Home Affairs, Government of India, 1947, National Archives, New Delhi.

[16] Bhaskar Rao, *The Story of Rehabilitation* (1967), p. 79.

[17] For discussions on the image of Indian women within the nationalist movement in late colonial India see Geraldine Forbes, *Women in Colonial India: Essays in Politics, Medicine and Historiography* (New Delhi: Chronicle Books, 2005), pp. 28–78; Partha Chatterjee, 'The Nationalist Resolution of the Women's Question', Sangari and Vaid (eds), *Recasting Women* (1989), pp. 233–53; Radha Kumar, *The History of Doing : An Illustrated Account of Movements for Women's Rights and Feminism in India 1800–1990* (New Delhi: Kali for Women, 1993), pp. 74–95 and Jasodhara Bagchi, 'Representing Nationalism: Ideology of Motherhood in Colonial Bengal', *Economic and Political Weekly*, 'Review of Women's Studies', 25:42/43, (1990), 65–71.

[18] Mridula Sarabhai was a Gandhian and a prominent member of the Indian National Congress from Gujarat. During and after partition, she followed Gandhi's example of working for communal harmony in riot-torn regions. For details, see Aparna Basu, *Mridula Sarabhai: Rebel With a Cause* (New Delhi: Oxford University Press, 2005).

[19] Durgabai Deshmukh, a Gandhian nationalist, lawyer and social worker from Andhra Pradesh, came to play a prominent role in building national organisations for the welfare of women and children through the patronage of Jawaharlal Nehru. For details see Durgabai Deshmukh, *The Stone That Speaketh* (Hyderabad: Andhra Mahila Sabha, 1979) and M. Garg, 'Durgabai Deshmukh: A Pioneer Social Builder,' *Social Welfare*, 54: 5 (2007), 28.

organisations in providing welfare. This pattern of inviting prominent social workers to participate in the rehabilitation of women on an advisory capacity was replicated in the 1950s in the eastern region. Seeta Chaudhuri, Romola Sinha and Ashoka Gupta became involved, on an advisory capacity, with an official drive to rehabilitate refugee women. All three women were prominent social workers who hailed from elite families and were married to powerful men who were high-ranking civil servants or politicians. Ashoka Gupta was the youngest of the three and alone in her involvement in the Gandhian movement.

The active participation of women in the relief and rehabilitation of refugee women was not limited to those from elite backgrounds, who had familial ties with the Congress government and the upper echelons of the bureaucracy. Women from a range of backgrounds came forward as volunteers. For example, Khorsed Italia from Delhi had no background in politics and was an honorary worker at the Lady Hardinge Medical College. She, along with other volunteers, responded to a call to care for the women among the refugees evacuated from Punjab and brought into the camp set up at the Old Fort in Delhi.[20] There were Gandhian women from ordinary middle-class backgrounds, such as Kamlaben Patel, who became Mridula Sarabhai's trusted associate.[21] Volunteers also included young women from prominent political families opposed to Gandhian principles, such as Sheila Sengupta, the niece of Subhash Chandra Bose.[22] Besides volunteers, many women worked as paid employees of the Ministry of Relief and Rehabilitation. Both Nalini Mitra and Durga Rani came to India as refugees, albeit in radically different circumstances. While the former had been a college lecturer in Dhaka, the latter came to India as a young widow with little education. Both became involved in the rehabilitation of refugees as government employees. Durga Rani spent most of her working life looking after partition's widows at the Karnal Mahila Ashram while Nalini Mitra became the principal of a women's industrial training home in Chunar, which catered to displaced women from eastern Pakistan.[23] Many more women became involved through various philanthropic and women's organisations that ranged from

---

[20] Interview with Khorsed Italia, conducted by Andrew Whitehead, January 1997, (http://www.andrewwhitehead.net/partition-voices.html, accessed on 10 August 2015).

[21] For details see Menon and Bhasin, Borders and Boundaries (1998).

[22] Interview with Sheila Sengupta, conducted by Andrew Whitehead, 1997, *Oral history interviews (sound recordings)*, OA3/01, Archives and Special Collections, School of Oriental and African Studies, London.

[23] 'Interview with Nalini Mitra', in *Seminar No. 510, Porous borders, divided selves: a symposium on partitions in the East*, February, 2002, <http://www.india-seminar.com/2002/510/510%20sujit%20chaudhuri.htm>, Last accessed 5 August 2015.

national and international organisations, such as the Young Women's Christian Association and All India Women's Conference (AIWC), to regional efforts, such as *Nari Seva Sangha* (Women's Service League) in Calcutta. Participation also cut across the political spectrum, with Communist women and Gandhian women contributing in equal measure to the task at hand. The scale of participation of non-official organisations, volunteers and 'public-spirited' women has led Menon and Bhasin to argue that 'the real work of rehabilitating women fell to women.'[24] While there is little doubt that the actual work of caring for refugee women was delegated to women, this delegation was not without its problems.

Most women who did the work of rehabilitating refugee women served as volunteers or as government employees. This left them with no say regarding the actual content of rehabilitation. A handful of women, such as Rameshweri Nehru, Mridula Sarabhai, Ashoka Gupta and Romola Sinha, were invited to participate in the actual formulation of policy, albeit as advisors and in an honorary capacity. They therefore had to depend on allies within the government and the bureaucracy, usually men, to influence policy. This structure left room for serious disagreement, not only between the official agenda of the state and the women who were expected to implement policy, but also between different social workers and advisers. These tensions and disagreements came to a head over the controversial policy of state-led recovery of abducted women. Mridula Sarabhai's passionate advocacy of compulsory recovery of all abducted women won the support of the state and eventually led to the passage of the draconian Abducted Persons (Recovery and Restoration) Act in 1949 that effectively denied refugee women their civic rights. Received wisdom clearly demonstrates that Sarabhai's position had little support among either the women who were being rescued, or the social workers who were charged with the unpleasant task of dragging unwilling women back to their putative homeland.[25] Rameshwari Nehru resigned from her position of honorary advisor of the Ministry of Relief and Rehabilitation once it became clear that the state was free to ignore her advice and the protests of refugee women who bore the brunt of policies driven by hetero-patriarchal nationalism. Thus, the participation of women in the work of rehabilitating women did not necessarily translate into a foregrounding of the needs and perspectives of refugee women. This was because while the post-colonial state was happy to delegate the implementation of schemes and policies targeting refugee women, it retained firm control over the direction of policy. This unequal and fraught partnership between the official regime of rehabilitation on one hand; and unofficial organisations

---

[24] Menon and Bhasin, *Borders and Boundaries* (1998), p. 170.   [25] Ibid.

and social workers on the other, became the standard pattern of administering to the needs of refugee women in independent India.

While the plight of abducted women is better known, 'unattached women' constituted a more numerous group among the refugees who came under the purview of the Women's Section. By 1949, there were 73,000 refugee women receiving some form of relief from the government of India. The large number of such women expanded the scale of operation of the Women's Section, eventually leading to its transformation from an independent advisory committee to an integral part of the Ministry of Relief and Rehabilitation. From March 1949, the Delhi-based Women's Section under the directorship of Rameshwari Nehru confined its activities to caring for unattached refugee women among refugees from West Punjab.[26] West Bengal had a separate Women's Section, attached to the state's Refugee Rehabilitation Directorate. Between 1949 and 1957, it cared for 25,830 refugee women.[27] In theory, the Women's Section was in charge of organising relief and rehabilitation for unattached refugee women. However, in the absence of its own personnel, the Women's Section had to rely on the cooperation of regular employees and staff of the provincial ministries in charge of refugee rehabilitation. Moreover, in West Bengal as well as in Delhi, social workers supposedly in charge of the rehabilitation of women worked in an advisory capacity. Their proposed schemes could become policy only if they met with the approval of the central minister in charge of relief and rehabilitation, who sanctioned the necessary funds. They soon found themselves at odds with the Ministry of Rehabilitation when it came to the formulation of policy towards unattached women.

The official take on the rehabilitation of unattached women is summarised by U. Bhaskar Rao in his state-sponsored and celebratory account of the achievements of the Ministry of Rehabilitation. According to him, the rehabilitation of 'such refugees' consisted of caring for them in transit camps, removing them to sites of permanent settlement, and finally, 'culminated in the establishment and maintenance of homes and infirmaries.'[28] The government of India agreed to bear all the costs of these homes and infirmaries, while its day-to-day administration was delegated to local bodies and frequently, to non-official organisations. This generosity of the state in stepping in as the missing provider came at the cost of a refusal to even attempt substantive rehabilitation for unattached women. While refugee rehabilitation was generally taken to

[26] Ibid., pp. 151–2.

[27] 'Women's Section Report, 1957', *Ashoka Gupta Papers, File 11*, Women's Studies Centre, Jadavpur University, Calcutta (henceforth, WSC, Calcutta).

[28] Bhaskar Rao, *The Story of Rehabilitation* (1967), p. 79.

mean integration with the host society and mainstream economy, for women, it meant their inclusion within government-sponsored homes. However, women like Rameshwari Nehru, Durgabai Deshmukh, Phulrenu Guha and Ashoka Gupta had very different ideas. They saw ameliorative work among refugee women as a means to participate in the larger project of nation-building. In Punjab, as well as in West Bengal, a variety of women's organisations came forward to provide training and opportunities of employment to refugee women.[29] The Women's Section collaborated with different training centres and philanthropic organisations to train educated women in useful professions such as nursing, midwifery, teaching and stenography; and uneducated women in embroidery, tailoring and minor handicrafts.

In dealing with refugee women, most unofficial organisations fell back upon their previous experience of promoting education and welfare among women in general.[30] A gendered conception of women's employment continued to inform the subjects taught, which either emphasised the 'natural' attributes of women as nurturers (as nurses, midwives and teachers) or taught them low-paid and home-based artisanal skills, which were considered appropriate since they did not involve uprooting Indian women from their proper place in the home. However, such artisanal skills, which at best provided auxiliary income, were wholly inadequate to the needs of women who had survived partition as homeless widows. The Women's Section was not entirely blind to the shortcomings of its activities. Rameshwari Nehru wanted women to be trained for professions such as agriculture and advanced industries, which were considered male preserves. She hoped that specially planned women's settlements, providing shelter and gainful employment not only to partition's widows, but to destitute women in general, would emerge in the long term. But the national government shared neither her vision, nor her optimism. While the Ministry of Rehabilitation was willing to fund non-official initiatives, such as Kasturba Seva Mandir's ambitious plans of training women in dairy farming and oil-pressing, it saw such schemes as 'experiments' rather than an essential component of rehabilitation.[31] The gap between

---

[29] For Punjab, see Menon and Bhasin, *Borders and Boundaries* (1998), pp. 169–201. For West Bengal, see Gupta, *In the Path of Service*, pp. 121–3 and 131–7 and Gargi Chakravartty, *Coming Out of Partition: Refugee Women of Bengal* (New Delhi: Bluejay Books, 2005), pp. 41–3 and 88–90.

[30] For a general background of women's movement for education and employment see Kumar, *The History of Doing* (1993), pp. 53–95 and for a Bengal-specific perspective see Dagmar Engels, *Beyond Purdah?: Women in Bengal, 1890–1930* (Delhi: Oxford University Press, 1999), pp. 158–93.

[31] Ritu Menon, 'Do Women Have a Country?', in Rada Ivekovic and Julie Mostov (eds), *From Gender to Nation* (New Delhi: Zubaan, 2006), pp. 43–62.

the vision of the Women's Section and the reluctant support of the Ministry of Rehabilitation is evident from Renuka Ray's complaint in the Constituent Assembly.

I do not think that the establishment of homes where some little occupation is given ... is enough ... Tinkering with the problem by doing a little here and there will not be sufficient.[32]

For the Ministry of Rehabilitation, the primary justification for training women was to keep them 'occupied' rather than to enable them to earn a living.

In West Bengal, the relief and rehabilitation of refugee women followed a slightly different pattern. Before the February riots of 1950, the government of India studiously avoided acknowledging that there was a refugee crisis in the east. As a result, between 1947 and 1950, West Bengal did not have a Women's Section. The initiative of providing for the specific needs of refugee women came entirely from a range of women's organisations. Established organisations such as the Bengal branch of the All India Women's Conference and All Bengal Women's Union were joined by younger formations, such as the *Nari Seva Sangha* (Women's Service League) and *Mahila Seva Samiti* (Association for the Service of Women). However, when it came to the actual content of the aid offered, there was not much to distinguish between the activities of social workers in West Bengal and those working in Delhi or Punjab. Adult education and vocational training, especially in tailoring and weaving, was the main thrust of these organisations' welfare work among refugee women. The social workers visited refugee camps, where they set up schools and ran courses of vocational training. At times they pitched in with money and encouragement to ensure that refugee girls completed their education.[33] Though no formal mechanism of collaboration between the state and social workers as yet existed in West Bengal, the authorities were quick to take advantage of the initiative, labour and organisational skills of volunteers. In 1947, the Premier of West Bengal, Dr P. C. Ghosh, encouraged social workers to come forward in the aid of partition refugees. Eighteen organisations came together to form the West Bengal Emergency Relief Committee, which eventually registered itself as a society under the name of *Mahila Seva Samity* (Association for the Service of Women). The association functioned under the guidance and patronage of Dr Rajagopalachari, the then Governor of West Bengal. The degree of gov-

---

[32] Cited in ibid., p. 48.
[33] Interview with Ashoka Gupta, conducted by Dr Subhoranjan Dasgupta, 2000, Personal Collection of Subhoranjan Dasgupta (henceforth, PCSD).

ernment patronage is evident from the fact that it set up office in an empty room in the Governor's House.[34] Other prominent organisations in West Bengal that relied on official patronage included a women's home at Uday Villa, established in 1949–50 by Abala Basu, and Ananda Ashram, a residential school for orphan refugee girls, established in 1950.[35]

Thus, in post-partition India, the interaction between the state and single and widowed refugee women was more often than not mediated through social workers or philanthropic organisations. Official accounts of rehabilitation and the reminiscences of social workers represent this mediation to be beneficial for refugee women. However, the social workers, who were frequently treated as 'experts' on the needs of refugee women, seldom consulted unattached refugee women regarding what their needs and aspirations were. The drive to provide education and training did not come from the refugee women. It originated in largely middle-class ambitions and aspirations regarding what constituted progress for Indian women. The social workers who worked with unattached refugee women often drew upon Gandhian ideals of service. Most had advocated education and training for women during the 1920s and 1930s and now drew upon these experiences to formulate new schemes.[36] In late colonial India, the women's movement had been based on a vision of the complementarity between men and women, rather than on any critique of gender inequality.[37] Unsurprisingly, schemes drawing upon this heritage continued to view women's work as supplementary and as an aspect of self-development, instead of a means of survival. For destitute widows, many of whom were overnight forced into the role of providers for their dependent children, training in feminised and low-paid artisanal skills did not offer a way forward.

The yawning gap between the needs of unattached women and the philanthropic activities of social workers becomes evident from a brief summary of the work of the *Mahila Seva Samiti*.[38] The association convinced the government of India to place its orders of woollen garments for Punjab's refugees with it, on the grounds that it could provide knitted

---

[34] Mahila Seva Samity, *Annual Report of the Year 2005–2006* (Calcutta, 2006).

[35] For details of the Women's Cooperative Industrial Home, popularly known Uday Villa, see Bolan Gangopadhyay, 'Reintegrating the Displaced, Refracturing the Domestic: A Report on the Experiences of "Uday Villa"', Pradip Kumar Bose (ed.), *Refugees in West Bengal: Institutional Practices and Contested Identities* (Calcutta: Calcutta Research Group, 2000), pp. 98–105.

[36] For example, in founding Uday Villa, the veteran social worker, Lady Abala Bose drew upon her long experience of promoting education and training to women through various organisations, such as the *Nari Siksha Samiti* (Women's Education Association) founded in 1919, and the Bengal Women's Education League, founded in 1927. Ibid.

[37] Kumar, *The History of Doing* (1993), pp. 54–73.

[38] Interview with Ashoka Gupta, 2000, PCSD.

woollens at cheaper rates than the market price. It distributed the wool supplied by the government to East Bengali refugee women, and later collected the finished garments for sale.[39] The income this scheme generated was meagre. Yet, it aroused great enthusiasm among the social workers as it combined helping East Bengali refugees with serving those from Punjab.[40] In true Gandhian tradition, women's work was seen as service to the nation, with income being a secondary consideration.[41] Thus, for philanthropic organisations, ideological commitments towards promoting a specific vision of women's role within society often overrode the actual needs of refugee women.[42] However, the visible needs of women thrown into the role of breadwinners led avowedly Gandhian women, such as Ashoka Gupta, to balance their ideals of national service with pragmatic schemes for generating income. She described at length the initiative of the All India Women's Conference to train refugee women to cook and manage canteens. The AIWC succeeded in setting up canteens at several government offices, hospitals and colleges of Calcutta, which were run by refugee women.[43] This scheme was born from the demand for 'rannar kaj' or employment as cooks among refugee widows. It was popular with refugee women, largely because it generated enough income to provide for families. Many other organisations in West Bengal not only provided training courses for refugee women, but also tried to find them gainful employment.

By 1957, there were two residential and thirty-three non-residential training courses for women run by various non-official organisations, that cumulatively advocated nineteen different kinds of vocations for refugee women.[44] These included, besides the usual low-paid work considered suitable for women, such as domestic service, hosiery knitting, spinning and weaving khadi, embroidery and condiments making, several practical and remunerative options, such as typewriting, bleaching and dyeing,

[39] Ibid.

[40] The relationship between ideals of service and citizenship was often more complicated than what has been explored by Carey Watt in Serving the Nation: Cultures of Service, Association and Citizenship in Colonial India (New Delhi: Oxford University Press, 2005). While this chapter does not focus on the motives and activities of the associations discussed by Watt, it does illustrate how the participation of social workers in nation-building through serving refugees compounded the marginalisation of refugee women.

[41] For Gandhi's views on women, see Sujata Patel, 'Construction and Reconstruction of Woman in Gandhi', Economic and Political Weekly, 23:8, (1988), 377–87 and Madhu Kishwar, 'Gandhi on Women', Economic and Political Weekly, 20:40, (1985), 1691–702.

[42] For a discussion on the impact of nationalist ideology on the lives of women, see Samita Sen, 'Histories of Betrayal: Patriarchy, Class and Nation', Sekhar Bandyopadhyay (ed.), Bengal: Rethinking History, Essays in Historiography (Delhi: Manohar, 2001), pp. 259–81.

[43] Interview with Ashoka Gupta, 2000, PCSD.

[44] Refugee Relief and Rehabilitation Department, Government of West Bengal, Relief and Rehabilitation of Displaced Persons in West Bengal, Calcutta, October 1957.

tailoring, teacher's training, compositor work, catering and confection-ary, nursing and goat and poultry keeping. Some initiatives, such as training women to be *sevikas* and in bookbinding reflected an attempt to design schemes keeping in mind the contemporary labour market.[45] There was a demand for women to work as *sevikas* or ground-level work-ers in the various community development schemes launched in the 1950s. Bookbinding had been traditionally dominated by Muslims and was likely to provide greater opportunities for employment in the post-partition context of Muslim emigration from Calcutta.[46]

Social Workers in post-partition India were well aware of the discrimi-nation women faced in the labour market and the wholly inadequate income that 'women's work', such a spinning and weaving, generated. In her autobiography, Ashoka Gupta confesses that sex work, which she alludes to as 'other means to earn some money' were far more effective than vocational training in enabling uneducated women to provide for their families.[47]

We tried to rescue some of them. We organised vocational training, gave sewing lessons and other such training to give them a respectable means of earning their living. But the truth was how much money could something like sewing bring in? Especially when one's very sustenance, the medical treatment of one's whole family, depended on it?[48]

Nevertheless, women's organisations kept to their task – largely because employment or income was not the only goal of these ventures. For social workers, training refugee women in productive economic activity had the symbolic value of opposing the reduction of refugee women to passive recipients of welfare.

In sum, the intervention of philanthropists and social workers bore mixed results for unattached refugee women. Dedicated social workers often succeeded in offering substantive help to the women they came into direct contact with. However, when it came to their advisory role in the sphere of framing policy, they failed to adequately represent the specific needs of unattached refugee women. Their emphasis on training and education inadvertently reinforced the official tendency to view all unat-tached refugee women as victims, who were incapable of social or eco-nomic autonomy and therefore, unfit for rehabilitation. For example, in

[45] Minutes of the Meeting of the sub-committee appointed in the advisory board for women's rehabilitation, 5 July 1951, Ashoka Gupta Papers, File No. 7, WSC, Calcutta.
[46] See Asok Sen, 'The Bindery Workers of Daftaripara-1: Forms and Fragments', *Occasional paper, No. 127* and 'The Bindery Workers of Daftaripara-2: Their Own Life-stories', *Occasional paper, No. 128, Centre for Studies in Social Sciences* (Calcutta: CSSS, Occasional paper series, 1991).
[47] Gupta, *In the Path of Service* (2005), p. 135.   [48] Ibid.

1953, while inaugurating an exhibition of handicrafts produced by refugee women trained at Uttarpara women's home, Renuka Ray, who was West Bengal's Minister of Relief and Rehabilitation and a great advocate for training refugee women, declared that 'the inmates of the Home, who had at one time been given up as hopeless in some quarters, were through systematic training now converted into good citizens of the Indian Union'.[49] This was a dangerous assertion for unattached refugee women. It made their inclusion within Indian society and polity dependent upon remedial training. It also left unchallenged their representation as economically dependent creatures, who lacked the ability to fully belong to the post-colonial nation in the absence of familial 'attachment' to adult men. In the long run, official failure to envision refugee women as individuals capable of socio-economic autonomy had a lasting and negative impact on the lives of refugee women. It was written into policy as soon as the focus shifted from provision of relief to permanent rehabilitation for refugees from western Pakistan.

Rehabilitation's Residue: Recasting Refugee Women as Permanent Liabilities

Between 1947 and 1949, while the Women's Section advocated training and economic independence for the refugee women in its care, the Ministry of Rehabilitation had moved ahead with ad hoc allotments of evacuee land to refugee men. By 1949, plans for permanent resettlement were finalised, and en masse allotment of land started in winter that year.[50] With this, the focus of state intervention shifted from temporary relief to permanent rehabilitation in Punjab. Immediately after this shift, in 1950, 'permanent liability' emerged as a distinct category of refugees who were unfit for rehabilitation. All 'unattached' refugee women were clubbed together with aged and infirm men and dependent children as permanent liabilities of the state. By stepping in as the provider and guardian of refugee women, the government of India drew the gendered nature of the regime of rehabilitation to its logical conclusion. As permanent liabilities of the state, unattached refugee women were entitled to perpetual relief, but were not deemed capable of being rehabilitated. Though the rhetoric remained one of providing care to women, it now

---

[49] *Hindustan Standard*, 3 January 1953.

[50] See Gyanesh Kudaisya, 'The Demographic Upheaval Partition: Refugees and Agricultural Resettlement in India, 1946-67', *South Asia*, 18, Special Issue, (1995), 73–94 and Gyanesh Kudaisya and Tai Yong Tan, *The Aftermath of Partition in South Asia* (London and New York: Routledge, 2000), pp. 128–33.

became official policy to deprive refugee women of the core benefits of rehabilitation, i.e., land and loans.

Special homes, often called *sevashrams* or hermitages of service, and training centres were set up for unattached women under this new policy. Older facilities, originally built for abducted women, were now converted into widows' homes. Many of these homes continued to offer vocational training and education for refugee women. However, with the reclassification of all unattached women as permanent liabilities, the training offered in these homes became a poor substitute for substantive rehabilitation, instead of the means to achieve the rehabilitation of single and widowed women. These institutions were a far cry from Rameshwari Nehru's vision of self-sufficient women's settlements. Through a gendered curriculum of training in crafts and professions considered appropriate for women, they promoted a brand of self-sufficiency specific to women.[51] The majority of the women, who were uneducated, were taught low-paid artisanal skills, such as embroidery, spinning, weaving and soap making. The aim, at most, was to enable women to earn their own subsistence. However, circumstances demanded much more of refugee women. Many felt the pressure to provide for their families. While the government of India stubbornly refused to acknowledge refugee women as breadwinners, the social workers who collaborated with the state also failed to ask for equal access for female-headed families in official schemes of refugee resettlement. In the process, socio-economic rehabilitation became a male preserve, while training in suitably feminine enterprises became the fate of unattached refugee women.

In Punjab, the disjuncture between the bureaucratic infantilisation of women and their actual capabilities was exposed by the compensation scheme. The Ministry of Rehabilitation suddenly 'discovered' that 'a fairly large number of persons in homes and infirmaries were eligible for compensation'.[52] Though treated as helpless victims by the state, these women had not only owned property and/or agricultural land in West Pakistan, but had also managed to negotiate the maze of bureaucratic regulations to apply for compensation. It is possible to speculate that at least some of them had the necessary skills for running small businesses or managing land as a productive economic unit. But for the ministry, the possibility of women receiving compensation constituted an unlikely and surprising discovery. It hastened to ensure that these women received compensation at a 'generous scale' and 'top priority' in payment.[53] This generosity was perhaps an attempt to gloss over the state's initial

---

[51] See Kumar, *The History of Doing* (1993), pp. 54–73.
[52] Bhaskar Rao, *The Story of Rehabilitation* (1967), p. 79.   [53] Ibid, p. 80.

exclusion of all women, irrespective of their skills, capabilities or backgrounds, from the enterprise of allotting land to refugees. The regime of rehabilitation thus followed an unwritten rule by which the mainstays of economic rehabilitation – land, houses and loans for starting businesses – could not be distributed to female-headed families.

A similar pattern of arbitrary exclusion of refugee women from rehabilitation schemes developed independently in West Bengal. In 1949, when B. C. Roy's government turned its attention to the refugee camps, it found 7,500 refugees 'unfit for rehabilitation.'[54] The government hastened to find land and resources for the 12,500 displaced families deemed fit for rehabilitation. In other words, in the eyes of the state, the male-headed family was the only viable unit of rehabilitation. These families were divided into occupational groups, such as professionals, traders, agriculturists or weavers, and rehabilitated accordingly. By January 1950, a residue of 'old, infirm or widow and their dependent children'[55] was left in refugee camps. They were divided into families headed by women and those headed by old or infirm men and sent off to separate camps in Titagarh and Ranaghat. The government continued to support these two camps after all the others were wound up in January 1950. Though the term 'permanent liability' was yet to be coined, in effect the government of West Bengal treated female-headed refugee families as permanent liabilities. They were not given lands, house-building loans or loans to set up businesses. As women, they were deemed to be incapable of productive economic activity and therefore, unrehabilitable.

After 1950, the increasing involvement of the central government in the rehabilitation of East Bengali refugees saw the institutionalisation of this exclusion. A branch of the Women's Section was opened in West Bengal to take charge of the relief and welfare of unattached women. Permanent liability (PL) camps were established in West Bengal. Single women and their dependants were pulled out from the general population of refugees and sent to these camps.[56] According to Hiranmoy Bandyopadhyay, the authorities considered it inappropriate to accommodate families consisting of widows and their children in the same camps as other PL families headed by aged and disabled men. 'Women's camps' were opened at Titagarh, Kartikpur, Bansberia and Bhadrakali and separate sections of Rupasreepalli and Dhubulia camps were reserved for unattached women and their children. By 1955, there were 11,828 unattached women and children in various women's camps in West Bengal.[57] New admissions to

[54] Bandyopadhyay, *Udvastu (Refugee)* (1970), p. 46.   [55] Ibid.
[56] Government of West Bengal, *Five Years of Independence, August 1947 – August 1952* (Calcutta, 1953).
[57] Report of the Committee Appointed by the West Bengal Government to Enquire into the Technical and Vocational Training of Displaced Persons from East Pakistan Now

the PL camps were halted in June 1957, at which time the total numbers of families headed by unattached women and living in various PL institutions came to 10,364.[58] These institutions, variously named as homes, camps and infirmaries, became a permanent feature of the regime of rehabilitation in West Bengal, largely due to the recurring pattern of migration of minorities from East Bengal. They continued to periodically admit new residents, as every new wave of refugees and every phase of rushed dispersal from camps repeated the bureaucratic process by which all 'unattached' women were reclassified as permanent liabilities of the state. By the end of 1973, there were eighteen PL homes and infirmaries in West Bengal with a total population of 16,861.[59] Despite promising perpetual care to these refugees, the government of India washed its hands of all PL camps in 1974, leaving the government of West Bengal to shoulder the financial burden of providing for this human residue, sedimented out as the unrehabilitable waste from successive processes of refugee resettlement.[60]

There are two ways to read this pattern of categorising unattached refugee women as permanent liabilities of the state. As the name suggested, the state was in effect promising to provide for these women in perpetuity. However, this promise of care came at a steep price. Women who entered PL camps were denied rehabilitation and had to give up any semblance of normal family life for a highly regimented existence in camps and homes. How historians have read this policy has depended upon whether they have focused on the promise of permanent relief, or on the denial of rehabilitation. However, the evolution of this particular policy clearly indicates that the blanket denial of rehabilitation to all refugee women preceded any promise of welfare. In Punjab, the ad hoc allotment of land to refugees bypassed female-headed families, while in Bengal the first attempt to close all camps in 1949 left behind unattached women and their dependants as an 'unrehabilitable' residue. In both cases, the bureaucrats and administrators who were charged with envisioning a new beginning for displaced families clearly believed that all women, irrespective of their background and abilities, were incapable of

Residing in West Bengal, Calcutta, June 1955, p. 3, *Ashoka Gupta Papers, File No.10*, WSC, Calcutta.

[58] 'Women's Section Report, 1957', *Ashoka Gupta Papers, File 11*, WSC, Calcutta.

[59] Committee of Review of Rehabilitation Work in West Bengal, *Report on Repair and Reconstruction of Permanent Liability Homes and Infirmaries for the Displaced Persons From Erstwhile East Pakistan in West Bengal* (New Delhi: Ministry of Supply and Rehabilitation, 1974), p. 2.

[60] Screening Committee, Government of West Bengal, *Problems of Refugee Camps and Homes in West Bengal (The Screening Committee Report, 1989)* (Calcutta: Refugee Relief and Rehabilitation Directorate, Government of West Bengal, 1989).

economic self-sufficiency and social autonomy. So they remained in camps and continued to receive relief while the rest of the refugee population was moved on to sites of rehabilitation. Reclassifying the women who were left behind as permanent liabilities was a postfacto rationalisation of this practice. The Ministry of Relief and Rehabilitation was quick to take credit for this act of patriarchal benevolence. However, it was not long before it came to resent the cost of providing for PL families.

By the mid-1950s, the government of India started reviewing existing policy, actively looking for a way out of playing the role of the missing male providers of unattached women. This was particularly true of West Bengal, where the population of unattached women in PL camps grew with the rising tide of refugees during the 1950s. In 1954, a Committee of Ministers recommended compulsory training followed by employment in production centres for all able-bodied refugees in the PL institutions of West Bengal.[61] Given that permanent liabilities consisted of unattached women and 'aged and infirm men', this recommendation was clearly aimed at refugee women. Though at first glance this recommendation appears to be a progressive step, in practice, it initiated a process of dispersal of refugee women from PL camps. The ministers of rehabilitation for Assam, Tripura and West Bengal responded to these recommendations by adopting a new classificatory schema that divided all residents of PL institutions into three categories: aged and infirm, partially employable, and fully employable.[62] The ultimate aim of training both 'partially employable' and 'fully employable' unattached women was to discharge them from the camps. The former, after receiving 'intensive training in usual trades suited to their aptitude', were to be 'encouraged to go out with rehabilitation benefits recommended by the Committee of Ministers'.[63] For the latter, a full course of training and intensive practical work in production centres was meant to prepare them for being discharged from the camps with the same 'rehabilitation benefits'. However, neither the training nor the 'rehabilitation benefits' offered to refugee women was adequate. Female-headed families continued to be denied access to land or housing in the numerous government-sponsored schemes for refugee resettlement. The recommended 'rehabilitation' for refugee women was a grant of Rs 1200, with which the government proposed to wash its hands off those who had once been promised permanent care.[64] The

---

[61] 'Reorganisation of Permanent Liability Camps, Homes and Infirmaries', *Ashoka Gupta Papers, File No. 11*, WSC, Calcutta.
[62] Ibid.   [63] Ibid.
[64] Refugee Relief and Rehabilitation Department, Government of West Bengal, *Relief and Rehabilitation of Displaced Persons in West Bengal* (Calcutta, October 1957).

only women who were not subject to this new policy were those who had sons and, therefore, could gain access to land and housing through them, once they reached adulthood.

Schemes of training refugee women had gained currency due to the intervention of social workers. For them, training was ideally meant to achieve self-sufficiency for refugee women. However, for the Ministry of Rehabilitation, it served an entirely different purpose. By 1959, the training of unattached refugee women had become the primary means through which the Indian state reneged on its promise of providing perpetual relief to unattached refugee women. In a memorandum submitted to the Central Social Welfare Board, Rameshwari Nehru advocated for the provision of secure accommodation for the 'large number of widows' who were being discharged after training from various PL homes and infirmaries in the western zone. She points out the obvious fact that their rehabilitation remained incomplete in the absence of secure and cheap accommodation.

Since these widows have no place to go, they are put to great hardship . . . many of them request for re-admission or they run the risk of being waylaid by undesirable persons who expose them to social and moral danger.[65]

Rameshwari Nehru suggested that the government should construct cheap tenements or mud huts within the grounds of existing PL institutions, which widows could buy through payment of monthly instalments spread out over a twenty-year period. Ashoka Gupta expressed a similar concern regarding the unattached women among East Bengali refugees. Her private papers yield an undated proposal for a hostel for 'trained refugee lone unattached women', submitted sometime between 1954 and 1962 to Mehr Chand Khanna, the central minister in charge of refugee rehabilitation.[66] This proposal claimed that 'under certain government orders' all unattached women who complete a year's training were being forced to leave, along with their children, 'on the very day' the training scheme was over. As most trainees were destitute widows, this policy forced them to seek shelter with distant relatives, who more often than not were unwilling to shelter them for long. Given that the government of India ultimately reneged on its promise of perpetual care, it is more likely that the initial decision to pay for the upkeep of unattached women and their dependants was an unintended consequence of the gendered logic of

[65] 'Memorandum submitted by Shrimati Rameshwari Nehru on the Needs of Displaced Women and Children, Old and Infirm, during the 3rd Five Year Plan', *Rameshwari Nehru Papers, Reports, No. 1*, Nehru Memorial Museum and Library, New Delhi.

[66] 'A Scheme for Hostel for Trained Refugee Lone Unattached Woman', *Ashoka Gupta Papers, File No. 11*, WSC, Calcutta.

rehabilitation, rather than a positive commitment intended to improve the lives and status of partition's widows.

The denial of rehabilitation to unattached refugee women was embedded in the very logic of rehabilitation of partition refugees. At the core of government policies designed to rehabilitate refugees from western Pakistan stood the principle of compensation. Besides relief, the extent of land and other benefits a refugee could claim from the state was determined by his socio-economic position in West Pakistan.[67] While compensation was denied to East Bengali refugees, their rehabilitation nevertheless mirrored erstwhile social status and occupational background. For example, displaced lawyers and doctors were entitled to maintenance grants of Rs 1,500 for a year and Rs 600 for six months respectively, while the agriculturists and small traders had to be satisfied with grants of Rs 50 per month.[68] Similarly, the state sought to provide agriculturists with arable land, while those who registered themselves as artisans were not entitled to claim any land other than homestead land. This is because once recognised as bona fide refugees, displaced Hindus from Pakistan were treated as citizens of India, who had been uprooted from their social milieu and rendered economically destitute. These were the gaps that the regime of rehabilitation sought to fill. The entire regime can be seen as an elaborate attempt to recreate the lost socio-economic status of the refugees. This emphasis on replicating past hierarchies, when combined with the ingrained patriarchal values of the vast majority of the bureaucratic and political elite who crafted policies, paved the way for the denial of rehabilitation to refugee women.

In a patriarchal society, the status of the family derives from the male head of the family. This is why, when it came to dealing with large numbers of female-headed families, governmental imagination, obviously influenced by contemporary social mores, ran out of ideas. The regime of rehabilitation in post-colonial India was blind to the social identities and economic backgrounds of single or widowed women. Instead of seeing them in their socio-economic context, it treated all unattached women as a homogenous group of victims. Their personal loss of family members was seamlessly translated into the loss of socio-economic identity. Seen through the eyes of the state, families that had

---

[67] Satya M. Rai, *Partition of the Punjab: A Study of its Effects on the Politics and Administration of the Punjab, 1947–56* (New York: Asia Publishing House, 1965). Also see Mohinder Singh Randhawa, *Out of the Ashes: An Account of the Rehabilitation of Refugees from West Pakistan in Rural Areas of East Punjab* (Chandigarh: Public Relations Department, Punjab, 1954). Also see Kudaisya and Tan, *The Aftermath of Partition in South Asia* (2000), pp. 128–33.

[68] For details see Refugee Relief and Rehabilitation Department, *Relief and Rehabilitation of Displaced Persons in West Bengal* (Calcutta, 1957).

lost their male heads had also lost their social and economic standing, i.e., a class or occupational group into which they could be slotted for rehabilitation. Moreover, this loss was deemed to be irrecoverable. These women, according to the Ministry of Rehabilitation 'bore scars that would not heal' and lived lives 'enveloped in misery and hopelessness'.[69] It followed that though unattached refugee women were entitled to relief, and to sympathetic treatment from the state, they were unfit for rehabilitation. To read this radical exclusion of unattached women as an act of welfare requires historians to take at face value the official assertion that all refugee women, once bereft of their husbands, had neither the desire for rehabilitation not the ability to achieve socio-economic autonomy. The reminiscences of unattached women as well as later reports and surveys of the conditions of PL camps and homes suggest otherwise.[70]

In sum, the decision to govern refugee women as perennial victims was a by-product of a governmentality of rehabilitation that idealised the hyper-masculine refugee. In post-colonial India, government help in rehabilitation was offered to only those who needed it, i.e., the poorer section of the refugees. As demonstrated in earlier chapters, the project of resettling refugees who entered government camps came to be permeated by the broader agenda of national development and sought to harness refugees to projects of agricultural expansion. As a result, self-sufficiency and economic productivity was equated with the capacity for hard manual labour. 'Able-bodied men' among the refugees remained the main concern of the state, whether as much-needed tillers of evacuee land in Punjab, or as the hapless East Bengali refugees who were expected to play the role of agricultural pioneers across the length and breadth of India. A rehabilitation regime designed with the hyper-masculine refugee in mind was both ablist and sexist, and bypassed, along with 'unattached' women, the aged and the infirm.

Becoming Permanent Liability: Negotiating Patriarchy in West Bengal

In West Bengal, state response to permanent liabilities stood at odds with the policy followed towards refugees in general. In the aftermath of the riots of 1950, those categorised as permanent liabilities were the only ones exempt from the government of India's desperate attempts to engineer a voluntary repatriation of refugees to East Bengal. Having promised

[69] Bhaskar Rao, *The Story of Rehabilitation* (1967), pp. 78–9.
[70] Of particular relevance is the *Screening Committee Report* (1989), which reported that almost all able-bodied women who lived in PL camps earned a living to supplement their meagre grants.

perpetual care and maintenance to unattached women, old and infirm men and their dependants, the state needed to separate them from the general population of refugees, who, at this stage, were expected to return to East Bengal. A bureaucratic system of sorting out and segregating PL families was put in place. The camps which were established to house the women selected through this process still exist in West Bengal. Interviews conducted with unattached women living in the PL camps in West Bengal in 2002 suggest that for many, the process of being categorised as permanent liability was scarred by bureaucratic violence that severed organic social bonds, imposed sexual segregation and constrained mobility. Yet, there were others who actively sought entry to PL camps as a means of negotiating widowhood. This section explores the constraints faced and choices made by unattached women living in PL camps of West Bengal.

The Ministry of Rehabilitation put in place a 'machinery for selection' to sort out those eligible for admission to permanent liability camps. This selection took place at interception points at the border areas. Later, centres for interception were also set up at the hubs of public transport where refugees arrived, such as Sealdah and Bongaon railway stations. Officials of the Ministry of Rehabilitation interrogated the refugees and issued a special class of interception slip to those who looked to the government for food and shelter. From among these refugees, aged and infirm men, unattached women and their dependants were pulled out for admission to PL camps. For unattached women this apparently innocuous system of categorisation often became the basis of compulsory separation from family members. This is largely because the bureaucratic definition of an 'unattached woman' privileged certain familial ties while marginalising others. In theory, only women who had no 'adult, able-bodied son, father, father-in-law or any other relative in a position to support them' were to be separated as permanent liabilities of the state.[71] However, in practice, the officials in charge of classification paid little heed to the relationships widowed and single women had with 'other' male relatives, or to familial ties between women. Women in PL camps of West Bengal spoke of separation from brothers, uncles, brother-in-laws or nephews before they were herded off to PL camps. In the process of isolating these women as recipients of special care, the state often compounded the disorientation and suffering of vulnerable women who had already lost family members to riots.

Several women living in the PL camps of West Bengal narrated such incidents of forced separation. Sonai Mali of Bhadrakali camp had

---

[71] Categories of displaced persons entitled to maintenance at government expenses and the definition of each category, Ashoka Gupta Papers, File No. 7, WSC, Calcutta.

witnessed rioters slaughter her husband, father and uncles in Barisal. She sought refuge in West Bengal along with her mother and five siblings. At Sealdah station, this widow of sixteen was separated from her surviving family and sent to the women's camp at Bhadrakali. It seems that being the archetypal partition widow, Sonai had been singled out as 'unrehabilitable'. The rest of her family were sent to a separate camp, as her unmarried sisters might have been considered 'rehabilitable' through marriage.[72] A similar pattern is repeated with Mukul Shil of Bhadrakali camp. She came to India as a young widow along with her sister and aged parents. The perverse logic of categorisation split this family into two, sending the parents off to Dhubulia and the sisters to a women's-only camp.[73] Binodini Haldar came to West Bengal in an extended family of six that included her daughter, an elder brother and his wife, and an elder sister and her son. At Sealdah station, Binodini and her two-year-old daughter were separated from the rest of the family and sent off to a women's camp in Asansol.[74]

Unlike Punjab, where widespread communal violence produced mass widowhood, most women who ended up in PL camps in West Bengal had not lost their husbands or families in riots. The East Bengali women segregated by the state were typically widows who had lived as dependants in extended families in rural East Bengal. According to Hiranmoy Bandyopadhyay, dependent widows were forced to turn to the government for shelter when their families suffered displacement.[75] However, from the reminiscences of the women who reached West Bengal as a part of larger family units, it is clear that familial ties often survived displacement from East Bengal. A married man's understanding of his family would include a range of dependants, such as an orphaned *bhaiji* (brother's daughter) a widowed *pishi* (father's sister), an aging uncle and even cousins. What refugee families could not withstand was the top-down imposition of rigid definitions of the limits of the familial upon more complex social realities.[76] As far as the state was concerned, a 'family' consisted of a married couple, their children and at most, also the husband's parents. This idealised nuclear family was a figment of bureaucratic imagination. Its indiscriminate application in classifying refugees had disastrous consequences for familial dependants. By refusing to

---

[72] Interview with Sonai Mali conducted by Debjani Datta and Subhasri Ghosh, 2002, PCSD.
[73] Interview with Mukul Shil, ibid.   [74] Interview with Binodini Haldar, ibid.
[75] Bandyopadhyay, *Ubvastu (Refugee)* (1970), p. 97.
[76] The Bengali notion of the family does not distinguish sharply between dependants who are part of the elementary, i.e., nuclear or minimal family, and dependants who might be more distantly related. See Ronald B. Inden and Ralph W. Nicholas, *Kinship in Bengali Culture* (New Delhi: Orient Blackswan, 2005).

recognise familial ties that exceeded the normative nuclear family, the regime of rehabilitation uprooted widows, elderly relatives and dependent children from their *atmiya-swajan*, i.e., their 'own-people'. In other words, the 'unattached' condition of the thousands of single and widowed women was produced by the regime of rehabilitation, rather than by the vicissitudes of partition.

Besides segregating single women, the regime of rehabilitation also corroded familial ties in general. Its regulations fixed the maximum monthly allowance available to any refugee family at Rs 60, irrespective of the number of family members. This penalised larger families and led many impoverished 'heads' of large families to reject familial dependants. According to Ashoka Gupta, the brunt of these rejections was borne by women. As an eyewitness, she squarely blamed the government's classificatory system for the liquidation of familial ties.[77] According to her, sending an 'unmarried sister or widowed aunt' to a separate camp marked the beginning of the fragmentation of the traditional joint family that had characterised the Hindu families of East Bengal.[78] Kanti B. Pakrasi's sociological study of the refugees from East Bengal lends some substance to these allegations. According to him, 'Perceptible disintegration of joint family structures was the social reality for the Hindu migrants from East Bengal.'[79] However, beyond alluding to partition migration as a causal factor, Pakrasi does not attempt to explain the changes he describes. The evidence from oral history suggests that the rarefied notion of family promoted by the state might have facilitated the erosion of familial ties. Herein lay the central paradox of the state's relationship to unattached women in the eastern region. By defining, classifying and segregating refugees, the state first reduced women to a state of abject victimhood; and then donned the garb of the patriarch to protect them.

Selection at reception centres was not the only route refugee women travelled to enter PL camps. A number of interviewees from Dhubulia camp lost their husbands or children, or both, at government camps. Insanitary conditions, arising from the government's failure to prevent overcrowding, lay at the root of these entirely avoidable tragedies. The refugee camps of West Bengal were rife with diseases.[80] A contemporary

---

[77] Ashoka Gupta, along with other volunteers of AIWC had helped officials at Sealdah station in their work of receiving and categorising refugees during the crisis of 1950. For details, see Gupta, *In the Path of Service* (2005), pp. 122–3.

[78] Interview with Ashoka Gupta, 2000, PCSD.

[79] Kanti B. Pakrasi, *The Uprooted: A Sociological Study of the Refugees of West Bengal, India* (Calcutta: Indian Statistical Institute, 1971), p. 73.

[80] Prafulla Kumar Chakrabarti, *The Marginal Men: The Refugees and the Left Political Syndrome in West Bengal* (Calcutta: Naya Udyog, 1999), pp. 156–61; Manikuntala Sen, *In Search of Freedom: An Unfinished Journey* (Calcutta: Stree, 2001), pp. 180–1.

report regarding mortality rates in Dhubulia camp for the period between 6 June and 7 July in 1950 presents an alarming picture. Among the 2,682 families surveyed, 2,703 refugees were registered as ill while no less than 685 refugees had died within the span of a month.[81] The Communist opposition scathingly criticised B. C. Roy's government for the inhuman conditions in refugee camps. There was, however, little concern for the women who survived the deaths of their husbands and sons. They were promptly reclassified as permanent liabilities and shifted to PL camps. After Pari Goswami's father died at Ghushuria camp, she was shifted along with her mother and two sisters to the PL camp at Dhubulia.[82] Mayarani Dutta's husband was claimed by cholera at Bongaon station.[83] When interviewed in 2000, Khuki Sarkar still rued the fact that when her husband died, all arrangements for their rehabilitation had already been made. However, as a widow with two daughters, she ended up at Champta PL camp struggling to make ends meet on government dole.[84]

Most unattached women who were pulled out from reception centres or transit camps and shifted to PL camps had little or no say in their relocation. However, there were significant exceptions to this pattern. Many widows actively sought entry to PL camps, largely because a refugee woman could directly claim government aid only as a permanent liability. The regulations provided for the entry of 'very deserving cases', such as families reduced to destitution due to the death or infirmity of the male earning member.[85] A number of widows utilised this provision to apply for admission to PL camps. Several inhabitants of Bansberia and Dhubulia PL camps had opted to enter these institutions, though they had not been rejected by their extended families. Many women who had initially sought shelter as dependants in the households of male relatives chose to leave with their children, at times going against the wishes of other family members. More often than not, this was a calculated choice. They hoped that entering a PL camp would give them greater control over their personal finances and ensure schooling for their children. Lilabati Ghosh, who came to West Bengal as a pregnant widow, is a case in point. She initially put up with her brother's family in Farakkah with her two sons, but left his household after giving birth to her daughter. She was convinced that her natal family lacked the generosity, if not the means, to provide for four additional members. She organised formal applications

[81] Tushar Singha, *Maranjayee sangrame vastuhara (Refugees in a Death-Defying Battle)* (Calcutta: 1999), p. 28.

[82] Interview with Pari Goswami conducted by Ghosh and Dutta, 2002, PCSD.

[83] Interview with Mayarani Dutta, ibid.   [84] Interview with Khuki Sarkar, ibid.

[85] Report on Technical and Vocational Training, 1955, Ashoka Gupta Papers, File No.10, WSC, Calcutta.

and obtained recommendations in order to gain entry to Bansberia camp. Lilabati preferred living in a PL camp as she feared abuse and neglect from her extended family. More importantly, it gave her some means, however meagre, to care for her three children.[86] Atashibala Das of Dhubulia camp used to live with her brother after her husband's death. Economic distress in his family led her to seek shelter in PL camps with her baby son.[87] Lakshmi Saha of Bansberia camp was similarly reluctant to be 'a burden' on her brother's household in East Bengal. Incredibly, she chose to become a refugee and travelled with her three-year-old daughter from Barisal to Bongaon, with the explicit intention of staying in a government camp.[88]

From the above reminiscences, it is clear that for some widows, especially those who had young children, PL camps provided a way out of a life of dependence on dubious charity from relatives. They saw themselves as an added burden on the household and felt constrained to claim a share of the household's resources for their children. Interestingly, they had no such qualms about accepting 'dole' from the government, which they came to see as an entitlement. Clearly, unattached refugee women had a very different interpretation of the official discourse of charitable relief. They increasingly claimed shelter and maintenance from the government as a matter of right, resorting to angry protests when the conditions in the PL camps did not meet their expectations.

Surabala Das of Bansberia, who left the home of her *deor* or husband's brother to enrol herself in a PL camp, expressed this sense of entitlement in no uncertain terms. The idea of living in a camp was put to her by her widowed mother, who was already a resident of Rupasreepalli camp at Ranaghat. The latter suggested that it would be easier for Surabala to educate and marry off her daughter if she went to a camp. Surabala decided to join her mother's camp but was denied entry to Rupasreepalli, where new admissions had been frozen. Determined to have her way, she resorted to an elaborate attempt to manipulate the bureaucratic system of classification and dispersal. She made her way to Bongaon station where she joined the crowd of fresh arrivals to be enlisted as a 'permanent liability'. The next stop was the overcrowded transit camp of Babughat. Surabala waited at this camp for three months in the vain hope that there would eventually be a call for new residents from Rupasreepalli. In her bid to manipulate the system, Surabala

---

[86] Interview with Lilabati Ghosh, conducted by Ghosh and Dutta, 2002, PCSD.
[87] Interview with Atashibala Das, ibid.   [88] Interview with Lakshmi Saha, ibid.

regularly hid from the officials who relocated refugee women to more permanent camps. However, after three months of waiting she gave up and was sent to Bhadrakali camp. Here, a far greater terror greeted the young widow. Bhadrakali was in the grip of a smallpox epidemic when she arrived:

There, every day two or three would die of pox. They used to leave (the bodies) stacked together, later cars would come to take the dead bodies away. Seeing this, I sent my daughter to my mother.[89]

Once the epidemic passed, she brought her daughter back. Clearly, the life Surabala had opted for was far from comfortable. Yet she did not regret leaving her in-laws, who she insisted had not deprived her in anyway. For her, the decision to enter a PL camp boiled down to a simple question: 'since the opportunity was there, why would I not take it?'[90]

Despite the overcrowding, disease and lack of privacy that charac-terised life in PL camps, widows like Surabala Das saw their eligibility for shelter in these camps as an 'opportunity'. But what opportunity could these camps provide that living with relatives did not? The scale of monthly maintenance was so meagre that it barely ensured subsis-tence. However, there were other benefits which had been promised by the independent state to its permanent liabilities. While unattached women were promised training towards gainful employment, their children were entitled to free primary education at these camps. The government treated these children as orphans and shouldered the entire cost of their secondary education. Even a cursory look at the evidence from oral history suggests that primarily widows with young children chose to leave their relations and live in PL camps. In a patriarchal culture, the joint family could be a hostile space for a widow with young children. Traditionally, Hindu widows were not only viewed as unwelcome burdens, but were also seen to be inauspi-cious. Discriminatory treatment of the children of dependent widows was far from uncommon. It is possible that refugee women saw these camps as means of obtaining free education for their children. Besides free education, the PL camps also promised training to unattached women, rehabilitation for their sons, and a marriage grant of Rs 200 for their daughters. For widowed women dependent upon male rela-tives, this combination of schemes appeared to offer a better future for their children. In order to access these schemes, they were prepared to

[89] Interview with Surabala Das, ibid.   [90] Ibid.

negotiate the overcrowded and restricted life of camps. In other words, for many young widows, entering PL camps became a way of negotiating patriarchy.[91] However, the government of West Bengal seldom kept its part of the deal. Administrative apathy and parsimonious budgets set the tone of life in women's camps. There was a huge gap between rhetoric and ground reality in the women's camps of West Bengal, where most promises, including that of education for children, remained unfulfilled. Unattached women responded with hunger strikes and protests, aggressively demanding as their right what the government sought to dole out as charity.

Broken Promises: Life in PL Camps

For refugee women, becoming permanent liabilities exacted a high price. Separated from their affective communities and segregated into women-only camps, they often lost contact with friends and family. Moreover, the living conditions in most PL camps of West Bengal were very poor. Families shared dormitories and women had no privacy. Instead of providing better accommodation, the government of West Bengal carried gender segregation in PL camps to extreme lengths, sending aged fathers to separate camps and adolescent sons to orphan homes. However, from the reminiscences of women living in the PL camps of West Bengal and stray eyewitness accounts gathered from autobiographies, newspaper reports and interviews of contemporaries, a more complicated picture emerges. Though refugee women suffered isolation and marginalisation within the regime of rehabilitation, they seldom suffered in silence. Instead, they refigured government charity as their right, and demanded their due in no uncertain terms.

The post-colonial state never came good on its promise of welfare to unattached women in the PL camps of West Bengal. In keeping with the sorry state of the majority of government-run camps in West Bengal, the conditions in the women's camps were also far from satisfactory. Set up during the crisis of 1950, these 'camps' consisted of a combination of make-shift barracks, constructed out of bamboo and corrugated iron sheets, and aluminium huts originally used for storing goods or grains during the Second World War. The government of West Bengal took over

---

[91] For a similar argument regarding PL camps in Bihar see Kathinka Sinha-Kerkhoff, 'Permanent Refugees: Female Camp Inhabitant in Bihar', Philomena Essed, Georg Frerks and Joke Schrijvers (eds), *Refugees and the Transformation of Societies: Agency, Policies, Ethics and Politics* (New York and Oxford: Berghahn, 2004), pp. 81–93.

these abandoned lands and structures from the Ministry of Defence and converted them into dormitories for refugees. For example, the Bansberia women's 'home' consisted of a string of 'twin tin sheds' with makeshift outdoors kitchens and none of the promised amenities (see Figure 5.1).[92] These camps provided little more than overnight shelter for thousands of women and their dependent children. Packed to capacity due to government inability to keep pace with the influx, the women's camps often lacked privacy, kitchens and any separate common space. Overcrowding, inadequate water supply and non-existent healthcare characterised the day-to-day lives of the residents.[93] They bore no resemblance to the 'homes' the government offered on paper. In theory, unattached women were entitled to permanent residence in full-fledged residential institutions providing not only 'shelter, water, lighting, electricity, sanitation and medical care' but also 'maintenance, clothing, education and facilities for work and vocational training'.[94] Such facilities could hardly be provided in the abandoned tin and bamboo structures which studded the West Bengal countryside as relics of the Second World War. These conditions persisted long after the crisis was over. According to a 1973 report, the residents of the remaining PL camps in West Bengal were still living in a combination of military sheds and makeshift structures. Periodic repairs had failed to halt the wear and tear of these shelters and most were so dilapidated that 'even with repairs, they cannot be made fit for safe dwelling'.[95]

Unattached women in West Bengal received little more than the bare minimum from the government. They were given two sets of clothes per annum and a monthly dole of Rs 12 for each adult and Rs 8 for every child below the age of eight. This scale of maintenance continued in the eastern sector long after it had been discarded in the western states, in 1951, as both insufficient and illogical.[96] Though the scale of assistance was

---

[92] *Screening Committee Report* (1989).

[93] Ashoka Gupta, Bina Das, Amar Kumari Varma, Sudha Sen and Sheila Davar, 'East is East, West is West', Jasodhara Bagchi and Subhoranjan Dasgupta (eds) *The Trauma and the Triumph: Gender and Partition in Eastern India* (Calcutta: Stree, 2003), p. 245.

[94] Letter No. RHAW-97 (1)/52, Ministry of Rehabilitation, Government of India, Ashoka Gupta Papers, File No. 11, WSC, Calcutta.

[95] Committee of Review of Rehabilitation Work, *Report on Repair and Reconstruction of Permanent Liability Homes and Infirmaries* (1974).

[96] In the Western states, children and adults were paid at the same rate, and the scale of payment *per capita* varied depending upon the number of members in a family as follows: 1 unit family – Rs 18, 1 unit family – Rs 18, 2 person family – Rs 16, 3 person family – Rs 15, 4 person family – Rs 14, 5 person family – Rs 13, and Rs 10 for every additional member thereon. See Gupta et al., 'East is East, West is West', Bagchi and Dasgupta (eds) *The Trauma and the Triumph* (2003), p. 245.

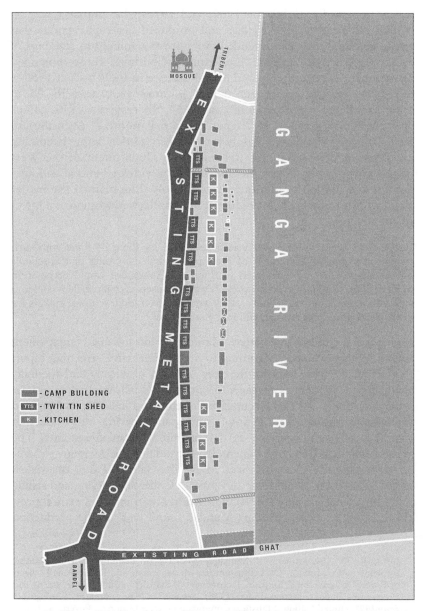

Figure 5.1: Sketch plan of Bansberia Women's Home, c.1989 (not to scale)
Source: Redrawn from *Problems of refugee camps and homes in West Bengal, the screening committee report*, Refugee Relief and Rehabilitation Directorate, Calcutta, 1989.

revised repeatedly during the 1960s and 1970s, the emphasis was on cutting costs rather than welfare and produced per capita grants that barely matched the recommended amount for a minimum standard of living. For example, in 1962, the Planning Commission recommended that the bare minimum required for subsistence in India was, at 1960–1 prices, Rs 20 per capita per month in rural areas and Rs 25 in urban locations.[97] Between 1960 and 1964, the residents of PL camps of West Bengal received Rs 21 per capita per month.[98] According to Nalini Mitra, who worked closely with refugee women before becoming the Director of the Refugee Rehabilitation Department of the West Bengal government, government concern for widowed and abandoned women was limited to granting monthly dole. She blamed the inadequacy of these payments for reducing the unattached women to a life of abject poverty:

The amount given as dole was insufficient. Can anything be done with such meagre amounts? The number of dropouts started increasing in the schools within camps. The mothers used to think that more use would come from children collecting *ghunte* (dried cakes of cow dung used as cheap fuel for cooking) than from their attending school . . . they would go from door to door, looking for work. They would not let their children go to school.[99]

Later reports confirm this pattern of informal and low-paid employment among refugee women. According to a comprehensive screening report conducted in 1989, 'barring the very old, the physically and mentally handicapped, all inmates are eager to work and actually do work to supplement their doles.'[100] The 'occupations' mentioned included making and selling paper packets, *bidi*-binding, spinning and weaving, basket and mat manufacturing; and working as day labourers or maid servants. The women interviewed in 2002 were mostly too old to work but many remembered working to make ends meet. Many, like Satirani Pal of Bhadrakali camp, found work as domestic servants.[101] Collecting, drying and selling cow dung as fuel was another common means of earning a few extra rupees. The lucky few, such as Pushpa Mandal, found work at the production

[97] Joshi, P. D. (Department of Statistics, Ministry of Planning and Programme Implementation, India). 'Conceptualisation, Measurement and Dimensional Aspects of Poverty in India, by P. D. Joshi, Department of Statistics, Ministry of Planning and Programme Implementation, India' (PDF). *Seminar on Poverty Statistics Santiago 7–9 May 1997*. United Nations Statistical Commission Expert Group on Poverty Statistics. Retrieved 7 September 2017.

[98] *Screening Committee Report* (1989).

[99] Interview with Nalini Mitra conducted by Subhoranjan Dasgupta, 2000, PCSD.

[100] *Screening Committee Report* (1989), p. 32.

[101] Interview with Satirani Pal conducted by Ghosh and Dutta, 2002, PCSD.

centre at Uttarpara.[102] Thus, the very regime of rehabilitation which pre-sented refugee women as passive recipients of government munificence, in practice forced them into a variety of informal and low-paid work.

Reminiscences of the residents of PL camps suggest that rudimentary primary education was provided in some of these camps. However, residential training for the women remained an empty promise until 1952, when Renuka Ray intervened. The central minister of rehabilita-tion remained 'doubtful' of the utility of such training; and despite her commitment to women's rights, West Bengal's Minister for Refugee Relief and Rehabilitation could only obtain sanction to set up a single centre on an 'experimental basis'.[103] A residential training centre was set up at Uttarpara, which trained unattached women in tailoring, weaving, calico printing, confectionary, bakery, bookbinding, brush-making and soap making. General administrative apathy combined with widespread bias against women's employment meant that this 'experiment', though successful, was not replicated. In 1955, Mehr Chand Khanna, the central Minister for Rehabilitation, admitted that provision for training existed only in some PL camps. Champta was one of the few PL camps where some provisions of training existed. However, by Khanna's own admission, even the standard of training was 'not very high' and it was 'intended more to discourage idleness than anything else.'[104]

The regime of rehabilitation in independent India was fraught with anxiety over the 'unsafe' sexuality of single women. Nalini Mitra's description of her work as the supervisor of Chunar fort, a women's residential training centre in erstwhile United Provinces, provides an insight into official anxiety regarding the 'safety' of 'young girls'.

I used to keep them under very strict discipline. Inside the fort, they are locked up. No one can do anything there. But young girls will always be a little restless, if I had allowed them to freely move outside, who knows what they could have done? Bengali girls would get a bad name! That's why I had taken a strict attitude. All those who wanted to go out had to take permission to do so. Leaving the fort was a difficult job![105]

PL camps were subjected to strict gender segregation. Even the sons of residents were considered to be a threat once they crossed the age of

---

[102] Interview with Pushpa Mandal conducted by Ghosh and Dutta, 2002, PCSD.

[103] Renuka Ray, *My Reminiscences: Social Development During the Gandhian Era and After* (Calcutta: Stree, 2005), p. 145.

[104] Reorganisation of Permanent Liability Camps, Homes and Infirmaries, Ashoka Gupta Papers, File No. 11, WSC, Calcutta.

[105] Interview with Nalini Mitra conducted by Dr Subhoranjan Dasgupta, 2000, PCSD.

fourteen and were removed from these camps. A series of restrictions curtailed the mobility of refugee women and adversely affected their opportunities of employment. For the camp superintendents, the need to prevent the consequences of uncontrolled female sexuality took precedence over the economic needs of the women. Frequently, the supervisors of women's camps prevented unattached women from working in adjoining cities or villages.[106]

In sum, the everyday lives of women in permanent liability camps of West Bengal had little connection with the rhetoric of welfare that was used to justify their confinement in these institutions. Unattached women were certainly aware of the gap between the facilities promised, and those delivered. They regularly complained to camp superintendents regarding the inadequacy of the monthly dole, overcrowding and insanitary conditions. Most supervisors of PL camps in West Bengal were junior clerks or 'un-gazetted' officers who had no authority to sanction funds, and little sympathy for their wards.[107] Their apathy led refugee women to devise other strategies for redress. Like their counterparts in generic camps and colonies, unattached refugee women also used both deputation and agitation to demand their due from the state. Asok Mitra's[108] description of a chance encounter with the women of Jamuria camp provides us with a glimpse of unattached women's negotiations with the state. During his brief tenure in 1954–5, as the District Magistrate of Burdwan, Asok Mitra was accosted by a group of women and children who stopped his car on the highway linking Burdwan to Asansol.[109] Feeling 'like a cad in my pullover and tweed jacket in front of women who were virtually in rags', he was led on a tour of Jamuria women's camp. The so-called camp was actually a 'cluster of tin-walled and tin-roofed empty warehouses on the nearby railway siding' into which these women and their children had been herded. Spending about three-quarters of an hour moving from room to room and peering into the kitchens, the baths, the toilets, the apology of a schoolhouse and dispensary, Mitra concluded that:

---

[106] Gupta et al., 'East is East, West is West', Bagchi and Dasgupta (eds), *The Trauma and the Triumph* (2003), p. 247.

[107] Ibid.

[108] Asok Mitra, who joined the Indian Civil Service in 1935, is better known as a demographer and for his contributions to successive census reports in independent India. He was Superintendent of the Census Report of West Bengal (1951) and later became the Registrar-General and Census Commissioner of India (1961).

[109] Asok Mitra was briefly posted as the District Magistrate of Burdwan between December 1954 and May 1955, Asok Mitra, *The New India: 1948–55, Memoirs of an Indian Civil Servant* (Bombay: Popular Prakashan, 1991), pp. 126–33.

These were only notional substitutes for the real things. None of them were even minimally furnished. There was no privacy anywhere. The entire camp was open to public gaze amidst surroundings that were inhospitable to say the least.[110]

However, what struck him was the ease with which he was able to remedy this neglect. Official request for provisions, clothes and training equipment received an uncharacteristically prompt response. By 19 January, new clothes and saris, blankets, sewing machines and other equipment had already reached Jamuria camp. Asok Mitra concluded that 'It was quite obvious that the sanctions had existed, but not been acted upon. What was worse was that nobody had made any noise over it either.'[111] Clearly, administrative apathy compounded the suffering of unattached women.

While the women of Jamuria camp petitioned senior state officials to intervene on their behalf, the women of Bhadrakali camp resorted to forming associations in order to protest. Tushar Sinha's account of these protests privileges the UCRC as the champion of refugee women. He chronicles the meetings and protests organised by refugee leaders in support of the inmates of Bhadrakali camp between 1954 and 1957. Despite this lopsided narrative, it is clear that the women of Bhadrakali camp had thrown up their own leader – a woman named Surabala Das. She not only led the protests against the authorities, but also organised the women into a committee for self-protection.[112] The camp authorities responded by unleashing a series of repressive measures. Surabala was expelled from the camp and charged with unlawful protest. The government punished her and sixteen other protesters by withholding their dole for months.[113] When interviewed in 2002, she recalled weathering this punishment by combining her earnings from domestic service with sympathetic donations from various refugee leaders. She claimed that the 'people who belonged to Congress gave nothing.'[114] She described marches and protests as a routine affair in both Bhadrakali camp and Bansberia camp, to which she was

---

[110] Ibid., pp. 128–9.   [111] Ibid., p. 129.

[112] This could have been influenced by the communist-led *Mahila Atmaraksha Samiti* (Women's Self-defence League) or MARS. Formed in the aftermath of the Bengal Famine, MARS had grown to a membership of 30,000 in undivided Bengal. For a history of MARS see Manikuntala Sen, *In Search of Freedom*, Calcutta (2001), pp. 72–146 and Renu Chakravartty, *Communists in Indian Women's Movement, 1940–50* (New Delhi: Peoples' Publishing House, 1980). MARS involvement with refugee women was usually confined to the colonies. See Chakravartty, *Coming Out of Partition* (2005), pp. 86–92 and Chakrabarti, *The Marginal Men* (1999), p. 49.

[113] Singha, *Maranjayee sangrame vastuhara* (Refugees in a Death-Defying Battle), pp. 29–30.

[114] Interview with Surabala Das conducted by Datta and Ghosh, 2002, PCSD.

later transferred. According to Surabala, these protests were essential to obtain 'mugs, buckets, soap and hurricane lamps' from the authorities.[115] In this respect, life in the PL camps of West Bengal was not very different from that in generic refugee camps. Government denial of what unattached women considered to be their right led to frequent protests and politicisation of many unattached women.

While protesting against government apathy, the residents of PL camps displayed a fair deal of militancy. Nalini Mitra vividly recalled their aggression, describing it as *'juddhang dehi bhab'* or a near declaration of war:

Their conviction was that we owed our jobs to them. We had been employed because they had chosen to come. They thought that the government allotted a lot of money for them, but we (government officials) did not distribute it. Such notions they had![116]

What Nalini Mitra saw as a misguided notion was in effect a radical expression of entitlement. Far from being grateful for government charity, unattached women saw it as their due. In the process, they radically inverted their relationship to state officials. They reminded Nalini Mitra that she owed her job to their misfortune, perhaps suggesting that it was she who should be grateful to the widows of PL camps. Thus, refugee women in West Bengal did not merely protest against specific policies or failures of administration. Their protests were driven by a radical re-interpretation of their position within the regime of rehabilitation. Not all women were equally militant in their protests. But almost all women in PL camps shared a sense of entitlement to state support. This is thrown into sharper focus by the common fear of being a 'burden' on their extended families. Yet, single and widowed refugee women seldom saw themselves as a burden on the state, or their monthly maintenance dole as charity. Instead, they aggressively demanded permanent relief as their due from the national government. By seeing themselves as bearers of rights, no matter how meagre, refugee women located themselves firmly within the social body of the nation and challenged their systematic exclusion from the regime of rehabilitation. Radical as this reinterpretation was, its expression remained fragmented and inchoate. It did not reach the national government, which refused to engage directly with unattached refugee women regarding their needs and grievances. More importantly, social workers and refugee leaders failed to take account of this reinterpretation of charity as rights, authored by unattached refugee women.

[115] Ibid.
[116] Interview with Nalini Mitra conducted by Subhoranjan Dasgupta, 2000, PC, SD.

Conclusion

Refugee rehabilitation in post-partition India was a sphere of state intervention into society that explicitly aimed at producing normal citizens out of the unsettled category of citizen-refugees. In theory, legal citizenship was guaranteed to all partition refugees and the work of the Ministry of Rehabilitation was limited to ensuring that *all* refugees attained economic self-sufficiency and joined the mainstream of Indian society. However, in practice, when faced with refugee women who were 'unattached' to adult men through ties of kinship, the post-colonial state responded by setting up a parallel regime for their relief, care and rehabilitation. The core belief that animated this response was that unattached women were 'unfit' for rehabilitation. In post-colonial India, the partition refugee's quest to substantively belong to his putative homeland passed through the regime of rehabilitation. Therefore, the pre-emptive exclusion of all unattached women from routine schemes and policies of rehabilitation speaks of a deeply gendered vision of citizenship. In the eyes of the state, refugee women were unfit to receive and make proper use of the key ingredients of an autonomous life – agricultural land, houses and homestead plots, and loans for starting a trade or business. This radical exclusion has gone largely unnoticed by historians because it was replaced by a host of schemes, purportedly designed to achieve the welfare of unattached refugee women. These schemes, however, owed more to the aspirations of social workers and philanthropists than to the needs of refugee women. They promoted the training and employment of refugee women in order to make them economically productive. Instead of demanding the full inclusion of women as autonomous citizens, such schemes aimed to merely demonstrate that women could perform the role of productive citizens.

Yet, no amount of training and acquisition of economic productivity qualified unattached refugee women for resettlement schemes. The only way for an unattached woman to officially access rehabilitation was to achieve 'attachment' to an adult man. This could be attained either through marriage, or through the adulthood of a son. Thus, contrary to received wisdom, the state did not facilitate the assimilation of unattached women, especially widows, 'into the economic and social mainstream as expeditiously as possible.'[117] They were either relocated within a patriarchal nuclear family, where an adult man could access rehabilitation on their behalf, or discharged with some training and a grant in lieu of substantive rehabilitation. Those who could not access either lingered

---

[117] Menon, 'Do Women Have a Country?', p. 49.

as unassimilable residues of a regime of rehabilitation that could not imagine women as autonomous citizens. The evidence of oral history suggests that the residents of women's homes and PL camps were well aware of the gendered texture of their marginalisation. For example, several widows of the Karnal Mahila Ashram summed up their lot with the pithy statement *'putran waliyan dhar gaiyan, thiyan waliyan mar gaiyan'*, meaning those with sons got settled while those with daughters were as good as dead.[118] This lament of a dead existence is echoed in the PL camps of West Bengal by the unfulfilled desire to live in one's own *sansar* or household among sonless widows and adult daughters of unattached women. If the voices of unattached women are privileged above the reminiscences of social workers, it becomes difficult to argue that official policy towards unattached women actually improved the social status of widows.

While the scholarship on Punjab's refugee crisis overestimates the beneficial impact of state policy towards unattached women, received wisdom on Bengal portrays the dislocation of partition as a blessing in disguise for East Bengali Hindu women. According to Jashodhara Bagchi, the refugee woman's 'historic assertion ... as the tireless breadwinner changed the digits of feminine aspiration of the Bengali *bhadramahila* and altered the social landscape irrevocably'.[119] Gargi Chakravartty argues that partition led to a fundamental rupture in social orthodoxies, which created space for the emergence of a new image of the Bengali woman, 'self reliant, independent ... who could challenge the rigidity of patriarchal domination.'[120] In these narratives, partition is seen to trigger a causal chain of socio-economic and cultural changes. Displacement led to the impoverishment of middle-class Hindu families from East Bengal. Women entered the job market due to economic compulsion, at times becoming the primary breadwinners for their families. Economic independence paved the way for the emancipation of refugee women, and through them, of all middle-class Bengali women.[121] This celebratory narrative suffers from a middle-class bias and problematically equates waged labour with the emancipation of women.[122] While surveys reveal a

---

[118] Menon and Bhasin, *Borders and Boundaries* (1998), p. 134.

[119] Jasodhara Bagchi and Subhoranjan Dasgupta, 'Introduction', Jasodhara Bagchi and Subhoranjan Dasgupta (eds) *The Trauma and the Triumph* (2003), p. 6.

[120] Chakravartty, *Coming Out of Partition* (2005), p. 91.

[121] A similar argument for Punjabi refugee women is made in Anjali Bhardwaj Datta, 'Gendering Oral History of Partition: Interrogating Patriarchy', *Economic and Political Weekly*, 41:22, (2006): 2229–35.

[122] For example, see Dagmar Engel's survey of working women in colonial Bengal, which illustrates how women's waged labour meant different things among different sections of the population. While most *adivasi* and low-caste women routinely worked along with

substantial rise in the number of 'gainfully employed' refugee women, there is scant evidence to suggest that such employment was emancipatory.[123] Interviews of middle-class women reveal contradictory emotions and experiences. While earning gave women greater confidence, it seldom translated to greater social or economic autonomy. Many women resented the double load of housework and waged labour and stopped working as soon as they could.[124] However, a far greater gap within received wisdom is the complete erasure of the experiences of thousands of refugee women who entered the PL camps.[125] Given the acute impoverishment that characterised life in the PL camps of West Bengal, there is a need for a more nuanced understanding of the impact of partition-induced dislocation upon Bengali refugee women.

Previous chapters have illustrated how the ability of partition refugees to access relief and rehabilitation varied significantly, depending on their caste, class background and ethnicity. However, for unattached refugee women, their gender identity overrode all other factors in defining their relationship to the post-colonial nation. Irrespective of ethnicity, caste or class background, refugee women were promised permanent relief, but denied rehabilitation. It was not just recovered abducted women who were seen as belonging to the community, before they could belong to the nation. For all refugee women, national belonging was mediated through the patriarchal institution of the heterosexual and patrilineal nuclear family. For single and widowed women, this meant a truncated form of belonging where the state recognised its obligation towards their welfare, but refused to provide them the means to recreate autonomous social lives. This refusal to allow unattached refugee women the means of social autonomy was in effect an assertion of patrilineal values, where social status and heredity pass along the male line. This gendered form of

their husbands as unskilled labourers, among upper castes, only women who had somehow lost social status or had been socially ostracised joined the labour market. Among middle-class Hindus, waged labour of married women continued to be unacceptable, while there was some tolerance for a widow earning her own living. Engels, *Beyond Purdah?* (1996), pp. 194–244. For the gendered construction of women's labour and its devaluation, see Samita Sen, *Women and Labour in Late Colonial India: The Bengal Jute Industry* (Cambridge and New York: Cambridge University Press, 1999).

[123] For an alternative reading of the meaning of employment for refugee women see Rachel Weber, 'Re(Creating)the Home: Women's Role in the Development of Refugee Colonies in South Calcutta', Bagchi and Dasgupta (eds) *The Trauma and the Triumph* (2003), pp. 59–79.

[124] Ibid and Ashok Mitra, 'Take a Girl Like Her', *Calcutta Diary* (London: Cass, 1976), pp. 16–20.

[125] The sole exception to this trend is Ishita Dey, 'On the Margins of Citizenship: Principles of Care and Rights of the Residents of the Ranaghat Women's Home, Nadia District', *Refugee Watch*, 33 (2009).

belonging, devoid of the right to create or reproduce social identity, was not just limited to refugee women. It informed the Citizenship Act of 1955, which limited citizenship by descent to those who had an Indian father.[126] While denying Indian women the ability to pass on citizenship to their children, in the absence of heterosexual 'attachment' to an Indian man, the home minister Pant declared that "We, in our country, have always thought on masculine terms, and that has been our attitude towards all matters".[127] The gendered belonging offered to unattached refugee women thus anticipated a gendered form of citizenship for all Indian women.

---

[126] Citizenship by descent was extended to include either parents by an amendment to the Citizenship Act in 1992. For details of the amendments, see India: Act No. 57 of 1955, Citizenship Act, 1955, 30 December 1955, <http://www.refworld.org/docid/3a e6b57b8.html> last accessed 7 March 2018.

[127] 'Citizenship Bill Referred to Joint Select Body', *Hindustan Times*, 10th August 1955.

Conclusion

Fifty years after the partition of India, Khorshed Italia, a member of one of the oldest Parsi families of Delhi and fondly remembered as the 'grand dame of CP',[1] recalled watching communal riots unfold from the balcony of her second storey apartment in Connaught Place, in Delhi. According to Mrs Italia, as the Muslim shops around Connaught Place started being looted, and rioters made off with their loot in *tongas*,[2] Jawaharlal Nehru himself arrived on the scene. Running around with a *'lathi'* (stick) trying to stop the *'chokra'* (boys),[3] Nehru was, she claimed, shouting: "Stop. *Bas karo, bas karo. Bas Karo! Bandh karo!*"[4] The interview with Mrs Italia was conducted by Andrew Whitehead for a BBC film documentary entitled *India: A People Partitioned* (1997), which featured her role as a volunteer working with refugee women at the Lady Harding Hospital.[5] The part of her interview about Nehru's attempt to suppress the rioters, however, did not make it to the final cut. It is not difficult to understand why. Though both scholars and contemporaries have noted Nehru's 'exemplary' personal response in rushing to the old city and Connaught Circus to reassure Muslim residents, it is almost impossible to fully verify this particular instance of dangerous heroics.[6] Ultimately, it matters little whether this reminiscence was a genuine recollection or an 'invented memory', unconsciously inserted into

---

[1] 'Khorshed Italia: The grand dame of CP', *Parsi Khabar*, 10 July 2006, https://parsikhabar .net/individuals/khorshed-italia-the-grand-dame-of-cp/434/. Accessed on 31 July 2017.

[2] A light horse-drawn two-wheel vehicle.

[3] *Chokra* literally means a youth or a teenage boy but is usually only used to describe youth from non-elite backgrounds, who are most frequently present in urban spaces.

[4] *Bas karo* literally means to desist or cease an activity while *bandh karo* means to stop.

[5] BBC World Radio Service, *India: A People Partitioned*, 1997, http://www.bbc.co.uk/pro grammes/p034m6hb<i>, last accessed on 26 August 2017. The full interview with Khorshed Italia is available on Andrew Whitehead's blog, http://www.andrewwhitehead .net/partition-voices.html, last accessed 26 August 2017.

[6] Sunil Khilnani, *The Idea of India* (New Delhi, New York and London: Penguin: 1998), p. 31.

personal reminiscences.[7] Its significance lies less in its accuracy, and more in the meanings it conveys. Mrs Italia's vision of Nehru as a lone and desperate figure, frantically and ineffectually trying to quell the violence in the aftermath of partition, encapsulates contemporary representations of the official response to the horrors of partition. Throughout the period, news and official publications represented Indian politicians and administrators as neutral figures, overwhelmed by the scale of violence. Within official narratives, well-intentioned bureaucrats struggle to cope with the scale of displacement unleashed by partition, trying, to the best of their abilities, to serve refugee needs. This book has told a different story.

Shifting the focus from the spectacular violence and the 'heroic saga' of rehabilitation in Punjab, to the prolonged struggle for belonging waged by refugees from eastern Pakistan, illuminates the insidious violence that permeated policies of rehabilitation. In West Bengal, rehabilitation was designed to somehow make the 'problem' of East Bengali refugees disappear. Treated as foreigners, denied legitimacy as 'genuine' refugees, crammed into unhygienic and dead-end camps, and earmarked either for repatriation to eastern Pakistan or for dispersal outside West Bengal, there is little doubt that East Bengali refugees experienced the regime of rehabilitation as bureaucratic violence. However, the roots of this violence ran deeper than local machinations of electoral politics,[8] or racist scorn for the 'slimy and crawling Bengali refugees'.[9] The violence of the regime of rehabilitation derived from the conflation of refugee rehabilitation with the broader project of nation-building in post-partition India. In the ultimate analysis, policies of rehabilitation were designed to transform citizen-refugees into developmental citizens – worthy members of a post-colonial nation wedded to planned economic transformation. Rehabilitation became a conditional reward for refugees willing and able to become grist for the mill of national development. This book has traced why and how refugee rehabilitation and national development became intertwined in post-colonial India, as well as the diverse strategies employed by Bengali refugees to negotiate a hostile regime of

[7] Such 'invented memories' are common in accounts of veterans of the First World War and are discussed at length in Jean Peneff's 'Myths in Life Stories' in Raphael Samuel and Paul Thompson (eds), *The Myths We Live By* (London and New York: Routledge, 1990). This analytical framework is used extensively in chapter 4.

[8] Joya Chatterji traces West Bengal's policies of rehabilitation to political motives of the Congress government in *The Spoils of Partition: Bengal and India, 1947–1967* (Cambridge and New York: Cambridge University Press, 2007).

[9] Prafulla K. Chakrabarti, *The Marginal Men: The Refugees and the Left Political Syndrome in West Bengal* (Calcutta: Naya Udyog, 1999), p. 211.

rehabilitation. In the process, it has generated new insights into the governmentality of rehabilitation, the agency of refugees and the limitations and
contradictions of Nehruvian India's vision of national development.

Governmentality of Rehabilitation: A New Answer to an Old Riddle

An enduring puzzle of partition historiography has been the difference in
official responses to the refugee crisis in Punjab and the one in divided
Bengal. Despite considerable popularity, Hindu demands for exchange of
population and compensation for lost properties found no traction in
West Bengal. The government of India, on its part, exempted the eastern
states of West Bengal, Assam and Tripura from the remit of the Evacuee
Property Ordinance.[10] In stark contrast, there is increasing evidence of
the complicity of the state in the expulsion of Muslim minorities from
India, conducted either under the cover of 'voluntary' military evacuation
or by using the Evacuee Property Ordinance promulgated in 1949.[11]
So much so, that historians have argued for a logic of rehabilitation that
demanded the evacuation of Muslim minorities to enable the rehabilitation of Hindu refugees.[12] However, if the Nehruvian government was
prepared to oversee the dispossession of Muslim minorities in order to
resettle Hindu and Sikh refugees from western Pakistan, what stayed its
hand in the eastern region? This was not, as received wisdom suggests,
a difference born of different levels of violence in the eastern and western
regions. A close study of West Bengal's refugee crisis reveals the gradual
crystallisation of a *singular* governmentality that informed the regime of
rehabilitation, but led to diametrically opposite policies in Bengal and
Punjab.

In Nehruvian India, determination to develop the national economy
took precedence over the rights and needs of citizen-refugees.
Bureaucrats saw refugees as additional population in a context where
overpopulation had already been identified as one of the main obstacles
to economic growth.[13] As a result, the ability of any region to absorb
refugees became dependent on the amount of land available. In divided
Punjab, an exchange of population made sense because the number of

---

[10] For details of this exclusion, see Joya Chatterji, 'South Asian Histories of Citizenship,
1946–1970,' *The Historical Journal* 55:4 (2012), 1049–71.
[11] See Vazira Fazila Zamindar, *The Long Partition and the Making of Modern South Asia:
Refugees, Boundaries, Histories* (New York: Columbia University Press, 2010) and Joya
Chatterji, ibid.
[12] Vazira Zamindar, ibid.
[13] The post-war emergence of this discourse has been mapped in some detail in chapter 1.

Hindu and Sikh refugees roughly approximated the number of Muslim evacuees. Though rehabilitation was organised along communal lines of transferring land from Muslim evacuees to Hindu refugees, the logic underpinning this solution was an economic one. In stark contrast, in West Bengal, an exchange of population made little economic sense as the Hindu population of eastern Pakistan exceeded West Bengal's Muslim population by 4 million. As a result, even a trickle of refugees from East Bengal raised fears of being burdened by millions of unwanted and 'extra' people. It is the dominance of these discourses of development and not the lack of violence in the eastern region that lay at the root of differential policy and the neglect of Bengali refugees.

In post-partition South Asia, bureaucrats and politicians usually resorted to calculations of available land, housing and employment to deny rehabilitation to refugees. Vazira Zamindar understands this pattern of mobilisation of economic factors as the violence of governmentality.[14] However, the governmentality that informed the regime of rehabilitation in post-colonial India was more complex than the periodic evocation of economics to withhold rehabilitation.[15] It consisted of the compulsion to align policies of rehabilitation to goals of national development and could take negative as well as positive forms. The conflation of rehabilitation with development was achieved with relative ease in divided Punjab, where the exchange of populations had freed up agricultural land.[16] Punjabi refugees could be easily absorbed into the national economy as extra hands to till abandoned fields. By contrast, in West Bengal, refugees were an unwanted burden on the economy. The dominant governmentality demanded their expulsion or repatriation. In the sphere of policy, it took the shape of the Nehru-Liaquat Ali Pact of 1950, encouraging Bengali Hindus to return to Pakistan. However, the refusal of Bengali refugees to return to East Pakistan forced the authorities to abandon their negative stance and turn to more creative attempts of recasting East Bengali refugees as agents of development. They were used to build dams, colonise 'backward' tracts, cultivate paddy in order to promote national self-sufficiency in food and to grow jute to increase India's foreign exports. In certain areas, such as the Andaman Islands, Bengali refugees served a clandestine agenda of increasing the proportion of the

---

[14] Zamindar, *The Long Partition* (2007).

[15] This pattern has also been noted in the Sindhi context by Sarah Ansari in Sarah F. D. Ansari, *Life After Partition: Migration, Community and Strife in Sindh, 1947–1962* (Oxford: Oxford University Press, 2005).

[16] See Mohinder Singh Randhawa, *Out of the Ashes: An Account of the Rehabilitation of Refugees from West Pakistan in Rural Areas of East Punjab* (Chandigarh: Public Relations Department, Punjab, 1954). Also see Gyanesh Kudaisya and Tai Yong Tan, *The Aftermath of Partition in South Asia*, (Hove: Psychology Press, 2000), pp. 128–33.

Hindu population, which was deemed necessary for national security. In sum, a singular governmentality of rehabilitation found different iterations in different contexts. It functioned negatively when officials withheld rehabilitation from East Bengali Hindus and sought to block the entry of Muslim refugees in Rajasthan. Its positive iterations can be seen in Randhawa's scheme of resettling Hindu and Sikh refugees in eastern Punjab and in various projects of resettlement of Bengali refugees outside West Bengal, including the colonisation of the Andaman Islands and the development of Dandakaranya.

This dominance of 'economic factors' over questions of religious or ethnic solidarity was not always visible within the regime of rehabilitation. Wherever local demographics allowed policy to be aligned with identity, popular ethno-nationalist solidarities obscured the economics of rehabilitation. The prime example of this is the bureaucratic violence of the Evacuee Property ordinances. These operated in both India and Pakistan and were designed to confiscate minority resources for the rehabilitation of the majority community. Though born of the economic necessity of creating resources for rehabilitation, there is no doubt that these policies disenfranchised religious minorities. Yet, this ran parallel to numerous instances, in both India and Pakistan, where the alignment between identity and policy broke down. Examples include the official refusal to take in non-Punjabi Muslims in Pakistan,[17] and the attempts to stop the emigration of Hindu minorities in Sind.[18] In West Bengal, this took the form of denial of rehabilitation and an insistence on the repatriation of East Bengali refugees. As Joya Chatterji has already noted, the accumulating evidence of cross-regional resonances suggests that Punjab's experience of genocidal violence followed by an exchange of population, despite its dominance in popular representations, was the exception rather than the rule of how partition unfolded in South Asia. This study has expanded on this insight to demonstrate why and how Punjab's experience of partition-induced migration came to be an exception to the 'drawn out, messy and chaotic' patterns seen 'elsewhere'.[19] In Punjab alone demographic conditions allowed partition refugees' aspirations to belong, based on religious identity, to be aligned with official policy that was wedded to an economic rationality. Everywhere else, the partition refugees' attempts to belong to their chosen homeland ran up against the governmentality of rehabilitation. The significance of West Bengal's refugee crisis lies in the stark visibility it lends to this governmentality.

[17] Zamindar, *The Long Partition* (2007).   [18] Ansari, *Life After Partition* (2005).
[19] Joya Chatterji, 'Partition Studies: Prospects and Pitfalls', *The Journal of Asian Studies* 73 (2), 2014, 309–12.

Agency and Subalternity: The Caste, Class and Gender of Rehabilitation

This book has mined the reminiscences of Bengali Hindu refugees primarily to understand how refugees from different class, caste and gender backgrounds negotiated the regime of rehabilitation from below. This has revealed some unexpected patterns of state-society interaction and identity formation that do not conform to dominant understandings of subaltern agency. The classic subaltern, usually equated to a broad spectrum of marginalised groups, such as Dalits, peasants, tribal groups and women, has long been treated as a repository of alternative and autonomous visions of politics.[20] There is a rich historiography of subaltern protest and politics which maps how its methods, goals and ideologies do not conform to elite visions of nationalism or nation-building.[21] When it comes to the East Bengali refugee's negotiation of the regime of rehabilitation, the oppositional relationship between subaltern agency and hegemonic discourse breaks down in unexpected ways. Within the population of East Bengali refugees, those most able to actualise an alternative vision of rehabilitation were the relatively elite *bhadraloks* from eastern Pakistan who had fallen upon hard times, but were far from destitute. In stark contrast, the most marginalised amongst the refugees – the *Namasudra* peasants of eastern Bengal – towed the line of official policy and completely internalised the hegemonic discourse of rehabilitation.

The *bhadralok* refugees were the architects of the squatters' colonies of Calcutta, which were built in defiance of official policies of dispersal and evacuation. Contrary to their image as left-wing radicals and underdogs, the micro-history of the establishment of Bijaygarh colony in chapter 4 reveals how cultural capital and elite connections enabled upper-caste refugees to give shape to their own vision of rehabilitation. The leaders and visionaries of urban squatting were not only proximate to state power; they were cogs in its wheels. Within the ranks of refugees were clerks and bureaucrats who were government employees. Their intimate knowledge of various departments of the government of West Bengal was crucial to

---

[20] The insistence on the autonomous nature of subaltern politics was a key aspect of Ranajit Guha's initial conceptualisation of subalternity in 'On Some Aspects of the Historiography of Colonial India' in Ranajit Guha (ed.), *Subaltern Studies I* (New Delhi: Oxford University Press, 1982). Later theorists of subalternity have moved away from this insistence on autonomy, without sacrificing the impetus to trace the texture of subaltern agency.

[21] The focus on mapping rich histories of subaltern protest is particularly prominent in *Subaltern Studies*, Volumes I to VII, before the cultural turn in subaltern theory led to a shift in focus. For a critical analysis of the shifting meanings of subalternity within the *Subaltern Studies* project see David Ludden, *Reading Subaltern Studies: Critical History, Contested Meaning and the Globalization of South Asia* (London: Anthem Press, 2002).

their ability to resist statist visions of rehabilitation. Within the squatters' colonies, refugees resisted being recast as productive labourers harnessed to projects of national development. Schools became the heart of the refugee colonies instead of the factories and training centres promoted by the Department of Rehabilitation. Education or *shiksha* followed by *chakri* or paid white-collar employment became the main pathway to becoming 'normal' citizens of the nation.

The poorest refugees had little option but to enter government-run camps and wait for rehabilitation. Lacking cultural capital, social status, and economic resources, they bore the full brunt of the regime of rehabilitation. They were either dispersed to 'empty lands' outside West Bengal, or forgotten at ex-camp sites when they refused to move. An overwhelming majority of the refugees dispersed to the Andaman Islands and to Dandakaranya were *Namasudras*.[22] Though they were far from passive recipients of state *diktat*, their negotiation of the regime of rehabilitation failed to throw up any alternative values or visions that could contradict statist models of development. As discussed in chapter 3, the reminiscences of refugees resettled in the Andaman Islands are replete with anecdotes of how they outsmarted officials when it came to key decisions, such as the selection of 'suitable' settlers for the Andaman Islands. Yet, these everyday acts of resistance did not amount to an alternative vision of rehabilitation. In fact, the illiterate *Namasudra* peasants, who were by any definition a subaltern group within East Bengali refugees, largely internalised official discourses of rehabilitation. They identified as settlers and took pride in their role as agricultural pioneers who had transformed the Andaman Islands. The poorest Dalit refugees thus came to embody the post-colonial fantasy of the hyper-masculine and productive citizen-refugee.

The most radical exclusion perpetuated by the regime of rehabilitation was of single and widowed refugee women. By classifying them as permanent liabilities of the state, the government of India promised them perpetual relief, but denied them rehabilitation. Driven by heteropatriarchal assumptions, the regime of rehabilitation could only see 'unattached women' as victims of partition who had permanently lost their place in society when they had lost the men they were 'attached' to.

---

[22] Not all Namasudra refugees entered government camps. Prominent Namasudra leaders, such as Jogendranath Mandal and P. R. Thakur, used their political and religious influence, respectively, to author their own resettlement in different terms. For details, see Sekhar Bandyopadhyay and Anusua Basu Ray Chaudhuri, 'Partition, Displacement and the Decline of the Scheduled Caste Movement in West Bengal', in Uday Chandra, Geir Heierstad, and K. B. Nielsen (eds), *The Politics of Caste in West Bengal* (Abingdon and New York: Routledge, 2016), pp. 60–82.

In sharp contrast, these women reinterpreted the state's charity as an entitlement. Several widows left their relatives to enter permanent liability camps, while many more joined hunger strikes and protests demanding better conditions at the women's homes. However, their subversion of the logic of rehabilitation went largely unnoticed by contemporaries and by historians. As discussed in chapter 5, the leaders of the refugee movement in West Bengal usually ignored the organised protests of unattached women. Social workers imposed upon them the dominant paradigm of productive citizenship by subjecting them to various training schemes. This book explores the unsuccessful demands and forgotten protests of unattached refugee women, to make explicit the critique of the dominant discourse of rehabilitation implicit in their words and actions. Unlike refugee men, and women located within the heteropatriarchal family, unattached women were essentially impossible to rehabilitate unless the very meaning of refugee rehabilitation shifted to accommodate the individual needs and rights of refugees. Their persistent demand for land and employment gave lie to official stereotypes of abject victimhood, while their critique of vocational training undermined the dominant governmentality of rehabilitation. Yet, the policies did not change and most unattached women were reduced to a life of poverty and isolation. To invoke Spivak, as subaltern subjects, unattached refugee women spoke, but were not heard.[23]

Through Refugee Eyes: The Violence of Nehruvian Development

Refugee rehabilitation in post-partition India was driven by the logic of national development. Today, in post-liberalisation India, an uncritical celebration of 'development' has paved the way for massive displacement of the poorest of India's agriculturists and tribal communities.[24] The standard critique of this onslaught of neo-liberal forces often indulges in an unconscious nostalgia regarding the Nehruvian nation. However, if the regime of rehabilitation is any indication, a planned

---

[23] Gayatri Chakravorty Spivak, 'Can the Subaltern Speak?' in Cary Nelson and Lawrence Grossberg (eds). *Marxism and the Interpretation of Culture* (Urbana and Chicago, IL: University of Illinois Press, 1988).

[24] The most striking examples are the state-led dispossession of peasants in Singur and Nandigram, in West Bengal, designed to establish Special Economic Zones, and the ongoing attempts by the mining giant, Vedanta, to establish a bauxite mine in Niyamgiri in Orissa, the sacred mountain of the *Dongriya Kondh* tribe. There is a vast literature on the impact of globalisation and neoliberal development in India. For a useful synthesis, see Aseem Shrivastava, *Churning the Earth: The Making of Global India* (London: Penguin, 2012).

national economy offered scant protection for the rights and liberties of Indian citizens. When viewed through the prism of refugee rehabilitation, Nehruvian development, despite its socialist pretensions, appears to be a violent and regressive discourse. It provided the justification for the marginalisation of the most vulnerable refugees, namely, single women, widows, the elderly and the disabled. Moreover, the violence of development did not only fall on refugee bodies. When harnessed to projects of development, refugees could become the handmaidens of statist violence. This is particularly true of the 'Colonisation and Development Scheme' implemented in the Andaman Islands, where Dalit refugees were used to expand agriculture. They provided the necessary manpower for state-led onslaught upon indigenous land. The consequences of such 'development' have been genocidal for the Onge and Jarawa tribes.[25]

The pattern of refugee-led development did not remain confined to the Andaman Islands. During the late 1940s and early 1950s, several schemes were envisioned that aimed to transform 'backward' areas or 'empty lands' using the labour of partition refugees. This included projects to grow jute in the Terai region, expansion of refugee settlements in Tripura and the infamous Dandakaranya Development Project. These projects have usually been evaluated in terms of their success or failure in meeting the needs of refugees. However, the true significance of these projects lay in initiating a pattern of development of tribal regions that was driven by settlers from outside. Such development amounted to the appropriation of tribal land by outsiders for purposes of settled agriculture. Such marginalisation of tribal communities was by no means new. It had a long history in India, especially in regions like Assam and Tripura. However, the presence of partition refugees transformed the pace and scale of such incursions. It also provided the necessary manpower for envisioning ambitious schemes of agricultural colonisation. In the Andaman Islands, administrative fantasies of expanding agriculture had long been derailed by the impossibility of finding a significant number of willing settlers from the Indian mainland. Even late colonial plans of reconstructing the Islands using demobilised soldiers foundered due to the lack of volunteers. The easy availability of 'willing settlers' in the refugee camps of West Bengal got rid of this obstacle. It completely transformed the realms of the possible when it came to planned development. Both the Dandakarnaya Development Project and Andaman's Colonisation Scheme were, in the ultimate analysis, utopic

---

[25] For the impact of refugee resettlement on Onges see Sita Venkateswar, *Development and Ethnocide: Colonial Practices in the Andaman Islands* (Copenhagen: International Work Group for Indigenous Affairs, 2004). For the impact of 'development' on Jarawas, see Uditi Sen, 'Developing Terra Nullius: Colonialism, Nationalism and Indigeneity in the Andaman Islands', *Comparative Studies in Society and History*, 59(4) 2017.

schemes of rapid transformation of 'backward' areas. These top-down fantasies of national development would have been impossible to imagine, let alone implement, without the presence of thousands of displaced Hindus, who in the eyes of the authorities, could be relocated at will. In this sense, the post-partition refugee crisis fed statist utopias.

These utopic visions of planned development largely focused on the transformation of territory. Within the regime of rehabilitation, they co-existed with a deeply conservative vision of rebuilding society. Though only refugees from western Punjab were officially entitled to compensation for property lost, the ethos of compensation permeated the entire regime of rehabilitation. For the Indian state, to rehabilitate was to restore refugees to their earlier socio-economic status. To do so, it classified refugees according to their occupational groups. Since occupations were often linked to caste identities, a regime of rehabilitation based on reinstating refugees to their erstwhile occupations was inherently regressive. In Punjab, the focus on compensating property owners left Dalit refugees in the cold. A single Dalit refugee colony was built, largely as an afterthought and at the intervention of Ramehswari Nehru, who stressed its symbolic importance given Gandhi's ideology of serving 'Harijans'.[26] When it came to the rehabilitation of refugees from eastern Pakistan, the social inequalities that divided Bengali refugees were projected onto the geopolitical map of India. The educated upper and middle classes drew upon their cultural capital and political knowhow to wrest resettlement in Calcutta and other urban sites in West Bengal. In stark contrast, poor and illiterate agriculturalists from depressed caste backgrounds were pushed out to marginal lands as agricultural pioneers. Far from being unconscious of these cleavages, the bureaucrats of independent India used caste as a convenient marker for sorting out 'genuine' agriculturists. The active selection of *Namasudra* refugees as 'suitable' colonisers relied upon colonial stereotypes regarding the attributes of particular caste groups, such as the greater physical resilience of Dalits. Thus, the regime of rehabilitation replicated the social inequities of caste and gender, which the post-colonial state had pledged to mitigate as part of its modernising role. Much like partition is the Janus face of independence in South Asia, the rehabilitation of partition refugees can be understood as the mirror twin of India's planned economic development. Inseparable from Nehruvian India's lofty plans of economic transformation, the regime of rehabilitation nevertheless reveals the many contradictions and limitations of this post-colonial project.

[26] Urvashi Butalia, *The Other Side of Silence: Voices from the Partition of India* (New Delhi: Penguin, 1998).

Appendix I   Questionnaire 1 given to H. R. Shivdasani by Mr Stooks of the Ministry of Home Affairs in Delhi

(1) The Andamans group consist of about 204 islands. How many of these are habitable and suitable for colonisation? Would disafforestation be necessary in all acres before making the lands fit for cultivation? Is potable water available in all the islands? Can streams be bunded to conserve the water? What are the possibilities of obtaining potable water by draw well or more wells?

(2) Which of these islands are in actual occupation of the aborigines (This will presumably be dependent on reports from forest camps)?

(3) Which areas do you consider should be set apart exclusively for aborigines? What steps would you suggest for their protection and welfare?

(4) Apart from timber are there other resources in the islands which could be commercially exploited?

(5) Would it be desirable to allow exploitation of any portion of forests by private enterprise? If so, in what terms?

(6) Would it be desirable to allow private persons or firms to export forest produce other than timber from the Islands? Would you consider it better to have one or more specified agents for the purchase of all the timber produced in the islands or would you recommend the sale to whosoever demand timber?

(7) For what industries are the islands suitable (A note of requirements of labour and machinery and financial implications would be useful)?

(8) An agricultural survey has been carried out – what are your suggestions for implementing the recommendations made therein?

(9) What is the approximate number of milch cattle in the island?
   (a) What breeds are suitable for these islands?
   (b) As an immediate measure how many heads of cattle would you suggest should be imported?
   (c) What steps would you recommend for preventing cattle disease?

    (d) Are there possibilities of making any of the islands into a cattle preserve for cows, buffaloes, goats, etc.

    (e) What are the possibilities of developing dairy farming?

    (f) What steps should be taken for encouraging poultry farming?

(10) A horticultural survey has also been carried out – What are your recommendations in this respect?

(11) Would you recommend the leasing out of large blocks of land for the growing of sugar cane and similar money crops to private individuals or firms? Would you recommend the leasing of large blocks for the cultivation of the oil palm which it is presumed would thrive in certain areas?

(12) What opportunities for employment are available in the islands for educated persons? What opportunities would be available in the future?

(13) What opportunities for trade and commerce are available now and will be available as development proceeds? Should any facilities be provided by the government for encouraging trade and commerce at present?

(14) Is it possible for doctors and lawyers to build up a useful practice in the islands?

(15) What in your opinion are the bottlenecks in the reconstruction programme and what steps should be taken to expedite reconstruction?

(16) Is the rebuilding programme with regard to office and residential accommodation for government servants too ambitious? Can any of the existing buildings be reconditioned and made to serve a useful term instead of demolishing them?

(17) Would it be desirable to entrust the whole work or reconstruction to private enterprise?

(18) There is at present only one means of communication between the mainland and the islands, the SS *Maharaja* – would there be an economic proposition to charter another steamer in the near future (Please examine with regard to traffic, passenger and cargo)? If so, of what tonnage should it be? If another steamer should be chartered at a later stage, can you indicate at what stage?

(19) The charter of the SS *Maharaja* will terminate within 18 months and there is proposal to build a ship to meet the requirements of the Government. Keeping in view the future development can you indicate capacity for passenger and cargo and facilities that should be provided on the ship?

(20) The question of a weekly air service is under consideration – can you indicate what income may be anticipated for passenger fares, freight and carriage of mails?

(21) What facilities would you recommend for inter-island communication?

(22) What are the possibilities of developing Port Blair as a holiday resort? What facilities should be given by the government?

(23) Would it be a reasonable proposition to suggest the construction of a light railway to link up Port Blair with the northern part of the main island?

(24) In view of the future developments do you consider that the present set up of the administration requires any change?

(25) Would you consider it desirable to entrust the entire development of the islands to a government corporation on the lines of Damodar Valley Project?

(26) In view of the recent constitutional changes in the country what amendments to the regulations affecting the islands are necessary and is there any need for any new regulations?

(27) What are the possibilities of settling refugees in the islands (Please see the enclosed questionnaire)?

(28) Would it be a workable proposition to construct a dry dock to provide docking facilities to commercial vessels?

Source: H. R. Shivdasani, Report on the Possibilities of Colonization and Development of the Andaman and Nicobar Islands, New Delhi, 1949, Appendix 1.

Appendix II   Questionnaire 2 given to H. R. Shivdasani by Mr Stooks of the Ministry of Home Affairs in Delhi

Colonisation

(1) What do you consider would be the total number of families (allowing for 5 in a family) that could be settled in the islands?

(2) What are the villages or areas or islands where this could be done (A rough sketch showing the area would be useful)?

(3) What is the incidence of malaria in these areas or in the neighbouring areas as collected from the statistics that may be available from in forest camps?

(4) What is the position with regard to water supply for drinking purposes in these areas? Would wells have to be dug, and if so, at what depth is potable water reported to be available? Are there any streams which would provide drinking water? Which is the nearest forest camp to each of these areas?

(5) What hospital and medical facilities would be necessary for these areas?

(6) What is the distance of each of these places from Aberdeen?

(7) Which area would you suggest be taken in hand first for colonisation?

(8) Assuming that the scheme will have to be a phased one what do you think would be a reasonable number of settlers for each phase?

(9) What in your opinion would be the nearest port or ports at which to disembark the settlers?

(10) What should be the tonnage and draft of the steamer carrying the settlers?

(11) Is there a jetty or pier alongside which the steamer could anchor?

(12) Presuming that this facility does not exist, how many jetties and piers would it be necessary to construct? And at what places? Can you give a rough indication of what each would cost?

(13) In the absence of jetties and piers what distance away from the land would the steamer have to anchor?

(14) In such a contingent, how many motor boats would be required to get 100 persons across from the steamer to land? What would be the cost exclusive of wages and personnel of the boat for each trip?

(15) What do you consider would be a workable limit of disembarkation per day?

(16) Would you consider it advisable to disembark settlers at Port Blair (Chatham) and send them on to the settlements by motor boats or steam launches or by road? If so, could the motor boat and launches and trucks available in the islands be used for this purpose? If they will not be available or they cannot be used what vessels would you suggest for the purpose and how many? What would be the strength of crew required for each vessel?

(17) If settlers are disembarked at Chatham, would it be necessary to construct a transit camp? If so, where and what should be the type of the building? Please give a rough indication of cost. Could any of the existing buildings be utilised for the purpose? For example, a cellular jail or Ross Island?

(18) If settlers are disembarked at ports, where would you suggest placing transit camps?

(19) How long do you reckon settlers should be maintained in transit camps? What would be the cost of maintaining each person per day?

(20) What assistance would each settler require for building houses – work, men? Timber, nails, thatch, zinc sheets, etc.

(21) Would it not be feasible to set settlers themselves on the job of building their temporary abodes?

(22) What do you consider should be the size of each dwelling? Please give a rough indication of cost?

(23) Assuming that each settler is given 10 acres of land what in your opinion would be the most economic method of cultivation? Would you suggest the growing of food crops mainly so as to make the settler self-sufficient in this respect, leaving an acre or two for horticultural produce or would you leave the kind of crop to be raised entirely to the discretion of the settler? Would you suggest the levy of any penalty for non-cultivation of any appreciable extent that is actually cultivable? Would you recommend the payment of any bonus for the cultivation of any specific crop? If so, what crop and how much? What should be the time limit under which the entire extent should be brought under cultivation?

(24) Would you suggest the opening of ration shops in the early stages under government auspices? If so, where should each shop be located? What arrangements would be necessary for provisioning these shops?

(25) Would you suggest the opening of shops for other consumer goods also under government auspices in the early stages or would you

leave it to individual enterprise? What suggestions have you for running these shops?

(26) Would it be necessary to store kerosene oil and petrol in bulk?

(27) Where would you recommend the location of police stations and what should be the strength of each in the initial stages (Presumably this would have to be considered along with he development of the scheme)?

(28) Would you recommend the use of tractors for cultivation? If so, what types and how many would be required at the initial stages? Assuming that each batch of settlers would consist of 200 families, what scheme would you suggest to ensure that every cultivator gets the benefit of the machines?

(29) Do you consider cooperative farming advisable and feasible? If so, please work out a scheme. If so, would agricultural colonies be formed? Would it be a workable proposition for government or a government-financed bank to make them long-term low interest loans for the purchase of machines, housing equipment and farm animals?

(30) What roads would be required in the areas to be settled? Please specify point to point and width of road. Should they not be tarmac considering the heavy rainfall?

(31) Should any of the roads be constructed before the settlers actually begin to arrive? If so, which?

(32) What labour is at present available in these islands for this purpose? What extra labour will be required?

(33) Would any machinery and material have to be brought from the mainland for road works (There is a certain amount of machinery already in the islands)? Would considerable blasting be necessary and if so, what quantity of explosives would be required? If these items have to be brought from India where do you suggest they should be stored?

(34) What tools should be supplied to each cultivator and what are the possibilities of making these tools in the Marine Workshop? Would the necessary steel and iron be available from the old Japanese stocks?

(35) What cattle should be supplied to each family? Should it be free of cost or should we recover the value?

(36) What transport would be required for the cultivators, e.g. carts?

Source: H. R. Shivdasani, Report on the Possibilities of Colonization and Development of the Andaman and Nicobar Islands, New Delhi, 1949, Appendix 2.

Select Bibliography

Primary Sources

Private Papers

A. K. Biswas, Personal Collection, Manglutan Village, Andaman Islands.

Ashoka Gupta Papers, Centre for Women's Studies, Jadavpur University, Calcutta.

Noel Kennedy Patterson Papers, Asia and Africa Records, British Library, London.

Prafulla K. Chakrabarti Papers, International Institute of Social History, Amsterdam.

Rameshwari Nehru Papers, Nehru Memorial Museum and Library, New Delhi.

Renuka Ray Papers, Nehru Memorial Museum and Library, New Delhi.

Syama Prasad Mookerjee Papers, Nehru memorial Museum and Library, New Delhi.

Oral History Transcripts and Interviews

Interviews by the Author

Amulya Sutar, interviewed by the author at Harinagar, Andaman and Nicobar Islands, 31 January 2007.

Ananta Kumar Biswas, interviewed by the author at Manglutan, Andaman and Nicobar Islands, 10 February 2007.

Benilal Samaddar, interviewed by the author at Rampur, Andaman and Nicobar Islands, 31 January 2007.

B. K. Samaddar, interviewed by the author at Nimbutala, Andaman and Nicobar Islands, 1 February 2007.

Dasharath Barui, interviewed by the author at Havelock, Andaman and Nicobar Islands, 29 January 2007.

Gokul Biswas, interviewed by the author at Havelock, Andaman and Nicobar Islands, 29 January 2007.

Haricharan Mistri, interviewed by the author at Ramkrishna Gram, Andaman and Nicobar Islands, 5 February 2007.

Jagabandhu Das, interviewed by the author at Dasarathpur, Andaman and Nicobar Islands, 1 February 2007.

Kalipada Mandal, interviewed by the author at Kalsi, Andaman and Nicobar Islands, 3 February 2007.

Kalipada Mandal, interviewed by the author at Kalipur, Andaman and Nicobar Islands, 5 February 2007.

Kalipada Shikdar, interviewed by the author at Urmilapur, Andaman and Nicobar Islands, 3 February 2007.

Kamalakanta Biswas, interviewed by the author at Harinagar, Andaman and Nicobar Islands, 31 January 2007.

Lakshmikanta Ray, interviewed by the author at Sabari, Andaman and Nicobar Islands, 1 February 2007.

Lalitmohan Pal, interviewed by the author at Madhupur, Andaman and Nicobar Islands, 6 February 2007.

Makhanlal Majumdar, interviewed by the author at Sitanagar, Andaman and Nicobar Islands, 7 February 2007.

Manoranjan Sutar, interviewed by the author at Billiground, Andaman and Nicobar Islands, 31 January 2007.

Narayan Dutta, interviewed by the author at Havelock Island, Andaman and Nicobar Islands, 28 January 2007.

Naren Haldar, interviewed by the author at Nimbutala, Andaman and Nicobar Islands, 1 February 2007.

Nimchand Majumdar, interviewed by the author at Harinagar, Andaman and Nicobar Islands, 31 January 2007.

Rajlakshmi Biswas, interviewed by the author at Sabari, Andaman and Nicobar Islands, 1 February 2007.

Sandhyabala Mridha, interviewed by the author at Kalsi, Andaman and Nicobar Islands, 4 February 2007.

Saralabala Pal, interviewed by the author at Madhupur, Andaman and Nicobar Islands, 6 February 2007.

Sujata Mandal, interviewed by the author at Jankayapur, Andaman and Nicobar Islands, 4 February 2007.

Sukharanjan Mridha, interviewed by the author at Kalsi, Andaman and Nicobar Islands, 4 February 2007.

Sumana Majumdar, interviewed by the author at Sitanagar, Andaman and Nicobar Islands, 7 February 2007.

Sushil Chandra Biswas, interviewed by the author at Kalsi, Andaman and Nicobar Islands, 7 February 2007.

Interview Transcripts and Recordings

India: A People Partitioned Oral Archive, Archives and Special Collections, School of Oriental and African Studies, London.

Transcript of interview with Ashoka Gupta conducted by Subhoranjan Dasgupta, Personal Collection of Subhoranjan Dasgupta, Calcutta, 2000.

Transcript of interview with Nalini Mitra conducted by Subhoranjan
    Dasgupta, Personal Collection of Subhoranjan Dasgupta, Calcutta,
    2000.
Transcript of interview with Phulrenu Guha conducted by Subhoranjan
    Dasgupta, Personal Collection of Subhoranjan Dasgupta, Calcutta,
    2000.
Transcripts of interviews with Kanan Moulik, Charubala Sarkar,
    Phulmati Biswas, Ujjwala Mandal, Pari Goswami, Alomati Debnath,
    Mihirkana Das, Bimala Karmakar, Mayarani Dutta, Atashibala Das,
    Lilabati Dutta and Ruchibala Das of Dhubulia PL camp, conducted
    by Subhasri Ghosh and Debjani Dutta, Personal Collection of
    Subhoranjan Dasgupta, Calcutta, 2002.
Transcripts of interviews with Khuki Sarkar, Binodini Haldar, Khuku
    Byepari, Shyamali Mandal, Arati Mandal, Saraswati Biswas, Suchitra
    Bairagi, Gouri De and Shishubala Das of Chamta PL camp,
    conducted by Subhasri Ghosh and Debjani Dutta, Personal
    Collection of Subhoranjan Dasgupta, Calcutta, 2002.
Transcripts of interviews with Lakshmi Saha, Surabala Das, Lilabati
    Ghosh, Maya Saha, Aruna Saha, Debal Kirtania, Amiya Dutta and
    Renu Ray of Bansberia PL camp, conducted by Subhasri Ghosh and
    Debjani Dutta, Personal Collection of Dr. Subhoranjan Dasgupta,
    Calcutta, 2002.
Transcripts of interviews with Sushila Das, Binota Majhi, Pushpa
    Mandal, Geeta Majhi, Sonai Mandal, Shashirani Das, Satirani Pal,
    Mukul Shil and Sukumari of Bhadrakali PL camp, conducted by
    Subhasri Ghosh and Debjani Dutta, Personal Collection of Dr.
    Subhoranjan Dasgupta, Calcutta, 2002.

Unpublished Official Records

Home Department Records, Home Confidential Political Department,
    Political Branch, West Bengal State Archives.
India Pakistan and Burma Association, India Subject Files, Asia, Pacific
    and Africa Collections, British Library, London.
Intelligence Branch, Bengal/West Bengal Police, Intelligence Branch
    Library, Calcutta.
Ministry of Home Affairs, Files of the Andamans Section, National
    Archives of India, New Delhi.
Ministry of Home Affairs, Files of the Rehabilitation Division, National
    Archives of India, New Delhi.
Report on Forest Administration in the Andamans, 1885–1948, Asia,
    Pacific and Africa Collections, British Library, London.

Published Official Records and Reports

Andaman and Nicobar Islands

Andaman and Nicobar Commission for Backward Classes, *Report of the Andaman and Nicobar Commission for Other Backward Classes*, 2001, http://www.and.nic.in/Citizen%20Services/tw/obcPart%20V.pdf, last accessed on 15 May 2014.

Report of the Expert Committee on Jarawas of Andaman Islands, June 2003, (http://www.and.nic.in/C_charter/Dir_tw/ecr/contents.htm), accessed on 14 July 2015.

Government of India

A Note on the Dandakaranya Scheme, Ministry of Rehabilitation, Government of India, Calcutta, 1958.

A Report on Recurrent Exodus of Minorities from East Pakistan and Disturbances in India, Indian Commission of Jurists, Committee of Enquiry, New Delhi, 1965.

Administration report on the Andaman and Nicobar Islands, 1945–46, Delhi, 1946.

Constituent Assembly of India, Debates (12 vols.), Lok Sabha Secretariat, Government of India Press, Faridabad, 1947–51.

Dandakaranya Project, Ministry of Rehabilitation, 97th Report of the Parliament Estimates Committee, 2nd Lok Sabha, 1957–1962, Government of India, New Delhi, 1960.

Dandakaranya Project, Ministry of Rehabilitation, 72nd Report of the Parliament Estimates Committee, 3rd Lok Sabha, 1962–67, Government of India, New Delhi, 1965.

Guha, B. S., *Memoir No. 1, 1954, Studies in Social Tensions Among the Refugees from Eastern Pakistan*, Department of Anthropology, Government of India, Calcutta, 1959.

Inter-Departmental Team, *Report on accelerated development programme for Andaman and Nicobar Islands*, New Delhi, 1966.

Luthra, P. N., *Rehabilitation*, Publications Division, New Delhi, 1972.

Rao, U. B., *The Story of Rehabilitation, Ministry of Information and Broadcasting, Publications Division*, Faridabad, 1967.

Reception, Dispersal and Rehabilitation of New Migrants Arriving in India from East Pakistan since 1st January 1964, Ministry of Rehabilitation, 71st Report of the Parliament Estimates Committee, 3rd Lok Sabha, 1964–65, Government of India, New Delhi, 1965.

Report of the Foodgrains Enquiry Committee, Ministry of Food and Agriculture, Department of Food, Government of India, Delhi, 1957.

Report of the Grow More Food enquiry committee, Ministry of Food and Agriculture, Delhi, 1952.

Reports of the Ministry of Rehabilitation, Government of India, 1950–51 to 1954–55.

Report on Development of Colonies of Displaced Persons from Erstwhile East Pakistan in West Bengal, Committee of Review of Rehabilitation Work in West Bengal, New Delhi, Ministry of Supply and Rehabilitation, Department of Rehabilitation, Government of India, 1974.

Report on Development of Fisheries for Rehabilitation of Old Migrant Families in West Bengal, 10th Report, Committee of Review of Rehabilitation Work in West

Bengal, New Delhi, Ministry of Supply and Rehabilitation, Department of Rehabilitation, Government of India, 1972.

Report on Establishment of Industrial Estates in West Bengal for the Rehabilitation of Displaced Persons from East Pakistan in West Bengal, Committee of Review of Rehabilitation Work in West Bengal, New Delhi: Ministry of Supply and Rehabilitation, Department of Rehabilitation, 1971.

Report on Medical Facilities for New Migrants from East Pakistan in West Bengal, Committee of Review of Rehabilitation Work in West Bengal, New Delhi: Ministry of Supply and Rehabilitation, Department of Rehabilitation, New Delhi, 1971.

Report on Rehabilitation of Displaced Persons from East Pakistan at Ex-Camp-Sites in West Bengal, Committee of Review of Rehabilitation Work in West Bengal, New Delhi: Ministry of Supply and Rehabilitation, Department of Rehabilitation, Government of India, 1969.

Report on Rehabilitation of Displaced Persons from East Pakistan Living at Bagjola Group of Ex-camp Sites in West Bengal, Committee of Review of Rehabilitation Work in West Bengal, New Delhi: Ministry of Supply and Rehabilitation, Department of Rehabilitation, Government of India, 1970.

Report on Rehabilitation of Displaced Persons from East Pakistan Squatting on Government and Requisitioned Properties in West Bengal, Committee of Review of Rehabilitation Work in West Bengal, New Delhi: Ministry of Supply and Rehabilitation, Department of Rehabilitation, 1970.

Report on Rehabilitation Loans to the Displaced Persons from Erstwhile East Pakistan in West Bengal, Committee of Review of Rehabilitation Work in West Bengal, New Delhi, Ministry of Supply and Rehabilitation, Department of Rehabilitation, 1974.

Report on Repair and Reconstruction of Permanent Liability Homes and Infirmaries for the Displaced Persons from Erstwhile East Pakistan in West Bengal, Committee of Review of Rehabilitation Work in West Bengal, Ministry of Supply and Rehabilitation, New Delhi, 1974.

Report of the Technical Sub-Committee to the Subject Committee on Transport on the Future of Road Transport and Road Rail Relations, Post-war Reconstruction, Government of India, November 1943.

Report of the Working Group on the Residual Problem of Rehabilitation in West Bengal, Committee of Review of Rehabilitation Work in West Bengal, Delhi, 1976.

Shivdasani, H. R., *Report on the Possibilities of Colonization and Development of the Andaman and Nicobar Islands*, New Delhi, 1949.

Sinha, S. C., *Report on the Possibilities of Further Resettlement of East Pakistan Refugees in Andaman Islands*, Anthropological Survey of India, Calcutta, 1952.

The Andaman and Nicobar Islands, Ministry of Information and Broadcasting, Government of India, Delhi, July 1957.

The Post-war Development Plan for Bihar, Post-War Reconstruction Board of Bihar, Government of India, Patna, 1945.

Government of West Bengal
Five Years of Independence, August 1947–August 1952, Calcutta, 1953.

Millions Came from Eastern Pakistan, Report on How They Live Again, Directorate of Publicity, Government of West Bengal, Calcutta, 1954.

Mitra, A., *The Tribes and Castes of West Bengal,* Alipore, 1953.

Problems of Refugee Camps and Homes in West Bengal, The Screening Committee Report, Refugee Relief and Rehabilitation Directorate, Calcutta, 1989.

Rehabilitation of Refugees: A Statistical Survey, 1955, State Statistical Bureau, Government of West Bengal, Alipore, 1956.

Relief and Rehabilitation of Displaced Persons in West Bengal, Refugee Relief and Rehabilitation Department, Government of West Bengal, Calcutta, 1957.

Report of the Committee Appointed by the West Bengal Government to Enquire into the Technical and Vocational Training of Displaced Persons from East Pakistan Now Residing in West Bengal, Calcutta, June 1955.

West Bengal Legislative Assembly Debates, 1947–1954, West Bengal Government, Alipore, 1947–54.

Other Published Primary Sources

An Alternative Proposal for Rehabilitation of Camp Refugees: Memorandum Submitted by UCRC to Dr B.C. Roy, Chief Minister, West Bengal, on 11. 8. 58, United Central Refugee Council Pamphlet, Calcutta, 1958.

Bengal Rehabilitation Organisation, Calcutta, *The Tragedy of East Bengal Hindus and How to Resettle and Rehabilitate Them (An Examination of the Working of the Indo-Pak Agreement),* East Bengal Relief Committee, Calcutta, 1950

Chopra, P. N. (ed.), *The Collected Works of Sardar Valabhbhai Patel in 10 volumes,* Delhi, 1998.

Das, D. (ed.), *Sardar Patel's Correspondence,* Volume 6, Ahmedabad, 1972.

Gopal, S. (ed.), *Selected Works of Jawaharlal Nehru, Second Series, 61 Vols.,* Jawaharlal Nehru Memorial Fund, New Delhi, 1988–2015.

Mahila Seva Samity, *Annual Report of the Year 2005–2006,* Calcutta, 2006.

Mansergh, N., and Lumby E. N. R., (eds), *Constitutional Relations Between Britain and India: The Transfer of Power 1942–47,* (12 vols.), London, 1970–83.

Memorandum on the Rehabilitation of Refugees from Eastern Bengal, East Bengal Relief Committee, 1955

Regent Colony Vastuhara Samiti, Subarna Jayanti Utsab, (Regent Colony Refugee Association, Golden Jubilee Celebrations), 1999–2000, n.p., 2000.

Rehabilitation of Camp Refugees, Statement issued by Dr. B.C. Roy, Chief Minister, West Bengal, Calcutta, 13 October 1958.

Roy, B. C., *Towards a prosperous India: Speeches and writings of Dr. Bidhan Chandra Roy,* Calcutta, 1964.

Sovani, N. V. and Rath, N., *Economics of a Multi-purpose River dam: Report of an Inquiry into the Economic Benefits of the Hirakud Dam,* Pune, 1960.

Censuses of India

Census of India, 1951, Vol. VI, part III, Calcutta City,

Census of India, 1951, Vol. XVII, The Andaman and Nicobar Islands by A. K. Ghosh, Delhi, 1955.

Census of India, 2001, series 36, paper 2, Andaman and Nicobar Islands, Final population totals, 2003.

Newspapers and Journals

Amrita Bazar Patrika
Anandabazar Patrika
Hindustan Standard
Hindustan Times
Jugantar
Statesman
Swadhinata

Secondary Sources

Agamben, G., *Homo Sacer: Sovereign Power and Bare Life* (Translated by Daniel Heller-Roazen). 1st edition. Stanford, CA, 1998.

Ahmad, N., *An Economic Geography of East Pakistan*, London, 1958.

Ahmed, A. S., *Jinnah, Pakistan and Islamic Identity: The Search for Saladin*, London, New York, 1997.

Ahmed, I., *Memories of a Genocidal Partition: The Haunting Tale of Victims, Witnesses and Perpetrators*, Colombo, 2002.

Aiyar, S., '"August Anarchy": The Partition Massacres in Punjab, 1947', *South Asia: Journal of South Asian Studies*, 18(1), 1995, 13–36

Alexander, C., Chatterji, J., Jalais, A., *The Bengal Diaspora: Rethinking Muslim Migration*, London, 2015.

Alexander, H. G., *New Citizens of India*, Bombay, 1951.

Amin, S., *Event, Metaphor, Memory: Chauri Chaura 1922–1992*, New Delhi, 2006.

Amin, S., 'Representing the Musalman: Then and Now, Now and Then', in S. Mayaram, M. S. S. Pandian and A. Skaria (eds), *Subaltern Studies XII: Muslims, Dalits, and the Fabrications of History*, New Delhi, 2005.

Anderson, B., *Imagined Communities: Reflections on the Origin and Spread of Nationalism*, London, 1983.

Anderson, C., *Legible Bodies: Race, Criminality and Colonialism in South Asia*, Oxford, 2004.

Anderson, C., *The Indian Uprising: Prisons, Prisoners and Rebellion*, London and New York, 2007.

Anderson, C., Madhumita M., Pandya, V., *New Histories of The Andaman Islands: Landscape, Place and Identity in The Bay of Bengal, 1790–2012*, Cambridge and New York, 2015.

Ansari, S., 'Partition, Migration and Refugees: Responses to the Arrival of Muhajirs in Sind During 1947–48', *South Asia*, 18, 1995.

Ansari, S., *Life after Partition: Migration, Community and Strife in Sindh, 1947–1962*, Karachi, Oxford, 2005.

Arendt, H., *The Origins of Totalitarianism*, London, 1986.

Austin, G., *The Indian Constitution: Cornerstone of a Nation*, New Delhi, 1996.

Baboo, B., *Technology and Social Transformation: The Case of the Hirakund Multi-Purpose Dam Project in Orissa*, New Delhi, 1992.

Bagchi, J., 'Representing Nationalism: Ideology of Motherhood in Colonial Bengal', *Economic and Political Weekly*, 'Review of Women's Studies', 25(42 &c43), 1990, 65–71.

Bagchi, J., and Dasgupta, S., *The Trauma and The Triumph: Gender and Partition in Eastern India*, Calcutta, 2003.

Bal, E., *They Ask If We Eat Frogs: Garo Ethnicity in Bangladesh*, Singapore, 2007.

Bandopadhyay, H., *Udvastu (Refugee)*, Calcutta, 1990.

Bandopadhyay, S., *Caste, Protest and Identity in Colonial India: The Namasudras of Bengal, 1872–1947*, London, 1997.

Bandyopadhay, S., 'The Riddles of Partition: Memories of the Bengali Hindus', in R. Samaddar (ed.), *Reflections on Partition in the East*, Calcutta, 1997.

Bandyopadhyay, S., 'Partition and the Ruptures in Dalit Identity Politics in Bengal.' *Asian Studies Review*, 33(4), 2009.

Bandyopadhyay, S., and Basu Ray Chaudhuri, A., 'Partition, Displacement and The Decline of The Scheduled Caste Movement in West Bengal', in U. Chandra, G. Heierstad, and K. B. Nielsen (eds) *The Politics of Caste in West Bengal*, London, 2015.

Banerjee, Sarbani, 'Different Identity Formations in Bengal Partition Narratives by Dalit Refugees', *Interventions*, 19(4), 2017, 550–65.

Bardhan, P., *The Political Economy of Development in India*, Delhi, 1984.

Bardhan Roy, M., *Calcutta Slums: Public Policy in Retrospect*, Calcutta, 1994.

Barua, S., *India Against Itself: Assam and the Politics of Nationality*, New Delhi, 1999.

Basu, A., *Mridula Sarabhai: Rebel With a Cause*, New Delhi, 2005.

Basu Ray Chaudhury, A., 'Women after Partition: Remembering The Lost World in a Life Without Future', Navnita Chadha Behera (ed.), *Gender, Conflict and Migration: Women and Migration in Asia*, vol. 3, New Delhi, 2006.

Basu-RoyChowdhury, S., 'Exiled to The Andamans: The Refugees from East Pakistan' in P. K. Bose (ed.), *Refugees in West Bengal: Institutional Processes and Contested Identities*, Calcutta, 2000.

Bayly, C. A., *Empire and Information: Intelligence Gathering and Social Communication in India, 1780–1870*, Cambridge, 1996.

Bayly, C. A., and Harper, T. N., *Forgotten Armies. The Fall of British Asia, 1941–45*, London, 2004.

Bhalla, A., *Stories about the Partition of India*, 3 Volumes, New Delhi, 1994.

Bhardwaj Datta, A., 'Gendering Oral History of Partition: Interrogating Patriarchy,' *Economic and Political Weekly*, 41(22), 2006.

Bhattacharya, G., *Refugee Rehabilitation and its Impact on Tripura's Economy*, New Delhi and Guwahati, 1988.

Bhattacharya, H., 'The Emergence of Tripuri Nationalism, 1948-50', *South Asia Research*, 9(11), 1989.

Bhattacharya, N., 'Colonial State and Agrarian Society' in B. Stein (ed.), *The Making of Agrarian Policy in British India 1770–1900*, Delhi, 1992.

Bhattacharya, P. K., and Sarkar, B. N., *Jarawa Contact: Ours With Them, Theirs With Us*, Calcutta, 2002.

Bhattacharya, S. and Zachariah, B., '"A Great Destiny": The British Colonial State and the Advertisement of Post-war Reconstruction in India', 1942-45', *South Asia Research*, 19(1), 1999.

Biswas, A. K., *The Namasudras of Bengal: Profile of a Persecuted People*, New Delhi, 2000.

Bose, M., *Land Reforms in Eastern India*, Calcutta, 1981.

Bose, N. K., *Calcutta: 1964, A Social Survey*, Bombay, 1968.

Bose, P. K., 'Partition – Memory Begins Where History Ends', in R. Samaddar (ed.), *Reflections on Partition in the East*, Calcutta, 1997.

Bose, P. K., *Refugees in West Bengal. Institutional Processes and Contested Identities*, Calcutta, 2000.

Bose, S., *Agrarian Bengal: Economy, Social Structure and Politics, 1919–1947*, Cambridge, 1986.

Bose, S. and Jalal, A., *Nationalism, Democracy and Development: State and Politics India*, Delhi, 1997.

Bose, T. K. and Manchanda, R., *States, Citizens and Outsiders. The Uprooted Peoples of South Asia*, Kathmandu, 1987.

Brass, P., 'The Partition of India and Retributive Genocide in The Punjab, 1946–47: Means, Methods, and Purposes,' *Journal of Genocide Research*, 5(1), 2003.

Brass, P., *The Politics of India Since Independence*, Cambridge, 1994.

Broomfield, J. H, *Elite Conflict in Plural Society*, Bombay, 1969.

Buchanan, A., and Moore, M., *States, Nations and Borders: The Ethics of Making Boundaries*, Cambridge, 2003.

Butalia, U., 'Community State and Gender: On Women's Agency During Partition' in *Economic and Political Weekly, Review of Women's Studies*, 28 (17), 1993, WS12–WS21.

Butalia, U., *Partition: The Long Shadow*, New Delhi, 2015.

Butalia, U., *The Other Side of Silence: Voices From The Partition of India*, New Delhi, 1998.

Byres, T. J., *The State and Developmental Planning in India*, Delhi, 1994.

Chakrabarti, P. K., *The Marginal Men. The Refugees and The Left Political Syndrome in West Bengal*, Calcutta, 1999.

Chakrabarti, T., Ray Mandal, N. and Ghoshal, P., *Dhangsa-o-Nirman: Bangiya Udvastu Samajer Svakathita Bibaran (Destruction and Creation: Self-descriptive Accounts of Bengali Refugee Society)*, Calcutta, 2007.

Chakrabarty, D., *Habitations of Modernity: Essays in the Wake of Subaltern Studies*, Chicago, IL, 2000.

Chakrabarty, D., 'Remembered Villages: Representations of Hindu Bengali Memories in the Aftermath of Partition', *Economic and Political Weekly*, 31 (32), 1996.

Chakrabarty, S., *With Dr. B.C. Roy and Other Chief Ministers: A Record Up to 1962*, Calcutta, 1974.

Chakravarty, S., *Development Planning: The Indian Experience*, Oxford, 1987.

Chakravartty, G., *Coming Out of Partition: Refugee Women of Bengal*, New Delhi, 2005.

Chakravartty, R., *Communists in Indian Women's Movement, 1940–50*, New Delhi, 1980.

Chand, G., *India's Teeming Millions: A Contribution to the Study of the Indian Population Problem*, London 1939.

Chatterjee, N., 'The East Bengal Refugees: A Lesson in Survival,' in S. Chaudhuri (ed.), *Calcutta: The Living City, Vol. II*, Calcutta, 1990.

Chatterjee, P., 'The Nationalist Resolution of the Women's Question', in K. Sangari and S. Vaid (eds), *Recasting Women: Essays in Indian Colonial History*, New Delhi, 1989.

Chatterjee, P., *The Nation and its Fragments: Colonial and Postcolonial Histories*, Princeton, NJ, 1993.

Chatterjee, P., *The Present History of West Bengal: Essays in Political Criticism*, Delhi, 1997.

Chatterjee, P., *The Politics of the Governed: Reflections on Popular Politics in Most of the World*, New York, 2004.

Chatterji, J., *Bengal Divided: Hindu Communalism and Partition, 1932–1947*, Cambridge, 1994.

Chatterji, J., 'The Decline, Revival and Fall of Bhadralok Influence in the 1940s: A Historiographic Review', in S. Bandyopadhyay (ed.), *Bengal: Rethinking History, Essays in Historiography*, Delhi, 2001.

Chatterji, J., 'The Fashioning of a Frontier: The Radcliffe Line and Bengal's Border Landscape, 1947-52', *Modern Asian Studies*, 33(1), 1999.

Chatterji, J., 'Right or Charity? The Debate Over Relief and Rehabilitation in West Bengal', in S. Kaul (eds), *The Partitions of Memory: The Afterlife of The Division of India*, Delhi, 2001.

Chatterji, J., 'Of Graveyards and Ghettos: Muslims in Partitioned West Bengal,' in M. Hasan and A. Roy (eds), *Living Together Separately: Cultural India in History and Politics*, New Delhi, 2005.

Chatterji, J., '"Dispersal" and The Failure of Rehabilitation: Refugee Camp-Dwellers and Squatters in West Bengal', *Modern Asian Studies*, 41(5), 2007.

Chatterji, J., *The Spoils of Partition: Bengal and India, 1947–67*, Cambridge, 2007.

Chatterji, J., 'South Asian Histories of Citizenship, 1946–1970', *The Historical Journal*, 55(4), 2012.

Chatterji, J., 'From Imperial Subjects to National Citizens: South Asians and the International Migration Regime since 1947' in Chatterji, J. and Washbrook, D. (eds), *Routledge Handbook of the South Asian Diaspora*, London and New York, 2013.

Chatterji, J., 'Dispositions and Destinations: Refugee Agency and '*Mobility Capital*' in the Bengal Diaspora, 1947–2007', *Comparative Studies in Society and History*, 55(2), 2013.

Chatterji, Joya., 'Partition Studies: Prospects and Pitfalls', *The Journal of Asian Studies* 73(2), 2014.

Chattha, I., *Partition and Locality: Violence, Migration, and Development in Gujranwala and Sialkot, 1947–1961*. Karachi, 2011.

Chaudhary, M., *Partition and The Curse of Rehabilitation*, Calcutta, 1964.

Chaudhuri, P., *Refugees in West Bengal: A Study of the Growth and Distribution of Refugee Settlements within the CMD*, Centre for Studies in Social Sciences Occasional Paper, Calcutta, 1983.

Chaudhuri, S., *Calcutta: The Living City, Vol. I and II*, Calcutta, 1990.

Chimni, B. S., *International Refugee Law: A Reader*, New Delhi, Thousand Oaks and London, 2000.

Chopra, R. N., *Food Policy in India: A Survey*, New Delhi, 1988.

Corbridge, S., Williams, G., Srivastava, M., and Veron, R., *Seeing The State: Governance and Governmentality in India*, Cambridge, 2005.

Das, S. K., 'State Response to The Refugee Crisis: Relief and Rehabilitation in The East', in Ranabir Samaddar (ed.), *Refugees and The State: Practices of Asylum and Care in India, 1947–2000*, New Delhi, 2003.

Das, V., *Critical Events: An Anthropological Perspective on Contemporary India*, Delhi, 1995.

Dasgupta, A., 'Denial and Resistance: Sylheti partition "Refugees" in Assam,' *Contemporary South Asia*, 10(3), 2010.

Dasgupta, A., 'The Puzzling Numbers: The Politics of Counting "Refugees" in West Bengal', *SARWATCII*, 2(2), 2002.

Datta, Antara. *Refugees and Borders in South Asia: The Great Exodus of 1971*, New York, 2012.

Datta, D., *Bijaygarh: Ekti udvastu upanibesh (A Refugee Colony)*, Calcutta, 2001.

Deshmukh, D., *The Stone That Speaketh*, Hyderabad, 1979.

Devji, Faisal, *Muslim Zion: Pakistan as a Political Idea*, London, 2013.

Dey, I., 'On the Margins of Citizenship: Principles of Care and Rights of the Residents of the Ranaghat Women's Home, Nadia District', *Refugee Watch*, 33, 2009.

Dhulipala, Venkat, *Creating a New Medina: State Power, Islam, and The Quest For Pakistan in Late Colonial North India*, New Delhi, Cambridge, 2014.

Eaton, R. M., *The Rise of Islam and The Bengal Frontier, 1204–1760*, Oxford, 1993.

Elahi, M., 'Refugees in Dandakaranya', *International Migration Review*, 15(1 & 2), 1981.

Engels, D., *Beyond Purdah? Women in Bengal, 1890–1930*, Delhi, 1996.

Essed, P., Frerks, G., and Schrijvers, J., *Refugees and The Transformation of Societies: Agency, Policies, Ethics and Politics*, New York and Oxford, 2004.

Farmer, B. H., *Agricultural Colonisation in India Since Independence*, London, 1974.

Feldman, S., 'Feminist Interruptions: The Silence of East Bengal in the Story of Partition', *Interventions*, 1(2), 1999.

Field, J. O., and Franda, M. F., *Electoral Politics in the Indian States. The Communist Parties of West Bengal*, Delhi, 1974.

Forbes, G., *Women in Colonial India: Essays in Politics, Medicine and Historiography*, New Delhi, 2005.

Foucault, M., 'Governmentality', in G. Burchell, C. Gordon and P. Miller (eds), *The Foucault Effect, Studies in Governmentality*, London, Toronto, Sydney, Tokyo, Singapore, 1991.

Foucault, M., *Security, Territory, Population: Lectures at The Collège de France, 1977–1978*, Basingstoke, 2009.

Franda, M., *West Bengal and The Federalizing Process in India*, Princeton, NJ, 1968.

Frankel, F. R. et al. (eds), *Transforming India: Social and Political of Democracy*, New Delhi, 2000.

Fuller, C. J. and John H., 'For an Anthropology of the Modern Indian State', in C. J. Fuller and V. Benei (eds), *The Everyday State and Society in Modern India*, London, 1999.

Furedy, C., 'Whose Responsibility? Dilemmas of Calcutta's Bustee Policy in the Nineteenth Century,' *Journal of South Asian Studies*, 5(2), 1982.

Gangopadhyay, B. 'Reintegrating the Displaced, Refracturing The Domestic: A Report on The Experiences of 'Uday Villa', in P. K. Bose (ed.), *Refugees in West Bengal: Institutional Practices and Contested Identities*, Calcutta, 2000.

Gangopadhyay, S., *Arjun*, Delhi, 1990.

Ganguly, I., *Colonysmriti: Udvastu colony pratishtar gorar katha, 1948–1954, (Memories of Colonies: An Account of the Early Period of the Establishment of Refugee Colonies)*, Calcutta, 1997.

Garg, M., 'Durgabai Deshmukh: A Pioneer Social Builder,' *Social Welfare*, 54(5), 2007.

Gayatri B., *Refugee Rehabilitation and its Impact on Tripura's Economy*, New Delhi, Guwahati, 1988.

Gellner, E., *Nation and Nationalism*, Oxford, 1983.

Ghosh, A., *The Shadow Lines*, Delhi, 1988.

Ghosh, A. K., 'Bengali Refugees at Dandakaranya: A Tragedy of Rehabilitation', P. K. Bose (ed.), *Refugees in West Bengal: Institutional Practices and Contested Identities*, Calcutta, 2000.

Ghosh, P., 'Partition's Biharis', *Comparative Studies of South Asia, Africa and the Middle East*, 17(2), 1997.

Ghosh, S., 'The Refugee and the Government: A Saga of Self-rehabilitation in West Bengal' in Daniel Coleman et al. (eds), *Countering Displacements: The Creativity and Resilience of Indigenous and Refugee-ed People*, Alberta, 2012.

Gilmartin, D., 'Partition, Pakistan and South Asian History: In Search of a Narrative', *The Journal of Asian Studies*, 57(4), 1998.

Gilmartin, D., 'The Historiography of India's Partition: Between Civilization and Modernity.' *The Journal of Asian Studies*, 74(1), 2015.

Gould, William. *Hindu Nationalism and The Language of Politics in Late Colonial India*, Cambridge, New York, 2004.

Greenough, P. R., *Prosperity and Misery in Modern Bengal: The Famine of 1943–44*, Oxford, 1982.

Guha, R., 'Adivasis, Naxalite and Indian Democracy.' *Economic and Political Weekly*, 42(32), 2007.

Guha, R., *India After Gandhi: The History of The World's Largest Democracy*, London, 2007.

Guha, R. and Spivak, G. C., *Selected Subaltern Studies*. Oxford University Press, 1988.

Guha, S., *Non-Muslims Behind The Curtain of East Pakistan*, Calcutta, 1950.

Guha Thakurta, M., 'Uprooted and Divided', J. Bagchi and S. Dasgupta (eds), *The Trauma and The Triumph: Gender and Partition in Eastern India*, Calcutta, 2003.

Gupta, A., 'Blurred Boundaries: The Discourse of Corruption, The Culture of Politics, and The Imagined State', *American Ethnologist*, 22, 2, 1995.

Gupta, A., *In the Path of Service*, Calcutta, 2005.

Gupta, A., Das, B., Varma, A. K., and Sen, S., 'East is East, West is West', in J. Bagchi and S. Dasgupta (eds), *The Trauma and The Triumph: Gender and Partition in Eastern India*, Calcutta, 2003.

Gupta, S. K., *Kichu smriti, kichu katha (A Few Memories, A Few Stories)*, Calcutta, 1994.

Hasan, M. (ed.), *India's Partition: Process, Strategy and Mobilization*, New Delhi, 1993

Hasan, M. (ed.), *India Partitioned: The Other Face of Freedom*, Vols. 1 and 2, New Delhi, 1995.

Hasan, M. (ed.), *Inventing boundaries: Gender, politics and the partition of India*, New Delhi and Oxford, 2000.

Hasan, M., and Roy, A. (eds), *Living Together Separately: Cultural India in History and Politics*, New Delhi, 2005.

Hazarika, S., *Rites of Passage. Border Crossings, Imagined Homelands: India's East and Bangladesh*, New Delhi, 2000.

Hobsbawm, E., 'Peasants and Politics', *Journal of Peasant Studies*, 1(1), 1973.

Hodges, S., 'Governmentality, Population and Reproductive Family in Modern India.' *Economic and Political Weekly*, 39(11), 2004.

Hodson, H. V., *The Great Divide: Britain, India, Pakistan*, London, 1969.

Inden, R. B. and Nicholas, R. W., *Kinship in Bengali Culture*, Second Edition, New Delhi, 2005.

Iqbal, I., *The Bengal Delta: Ecology, State and Social Change, 1840–1943*, Basingstoke, 2010.

Ishaque, A. H. M., *Agricultural Statistics by Plot to Plot Enumeration in Bengal, 1944–45, 3 Parts*, Calcutta, 1946.

Jaffrelot, C., *Hindu Nationalist Movement and Indian Politics, 1925 to the 1990s*, London, 1996.

Jain, L. C., *The City of Hope: The Faridabad Story*, New Delhi, 1998.

Jalais, A., 'Dwelling on Morichjhanpi: When Tigers Become "Citizens" and Refugees "Tigerfood"', *Economic and Political Weekly*, 40(17), 2005.

Jalal, A., *The Sole Spokesman. Jinnah, the Muslim League and the Demand for Pakistan*, Cambridge, 1985.

Jayal, N. G., *Citizenship and Its Discontents: An Indian History*, Cambridge, London, 2013.

Karlekar, M., *Voices From Within: Early Personal Narratives of Bengali Women*, Delhi, 1991.

Kaul, S. (ed.), *Partitions of Memory. The Afterlife of The Partition of India*, New Delhi, 2001.

Kaur, R., 'Distinctive Citizenship: Refugees, Subjects and Post-Colonial State in India's Partition', *Cultural and Social History*, 6(4), 2009.

Kaur, R., *Since 1947: Partition Narratives Among Punjabi Migrants of Delhi*, New Delhi, 2007.

Kaur, R., 'The Last Journey.' *Economic and Political Weekly*, 41(22), 2006.

Keller, S.L., *Uprooting and Social Change: The Role of Refugees in Development*, Delhi, 1975.

Khalidi, O. 'From Torrent to Trickle: Indian Muslim Migration to Pakistan, 1947-97', *Bulletin of the Henry Martin Institute of Islamic Studies*, 16(1 & 2), 1997.

Khan, M. I., 'The Significance of the Dargah of Hazratbal in the Socio-religious and Political Life of Kashmiri Muslims', C. W. Troll (ed.), *Muslim Shrines in India: Their Character, History and Significance*, New Delhi, 1992.

Khan, Yasmin, *The Great Partition: The Making of India and Pakistan*, New Haven, CT and London, 2008.

Khilnani, S., *The Idea of India*, London, 1997.

Khosla, G. D., *Stern Reckoning: A Survey of the Events Leading up to and Following the Partition of India*, New Delhi, 1949.

Kishwar, Madhu, 'Gandhi on Women', *Economic and Political Weekly*, 20 (40), 1985.

Knight, H. F., *Food Administration in India, 1939–47*, Stanford, CA, 1954.

Kohli, A., *Democracy and Discontent: India's Growing Crisis of Governability*, Cambridge, 1990.

Kosinski, L. A. and Elahi, K. M. (eds), *Population Redistribution and Development in South Asia*, Dordrecht, 1985.

Kudaisya, G. and Yong, Tan Tai, *The Aftermath of Partition in South Asia*, London and New York, 2000.

Kudaisya, G., 'The Demographic Upheaval Partition: Refugees and Agricultural Resettlement in India, 1946-67', *South Asia*, XVIII, Special Issue, 1995.

Kumar, N., *Friends, Brothers, and Informants: Fieldwork Memoirs of Banaras*, Berkley, Los Angeles, London, 1992.

Kumar, R., *The History of Doing: An Illustrated Account of Movements for Women's Rights and Feminism in India 1800–1990*, New Delhi, 1993.

Kymlicka, W., and Norman, W., 'Return of the Citizen: A Survey of Recent Work on Citizenship Theory', *Ethics*, 104(2), 1994.

Lal, P., *Andaman Islands: A Regional Geography*, Calcutta, 1976.

Laushley, D. M., *Bengal Terrorism and the Marxist Left: Aspects of Regional Nationalism in India, 1905–42*, Calcutta, 1975.

Lipsky, M., *Street-Level Bureaucracy: The Dilemmas of the Individual in Public Service*, New York, 1983.

Low, D. A., and Brasted, H. (eds), *Freedom, Trauma, Continuities: Northern India and Independence*, New Delhi, 1998.

Lummis, T., 'Structure and Validity in Oral Evidence', *International Journal of Oral History*, 2(2), 1983.

Major, A. 'The Chief Sufferers: Abduction of Women During the Partition of Punjab' in D. A. Low and H. Barsted (eds), *Freedom, Trauma and Continuities: Northern India and Independence*, New Delhi, 1998.

Mallick, R., *Indian Communism. Opposition, Collaboration and Institutionalisation*, Delhi, 1994.

Mallik, R., 'Refugee Resettlement in Forest Reserves: West Bengal Policy Reversal and the Marichjhapi Massacre', *Journal of Asian Studies*, 58(1), 1999.

Mandal, J., *Mahapran Jogendranath Mandal*, Vols. 1 and 2, Calcutta, 1975.

Mathur, L. P., *Kalapani: History of Andaman and Nicobar Islands With a Study of India's Freedom Struggle*, Delhi, 1985.

Mazumdar, M, and Pandya, V., 'Making Sense of the Andaman Islanders: Reflections on a New Conjuncture', *Economic and Political Weekly*, 47(44), 2012.

Menon, R., 'Do Women Have a Country?', in R. Ivekovic and J. Mostov (eds), *From Gender to Nation*, Ravanna, 2002.

Menon, R., and Bhasin, K., *Borders and Boundaries: Women in India's Partition*, New Delhi, 1998.

Menon, R. and Bhasin, K., 'Recovery, Rupture, Resistance: Indian State and Abduction of Women During Partition', *Economic and Political Weekly*, 'Review of Women's Studies', 28(17), 1993, WS2–WS11.

Misri, Deepti, *Beyond Partition: Gender, Violence, and Representation in Postcolonial India*, Champaign, IL, 2014.

Mitra, A., *The New India 1948–1955. Memoirs of an Indian Civil Servant*, Bombay, 1991.

Mitra, A., 'Take a Girl Like Her', *Calcutta Diary*, London, 1976.

Mookerjee, S. P., *Leaves From a Diary*, Calcutta, 1993.

Moon, P., *Divide and Quit*, London, 1961.

Moore, R. J., *Escape from Empire: The Attlee Government and The Indian Problem*, Clarendon and Oxford, 1983.

Mukerjee, R., *The Political Economy of Population*, New York: 1943.

Mukerji, K., *Agriculture, Famine and Rehabilitation in South Asia: A Regional Approach*, Calcutta, 1965.

Mukhopadhyay, K., *Shikarer Sandhane (Quest for Roots)*, Kolkata, 2002.

Nair, N., *Changing Homelands: Hindu Politics and The Partition of India*, Cambridge, 2011.

Nakazato, N. and Hasan, M. (eds), *The Unfinished Agenda: Nation Building in South Asia*, New Delhi, 2001.

Nandy, A., *The Romance of the State and The Fate of Dissent in The Tropics*, Oxford University Press, 2003.

Naqvi, T. H., 'The Politics of Commensuration: The Violence of Partition and the Making of the Pakistani State', *Journal of Historical Sociology*, 20(1 & 2), 2007.

Nehru, R., *Gandhi is My Star: Speeches and Writings*, Delhi, 1950.

Newbigin, E., *The Hindu Family and the Emergence of Modern India: Law, Citizenship and Community*, Cambridge and New York, 2013.

Nicholson, N. K., 'Political Aspects of Indian Food Policy', *Pacific Affairs*, 41(1), 1968.

O'Leary, B., L'ustick, I. S., and Callaghy, T. (eds), *Right-Sizing the State. The Politics of Moving Borders*, Oxford, 2001.

Oberoi, P., *Exile and Belonging: Refugees and State Policy in South Asia*, New Delhi, 2006.

Pakrasi, K. B., *The Uprooted: A Sociological Study of the Refugees of West Bengal, India*, Calcutta, 1971.

Pal, B. K., *Barishal theke Dandakaranya: Purbabanger krishijibi udvastu-r punarbasan itihas (From Barishal to Dandakaranya: The History of Rehabilitation of East Bengal's Refugee Agriculturists)*, Calcutta, 2010.

Pandey, G., 'Community and Violence: Recalling Partition', *Economic and Political Weekly*, 32(32), 1997.

Pandey, G., 'Can a Muslim be an Indian?,' *Comparative Studies in Society and History*, 41(4), 1999.

Pandey, G., *Remembering Partition: Violence, Nationalism and History in India*, Cambridge, 2001.

Pandit, T. N., and Sarkar, B. N. (eds), *People of India, Volume XII, Andaman and Nicobar Islands*, Madras, Delhi, 1994.

Pandya, V., 'Jarwas of Andaman Islands: Their Social and Historical Reconstruction', *Economic and Political Weekly*, 37(37), 2002.

Patel, S., 'Construction and Reconstruction of Woman in Gandhi', *Economic and Political Weekly*, 23(8), 1988.

Portelli, A., 'History-telling and Time: An Example from Kentucky', *The Oral History Review*, 20(1 & 2), 1992.

Portelli, A., *The Death of Luigi Trastulli and Other Stories: Form and Meaning in Oral History*, Albany, NY, 1991.

Prabhakar, V. K., *Encyclopaedia of Environmental Pollution and Awareness in the 21st Century*, New Delhi, 2000.

Racine, J., *Calcutta 1981. The City, Its Crisis and the Debate on Urban Planning and Development*, New Delhi, 1990.

Rahman, M., and van Schendel, W., '"I am Not a Refugee": Rethinking Partition Migration', *Modern Asian Studies*, 37(3), 2003.

Rai, S. M., *Partition of the Punjab: A Study of Its Effects on the Politics and Administration of the Punjab, 1947–56*, London, Bombay, 1965.

Randhawa, M. S., *Out of the Ashes: An Account of the Rehabilitation of Refugees from West Pakistan in Rural Areas of East Punjab*, Chandigarh, 1954.

Rao, M., *From Population Control to Reproductive Health: Malthusian Arithmetic*, New Delhi, 2004.

Ray, M., 'Growing Up Refugee', *History Workshop Journal*, 53(1), 2002.

Ray, R., *My Reminiscences: Social Development During the Gandhian Era and After*, Calcutta, 2005.

Ray, S., *Bwadwip (Delta)*, Calcutta, 1972.

Roselli, J., 'The Self-image of Effeteness: Physical Education and Nationalism in Nineteenth Century Bengal', *Past and Present*, 86, 1980.

Rosler, M. and Wendl, T. (eds), *Frontiers and Borderlands: Anthropological Perspectives*, Frankfurt am Main, 1999.

Roy, A., *Mapping Citizenship in India*, New Delhi, Oxford, New York, 2010.

Roy, A. G., and Bhatia, N., *Partitioned Lives: Narratives of Home, Displacement, and Resettlement*, New Delhi, 2008.

Roy, H., *Partitioned Lives: Migrants, Refugees, Citizens in India and Pakistan, 1947–65*, Delhi, 2013.

Roy, R., *The Agony of West Bengal*, Calcutta, 1971.

Rudolph, L. and Rudolph, S., *In Pursuit of Lakshmi: The Political Economy of the Indian State*, Chicago, IL, 1987.

Sadasivan, S. N., *Political and Administrative Integration of Princely States*, New Delhi, 2005.

Sadhak, D., 'Diglipurer pratham Durga Pujo – 1958 (The First Durga Pujo of Diglipur)', *Dwip Bangla, sharadiya sankhya, 1413*, Island's Bengal, Autumn edition, 2006.

Sammadar, R., *Reflections on Partition in The East*, New Delhi, Calcutta, 1997.

Samaddar, R. (ed.), *Refugees and the State: Practices of Asylum and Care in India, 1947–2000*, New Delhi, London, 2003.

Samaddar, R., *The Marginal Nation: Transborder Migration From Bangladesh to West Bengal*, New Delhi, 1999.

Sangari, K., and Vaid, S., *Recasting Women: Essays in Indian Colonial History*, New Delhi, 1989.

Sanyal, R., 'Contesting Refugeehood: Squatting as Survival in Post-partition Calcutta,' *Social Identities*, 15(1), 2009.

Sarkar, S., 'The Women's Question in Nineteenth Century Bengal', in K. Sangari and S. Vaid (eds), *Women and Culture*, Bombay, 1985.

Sarkar, T., *Hindu Wife, Hindu Nation, Community, Religion, and Cultural Nationalism*, New Delhi, 2001.

Sarkar, T., and Bandyopadhyay, S., *Calcutta: The Stormy Decades*, 2015.

Sarkar, T., and Butalia, U., *Women and Right-wing Movements: Indian Experiences*, Kali, New Delhi, 1995.

Scott, J. C., *Weapons of the Weak: Everyday Forms of Peasant Resistance*, New Haven, CT, 1985.

Sekhsaria, P., and Pandya, V., *The Jarawa Tribal Reserve Dossier: Cultural & Biological Diversities in the Andaman Islands*, Paris, 2010.

Sen, A., *The Bindery Workers of Daftaripara-1: Forms and Fragments*, Centre for Studies in Social Sciences Occasional Paper, 127, Calcutta, 1991.

Sen, A., *The Bindery Workers of Daftaripara-2: Their Own Life-stories*, Centre for Studies in Social Sciences Occasional Paper, 128, Calcutta, 1991.

Sen, A., *Life and Labour in a Squatters Colony*, Centre for Studies in Social Sciences Occasional Paper, 138, Calcutta, 1992.

Sen, A. and Banerjee, A., *Migrants in the Calcutta Metropolitan District 1951–71*, Centre for Studies in Social Sciences Occasional Paper, 62, Calcutta, 1983.

Sen, A. K., *Tales of Nowhere People*, Kolkata, 2001.

Sen, E., *Darkening Days, Being a Narrative of Famine-stricken Bengal, With Drawings From Life by Zainul Abedin*, Calcutta, 1944.

Sen, M., *In Search of Freedom: An Unfinished Journey*, Calcutta, 2001.

Sen, P. K., *Land and People of the Andaman: A Geographical and Socio-Economical Study With a Short Account of the Nicobar Islands*, Calcutta, 1962.

Sen, S., *Disciplining Punishment: Colonialism and Convict Society in the Andaman Islands*, New Delhi, 2000.

Sen, S., 'Histories of Betrayal: Patriarchy, Class and Nation', in S. Bandyopadhyay (ed.), *Bengal: Rethinking History, Essays in Historiography*, Delhi, 2001.

Sen, S., *Women and Labour in Late Colonial India: The Bengal Jute Industry*, Cambridge, 1999.

Sen, U., 'Dissident Memories: Exploring Bengali Refugee Narratives in the Andaman Islands' in P. Panayi and P. Virdee (ed.) *Refugees and the End of Empire: Imperial Collapse and Forced Migration during the Twentieth Century*, Basingstoke and New York, 2011.

Sen, U., 'The Myths Refugees Live By: Memory and History in the Making of Bengali Refugee identity', *Modern Asian Studies*, 48(1), 2014.

Sen, U., 'Developing *Terra Nullius*: Colonialism, Nationalism and Indigeneity in the Andaman Islands', *Comparative Studies in Society and History*, 59(4), 2017.

Sen Gupta, P., *The Congress Party in West Bengal. A Study of Factionalism 1947–1986*, Calcutta, 1986.

Sengupta, D., 'From Dandakaranya to Marichjhapi: Rehabilitation, Representation and the Partition of Bengal (1947).' *Social Semiotics*, 21(1), 2011.

Sengupta, D., *The Partition of Bengal: Fragile Borders and New Identities*, Delhi, 2016.

Sengupta, J., *Eclipse of East Pakistan: Chronicles of Events Since Birth of East Pakistan Till October 1963*, Calcutta, 1963.

Sengupta, N., *History of the Bengali-speaking People*, New Delhi, 2001.

Shaikh, F., *Community and Consensus in Islam: Muslim Representation in Colonial India, 1860–1947*, New York, 1989.

Shani, O., 'Conceptions of Citizenship in India and the "Muslim Question"', *Modern Asian Studies*, 44(1), 2010, 145–173.

Shani, O., *How India became Democratic: Citizenship and the Making of the Universal Franchise*, Cambridge, New York, Melbourne, New Delhi, Singapore, 2018.

Sharma, R. K., *Demography and Population Problems*, Delhi, 1997.

Sharma, S., *Famine, Philanthropy, and the Colonial State: North India in the Early Nineteenth Century*, Delhi, 2001.

Sherman, T. C., 'From Hell to Paradise? Voluntary Transfer of Convicts to the Andaman Islands, 1921–1940,' *Modern Asian Studies*, 43(2), 2009.

Sherman, T. C., *Muslim Belonging in Secular India: Negotiating Citizenship in Postcolonial Hyderabad*, Cambridge, 2015.

Sherman, T. C., Gould, W., and Ansari, S., *From Subjects to Citizens: Society and the Everyday State in India and Pakistan, 1947–1970*, New York and Delhi, 2014.

Siddiqui, M. K. A., 'Life in the Slums of Calcutta: Some Aspects,' *Economic and Political Weekly*, 4(50), 1969.

Singer, W., *Creating Histories: Oral Narratives and the Politics of History-making*, Delhi, Oxford, 1997.

Singh, A., Iyer, N., and Gairola, R. K., *Revisiting India's Partition: New Essays on Memory, Culture, and Politics*, Lanham, MD, 2016.

Singh, K., *Unending Trail*, Delhi, 1957.

Singh, N. I., *The Andaman Story*, New Delhi, 1978.

Sinha, A., *Pashchim Bange udvastu upanibesh, (Refugee Colonies of West Bengal)*, Calcutta, 1995.

Sinha, D., 'Adjustment and Transition in a Bengali Refugee Settlement: 1950–1999' in P. K. Bose (ed.), *Refugees in West Bengal: Institutional Practices and Contested Identities*, Calcutta, 2000.

Sinha, D., 'Foundation of a Refugee Market: A Study in Self-reliance Initiative' in Bose, P. K., (ed.), *Refugees in West Bengal: Institutional Practices and Contested Identities*, Calcutta, 2000.

Sinha, M., *Spectres of Mother India: The Global Restructuring of an Empire*, Durham and London, 2006.

Sinha, T., *Maranjayee sangrame vastuhara, (Refugees in a Death-Defying Battle)*, Calcutta, 1999.

Sinha-Kerkhoff, K., 'Permanent Refugees: Female Camp Inhabitant in Bihar', in P. Essed, G. Frerks and J. Schrijvers (eds), *Refugees and The Transformation of Societies: Agency, Policies, Ethics and Politics*, New York, Oxford, 2004.

Sivaswamy, K. G., 'Indian Agriculture – Problems and Programmes', *Pacific Affairs*, 23(4), 1950.

Skaria, A., *Hybrid Histories: Forests, Frontiers and Wildness in Western India*, Delhi, Oxford, 1999.

Sundar, N., *Subalterns and Sovereigns: An Anthropological History of Bastar, 1854–1996*, Delhi, 1997.

Talbot, I. and Singh, G, *Region and Partition: Bengal, Punjab and the Partition of The Subcontinent*, Karachi, 1999.

Thompson, P., *The Voice of the Past: Oral History*, 3rd Edition, Oxford, 2000.

Tuker, F., *While Memory Serves*, London, 1950.

Usuda, M., 'Pushed Towards the Partition: Jogendranath Mandal and the Constrained Namasudra Movement' in H. Kotani (ed.), *Caste System, Untouchability and The Depressed*, New Delhi, 1997.

Vaidik, A., *Imperial Andamans: Colonial Encounter and Island History*, Basingstoke and New York, 2010.

Vaidik, A., 'Working the Islands: Labour Regime in Colonial Andamans (1858–1921)' in M. van der Linden and P. Mohapatra (eds), *Towards Global History: New Comparisons*, New Delhi, 2009.

Vakil, C. N., *Economic Consequences of Divided India. A Study of the Economy of India and Pakistan*, Bombay, 1950.

van Schendel, Willem, 'Stateless in South Asia: The Making of the India-Bangladesh Enclaves', *The Journal of Asian Studies*, 61(1), 2002.

van Schendel, W., *The Bengal Borderland. Beyond State and Nation in South Asia*, London, 2005.

van Schendel, Wilhem, 'Working Through Partition: Making a Living in the Bengal Borderlands,' *International Review of Social History*, 46, 2001.

Vansina, J., *Oral Tradition as History*, London, 1985.

Venkateswar, S., *Development and Ethnocide: Colonial Practices in The Andaman Islands*, Copenhagen, 2004.

Vernant, J., *The Refugee in the Post-war World*, New Haven, CT, 1953.

Watt, C. A., *Serving the Nation: Cultures of Service, Association and Citizenship in Colonial India*, New Delhi, 2005.

Watt, C. A., and Mann, M., *Civilizing Missions in Colonial and Postcolonial South Asia: From Improvement to Development*, London and New York, 2011.

Weber, R., 'Re(Creating) the Home: Women's Role in the Development of Refugee Colonies in South Calcutta', J. Bagchi and S. Dasgupta (eds), *The Trauma and the Triumph: Gender and Partition in Eastern India*, Calcutta, 2003.

Zachariah, B., *Developing India: An Intellectual and Social History, c. 1930–1950*, New Delhi, 2005.

Zakaria, R., *Sardar Patel and Indian Muslims: An Analysis of his Relations with Muslims Before and After India's Partition*, Mumbai, 1996.

Zamindar, V. F., *The Long Partition and the Making of Modern South Asia: Refugees, Boundaries, Histories*, New York, 2007.

Zehmisch, P., 'A Xerox of India? Policies and Politics of Migration in an Overseas Colony', *Working Papers in Social and Cultural Anthropology, LMU Munich*, 2 (1), 2012.

Zehmisch, P., *Mini-India: The Politics of Migration and Subalternity in The Andaman Islands*, New Delhi, 2017.

Zolberg, A., 'The Formation of New States as a Refugee-Generating Process', *Annals of the American Academy of Political and Social Science*, 467, 1983.

Zolberg, A. R., Suhrke, A., and Aguayo, S., *Escape from Violence. Conflict and The Refugee Crisis in the Developing World*, New York and Oxford, 1992.

Index

Abducted Persons (Recovery and
    Restoration) Act 1949, 208
abducted women, 201, 202
    recovery of, 202, 206, 208
'accelerated development' programme, 155
Agamben, Giorgio, 5
agradut, 71
Airways India Limited, 43
Alipore camp, 33
All Bengal Women's Union, 211
All India Women's Conference (AIWC),
    208, 213
    Bengal branch, 211
Amkunj, 129
'*Amra kara? Bastuhara!*' ('Who are we?
    The Refugees!'), 182
Anandabazar Patrika, 63, 142
Andaman Islands, 18
    agriculturists, 38, 48
    as British colony, 77, 78–80
    batches, 47
    bhadraloks, 192
    choice and agency, 137–46
    dispersal, 137
    displaced families in, 106–7
    forests, 124, 126
    Hindus, 244, 245
    Japanese occupation, 78–9, 102,
        119, 126
    '*karmatha*', 135
    map, 114
    Namasudras, 18, 247
    national development, 49, 68, 71–112,
        249–50
    'new Bengal', 84
    '*parisrami*', 135
    Penal Settlement, 78
    refugee resettlement, 87
Andaman Padouk (Pterocarpus
    Dalbergioides), 124
Andul transit camp, 71
Anglo-Indians, 102

Ansar Bahini (Volunteer Army) of
    Pakistan, 101
Anthropological Survey of India, 122,
    167–8
anuprobeshkaris, 66
Arendt, Hannah, 1, 4–5
Article 5, 8
Asansol camp, 224
Ashoknagar camp, 145
Ashram, Ananda, 212
Assam, 38
    abducted women, 202
    ethno-nationalist fear, 23, 107, 108
    Evacuee Property Act, 163
    Evacuee Property Ordinance, 243
    Hindus, 104
    marginalisation, 1, 249
    PL institutions, 219
    planned rehabilitation, 88
    saturation, 63
    unattached women, 203
Association for the Service of Women
    (*Mahila Seva Samiti*), 211, 213
associations, 164, 235
Auckland House, 199
Azadgarh colony, 167–8, 176

B.R.O camp, 33, 169
Babughat transit camp, 227
'backward' areas, 52, 249
Bagchi, Jashodhara, 238
Bagerhat district, Khulna, 42
Bagjola camp, 143
Bairagi, Manipada, 145
Baluchistan, 12
Bandyopadhyay, Hiranmoy
    Bijoygarh colony, 172, 175, 178, 186, 190
    Dr Roy, 35
    Jalpaiguri, 26
    optees, 184–5
    PL camps, 217, 224
    population exchange, 45

selection, 132
squatters' colonies, 166, 171
Bangiya Jatiya Rakshi Dal (Bengal National
  Protection Brigade), 101
Bangladesh, 24
banibahak, 71
Bannerjee, Amulya, 99, 185
Bannerji, Madhu, 179
Banpur reception centre, 64
Bansberia camp, 203, 217, 226, 227, 230
Baratang Islands, 72
Bardolai, Gopinath, 93, 104
Barisal, 42, 43, 227
Barui, Dasharath, 146
Bastar, Madhya Pradesh, 52, 94
Basu, Abala, 212
batches, 116–17, 119, 142
Bengal famine 1943, 27, 204
Bengal National Protection Brigade
  (Bangiya Jatiya Rakshi Dal), 101
Betapore, 120
Bettiah camp, Bihar, 195
Bhadrakali camp, 203, 217, 223, 228,
  232, 235
bhadraloks, 189
  Andaman Islands, 136
  Bijoygarh colony, 19, 246–7
  education, 189, 190
  rehabilitation loans, 191–8
  selection, 132, 134
  stereotypes, 135
bhadramahila, 238
Bhantus, 73, 78, 80
Bhasin, Kamla, 20, 208
Bihar, 38, 47, 50, 139, 161, 192
  citizenship, 23
  deserters, 198
  Dr Roy, 39
  Muslims, 26
Bijoygarh colony, 19, 34, 172–82, 187, 246
Bijoygarh Vidyapeeth, 188
Bijoygarh: Ekti Udvastu Upanibesh (a refugee
  colony), 172
Billiground, 121, 122
Biswas, Ananta Kumar, 122, 155
Biswas, Gokul, 138, 140, 145
Biswas, Hemanta, 54
Biswas, Rajlakshmi, 146, 149
Biswas, Sushil Chandra, 122
Bomlungta, 129
Bongaon, 227
Bongaon station, 227
Bongaon transit camp, 54
Boral, Dhiren, 143
Bose, Sarat, 35

Bose, Subhash Chandra, 207
Burma, 89
Burmese, 102
Butalia, Urvashi, 20
Byapari, Upen, 151
Bynanama scheme, 47

Calcutta, 17, 19, 25, 33, 161–200, 250
  rally of refugees, 35–6
  riots 1946, 25, 26, 27
caste, 19, 92, 130–37, 195
Catholic Labour Burueau, Ranchi, 78
cellular jail, 72, 78–9
Central Provinces, 88
Central Social Welfare Board, 206, 220
Central Tractor Organisation, 91
Chakrabarti, Prafulla, 168, 171, 172, 175,
  191, 195
Chakrabarty, Saroj, 34
Chakraborty, Benoy, 133
Chakravartty, Gargi, 238
Champta PL camp, 203, 226, 233
Chand, Gyan, 32
Chatterji, Joya, 16, 36, 111, 167, 245
Chaudhuri, Seeta, 207
children, 180
Chittagong, 43
Chotonagpur region, Bihar, 78, 105
Chouhatta village, 37
Chowdhury, Dhirendranath (alias
  Kalabhai), 190
Chowdhury, Dhirendranath Ray (alias
  Kalabhai), 181, 184–6
Chowdhury, Girin Ray, 185
Chowdhury, Sailen, 190
Christians, 102
Chunar, 207
Chunar fort, 233
cinema, 140
citizenship, 7–13
  diverse, 16
  jus sanguinis, 16
  jus soli, 16
  moral, 6
  'thick', 13–20
Citizenship Act 1955, 10, 16,
  240
Citizenship Bill, 8
Colonisation and Development Scheme,
  75, 86, 105, 140, 249
Committee of Ministers, 219–20
Communist Party of India (CPI), 176,
  179, 191
Communist Party of India (Marxist)
  (CPI (M)), 46, 67

Communists
  Andaman Islands, 139, 145
  anti-establishment, 177
  Eviction Bill, 50
  opposition, 226
  population exchange, 45–6
  propaganda, 140
  refugee associations, 191
  refugee organisations, 108
  refugee rights, 68
  votes, 58–9
  women, 208
compensation, 216–17, 221
Congress Socialist Party, 181
  Jayprakash faction, 187
Connaught Place riots, 241
Constituent Assembly, 16
contributory house-building loan, 59
Coochbehar, 38, 101
Coopers Camp, Ranaghat, 46
CPI (Communist Party of India), 176,
  179, 191
CPI (M) (Communist Party of India
  (Marxist)), 46, 67
'criminal tribes', 73, 78, 80

Dakhsin Kalikata Bastuhara Samgram
  Parishad (DKBS), 33, 177
Dalbhum, 39
Dalit refugees, 247, 249, 250
Dalits, 19, 135, 249, 250, see also
  Namasudra
dals (associations), 143, 164
Dandakaranya
  alienation of locals, 109
  colonisation, 245
  compulsory dispersal, 67
  'desert land', 142
  dispersal, 137
  Gokul Biswas, 145
  Namasudras, 247
  national development, 108
  refugees' agency, 139
  squatters, 169, 192
Dandakaranya Development Authority,
  40, 50
Dandakaranya Project
  agriculturists, 94–5
  'backward' areas, 109, 249
  failure, 159–60
  final dispersal, 52–6
  Gokul Biswas, 145
  national development, 49, 50–1, 110
  Prafulla Chandra Sen, 61
  'residual', 139

Saibal Kumar Gupta, 110
saturation, 67
  udvastu, 62
Das, Atashibala, 227
Das, B. K., 8
Das, Chittaranjan, 174
Das, Jagabandhu, 138, 143, 148
Das, Jatindranath, 196
Das, Surabala, 227–28, 235
Dasgupta, Nalini Mohan, 174, 188
Datta, Debabrata, 186
Datta, Jiten, 197
Datta, Santosh, 174, 175–7, 184
Debi, Basanti, 174
Debnath, Bharat Chandra, 192
Debray, Ashish, 173
deer, 150–51
Delhi, 161–2, 163, 164
denial of relief, 25–33
Department of Relief and
  Rehabilitation, 169
Desai, Morarji, 197–8
Deshbandhu colony, 190, 193
Deshmukh, Durgabai, 206, 210
Development Committee, 165
Development Programme, 27–8
Devi, Basanti, 174
Dhaka, 43, 162, 207
Dhangsa-o-Nirman (Destruction and
  Creation), 172
Dhubulia camp, 203, 217, 224, 225,
  226, 227
Diglipur, 115, 120
  Durga Puja, 135
  jungles, 148
  oral history, 116, 117, 122
  selection, 144
  transport, 130
disease, 85, 146, 225, 228
dispersal 1949, 33–41
District Magistrate of Burdwan, 234
DKBS (Dakhsin Kalikata Bastuhara
  Samgram Parishad), 33, 177
dole, 230, 232, 236
Durga Puja, 135, 192
Durgapur camp, 33
Dutta, Debabrata, 188
Dutta, Dr Aparnacharan, 174
Dutta, Mayarani, 226
Dutta, Narayan, 136, 154
Dutta, Santosh, 173

East Punjab's Rehabilitation Board, 82
education, 211
elephants, 148, 150, 151

Emergency Cabinet Committee, 81
employment, 25, 187
  'fully employable', 219
  'partially employable', 219
  women, 210–11, 213–15
'empty lands', 141, 247, 249
Engel, Dagmar, 238
Evacuee Property Act, 163–4
Evacuee Property Ordinance, 243, 245
Eviction of Persons in Unauthorised
  Occupation of Land Bill, 50, 165,
  171, 178
ex-campsites, 64, 69, 157, 169, 170
ex-servicemen, 79–81, 83

family, 223–5
famine
  Bengal 1943, 27, 204
Famine Code 1880, 204
Feni, Noakhali, 43
Ferrargunj region, 121
forced separation, 223–4
forest clearance, 124, 126–9
Forest Department, 78, 91, 121, 124,
  126–9, 151
Foucault, Michel, 24

Gandhi colony, 33, 194
Gandhian
  ideals of service, 212
  movement, 207, 213
  women, 208
Gandhian movement, 174, 206
Ganguly, Indubaran, 173, 175–7, 183, 193,
  194, 196
Gayeshpur, 37
gender, 201–40
  difference, 19
  violence, 20, 201
Geneva Convention, 9
genocidal violence, 245
Ghosh, A. K., 97, 103, 130
Ghosh, Atulya, 63
Ghosh, Dr Prafulla Chandra, 25, 26, 183,
  194, 211
Ghosh, Dr Subratesh, 192
Ghosh, Lilabati, 226–7
Ghushuria camp, 226
Ghusuri camp, 145
GOC Eastern Command, 186
goondas, 165, 171
Goswami, Pari, 151, 226
government loans, 196–7
Great Andamanese, 74
Grow More Food campaign, 89–91

gruel kitchens, 204
Guha, B. S., 167–8
Guha, Phulrenu, 210
Guha, Shombhu, 181, 192, 194
Gupta, Ashoka, 207, 208, 210, 213, 214,
  220–1, 225
Gupta, S. K., 91, 99, 110, 128

Habra, 37
Haldar, Binodini, 224
Haldar, Naren, 134–5, 137, 138, 143
Hamilton, A. P., 125
Hanspuri, 153
Harithakur, 136
Hasnabad reception centre, 64
Havelock Island, 116, 117, 121, 122,
  136
  houses, 138
Hazratbal riots 1964, 56, 63, 158
Herobhanga scheme, 54
Hindu Raj, 10
Hinduisation, 71–112
Hindus
  anti-Hindu riots, 75
  anti-Hindu sentiments, 35
  compensation, 221
  Evacuee Property Act, 163
  Evacuee Property Ordinance, 243–4
  families, 225
  in Sind, 245
  marginalisation, 202
  Namasudras, 136
  population exchange, 7–13
  Punjab, 3, 245
  sexual harassment, 202
  widows, 228
  women, 239
  Women's Section, 205
Hirakud Dam, 48, 49
Hooghly district, 179
Hossain, Janab Mudassir, 16–17
Hossain, Janab Musharruf, 28–9
Howrah station, 199
Hyderabad 'accession', 35, 101

illiteracy, 133, 157
India: A People Partitioned (1997) BBC
  documentary, 23, 241
Indira-Mujib Agreement 1972, 66
infiltrators, 24, 66, 101
infirmaries, 209, 216, 218, 220
insanitary conditions, 225
Ishaque Report, 40–1
Ishaque, A.H.M., 40
Italia, Khorshed, 207, 241–2

jabardakhal (forced acquisition) movement, 25, 168, 169, 171, 175, 177, 193, 195
jabardakhal colonies, 170, 175, 192, 193, 198
Jadavpur Bastuhara Banipeeth, 188
Jadavpur Bastuhara Bidyapith (Jadavpur Refugee School), 174
Jadavpur Bastuhara Vidyapeeth, 188
Jadavpur camp, 33, 187
Jadavpur colony, 179, 192
Jadavpur Engineering College, 181
Jadavpur Refugee Camp Association, 33, 173–4, 184–6, 188, 194
Jain, Ajit Prasad, 13, 46
Jalais, Annu, 19
Jalpaiguri, 26, 28
Jamalpur, 43
Jamuria camp, 234–5
Jarawas, 74, 147, 148, 150, 151–4, 249
    deer, 150
    police, 152
Jayal, Niraja, 16–17
Jayprakash faction, Congress Socialist Party, 187
Jewish refugees, 4
Jinnah, Muhammad Ali, 6
Jirat, 167–8
Joint Meeting of Refugees (*Sanjukta Bastuhara Sammelan*), 179
Junagadh, 101
jute, 85–95, 249

Kadamtala, 151
Kalabhai, 181, 184–6, 190
Kalahandi, 94
Kalahandi, Orissa, 52
kalapani (black waters), 73, 77, 89, 138, 140, 145
Kalpong river valley, 120
Kalsi village, 122, 148, 152
Karachi, 162, 163, 164
Karachi Co-operative Housing Society Union, 164
Karens, 73, 102, 125
Karnal Mahila Ashram, 207, 238
Kartikpur camp, 217
Kashmir, 101
Katchal, 121
Katju, Dr, 190
Kaur, Ravinder, 17, 19
Kerala, 105
Khanna, Mehr Chand, 63, 220, 233
Kharia, 78
khasmahal lands, 26
Kichchha village, Nainital district, 94

Kidderpore dock, Calcutta, 71
kisans, 154
Kishoreganj, 43
Konar, Hare Krishna, 58
Koraput, 94
Koraput, Orissa, 52

Lady Hardinge Medical College, 207
Lahore, 162
Lake Jodhpur camp, 33
landscape, 146–57
Layalka, 174, 181, 184–6
LCT or Landing Craft Tank, 129
Liberation War, East Pakistan, 66
Lipsky, Michael, 14
Local Born, 73, 78, 95, 96–7, 100, 119, 124
Local Born Association, 96

Madhupur village, 149, 155
Madhya Pradesh, 50, 52, 94, 123, 139, 146
Mahila Atmaraksha Samiti (Women's Self-defence League), 235
Mahila Seva Samiti (Association for the Service of Women), 211, 212–13
Maitra, S. N., 129, 131
Maity, Abha, 62–3, 64
Maity, Nikunja Behari, 31, 38
Majherchar, 37
Majid, Inam-ul, 96, 97, 99, 100, 103, 127
Majumdar, Mohanlan, 149
Majumdar, Sumana, 156
Mali, Sonai, 223
Mallick, Ross, 46
Mana, 64
Manbhum, 39
Mandal, Jogendranath, 54, 134–5, 140
Mandal, Kalipada, 151
Mandal, Pushpa, 232
Mandal, Sujata, 140, 145, 151, 152
Mandir, Kasturba Seva, 210
Manglutan village, 155
Mappilas, 73, 78, 80, 97–8, 99
'marginal men', 69
Marginal Men, 172
marginalisation, 1, 26, 155
Marichjhapi region, 19
martyrdom, 179–80
mass slaughter, 3
massacre of refugees, 19
Matua sect, 133
Mayabunder (Port Bonington), 73, 116, 125, 129
Mazumdar, Apurbalal, 54, 195
Mellow, De, 125
Menon, Ritu, 20, 208

migration certificates, 51–2
militancy, 236
Ministry of Finance, 90
Ministry of Home Affairs, 71, 73, 80, 81,
    82, 83, 91
Ministry of Refugee Relief and
    Rehabilitation, 36, 233
Ministry of Rehabilitation, Calcutta, 46
Ministry of Relief and Rehabilitation, 31
    Andaman Islands, 81
    creation of, 12, 81
    dispersal, 40
    dissolution of, 23
    Dr Roy, 35–6
    housing, 164
    loans, 196
    Nehru, 14
    permanent liabilities, 219
    proposed dissolution of, 57–8
    Rameshwari Nehru, 208
    reconstitution of, 75
    unattached women, 203, 222
    volunteers, 207
    Women's Section, 209
Ministry of Works Housing and
    Supply, 55
Minority Affairs Minister, 44
Mitra, Asok, 45, 234–5
Mitra, Binapani, 179
Mitra, Haridas, 58
Mitra, Nalini, 207, 232, 233, 236
Monglutan village, 122
Mookerji, Syama Prasad, 29
Morichjhanpi massacre, 67–8, 159
Mridha, Sukharanjan, 138, 141, 142, 148,
    152–4
Mukerjee, Radhakamal, 32
Mukhopadhyay, Kaliprasad, 172,
    180–1
Mukhopadhyay, Samar, 58
Munda, 78
Muslim League, 28–30
    National Guards, 101
Muslims
    bhadraloks, 134
    Connaught Place, 241
    employment, 214
    Evacuee Property Act, 84, 163–4
    Evacuee Property Ordinance, 243
    evacuees, 169, 243–4
    harassment of, 29
    Hindus and, 245
    Majid, 97
    men, 202
    non-Punjabi in Pakistan, 245

    as outsiders, 3
    screening, 96
    violence, 202
Mymensingh district, 43, 183

Nadia, 44, 170
Naktala No. 1 colony, 190
Namasudras
    agriculturists, 92
    Andaman Islands, 18
    caste, 132–7, 193, 195
    dispersal, 54, 247
    marginalisation, 195, 246
    resettlement on own terms, 247
    selection, 157, *see also Dalits*
Nandigram, 248
Nari Seva Sangha (Women's Service
    League), 208, 211
National Development Corps (*Rashtriya
    Viaks Dal*), 121
nationalism, 5, 246
NBVK (Nikhil Banga Vastuhara Karma
    Parishad), 33
Nehru colony, 122
Nehru, Jawaharlal
    Connaught Place, 241–2
    crisis 1950, 43
    Delhi, 161
    dispersal, 68
    Dr Roy, 14, 39
    Muslims, 10–11
    Pakistan, 30
    Rehabilitation and Development Board,
        82, 86–8, 94
Nehru, Rameshwari, 204
    Dalits, 250
    patriarchy, 208
    training, 210, 216
    unattached women, 206
    widows, 220
    Women's Section, 204, 209
Nehru-Liaquat Ali Pact 1950, 44–5, 48,
    164, 244
Neil Island, 121
Neogy, K. C., 161
Netaji Nagar colony, 193, 194–5
Nicobar archipelago, 72
Nikhil Banga Vastuhara Karma Parishad
    (NBVK), 33
Nikhil Vanga Bastuhara Karma Parishad
    (NVBKP), 35
Nimbutalla, 129
Niyamgiri, Orissa, 248
Noakhali, 99
Noakhali riots 1946, 202

North West Frontier Provinces, 10
NVBKP (Nikhil Vanga Bastuhara Karma
    Parishad), 35, 180

Old Fort, Delhi, 207
Onges, 74, 109, 249
optees, 183–4, 185
oral history, 203, 225, 228, 238
Oraon, 78
Orissa
    Andaman Islands, 123
    crisis 1951, 47
    Dandakaranya Project, 52, 94
    deserters, 198
    dispersal, 23, 38, 50, 139, 192
    Dr Roy, 39
    Hirakud Dam, 48
    planned rehabilitation, 88
    rehabilitation failure, 139

Pakrasi, Kanti B., 225
Pal, Atul, 144
Pal, Lalitmohan, 143, 144
Pal, Manindra, 181, 185
Pal, Saralabala, 149, 155
Pal, Satirani, 232
Panchwati, 129
Pandey, Gyan, 11
Pant, Pandit, 8
passports, 51
Patel, Kamlaben, 207
Patel, Sardar, 6, 10, 63, 93, 99, 104, 107
patriarchy, 222–9, 238
    'new patriarchy' of nuclear families, 205
permanent liabilities (PL), 222–9, 247–8
    camps, 217–36
    compulsory training of, 219–20
Petrapole reception centre, 64
Philips, R.N., 81, 99–100, 103
Planning Commission, 232
police, 165, 171, 184
    harassment, 42
Port Blair, 72, 116
    cellular jail, 79
    education, 133
    employment, 121
    ex-convicts, 73
    forest clearance, 124
    oral history, 116, 117, 122
    small pox, 85
    transport, 129, 130
    tribes, 74
Port Bonington (Mayabunder), 73, 116,
    125, 129
Port Cornwallis, 77, 129

Praja Socialist Party, 177
Prasad, Rajendra, 89
Prasuti Sadan (Maternity Home), 174
protests, 54, 235
Pterocarpus Dalbergioides (Andaman
    Padouk), 124
public transport, 129
Punjab
    model of rehabilitation, 12
Punjabification, 162
puraton lok, 117, 123

Quest for Roots (Shikorer Sandhane), 172

Radcliffe Award, 101
Raha, Sadhan, 131–5, 137, 140, 144
    Rahasaheb, 132
Rahababu, 135, 144
Raj Bhavan conference, Calcutta, 44
Rajasthan, 50, 245
Rajshahi riots, 62
Ramamurthy, S. V., 94
Ranaghat, 217, 227
Ranchi labourers, 125, 153, 154
Randhawa, Mohinder Singh, 245
Rangat
    batches, 127, 143
    cinema, 140
    colonisation, 120, 129
    forest, 148
    forest clearance, 128
    houses, 138
    jungles, 148
    oral history, 116, 117, 122
    transport, 129
Rangat Bay, 121
Rani, Durga, 207
Rao, P. V. R., 96
Rao, U. Bhaskar, 84, 166, 209
rape, 202
rapes, mass, 201
Rashtriya Viaks Dal (National Development
    Corps), 121
Ray, Ashish Deb, 186
Ray, Chinta Haran, 185–6
Ray, Hemanta, 143
Ray, Jashoda Kanta, 184
Ray, Kamalkrishna, 183
Ray, Lakshmikanta, 133, 144, 148
Ray, Manas, 189, 193, 194–5, 198
Ray, Renuka, 40, 48, 197, 210–11,
    214–15, 233
RCRC (Refugee Central Rehabilitation
    Council), 50
reception centres, 64, 67

recovery of abducted women, 202, 208
Refugee Rehabilitation Directorate, 209
refugees
    agency, 163–72
    anti-establishment stance, 177–82
    choice and agency, 137–46
    'curse' of, 4
    identity, 191–8
    massacre of, 19
    memories of, 156–7
    non-camp, 56–9
    'refugee power', 177, 182–91
    resistance, 180–2
    screening, 53
    tagging, 53
Registrar of Firms, Societies and Non-
        trading Corporations of West
        Bengal, 187
registration, 8, 12, 16
rehabilitation, 13–20
    loans, 60
    'new migrants', 64–6
    of criminals, 73
    'old migrants', 65
    'residual', 56–62
Rehabilitation and Development Board, 82,
        83, 86–8
rehabilitation loans, 191–8
Rehabilitation of Displaced Persons and
        Eviction of Persons in Unauthorised
        Occupation of Land Act, 165
rehabilitation schemes, 26, 141, 142, 146,
        166, 205, 217
Relief Department, 25
religion, 95–107, 136
Revolutionary Socialist Party, 177
riots, 1
    anti-Hindu, 75
    Calcutta 1946, 25, 26, 27
    Connaught Place, 241
    East Bengal 1950, 43, 46
    Hazratbal 1964, 56, 63, 158
    Nadia, 44
    Noakhali 1946, 202
    Rajshahi, 62
Rizvi, Mr, 98
Roy, Anupama, 16
Roy, Dr B. C.
    Andaman Islands, 71, 74, 83–4, 108, 124
    Biyoygarh colony, 178
    conference, 46
    Dandakaranya Project, 94
    Datta, 174, 175–7
    denial of relief, 34
    dispersal, 141

Evacuee Property Act, 164
Eviction Bill, 50
Ishaque Report, 35–41
    marginalisation, 26
    migration certificates, 50–2
    Nehru, 14, 30, 43
    Raha, 132
    saturation, 139
    squatters, 165
    unfit camps, 217, 226
Roy, J. K., 38
Roy, S. B. S., 186
rubber plantation, 121
Rupasreepalli camp, 217, 227

S. S. Maharaja, 129
Sadhak, Dhirendranath, 135
Saha, Lakshmi, 227
Saksena, Mohanlal, 44
Samaddar, B. K., 140
Samaddar, Benilal, 121, 133
Sanjukta Bastuhara Sammelan (Joint
        Meeting of Refugees), 179
Santal families, 62
Sarabhai, Mridula, 206, 207, 208
Sarkar, Khuki, 226
Sarkar, Nalini Ranjan, 26–7
saturation, 49, 67, 87, 139, 164
Schedule Caste Federation, 134
schools, 188–90
Sealdah station, 35, 192, 199, 224
Second Foodgrains Policy Committee, 90
security, 95–107
self-identification as settlers, 123, 155–6
Sen, Kalu, 173
Sen, Prafulla Chandra, 61–2, 63, 64, 69
Sen, Shanti, 173, 187–8
Sen, Shantiranjan, 173, 180, 181
Sengupta, Sheila, 207
Sengupta, Sushil, 186
Sentinelese, 74
Sethi, R. L., 125
sevashrams (hermitages of service), 216
sexuality, 233
Shakho camp, 140
Shani, Ornit, 16
Shikarer Sandhane, 180–1
Shikdar, Kalipada, 148
Shikorer Sandhane (Quest for Roots), 172
Shil, Mukul, 224
Shivdasani Report, 91–2, 125–8
Shivdasani, H. R., 91–2, 125–8
Shoal Bay region, 128
Sikhs, 3, 205, 243, 244, 245
Sind, 12, 88

Sind-Rajputana border, 11
Singh, Iqbal, 102
Singur, 248
Sinha, Nanigopal, 199
Sinha, Romola, 207, 208
Sinha, Surajit Chadra, 128
Sinha, Tushar, 235
smallpox, 85, 228
social workers, 203–15, 220
Society Act of 1886, 187
Sonarpur transit camp, 54
Sonarpur-Bagjola scheme, 44
South Andaman Island, 120
South Andamans, 126
South Suburban Calcutta Refugee
    Association, 177
Special Economic Zones, 248
Spivak, Gayatri Chakravorty, 248
squatters, 25, 50, 161–200
    associations, 33–4
    colonies, 122, 163–72, 246–7
state paternalism, 20
stereotypes, 135
subalternity, 246
Sunderbans, 19, 54
Supur Ambagan camp, 144
Sutar, Manoranjan, 146
Swadhinata, 179
swaraj (self-rule), 87
Sylhet, 43

Tamils, 155
tehsil, 115, 116, 120
tehsildar, 132
Telegus, 155
Terai region, 94, 249
Thakur, Harichand, 133, 136
Thakurdas, Sir Purshottamdas, 90
Thakurta, Shombhu Guha, 173, 186
tigers, 148
Tippera, 43
Titagarh camp, 217
Tiwari, Durga Prashad, 98–9, 100
Tollygunge Refugee Association, 33
Tollygunge region, 169
Tollygunj colony, 192
Tollygunj Police Station, 185
Tollygunje constituency, 58
Tomachaung, 129
training
    compulsory for permanent liabilities,
        219–20
    women, 210–11, 213–15
trains, 43
transport, 126

Travancore-Cochin, 105
Tripura
    abducted women, 202
    alienation of locals, 109
    dispersal, 38
    division of territory, 101
    ethno-nationalist fear, 23
    Evacuee Property Act, 163
    Evacuee Property Ordinance, 243
    expansion, 249
    Hindus, 13
    marginalisation, 249
    Pakistan, 101
    PL institutions, 219
    saturation, 63
    unattached women, 203
tuberculosis, 146
Tully, James, 16
Type D province, 73, 102

UCRC (United Central Refugee
    Council), 40–1
    caste, 195
    colony committees, 192
    Communists, 108
    Congress Ministry, 58
    Dr Roy, 45–6
    Eviction Bill, 50, 165, 171, 178
    police, 179
    women, 235
Uday Villa, 212
udvastu, 9, 62, 123, 172
Udvastu (Refugee), 35
unattached women, 201–40, 247
unending trail, 41–8
Union of India, 73
United Central Refugee Council. *See* UCRC
United Nations Relief and Rehabilitation
    Administration, 9
Urmilapur, 148, 151
USAF Camp, 169
Uttar Pradesh, 139
Uttaranchal, 93, 139
Uttarpara training centre, 233, 233
Uttarpara women's home, 215

vagrants, 199
Vindhya Pradesh, 50
volunteers, 207

war widows, 202
Webi region, 73
West Bengal Emergency Relief Committee,
    211–12
Whitehead, Andrew, 23, 241

wild boars, 148
willing settlers, 76–85
'withouts', 122
women
    abducted, 201, 202
    as permanent liabilities, 215–22
    caste, 238
    Communist, 208
    employment, 211, 215, 238
    Gandhian, 208
    Hindu widows, 228
    industrial training home, 207
    recovery of abducted, 202, 206, 208
    resistance, 180
    rights and education, 206

social respectability, 149
training, 211, 215
unattached, 201–40, 247–8
Women's Section, 203–15, 217
Women's Self-defence League (*Mahila Atmaraksha Samiti*), 235
Women's Service League (*Nari Seva Sangha*), 208, 211
work-site camps, 48–9
World War II, 78–9, 83

Young Women's Christian Association, 208

Zamindar, Vazira, 11–12, 244
Zolberg, Aristide, 5